Sustainable Finance

Sustainable Finance is a concise and authoritative reference series linking research and practice. It provides reliable concepts and research findings in the ever growing field of sustainable investing and finance, SDG economics and Leadership with the declared commitment to present the theories, methods, tools and investment approaches that can fulfil the United Nations Sustainable Development Goals and the Paris Agreement COP 21/22 alongside with de-risking assets and creating triple purpose solutions that ensure the parity of profit, people and planet through choice architecture passion and performance. The series addresses market failure, systemic risk and reinvents portfolio theory, portfolio engineering as well as behavioural finance, financial mediation, product innovation, shared values, community building, business strategy and innovation, exponential tech and creation of social capital. Sustainable Finance and SDG Economics series helps to understand keynotes on international guidelines, guiding accounting and accountability principles, prototyping new developments in triple bottom line investing, cost benefit analysis, integrated financial first plus impact first concepts and impact measurement. Going beyond adjacent fields (like accounting, marketing, strategy, risk management) it integrates the concept of psychology, innovation, exponential tech, choice architecture, alternative economics, blue economy shared values, professions of the future, leadership, human and community development, team culture, impact, quantitative and qualitative measurement, Harvard Negotiation, mediation and complementary currency design using exponential tech and ledger technology. Books in the series contain latest findings from research, concepts for implementation, as well as best practices and case studies for the finance industry.

Vu Quang Trinh
Editor

Climate Governance and Corporate Eco-innovation

A Framework for Sustainable Companies

Springer

Editor
Vu Quang Trinh
Newcastle University Business School
Newcastle University
Newcastle upon Tyne, UK

ISSN 2522-8285 ISSN 2522-8293 (electronic)
Sustainable Finance
ISBN 978-3-031-56422-2 ISBN 978-3-031-56423-9 (eBook)
https://doi.org/10.1007/978-3-031-56423-9

This Springer imprint is published by the registered company Springer Nature Switzerland AG
The registered company address is: Gewerbestrasse 11, 6330 Cham, Switzerland

Preface

The Era of Climate Governance and Eco-Innovation

Climate Change

… has become a significant global environmental concern in recent years, affecting all business stakeholders, including the global business community, governments, managers, shareholders, consumers, media, suppliers, and employees. Consequently, addressing climate change should be integral to businesses' policies, activities, and investments. There has been also a growing demand from governments worldwide, particularly following the COP26[1] conference in Glasgow (2021) and the subsequent COP28[2] in Dubai (2023), for businesses to demonstrate their responsibility and accountability by enhancing their corporate practices related to climate change commitments and solutions.

The latest COP28 conference, attended by more than 70,000 delegates, including member states (or Parties) of the UN Framework Convention on Climate Change (UNFCCC), business leaders, young people, climate scientists, Indigenous Peoples, journalists, and various other experts and stakeholders, resulted in a new agreement to address climate change. Notably, countries have agreed on the necessity to transition away from fossil fuels in their energy systems for the first time. Certain groups, including the USA, European countries, and others particularly vulnerable to

[1] 2021 United Nations (UN) Climate Change Conference: "brought together 120 world leaders and over 40,000 registered participants, including 22,274 party delegates, 14.124 observers and 3.886 media representatives. For 2 weeks in 2021, the world was riveted on all facets of climate change—the science, the solutions, the political will to act, and clear indications of action" (see https://www.un.org/en/climatechange/cop26).

[2] 2023 United Nations (UN) Climate Change Conference: "In a demonstration of global solidarity, negotiators from nearly 200 Parties came together in Dubai with a decision on the world's first 'global stocktake' to ratchet up climate action before the end of the decade—with the overarching aim to keep the global temperature limit of 1.5 °C within reach" (see https://unfccc.int/cop28).

climate change, have advocated for even more ambitious commitments. They are pushing for a complete phase-out of fossil fuels.

At the corporate level, businesses are increasingly expected to adopt more innovative and effective policies and solutions to align with the agreements reached during COP28. In an era of constraints on natural resources and socio-environmental pressures, businesses worldwide have incorporated their voluntary and legal commitments to improve climate change practices into their decision-making processes. For instance, they can implement new practices, such as eco-innovation, to mitigate or entirely prevent ecological damage while accelerating waste recycling and energy conservation. Eco-innovation, in particular, stands out as one of the most effective solutions to enhance businesses' energy efficiency, thus reducing their energy consumption and carbon emissions during the production process. Another viable solution is the transformation of the traditional corporate governance system (i.e., mechanisms that do not necessarily reflect corporate commitment to climate change issues) into a climate governance system (i.e., a new governance system that comprehensively addresses corporate responsibility to climate change issues).

Eco-innovation and climate governance are approaches businesses can adopt to bolster their environmental sustainability efforts. They operate within the theoretical framework of the resource-based perspective, which posits a direct link between businesses' sustained competitive advantages and their "valuable, rare, imperfectly imitable, and non-sustainable" resources and capabilities,[3] such as management skills, organizational processes, and corporate governance mechanisms. However, it is essential to recognize that not all businesses with superior resources can effectively turn these resources into competitive advantages. This requires looking beyond merely owning and controlling superior assets and resources from a resource-based perspective. It necessitates considering managerial intention and corporate capability to "effectively and continuously reconfigure and upgrade critical resources to address the fast-changing environment", often called dynamic capability.[4] Dynamic capability refers to the conversion of businesses' resources into their competence and competitive advantage.

Academics have emphasized the role of organizational factors in developing dynamic capabilities and making them actionable. They also underscore the role of eco-innovation, driven by both internal and external knowledge and resources, in improving production processes and building green competence. Additionally, the significance of corporate governance systems and mechanisms should be considered, as they play a crucial role in setting priorities and stimulating the capability deployment process through executives and managers. Governance shapes and monitors corporate operations and supports corporate dynamic capabilities.

In this edited book, we explore how climate governance and green innovation can support businesses in the era of climate change mitigation. We highlight that companies with robust climate governance mechanisms and a greater engagement

---

[3] See Albitar et al. (2023), p. 3.

[4] See Albitar et al. (2023), p. 3.

with eco-innovation activities and strategies are more adept at identifying and adapting to the rapidly changing climate change requirements, giving them an edge over their competitors. These approaches are not just the outcome of businesses' efforts to build their green competence but also the input that makes businesses' climate engagement more actionable. Consequently, they enable businesses to utilize their existing resources and know-how better to commit to addressing climate change, outperforming their competitors.

This book is structured into two main parts. Part I (five chapters—Chapters 1–5) covers systematic review, perspectives, and practices of climate governance and eco-innovation. Part II (eight chapters—Chapters 6–13) provides case studies and empirical research evidence on those aspects.

Part I

"Climate Governance and Eco-innovation: Systematic Review, Perspectives, and Practices".

Chapter "Understanding the Antecedents and Consequences of Corporate Eco-Innovation" provides readers with an overview of empirical research on corporate decision-making about the distribution of resources to implement ecologically innovative practices (i.e., corporate eco-innovation). Through a systematic review of 100 scholarly studies, the authors illuminate the past and present state of the research on corporate eco-innovation. They first address the divergence in the terminologies and definitions for eco-innovations in business contexts and the measurements of corporate eco-innovation using quantitative regression analysis. Though the existing research on the topic is limited, it has yielded numerous exciting insights, and our aim here is to provide an overview of the influential factors, driving forces, and motivations underlying firms' eco-innovation decision-making as well as the impact of this decision-making on corporate structure and processes, organizing strategies, and operational efficiency. They conclude with some suggestions for future research on corporate eco-innovation.

Chapter "Navigating the Green Path: The Role of Climate Incentives in Shaping Eco-Innovation and Firm Policies" overviews the dynamic connection between climate incentives and eco-innovation. It explores how financial and non-financial climate incentives affect the trajectory of eco-innovation within firms. By tracing the historical evolution of climate incentives, this research elucidates their transformative impact on firm policies. This chapter employs bibliometric analysis to shed light on various aspects of the current research landscape concerning climate incentives and eco-innovation. Despite the evident potential of climate incentives, their implementation faces significant challenges. This chapter critically examines these challenges, offering insights into the complexities of design, global coordination, and equity concerns. In addition, the research critiques the effectiveness and fairness of these incentives, fostering a holistic understanding of the subject. Further, this research underscores the promising future research directions for climate incentives and emphasizes their pivotal role in steering the next wave of eco-innovations.

Chapter "Climate Governance Practices and the Evolutionary Trends in Corporate Eco-Innovation" provides readers with an overview of climate governance practices at global, national, and organizational levels, as well as the evolutionary trends in corporate eco-innovation. This study primarily centres on applying resource-based and institutional theories to clarify the complex connection between corporate governance and eco-innovation. Companies, often constrained by limited resources, operate within the dynamic interaction of social pressures and institutional regulations in sustainable development and green investments. Effectively allocating these resources to align with societal expectations and governmental mandates, particularly in the pursuit of net-zero emissions and carbon neutrality, requires the development of robust climate governance strategies and substantial investments in eco-innovation.

Chapter "Power Dynamics in Climate Governance and Eco-Innovation" overviews the importance of eco-innovation and the involvement of business actors in climate governance. The study highlights significant disparities in the Power and influence of various business organizations within climate governance structures, operating at the levels of nation-states, supranational entities, and individual actors. These disparities are categorized into two key concepts of Power: Structural Power and Discourse Power. Structural Power pertains to the capacity of business entities to shape agendas and establish regulations within the global climate governance framework, thereby showcasing their influential capabilities. Discourse Power explores how individual consumers exert influence by shaping their perceptions of climate change and influencing the decision-making processes of business actors. Business entities can use different forms of Power to influence climate-related matters.

Chapter "Climate Governance in the Digital Era" provides insights into climate governance and the implications of emerging technologies such as Artificial Intelligence (AI) and Blockchain in influencing corporate environmental outcomes. The study first offers an overview of the traditional corporate governance mechanisms in the context of increasing environmental challenges worldwide. It next defines climate governance and discuss various mechanisms and prior findings on their effectiveness. The research finally reviews the roles of the two cutting-edge technologies (AI and Blockchain) in climate governance. Potential applications are also discussed in this chapter.

Part II

"Case Studies and Research on Climate Governance and Eco-innovation".

Chapter "Achieving the Impossible: Perils of Eco-Innovation and Transformational Impact of Charismatic Leadership" provides an overview of the role of charismatic leadership in corporate eco-innovation. In our pursuit of elucidating the concept of eco-innovation, we explore how charismatic leadership can catalyse corporate strategies in the realm of sustainability and contribute to establishing a robust framework for eco-innovation. The exploration is rooted in a theoretical discourse. It aims to illuminate the theoretical linkage between charismatic leadership attributes and their hypothesized impact on fostering sustainability-oriented initiatives within organizational structures, as well as elucidating the potential pathways through which charismatic leadership might facilitate and encourage eco-innovation strategies. Through systematically exploring this subject, we aim to provide a more insightful and professionally grounded perspective on the intersection of charismatic leadership, sustainability, and eco-innovation.

Chapter "Climate Governance in South Asia" provides readers with an overview of the pressing necessity for strong climate governance in South Asia, analysing global and local aspects. South Asia nations have taken proactive measures by implementing domestic regulations, engaging in international initiatives, and developing technical solutions to address climate-related concerns. However, enduring political, socioeconomic, and governance barriers necessitate strategic resolutions. Regional cooperation is crucial for successful climate measures, requiring skilled diplomacy. The chapter thus highlights the importance of South Asia in global efforts to reduce climate change, focusing on the transition to renewable energy and active engagement in international advocacy. Enduring endeavours, collaborative initiatives, and fair settlements are the key as they will convert the goal of climate resilience in South Asia from a mere ambition to a binding commitment that surpasses national boundaries and temporal limitations.

Chapter "Promoting Sustainable Development Through Improving Green Banking Behaviour" provides readers with empirical evidence on green banking behaviour in Vietnam. Green banking has recently emerged as an ideal future model for banks, serving as a foundation for transitioning to a green economy and sustainable development. The study finds that subjective norms, attitudes towards the green bank, perceived behavioural control, and top management support directly affect green banking intention. Subjective norms had the most significant impact of all. All independent variables were found to affect green banking behaviour through the indirect contribution of green banking intention. Furthermore, green banking intention significantly influences green banking behaviour. The research findings imply effective solutions for promoting green banking behaviour in developing countries.

Chapter "Carbon Discourse, Climate Governance and Audit Fees" provides readers with empirical evidence on whether the audit fees would be affected by the firms' carbon disclosure. The findings show that firms disclosing carbon emission information can significantly reduce audit fees. Further analysis reveals that the state-owned firms' disclosure of carbon emissions has a more significant impact on audit fees than non-state-owned firms. In addition, the following industries drive the primary results: scientific research and technology services and metal, nonmetal, and machinery.

Chapter "Business Ecosystem and Sustainable Innovative Practices" provides evidence of how the business ecosystem affects companies adopting innovative approaches for sustainable outcomes. The study contends that companies alone cannot achieve sustainable outcomes and require collaborative approaches to innovate processes. It identifies various internal and external factors in the business ecosystem which could either facilitate or hinder the company's sustainable innovation approaches. Using multiple case study designs, documentary analysis, and semi-structured interviews, the chapter explores various crucial external factors, e.g., the country's regulatory framework, culture, available resources, and collaboration of companies with stakeholders, in developing sustainable, innovative approaches. These sustainable innovations (e.g., digitization, training on health, education, drip irrigation, and water sense technologies) help firms improve their existing products and processes and contribute positively to the environment and society.

Chapter "The Challenges in Constructing Effective Climate Governance in Southeast Asia: Evidence from Vietnam" provides readers with an overview of regional climate governance in Southeast Asia and climate governance in Vietnam. It then identifies and examines existing shortcomings in climate governance in this country, focusing on its current legal framework and practice of corporate responsibility for climate change adaptation. Based on the analyses and evaluations in the preceding parts, the chapter discusses and proposes practical solutions for policymakers and stakeholders to improve the legal framework and monitoring and enforcement mechanisms, which, in turn, enhance and strengthen effective climate governance.

Chapter "Eco-Innovative Actions and Small Business Performance" presents evidence regarding the association between eco-innovative actions and the sustainability performance of small businesses in Nigeria, which is Africa's largest economy. It also examines the extent to which small businesses implement eco-innovative actions. Based on a survey of 480 owners-managers, we identify a significant relationship between eco-innovative actions and the sustainability performance of Nigerian small businesses. These eco-innovative actions are found to enhance the resources needed for sustainability performance. Therefore, it is recommended that businesses incorporate eco-innovative actions and sustainability practices into their strategic vision. This alignment with SDG13 is critical and may offer advantages for the environment.

Chapter "Unboxing Eco-Innovation and ESG for Circular Economy" provides empirical evidence on the association between eco-innovation and ESG in Malaysia. First, this study proposes an econometric model based on the emerging Malaysian economy with the resource-based view theory. It then develops a multiple regression for the panel data for 6 years from 2016 to 2021 to test the econometric model and proposed hypothesis. The analysis reveals a positive and significant relationship between eco-innovation and ESG. This finding indicates that eco-innovation enhances ESG practices in the firm and contributes to circular economy practices in the industrial sector.

Newcastle upon Tyne, UK Vu Quang Trinh

Acknowledgements

I would like to express my gratitude to all authors for their valuable contributions to this edited book related to climate governance and corporate eco-innovation. I also would like to thank Rocio Torregrosa, Associate Editor for Business & Economics at Springer, and Parthiban Gujilan Kannan, Project Coordinator, for their continuous support and patience during the book publication process from its initial stages. Finally, I would like to send my special thanks to my family and loved ones for their patience and support during this book project.

The views expressed in this book are the author's own and do not necessarily reflect those of their affiliations.

Declaration of the Use of Generative AI and AI-Assisted Technologies in the Writing Process:

- Editor: The editor utilized ChatGPT (Premium GPT-4.0) and/or Grammarly (for specific chapters) for proofreading and detecting typos and inconsistencies.
- Authors: The authors refrain from employing AI to generate new and original content. However, some of them utilize AI to check for grammatical errors. This utilization has been confirmed by all contributing authors to this edited book.

Detailed declarations for each chapter are provided at the end of each chapter (prior to the reference list), following the declaration and approval process by the authors.

Contents

Part I Climate Governance and Eco-innovation: Systematic Review, Perspectives, and Practices

Understanding the Antecedents and Consequences of Corporate Eco-innovation 3
Yudian Chen and Teng Li

Navigating the Green Path: The Role of Climate Incentives in Shaping Eco-innovation and Firm Policies 65
Phuong Le, Thao Ngoc Nguyen, and Chau Le

Climate Governance Practices and the Evolutionary Trends in Corporate Eco-innovation 97
Kim Nguyen

Power Dynamics in Climate Governance and Eco-innovation 113
Monika Malik and Shelley Oberoi

Climate Governance in the Digital Era 141
Linh Thi My Nguyen, Devmali Perera, and Dao Le Trang Anh

Part II Case Studies and Research on Climate Governance and Eco-innovation

Achieving the Impossible: Perils of Eco-innovation and Transformational Impact of Charismatic Leadership 167
Tabish Zaman, Ngan Duong Cao, and Thi Tuong Giang Trinh

Climate Governance in South Asia 185
Maryam Eqan and Junfeng Wan

Promoting Sustainable Development Through Improving Green Banking Behaviour 215
Sang Tang My

Carbon Discourse, Climate Governance, and Audit Fees 237
Chengruizhi Ma and Yifei Bi

Business Ecosystem and Sustainable Innovative Practices 261
Meryem Altaf and Nosheen Jawaid Khan

The Challenges in Constructing Effective Climate Governance in Southeast Asia: Evidence from Vietnam 289
Phuong Dung Nguyen and Truc Hanh Vu

Eco-Innovative Actions and Small Business Performance 329
Olubiyi Timilehin Olasoji, Ravinder Rena, Valerie Onyia Babatope, Omoyele Olufemi Samuel, Jubril Bolaji, and Akinlabi Hameed Babatunde

Unboxing Eco-Innovation and ESG for Circular Economy 353
Md. Abu Toha, Parvez Alam Khan, Fatima Irfan, Mohd Salim, and Mantasha Khan

About the Editor

Vu Quang Trinh is a Senior Lecturer (Associate Professor) in Accounting and Finance at Newcastle University Business School, Newcastle University (UK), and holds the position of Visiting Professor of Finance at the University of Economics Ho Chi Minh City (Vietnam). Trinh also serves as the Deputy Director of the Finance and Banking Network (FBNet, AVSE Global). Trinh has a substantial publication record in corporate governance, corporate financial strategies, and sustainability. Trinh's work has appeared in leading academic journals, including those with 4/3* ABS ratings, such as the *British Journal of Management (4-ABS), Annals of Tourism Research (4-ABS), European Journal of Finance (3*-ABS), Journal of International Financial Markets, Institutions and Money (3*-ABS), International Review of Financial Analysis (3*-ABS), International Journal of Finance and Economics (3*-ABS), Accounting Forum (3*-ABS), Journal of International Accounting, Auditing, and Taxation (3*-ABS), Review of Quantitative Finance and Accounting (3*-ABS),* and *Business Strategy and the Environment (3*-ABS).* In addition to research contributions, Trinh holds significant editorial board positions for several scholarly journals, including *Section Editor, Associate Editor, Guest Editor,* and *Academic Editor*. Trinh's research findings have also been accepted for presentation at prestigious conferences, including the *IFABS Oxford Conference, the British Accounting and Finance Association (BAFA), the Financial Management Association (FMA),* and *the European Accounting Association (EAA).*

List of Figures

Navigating the Green Path: The Role of Climate Incentives in Shaping Eco-innovation and Firm Policies

Fig. 1 Financial versus non-financial incentives to promote the transition to a net-zero economy ... 70
Fig. 2 Number of publications over the years ... 78
Fig. 3 Top 10 Journals with the most publications ... 79
Fig. 4 Top 10 Authors with Most Publications ... 79
Fig. 5 Top 10 Research Areas ... 80
Fig. 6 Thematic clusters of keywords in climate incentives and eco-innovation research ... 81

Achieving the Impossible: Perils of Eco-innovation and Transformational Impact of Charismatic Leadership

Fig. 1 The three pillars of sustainability ... 168
Fig. 2 Theoretical framework linking eco-innovation and sustainability mediated by charismatic leadership ... 174

Climate Governance in South Asia

Fig. 1 Countries in South Asia ... 186
Fig. 2 Mean temperature in South Asia (1991–2020) ... 187

Promoting Sustainable Development Through Improving Green Banking Behaviour

Fig. 1 Theory of reasoned action ... 217
Fig. 2 Theory of Planned Behaviour ... 219
Fig. 3 Proposed research model ... 223
Fig. 4 The structural model assessment ... 231

Eco-Innovative Actions and Small Business Performance

Fig. 1 Authors' conceptual model (2023) ... 341

List of Tables

Understanding the Antecedents and Consequences of Corporate Eco-innovation
Table 1 Different terminologies relevant to corporate eco-innovation 5
Table 2 Various definitions of corporate eco-innovation 8
Table 3 Measurements and databases of corporate eco-innovation 10

Navigating the Green Path: The Role of Climate Incentives in Shaping Eco-innovation and Firm Policies
Table 1 A brief of related literature on the impacts of climate incentives on eco-innovation and firm policies 76
Table 2 Search strings relating to climate incentives and eco-innovation 77
Table 3 Overview of challenges, critiques, and future research directions 82

Promoting Sustainable Development Through Improving Green Banking Behaviour
Table 1 Survey questionnaire 225
Table 2 Construct reliability 226
Table 3 Cross loadings 227
Table 4 Heterotrait–Monotrait ratio (HTMT) 227
Table 5 Fornell and Lacker criteria 228
Table 6 Strength of effect (f^2) 228
Table 7 Results of the direct, indirect, and total effect 229

Carbon Discourse, Climate Governance, and Audit Fees
Table 1 Timeline of key corporate sustainability Reporting Requirements in China 242
Table 2 Summary statistics 248

Table 3 Correlation matrix 249
Table 4 The relationship between total audit fees and carbon information disclosure 250
Table 5 Disclosure percentage of sample firms in different industries 252
Table 6 The relationship between total audit fees and carbon information disclosure in scientific research and technology services industry 253
Table 7 The relationship between total audit fees and carbon information disclosure in metal, nonmetal, machinery industry 254

Business Ecosystem and Sustainable Innovative Practices

Table 1 Coding of data 272
Table 2 Innovative approaches and their outcomes 280

Business Ecosystem and Sustainable Innovative Practices

Table 1 The 17 Sustainable Development Goals (SDGs) 333
Table 2 Response Rate 343
Table 3 Multiple Regression result of innovative actions (eco-products, eco-business process, eco-organizational structure, and eco-technological capability) and sustainability performance of SMEs in Lagos State, Nigeria 344

Unboxing Eco-Innovation and ESG for Circular Economy

Table 1 Brief literature 355
Table 2 Eco-innovation and Circular Economy 362
Table 3 The mediating effect of ESG 362

Part I
Climate Governance and Eco-innovation: Systematic Review, Perspectives, and Practices

Understanding the Antecedents and Consequences of Corporate Eco-innovation

Yudian Chen and Teng Li

Abstract This Chapter provides readers with an overview of empirical research on corporate decision-making about the implementation of ecologically innovative practices (i.e., corporate eco-innovation). Through a systematic review of 100 academic publications, we shed light on the past and present state of corporate eco-innovation research. We initially address the divergency of the terminologies and definitions for eco-innovations in business contexts and its measurements used in quantitative regression analysis. Despite the paucity of prior research on this subject, we aim to provide an overview of the influential factors, driving forces, and motivations that underpin firms' eco-innovation decision-making, as well as its impact on corporate structure and processes, organizing strategies, and operational efficiency and other performance. We conclude with some suggestions for future research on corporate eco-innovation.

1 Introduction

Recently, eco-innovation (or environmental innovations or environmentally friendly activities with fundamental changes) has become a buzzword for corporate managers, policymakers, and members of the public. Corporate eco-innovation represents a crucial aspect of sustainable business development and environmental conservation, encompassing the proactive efforts of organizations to develop and implement environmentally friendly products, processes, and strategies. However, the

Y. Chen
Accounting and Finance Subject Group, Newcastle University Business School, Newcastle University, Newcastle Upon Tyne, UK
e-mail: y.chen203@newcastle.ac.uk

T. Li (✉)
Accounting Group, Essex Business School, University of Essex, Colchester, UK
e-mail: Teng.li@essex.ac.uk

V. Q. Trinh (ed.), *Climate Governance and Corporate Eco-innovation*, Sustainable Finance, https://doi.org/10.1007/978-3-031-56423-9_1

empirical evidence for the motivations behind eco-innovation and its impacts on individual organizations and society at large remains scant, as does the theoretical basis for interpreting these impacts. We help to close this gap in the literature with a systematic review of 100 scholarly articles published in prestigious academic journals such as the *Journal of Corporate Finance*, *International Review of Financial Analysis*, *The Leadership Quarterly*, *Research Policy*, *British Journal of Management*, *Journal of Business Ethics*, *Journal of Product Innovation Management*, and *Journal of Cleaner Production* (see Appendix 1 for a summary of all literature reviewed) that reveal trends in the research on corporate eco-innovation over the last two decades.

In the following sections, we consider the divergence in the terminology for and definitions of the eco-innovations that business entities have implemented and the proxies for corporate eco-innovation. Our summary of relevant academic publications shows that, despite the limitations of the extant research, scholars have developed considerable insight into this topic. The focus of this review is on the terminologies, definitions, and concepts related to eco-innovation used in the existing literature, academic inquiries regarding the factors, forces, and motivations that influence firms' eco-innovation investment, and the impact of this form of investment on businesses' structure and processes, organizing strategies, and operational efficiency. We conclude by offering some suggestions for future research on corporate eco-innovation.

2 Terminology and Definitions of Corporate Eco-innovation

As with other emerging research topics, there is no universally accepted term for a firm's ecologically responsible and environmental sustainability practices that are accompanied by substantial structural changes in business organization. Thus, we find that prior studies have used various terms and definitions to refer to such corporate activities but that, recently, *corporate eco-innovation* has emerged as the most common (Albitar et al., 2023; Kim et al., 2020; Ouyang et al., 2022; Zhou et al., 2023). As Table 1 shows, some researchers tend to describe this type of activity as *green, environmental,* or *sustainable*, including green products, technologies, competence innovation, and patents (Chen, 2007; Cheng & Yu, 2023; Fabrizi et al., 2018; Kim et al., 2021), corporate environmental ethics (Chang, 2011), environmental sustainability orientation (Adomako et al., 2022), environmental management systems (Valero-Gil et al., 2023), or sustainable innovation (Delmas & Pekovic, 2016; Juntunen et al., 2018).

The various terms for firms' ecologically sustainable practices share similar meanings and implications. Overall, our literature review suggests that *the primary objective when distributing resources to facilitate eco- and environmental-related practices is maintaining and increasing firms' competitive advantages and economic benefits*. For example, Kim et al. (2021, pp. 2–3) include in their definition of green innovation "*multidimensional plans and actions to achieve a competitive*

Table 1 Different terminologies relevant to corporate eco-innovation

No.	References	Terminology	Explanations
1	Kim et al. (2021), pp. 2–3	Green innovation activities	"Green innovation activities involve multidimensional plans and actions aimed at achieving a competitive advantage in the product market (i.e., through green product development), along with preserving the environment in terms of energy savings, pollution reduction, and waste recycling."
2	Albitar et al. (2023), p. 1	Climate governance	Climate governance consists of three proxies, namely: the existence of an environmental committee, climate incentives and the existence of sustainability reports
3	Horbach (2008), p. 167	Environmentally impactful practice	Firm offering goods or services related to the reduction of environmental impacts
4	Ziegler and Nogareda (2009), p. 887	Technological environmental innovations	A specific kind of technological innovations consist of new products and processes to avoid or reduce environmental burden
5	Fabrizi et al. (2018), p. 1024	Green patents	A technology that allows the identification of technologies related to environmental management (e.g., human and ecosystem health), water-related adaptation and climate change mitigation
6	Doblinger et al. (2022), p. 1	Long-term clean energy innovation	Aaddressing climate change mitigation goals (i.e., long-term net-zero targets and emission reduction) and economic and development goals (i.e., competitiveness and employment in rapidly expanding green industries)
7	Valero-Gil et al. (2023), p. 2	Environmental management systems (EMS)	EMS allows the development of new green technological knowledge that nurtures the firm's eco-innovation capacity to develop solutions that will reduce environmental impact
8	Valero-Gil et al. (2023), p. 6	Environmental performance	It is rated based on quantitative data on consumption, emissions, pollution, and impact, and also includes a more qualitative assessment of companies' current policies and programs as well as their involvement in environmental controversies
9	Cainelli et al. (2020), p. 3	Circular economy	New or improved socio-technical solutions that preserve resources, mitigate environmental degradation and/or allow recovery of value from substances already in use in the economy
10	Veugelers (2012), p. 1771	Clean innovation	A substantial improvement for the environment include CO2 emission reduction for climate change, but also involve other types of pollution reduction, waste treatment as well as the environmental gains from a better use of resources
11	Chen (2007), p. 533	Green core competence	The collective learning and capabilities about green innovation and environmental management in an organization

(continued)

Table 1 (continued)

No.	References	Terminology	Explanations
12	Chen (2007), p. 535	Green product innovation performance	The performance of hardware and software involved in the innovation that a company carries out in relation to green products or processes, including the innovation in technologies in energy-saving, pollution-prevention, waste recycling, green product designs or corporate environmental management
13	Chen (2007), p. 534	Green process innovation performance	The performance in process innovation that is related to energy-saving, pollution-prevention, waste recycling, or no toxicity
14	Chen (2007), p. 538	Green image	It is measured based on green reputation and green credibility. These measures include, among other things, a company's performance on environmental management
15	Chang (2011), p. 362	Corporate environmental ethics	Corporate environmental ethics formalizes corporate value and expectation for ethical behavior, so it is a driving force for green innovation and competitive advantage
16	Delmas and Pekovic (2016), p. 1072	Sustainable innovation	Sustainable innovation is defined as product, process, marketing, and organizational innovations that lead to a noticeable reduction of environmental burdens
17	Adomako et al. (2022), p. 303	Environmental sustainability orientation (ESO)	ESO reflects a firm's proactive stance towards: 'the integration of environmental concerns and practices into their strategic, tactical and operational activities'
18	Adomako et al. (2022), p. 299	Eco-product innovations	Eco-product innovations include improvements to product recyclability and the substitution of virgin inputs with recycled ones
19	Bellamy et al. (2020), p. 899	Administrative environmental innovations (AEIs)	AEIs comprises both internal and external practices connoting whether the firm has implemented environmental management practices or systems internally within its boundaries or externally within its supply chain
20	Olson (2013), p. 782	Green innovation value chain	Green innovation value chain as a tool for analyzing the financial viability of green products using a multi-stakeholder perspective that includes manufacturers, distribution channels, consumers, the environment, and governments as separate links in the chain
21	Juntunen et al. (2018), p. 331	Sustainability innovations	Sustainability innovations are aimed at improving the environmental, social, and economic performance of the innovated solution
22	Cheng and Yu (2023), p. 4	Green technology innovation	It represents technologies, products and processes for reducing pollutant emissions and energy use

advantage in the market through developing greener products and preserve the natural environment via energy saving, pollution reduction, and waste cycling", and Olson (2013, p. 782) relates green innovation to firms' "*financial viability through a multi-stakeholder perspective, including manufacturers, distribution channels, consumers, the environment, and governments*". Likewise, Valero-Gil et al. (2023, p. 2) argue that firms adopt an environmental management system to "*reduce environmental impacts by developing knowledge of new green technologies and fostering corporate eco-innovation capability*", and Adomako et al. 2022, p. 303) assert that an environmental sustainability orientation can "*reflect a firm's proactive stance towards the integration of environmental concerns and practices into their strategic, tactical and operational activities*".

Box 1
The primary objective when distributing resources to facilitate eco- and environmental-related practices is maintaining and increasing firms' competitive advantages and economic benefits.

Thus, recent studies agree that the term corporate eco-innovation is best suited to describe these efforts, and a consensus is emerging regarding its definition. There is agreement that *eco-innovation should change a firm's production process, business models, and management systems fundamentally to mitigate its environmental externalities*. For instance, Chen et al. (2006, p. 333) argue that eco-innovation should include "*hardware and software innovation that is related to green products or processes, including technological innovation involving in energy, saving, pollution-prevention, waste recycling, green product designs, and corporate environmental management*", and Yang and Yang (2015, p. 1003) define it as "*the process of developing or implementing new products, processes or organizational arrangements which significantly decrease environmental impact but provide increased competitiveness of the users*". For Konara et al. (2021, p. 1), eco-innovation describes "*new or modified processes, techniques, practices, systems and products [intended] to avoid or reduce environmental harms*"; for Holzner and Wagner (2022, p. 2), it is the process of developing "*new ideas, behaviour, products, and processes, apply[ing] or introduc[ing] them[,] and which contribute[s] to a reduction of environmental burdens or to ecologically specified sustainability targets*". See Table 2 for the summary of various definitions of corporate eco-innovation.

Box 2
Eco-innovation should change a firm's production process, business models, and management systems fundamentally to mitigate its environmental externalities.

Table 2 Various definitions of corporate eco-innovation

No.	References	Definitions
1	Kim et al. (2021), pp. 2–3	Green innovation involves multidimensional plans and actions aimed at achieving a competitive advantage in the product market (i.e., through green product development), along with preserving the environment in terms of energy savings, pollution reduction, and waste recycling
2	Albitar et al. (2023), p. 2	Eco-innovation can improve energy efficiency and consequently reduce energy consumption and carbon emissions in the production process
3	Costantini et al. (2015), p. 578	Eco-innovation consists of new or modified processes, techniques, systems and products for avoiding or reducing environmental damage
4	Horbach (2008), p. 163	Environmental innovations may lead to a so-called 'win-win' situation characterized by both economic and environmental benefits
5	Marin (2014), p. 302	Eco-innovation is the production, assimilation or exploitation of a product, production process, service or management or business method which results, throughout its life cycle, in a reduction of environmental risk, pollution and other negative impacts of resources use (including energy use)
6	Vasileiou et al. (2022), p. 1	Green innovation includes green organizational changes and marketing with environmental benefits
7	Kesidou and Demirel (2012), p. 862	It is innovation that reflects the concept's explicit emphasis on a reduction of environmental impact, whether such an effect is intended or not. And, it is not limited to innovation in products, processes, marketing methods and organisational methods, but also includes innovation in social and institutional structures
8	Kunapatarawong and Martínez-Ros (2016), p. 1219	Green innovations may be developed with or without the explicit aim of reducing environmental damage. They also may be motivated by usual business goals such as reducing costs or enhancing product quality. Many green innovations combine environmental benefits with a benefit for the establishment or user
9	Chen et al. (2006), p. 333	It is hardware or software innovation that is related to green products or processes, including the innovation in technologies that are involved in energy-saving, pollution-prevention, waste recycling, green product designs, or corporate environmental management
10	Ren et al. (2022), p. 2	Green innovation refers to the invention of new designs and the creation of novel products and processes to reduce environmental pollution
11	Yang and Yang (2015), p. 1003	Eco-innovation is defined as the process of developing or implementing new products, processes or organizational arrangements which significantly decrease environmental impact but provide increased competitiveness of the users
12	Konara et al. (2021), p. 1	Innovation in new or modified processes, techniques, practices, systems and products to avoid or reduce environmental harms
13	Zhou et al. (2023), p. 5	Green innovation is a typical kind of innovation that mainly focuses on green production and transformation

(continued)

Table 2 (continued)

No.	References	Definitions
14	Kirikkaleli and Adebayo (2022), p. 2	Green innovation must reduce environmental degradation by recycling natural resources, employing purifying methods and monitoring green practices
15	Kyaw (2022), p. 8	Environmental innovation may include innovations in the products businesses offer (e.g., the use of environmentally friendly packaging), the production process (e. g., an increased use of renewable energy), and/or the business model (e. g., retake/recycling program)
16	Zhao et al. (2022), p. 199	Firms can adopt green innovation to mitigate environmental degradation and achieve sustainability by developing green products or processes or optimizing organizational management
17	Javed et al. (2023), p. 3	The process of mitigating the adverse effects of business activities on the natural environment
18	Ouyang et al. (2022), p. 2	Green innovation reduces pollution emissions and energy consumption in business activities through developing green products and technologies and improving production processes
19	Wu et al. (2023), p. 5	Eco-innovation reduces environmental pollution and reducing energy consumption, while reducing production costs, improving production efficiency, and enhancing product competitiveness, to promote enterprise economic growth
20	Holzner and Wagner (2022), p. 2	Green innovation develops new ideas, behaviour, products, and processes, apply or introduce them and which contribute to a reduction of environmental burdens or to ecologically specified sustainability targets
21	Xu et al. (2022), p. 2	A new product or process that significantly reduces environmental impacts and can add value to individuals or companies

Regarding measuring corporate eco-innovation, empirical researchers have encountered numerous challenges in identifying suitable metrics or proxies. Naturally, researchers' perceptions and understanding of relevant practices affect such metrics. As mentioned, *eco-innovation is associated with a firm's investment in and allocation of resources to prevent and reduce environmental pollution and other environmental preservation activities*. Therefore, researchers use corporate *environmental expenditures* as a proxy for corporate eco-innovation in quantitative studies. More specifically, some investigate the number and citations of environmental protection patents sourced from a variety of databases (Darendeli et al., 2022; Fabrizi et al., 2018; Javed et al., 2023; Kim et al., 2020; Kirikkaleli & Adebayo, 2022; Ouyang et al., 2022; Quan et al., 2021; Su et al., 2022; Vasileiou et al., 2022; Wang et al., 2023; Wang & Li, 2022; Xing et al., 2021). When information about environmental patents is unavailable, researchers may rely on a firm's spending on environmental activities (Abid et al., 2022; Kesidou & Demirel, 2012) or the eco-innovation or environmental product innovation scores from the Eikon database or Thomson Reuters Asset4 (Albitar et al., 2023; Arena et al., 2018) as a proxy for eco-innovation measures (Table 3 describes the databases for eco-innovation). In addition to such quantitative approaches, a few researchers have

Table 3 Measurements and databases of corporate eco-innovation

No.	References	Measurements	Databases
Quantitative Methodology			
1	Kim et al. (2020)	The number of patents associated with environmental protection	Patent Network Dataverse managed by the Harvard Business School
2	Leoncini et al. (2016)	A dummy variable if the firm introduced an environmental innovation entailing CO2 abatement during the 2006–2010 period	An original database developed in 2011 by the Universities of Bologna and Trento (Italy)
3	Albitar et al. (2023)	Eco-innovation score	Eikon database
4	Fabrizi et al. (2018)	The number of green patents	OECD PATSTAT database
5	Vasileiou et al. (2022)	The number of forward citations of patents	PATSTAT
6	Kunapatarawong and Martínez-Ros (2016)	Factor analysis (principal-component method) on four green innovation objectives	the Spanish National Statistics Institute (INE), the Spanish Science and Technology Foundation (FECYT), and the Foundation for Technological Innovation (COTEC)
7	Kesidou and Demirel (2012)	Environmental research and development expenditures	Department for Environment Food and Rural Affairs
8	Leyva-de la Hiz et al. (2018)	The number of environmental patents	European Patent Office (EPO)
9	Quan et al. (2021)	The number of green patents and the number of green invention patents	Chinese National Intellectual Property Administration
10	Arena et al. (2018)	the score for environmental product innovation	Thomson Reuters Asset4
11	Darendeli et al. (2022)	Bad green news; environmental violations; green patents	WRDS and US Patents
12	Bellamy et al. (2020)	A binary measure: whether or not a firm has initiated internal environmental management practices or has launched an environmental management system	Bloomberg's ESG data
13	Xing et al. (2021)	The number of green patents	CSMAR
14	Wang et al. (2023)	Number of green patents	Chinese Research Data Services (CNRDS) database
15	Wang and Li (2022)	The green patent application	CRDS
16	Kirikkaleli and Adebayo (2022)	Patents on environment technologies	OECD database
17	Javed et al. (2023)	The number of green patents	National Intellectual Property Administration (NIPA)

(continued)

Table 3 (continued)

No.	References	Measurements	Databases
18	Ouyang et al. (2022)	The number of patent applications and the number of valid invention patents; the entropy method based on the pollution emission indicators	China Industrial Statistical Yearbook and China Science and Technology Statistical Yearbook
19	Abid et al. (2022)	research and development expenditure (R&D) related to environmental protection	OECD stats
20	Su et al. (2022)	the quantity and quality of green patents	World Intellectual Property Organization (WIPO)
Qualitative Methodology			
1	De Marchi (2012)	A question of "importance of reduced environmental impacts or improved health and safety"	
2	Ziegler and Seijas Nogareda (2009)	A question of if the company realized at least one of the respective technological environmental innovations	
3	Chen et al. (2006)	Likert five-point scale	
4	Antonioli et al. (2013)	MEI project	CIS5
5	Borghesi et al. (2015)	Dummy variable based on pollution data	CIS data
6	Cainelli et al. (2020)	Environmental benefits from the production of goods or services within an enterprise	Community Innovation Survey (CIS)
7	Kam-Sing Wong and Bigliardi (2012)	Seven-point Likert scale	
8	Juntunen et al. (2018)	A configurational approach and fuzzy-set qualitative comparative analysis (fsQCA)	

employed qualitative methodologies, for instance, collecting data through questionnaires on eco-innovation with the answers scored using five- or seven-point Likert scales (Cainelli et al., 2020; Chen et al., 2006; Juntunen et al., 2018; Kam-Sing Wong & Bigliardi, 2012; Ziegler & Seijas Nogareda, 2009). The following discussion summarizes the major empirical findings of prior eco-innovation studies using various research methods in different contexts.

Box 3
Eco-innovation is associated with a firm's investment in and allocation of resources to prevent and reduce environmental pollution and other environmental preservation activities.

3 The Driving Forces Behind and Barriers to Corporate Eco-innovation

Our review of the relevant literature identified several drivers of firms' allocation of resources to the application and implementation of ecologically responsible initiatives. We generally find that + include: increasing pressure from stakeholders with environmental concerns, the formulation of strict environmental protection regulations and policies, the adoption of additional requirements in global supply chains and/or the host countries in which firms operate, the implementation of new management and governance strategies, and the influence of top corporate executives such as CEOs. The following discussion considers each of these motivations in turn.

Box 4
The primary motivations for corporate eco-innovation practices include:

- Increasing pressure from stakeholders with environmental concerns
- The formulation of strict environmental protection regulations and policies
- The adoption of additional requirements in global supply chains and/or the host countries in which firms operate
- The implementation of new management and governance strategies
- The influence of top corporate executives such as CEOs

3.1 Increasing Demands and Expectations of Shareholders

Firms' stakeholders (e.g., customers, investors, and NGOs) play pivotal roles in motivating them to embrace eco-innovation and enhance their corporate image and reputation. Kim et al. (2020) examine the influence of institutional shareholders' political polarization on corporate engagement in activities relating to the environment in general and environmental disclosure and performance in particular. Using a sample of U.S. firms between 1999 and 2016, they find that when their major institutional shareholders are inclined to the Republican political ideology, firms are less likely to issue environmental reports, establish environmental management committees, or implement environmental and eco-innovation activities. This result suggests that institutional shareholders' political values can be crucial in encouraging or discouraging ecological decisions.

Similarly, Zhao et al. (2022) study the effect of various types of institutional investors on green innovation using a sample of Chinese-listed manufacturing firms between 2013 and 2019 and find that the impact of institutional investors on firms' green innovation depends on the investors' shareholding as well as their portfolio characteristics. Thus, investors with high equity independence and portfolio concentration are positively associated with green innovation while targeted institutional investors prefer to pursue the long-term benefits of implementing green innovation enjoyed by firms with satisfactory financial and social performance. By contrast, temporary institutional investors discourage firms with unsatisfactory economic and social performance from implementing green innovations to avoid short-term risks.

3.2 Regulations, Policies, and Other Institutional Pressures

Many studies have highlighted the significant positive impact of environmental regulations and policies on corporate eco-innovation. In general, firms that operate in regions with stringent environmental regulations are more likely to engage in eco-innovations to comply with legal requirements. Kim et al. (2021) study the relationship between multinationality and green innovation using a sample of 29 countries (the 23 OECD countries plus Brazil, China, India, Indonesia, Russia, and South Africa) from 1990 to 2012 and find that high exposure to foreign markets with more stringent environmental regulations stimulates the filing of green patent applications by multinational corporations (MNCs) and that green innovation is positively associated with the firm value in the long run and more so in the mining and oil and energy (i.e., more polluting) sectors than in the sales and service (i.e., less polluting) sectors. These researchers also find the environmental competitive advantages of MNCs associated with green innovation activities to be more pronounced in host countries with long-term and female orientation.

Rogge and Schleich (2018) focus on the role of policy mix characteristics in low-carbon innovation among German manufacturers of technologies for generating renewable power. They create a dataset using a questionnaire and computer-assisted telephone survey, the results of which show a positive relationship between the consistency and credibility of a firm's policy mix and innovation expenditures for renewable energies. However, they find neither the comprehensiveness of the instrument mix nor the coherence of the policy processes to be related to innovation expenditures. These results suggest that future research on low carbon and eco-innovation should extend beyond policy instruments to the characteristics of the policy mix.

Kesidou and Demirel (2012) examine the drivers of eco-innovation based on data from 1566 U.K. firms that responded to the 2006 Government Survey of Environmental Protection Expenditure by Industry. They find that demand factors affect the corporate decision to undertake eco-innovations but have no impact on the level of investment in eco-innovations. Their findings also suggest that customer and societal requirements motivate firms to embark on eco-innovation while cost savings, organisational capabilities, and strict regulations motivate them to increase their investment in eco-innovation. Interestingly, these researchers also find that less innovative companies invest in eco-innovation in order to increase efficiency and reduce production costs, whereas more innovative companies invest in eco-innovation to gain a first-mover advantage in green technologies and products.

Box 5
A Case Study for the U.K. context (see Kesidou & Demirel, 2012):

- Customer and societal requirements motivate firms to embark on eco-innovation while cost savings, organisational capabilities, and strict regulations motivate them to increase their investment in eco-innovation.
- Less innovative companies invest in eco-innovation in order to increase efficiency and reduce production costs, whereas more innovative companies invest in eco-innovation to gain a first-mover advantage in green technologies and products.

Ren et al. (2022) study the effect of mandatory corporate social responsibility (CSR) reporting on green innovation in China using the country's 2008 mandatory CSR reporting policy as a quasi-natural experiment and employing the difference-in-differences estimation approach to examine whether mandatory reporting can trigger substantive environmental activities by firms. The policy subjects firms to mandatory CSR reporting requirements to show substantially higher green innovation engagement in order to produce material reports for the public. The effect that they observe is stronger for firms located in areas with strong environmental enforcement, for state-owned enterprises, and for firms with high levels of media coverage in the Chinese context.

Berrone et al. (2013) also examine the effect of regulatory and normative pressures on environmental innovation. Based on data from 326 publicly traded U.S. companies from the 20 most-polluting sectors according to the Toxic Release Inventory program run by the U.S. Environmental Protection Agency between 1997 and 2001, they argue that institutional regulatory and normative pressures concerning environmental issues positively influence companies' propensity to engage in environmental innovation, especially companies that pollute relatively more than their industry peers or that have relatively large investments in specific assets. These researchers also find that normative pressures have a greater positive impact on environmental innovation in firms with more organizational slack, while regulatory pressures have less impact. Further, a study by Kyaw (2022) of the effect of policy uncertainty on environmental innovation using data from 1024 U.S. firms between 2002 and 2020 shows that, from a long-term perspective, policy uncertainty is negatively associated with environmental innovation because, along with regulatory uncertainty, it discourages firms' investment in environmental R&D and hence decreases environmental innovation.

Box 6
A Case Study for the U.S. context:

- Institutional regulatory and normative pressures concerning environmental issues positively influence companies' propensity to engage in environmental innovation, especially companies that pollute relatively more than their industry peers or that have relatively large investments in specific assets. (See Berrone et al., 2013).
- From a long-term perspective, policy uncertainty is negatively associated with environmental innovation because, along with regulatory uncertainty, it discourages firms' investment in environmental R&D and hence decreases environmental innovation. (See Kyaw, 2022).

Wang et al. (2023) investigate the impact of ESG ratings, as an institutional normative force or pressure, on green innovation using the ratings of an independent third-party agency (SynTao Green Finance) in China as a quasi-natural experiment. Their results show that being covered by an ESG credit rating agency promotes corporate green innovation, as reflected in the number of applications for green invention patents filed, and that the positive impact of ESG ratings on green innovation is more pronounced among non-state-owned firms, firms with less myopic investors, and firms with tighter financing constraints.

3.3 Internal Governance Mechanisms, Ownership, and Leadership

The relationship between internal governance mechanisms, ownership structure, and corporate eco-innovation is complex and multifaceted. Internal governance mechanisms refer to the controls, structures, and processes that organizations use to monitor and manage their operations, and ownership structure refers to the distribution of ownership rights and control within a company. These factors can significantly influence a firm's ability and willingness to engage in eco-innovation.

Chen and Hung (2014) study the effect of environmental collaboration across organizational boundaries on green innovation from a *social capital perspective*, using the structural equation modelling method to analyse the innovation performance of 237 Taiwanese firms. Their findings show that structural and cognitive capital have a positive influence on relational capital that facilitates knowledge-sharing and, thus, encourages firms to implement more green innovation and enjoy additional competitive advantages through environmental collaboration. Konara et al. (2021) study the relationship among *home-ecological institutions*, the *subsidiaries*' mode post-establishment experience, and environmental innovation in foreign subsidiaries using a sample of foreign subsidiaries in Spain from 2003 to 2015 and find that the extent to which the foreign subsidiaries of multinational enterprises engage in environmental innovation depends on the strength of a multinational enterprise's home-ecological institutions.

The results of our review of the literature indicate that global supply chain adjustments can significantly influence corporate eco-innovation. Various factors may drive these adjustments, including changes in market demand and geopolitical dynamics and, notably, the growing emphasis on sustainability and environmental responsibility. Some researchers have focused on the potential influence of adjustments to global supply chains and suppliers' new requirements for firms' eco-innovation. Doblinger et al. (2022) examine the influence of firms' geographic changes in global value chains on long-term eco-innovation in the wind energy sector based on data from 358 global wind suppliers between 2006 and 2016 and find that supply-side value chain shifts and policy-driven growth in the demand for clean energy have led companies to emphasize long-term green innovation and sustainable development. Similarly, Cheng (2018) investigates whether green suppliers' sustainability orientation affects their green innovation performance and finds that such suppliers can enhance the positive impact of their sustainability orientation on green innovation performance as a knowledge source and co-creator.

Zhang and Jin (2021) examine the effect of firms' *R&D expenditures* on green innovation and the facilitating role of financial constraints. They collect data from listed companies in China from 2007 to 2019 and find that increasing R&D expenditures improves green innovation as measured by the number of green patents granted. They also find that financial constraints discourage green innovation while financial constraints facilitate R&D investment efficiency, leading to an increase in the positive effect of R&D on green innovation. Ning and Guo (2022) investigate the effect of *technological relatedness and the ability to integrate prior knowledge* on environmental innovations in 1990 high-tech Chinese firms between 2006 and 2016 and find that climate and ecological challenges motivate firms to diversify into environmental domains. These researchers find an inverted U-shaped relationship between green technology and inventions and that the green-related attributes of a firm's pre-existing technological resources contribute to the impact of its innovations when the resources are moderately relevant to the targeted green areas. Overall, a deep knowledge of integration capabilities seems to accelerate the utilisation of relevant technological resources to create a greener impact.

Galbreath (2017) examines the impact of the *export intensity*, *women leaders, and absorptive capacity* in 649 Australian firms on green innovation and finds that export intensity is positively associated with green innovations, that the strength of this association increases with the number of women in leadership, and that absorptive capacity is positively associated with the strength of the relationship between export intensity and green innovation. Bammens and Hünermund (2020) explore the relationship between firms' *ownership structure* and eco-innovation in German manufacturing and service industries and suggest that family ownership is positively related to the implementation of eco-innovation and reputational concerns, especially when the ownership of a firm transfers to the next generation. Moreno-Ureba et al. (2022) study the relationship between *board gender diversity* and environmental innovation in the FTSE 250 between 2013 and 2018 and find that a positive impact on environmental innovation when at least three women serve on a board, especially when firms have CSR management boards, though this positive effect diminishes with the length of the tenure of the board members. Flammer et al. (2019) explore the effectiveness and implications for firms of the rise of integrating CSR criteria into *executive compensation* by constructing a database of executive compensation incentives for CSR from the annual proxy statements filed with the SEC for each firm in the Standard & Poor's 500 Index (S&P 500) for the years 2004 through 2013. These researchers argue that integrating executive compensation into CSR helps management focus on stakeholders, enhances corporate governance, results in long-term corporate development, and significantly increases green innovation and firm value.

Box 7
The relationship between internal governance mechanisms, ownership structure, and corporate eco-innovation is complex and multifaceted. Internal governance mechanisms refer to the controls, structures, and processes that organizations use to monitor and manage their operations, and ownership structure refers to the distribution of ownership rights and control within a company. These factors can significantly influence a firm's ability and willingness to engage in eco-innovation.

3.4 CEOs' Personal Characteristics

The top corporate executives naturally play a key role in firms' decision-making processes, including eco-innovation. In particular, CEOs can promote corporate eco-innovation by providing leadership, resources, and a clear strategic direction so that their commitment to sustainability influences the entirety of their organizations in driving positive environmental and business outcomes, including eco-innovation. Cheng (2018) examines whether and, if so, how CEOs' foreign experience affects corporate green innovation in China using evidence from all of the manufacturing firms listed on the Shanghai and the Shenzhen Stock Exchanges from 2007 to 2018 and finds that such experience increases corporate green innovation, especially in less financially constrained firms, state-owned enterprises, and less competitive industries. They find that multinational enterprises in countries with better ecological performance or more stringent environmental policies engage in more innovation than enterprises in countries with worse ecological performance and less strict environmental policies at the level of their foreign affiliates.

Arena et al. (2018) examine the influence of a personal trait of the CEOs, hubris, on their firms' environmental innovation, looking specifically at U.K. companies in the oil, gas, alcohol, beverage and tobacco, paper products, cement, and biotech industries that have sizable environmental impacts. These researchers find that CEOs' hubris facilitates engagement in green innovative projects. They argue that environmental innovation is characterized by high investment and high risk and that the broader social impact of environmental innovation can attract arrogant CEOs whose self-evaluation and consequent tendency to overestimate their chances of success mitigate the perception of the risks that environmental innovation projects entail. However, the effect of CEO hubris on environmental innovation that these researchers observe is not uniform but strengthens with organizational slack and weakens with environmental uncertainty. A study by Zhang et al. (2022a, b) on the effect of the military experience of executives (CEOs and chairpersons) on their firms' pollution and environmental innovation using a sample of 1509 Chinese-listed firms from heavily polluting industries from 2013 to 2017 suggests that such experience is associated with a strong sense of compliance and collective management and executives' military experiences are negatively (positively) related to environmental pollution (innovation).

Javed et al. (2023) investigate Chinese-listed firms from 2008 to 2016 and find that female CEOs are more inclined to implement green innovations than male CEOs, especially those who lead state-owned enterprises, companies in more developed regions, large corporations, and those in environmentally sensitive industries. Ren et al. (2020) use a sample of Chinese firms in heavily polluting industries firms to show that the CEO's hometown identity motivates green innovation performance in terms of increasing their attention to the local environment and implementing necessary eco-innovation practices and that market complexity reinforces this positive effect while institutional ownership may weaken it.

4 Organizational Effects of Implementing Eco-innovations

4.1 Effect on Corporate Management

Corporate eco-innovation, defined as the development and implementation of environmentally friendly products, processes, and strategies, profoundly affects on various aspects of corporate management. Our review of the relevant literature suggests that, when integrated effectively, corporate eco-innovation has a transformative impact on corporate management by requiring a holistic approach to sustainability that encompasses strategic reorientation, cultural change, and proactive risk management. Effective eco-innovation is not simply a technological endeavor but also a management philosophy involving the integration of environmental responsibility into a company's core values and decision-making processes.

Albitar et al. (2023) analyse a sample of firms listed on the London Stock Exchange from 2014 to 2020 and find a positive association between corporate eco-innovation and firms' climate-related governance and commitments to curb emissions and global warming. Simply put, companies that use innovative approaches to deal effectively with pollution and resource consumption take climate change more seriously, and those that integrate climate change considerations into their governance are more committed to addressing climate issues. Kunapatarawong and Martínez-Ros (2016) use data from the Spanish Technological Innovation Panel between 2007 and 2011 to show a positive relationship between green innovation and *employment*, especially in high-pollution industries, that is affected by whether firms voluntarily implement eco-innovations. Delmas and Pekovic (2016) analyse data collected from 4640 employees in 1764 French firms and find that social interactions during employees' work practices enhance sustainable innovation performance when they control for job strain and pay satisfaction and that extrinsic incentives such as remuneration can counteract negative impact of work stress on sustainable innovation. These results suggest that the synergistic effect of intrinsic and extrinsic rewards is conducive to sustainable innovation.

Bellamy et al. (2020) analyse the effect of environmental innovations on environmental information disclosure empirically based on Bloomberg's data for multi-industry supply chain relationships and ecological and financial performance for U.S. and international firms. These researchers argue that knowledge and information flows are critical for the implementation of both eco-innovation and environmental disclosure and that the implementation of eco-innovations reinforces pro-environmental beliefs and motivates responsive actions by organisational members, in turn improving such organisational outcomes as environmental information disclosure. Their results also show that the enhancing effect of eco-innovation on environmental disclosure is stronger when firms have access to information about the supply network.

Box 8
When integrated effectively, corporate eco-innovation has a transformative impact on corporate management by requiring a holistic approach to sustainability that encompasses strategic reorientation, cultural change, and proactive risk management. Effective eco-innovation is not simply a technological endeavor but also a management philosophy involving the integration of environmental responsibility into a company's core values and decision-making processes.

4.2 Effect on Competitive Advantage and Operational Efficiency

Beyond environmentally responsible behavior and policies, corporate eco-innovation can play a strategic role in gaining a competitive advantage. Businesses that invest in sustainability develop innovative solutions and are aligned with the values and preferences of their stakeholders, which can position themselves as leaders in their industries and create a sustainable competitive edge. Thus, for instance, Chen et al. (2006) administer a questionnaire-based survey to workers in Taiwan's information and electronics industries and find green product innovation and green process innovation to correlate positively with firms' competitive advantage. Researchers have devoted considerable attention to the relationship among firms' operational efficiency, financial performance, and, in turn, competitive advantage. However, relatively little research has directly explored the relation between eco-innovation and a corporation's competitive advantage.

For example, Xing et al. (2021) examine the impact of corporate green innovation in the context of environmental reporting on green loans by collecting data from 1086 listed Chinese manufacturing enterprises between 2012 and 2017. They find that implementing green innovation indicates a firm's tendency to be eco-friendly and, thereby, its likelihood of attracting favourable attention from banks consistent with green credit policies. However, environmental disclosure cannot secure more favourable conditions in terms of corporate lending because of the suspicion of greenwashing. Because banks can gather adequate information about borrowers and avoid decisions about lending to greenwashed firms, these researchers argue, firms with better internal green innovation performance are more likely to comply with green policies and, again, to attract positive attention from lenders than firms with external disclosure without substantial internal changes.

Box 9
Businesses that invest in sustainability develop innovative solutions and are aligned with the values and preferences of their stakeholders, which can position themselves as leaders in their industries and create a sustainable competitive edge.

4.3 Effect on Financial Performance

Vasileiou et al. (2022) examine the relationship between green innovation and financial performance using CIS data for a sample of Italian firms from 2006 to 2008 by distinguishing four areas of innovation, namely, products, processes, organization, and marketing. They find that the impact of environmental innovation on financial performance is moderated by the co-existence of innovation in other domains. Further, the interaction between environmental innovation and product innovation positively affects the profitability resulting from environmental innovation, and this effect is also evident as a result of process and organizational innovation, though not as a result of marketing innovation. In addition, Huang and Li (2015) use a questionnaire to collect data from workers in the information and communication technology industry in Taiwan for a study of the effect of green innovation on performance from the perspectives of organizational capability and social reciprocity. They find that dynamic capability, coordination capability, and social reciprocity are significant drivers of both green product innovation and process innovation, with dynamic capability relating more to the former and coordination capability pertaining more to the latter.

Leyva-de la Hiz et al. (2018) confirm that corporate slack resources influence the relationship between firms' environmental innovation and financial performance using a sample of 75 companies in the electrical components and equipment industry worldwide. They distinguish focused from diversified environmental innovations as being less uncertain and find that high levels of slack resources increase managers' moral hazard and attenuate the positive relationship between focused environmental innovations and financial performance. Adomako et al. (2022) collect data from Vietnam and Ghana, developing countries that are facing growing environmental pressure and rising levels of eco-product innovation, and find the positive effect of stakeholder pressures on new green production performance to be mediated by an orientation toward environmental sustainability on the part of stakeholders and eco-product innovation. They argue that weak institutional environments create barriers for domestic firms to act on pressure from stakeholders, and their findings suggest that resource constraints and weak institutions are inherent hindrances to the performance of new green production processes in developing countries. Banerjee et al. (2020) examine the effect of environmentally sustainable practices on firms' financial constraints using a sample of 24,393 firms from 41 high, medium, and low-income countries between 2002 and 2013. Their results indicate that companies are less financially constrained after adopting environmentally sustainable practices, especially those operating in countries with high institutional quality, high-emission industries, and less competitive environments.

Box 10

A Case Study for the Italian context (see Vasileiou et al., 2022):

- Four areas of innovation: products, processes, organization, and marketing.
- The impact of environmental innovation on financial performance is moderated by the co-existence of innovation in other domains.
- The interaction between environmental innovation and product innovation positively affects the profitability resulting from environmental innovation, and this effect is also evident as a result of process and organizational innovation though not as a result of marketing innovation.

4.4 *Effect on the Natural Environment*

Corporate eco-innovation can also have a profound positive effect on the natural environment since the development and implementation of sustainable practices and technologies can help companies reduce their environmental impact, contribute to biodiversity conservation, and promote a harmonious relationship between business operations and the ecosystems that sustain life on earth. For instance, Kirikkaleli and Adebayo (2022) positively assess the collective effects of green innovation, green finance, economic growth, political risk, and social globalization on environmental quality in Brazil. Abid et al. (2022) use data from a comprehensive index for green innovation, financial development, and environmental sustainability worldwide for the period from 2000 to 2019 and find that green innovation is conducive to reducing environmental pollution and achieving environmental sustainability and that financial development and green innovation have substantial long-term impacts on environmental sustainability in leading economies. Nevertheless, the empirical research on these issues remains scant.

In general, then, corporate eco-innovation, which, again, involves the development and implementation of environmentally friendly products, processes, and strategies, has a range of effects on businesses, society, and the environment. These effects are multifaceted and extend beyond companies to encompass environmental conservation, economic benefits, social improvements, enhanced reputation, technological advancements, and policy influence. In these ways, eco-innovation is vital in addressing environmental challenges and creating sustainable and responsible business practices.

Box 11
Corporate eco-innovation can have a positive effect on the natural environment since the development and implementation of sustainable practices and technologies can help companies reduce their environmental impact, contribute to biodiversity conservation, and promote a harmonious relationship between business operations and the ecosystems that sustain life on earth.

4.5 *Shortcomings of Existing Eco-innovation Studies and Directions for Future Research*

Corporate eco-innovation is an essential area of study. Still, the research is subject to certain limitations and challenges that need to be recognized and of which the following appear to be the most significant.

(i) *Complexity and heterogeneity*. Eco-innovation is a multifaceted and context-specific concept. It encompasses a wide range of activities, making it challenging to define and measure consistently across industries and organizations.

(ii) *Data availability.* Data on eco-innovation practices and their outcomes may not always be readily available or may be proprietary, for which reason the ability to conduct empirical research may be limited.

(iii) *Time lag.* Eco-innovation often has long-term effects that can make it difficult to assess its impact within the typical timeframe of research projects.

(iv) *Causality and endogeneity.* Establishing a causal relationship between eco-innovation and certain outcomes, such as financial performance, can be challenging because of the presence of various confounding variables and the potential endogeneity of eco-innovation decisions.

(v) *Measurement challenges.* Determining appropriate indicators and metrics for eco-innovation can be difficult, especially regarding qualitative impacts on brand reputation.

(vi) *Sample bias.* Studies often focus on large firms or industries with large environmental impacts, potentially resulting in sample bias and limiting the generalizability of the findings to smaller companies and other sectors.

(vii) *Self-reported data.* This type of research often relies on self-reported data from firms that may be subject to bias and reporting inaccuracies, especially when companies wish to present themselves in a positive light.

(viii) *Lack of longitudinal data.* Longitudinal data are essential to assess the long-term effects of eco-innovation, but such data can be scarce, particularly for small or privately held companies.

(ix) *Resource constraints.* Comprehensive research on eco-innovation may require significant resources, including access to extensive data, and such requirements can limit the efforts of some researchers.

(x) *Regional and cultural variation.* Significant variations in the drivers of and barriers to eco-innovation by region and culture may make it challenging to draw universal conclusions.

(xi) *Trade-offs and conflicts.* Researchers must consider the potential trade-offs between economic performance and environmental sustainability in eco-innovation and their implications.

(xii) *Lack of standardization.* The absence of standardized definitions of and criteria for eco-innovation can lead to inconsistencies in research findings and hinder cross-study comparisons.

(xiii) *Publication bias.* The greater likelihood that positive findings will be published could lead to publication bias and an incomplete view of eco-innovation research.

(xiv) *Ethical considerations.* Research on eco-innovation may raise ethical questions, particularly studies of the effects of innovations with potentially negative consequences, such as biofuel production from food crops.

(xv) *Dynamic nature.* Eco-innovation evolves as new technologies and practices emerge, so research findings may quickly become outdated.

In conclusion, corporate eco-innovation is a critical strategy for firms looking to address environmental challenges, gain a competitive edge, and enhance their reputation. Understanding the drivers, outcomes, and implications of eco-innovation and barriers to it is essential as researchers and practitioners seek to navigate the evolving landscape of sustainable business practices. As long as societies prioritize environmental sustainability, eco-innovation will remain a focal point of corporate strategy and research. Addressing these challenges to corporate eco-innovation research can generate increasingly robust and comprehensive insights into the role of eco-innovation in sustainable business practices and environmental conservation. Researchers should, therefore, work diligently to overcome these limitations by continuing to contribute to this critical area of study.

Declaration of Generative AI and AI-Assisted Technologies in the Writing Process for This Chapter The editor only used Grammarly to proof-read and check for typos and inconsistencies. There is no further declaration from the authors.

Review of the Literature on Corporate Eco-innovation

No	References	Definitions of EI	Research questions	Theory	Contexts	Sample	Databases	Main findings
1	Kim et al. (2020), p. 101704	Green innovation involves multidimensional plans and actions aimed at achieving a competitive advantage in the product market (i.e., through green product development), along with preserving the environment in terms of energy savings, pollution reduction, and waste recycling	Drivers	Agency Theory: As Friedman (1970) noted, managers may engage in CSR activities mainly to exploit personal benefits arising from social engagement (Borghesi et al. (2015); stkeholder theory: ESG plays a pivotal role in resolving conflicts among different types of stakeholders, and thus increasing long-term firm value	US	All	Patent Network Dataverse managed by the Harvard Business School	Institutional shareholders' Republican-oriented political values are negatively associated with their investee firms' environmental performance and green innovations
2	Kim et al. (2021), p. 101996	Involve multidimensional plans and actions aimed at achieving a competitive advantage in the product market (i.e., through green product development), along with preserving the environment in terms of energy savings, pollution reduction, and waste recycling	Influential factor	Multinational corporations diversifying operational risk, tax benefits, foreign resources, institutional arbitrage theory; liability-of-foreignness view, high additional costs	23 OECD countries plus Brazil, China, India, Indonesia, Russia, and South Africa)	MNC	Patent Network Dataverse managed by Harvard University	Relatively high exposure to foreign markets with more (less) stringent environmental regulations stimulates (stymies) MNCs' green patent applications; Moderators:The environmental standards of the operating countries will increase between green innvoation and firm value

No	References	Definitions of EI	Research questions	Theory	Contexts	Sample	Databases	Main findings
3	Geffen and Rothenberg (2000), pp. 166–186	Successful implementation of radical environmental innovation requires a commitment to innovation, a strong environmental policy, and the capacity to implement these new technologies at the operating level	Drivers	This study reinforces the emerging view that partnerships that build long- term relationships of trust and give greater responsibility to suppliers can be important to achieving improved performance in manufacturing facilities	US	Three case studies of US assembly plants		Suppliers represent a significant element of the successful application of innovative environmental technologies
4	Nameroff et al. (2004), pp. 959–974		Effect		US	26 sectors including chemical sector	CHI's Patent Citation Indicators database	US focuses on green chemistry patents to increase competitive advantage, pushes for environmental law changes
5	Costantini et al. (2017), pp. 799–819	Refer to Kemp and Pearson (2007, p. 7)	Influential factor	Different policies in several countries aim to enhance energy efficiency in the residential sector; new energy-efficient technologies play in achieving EE gains in the res- idential sector	23 OECD countries	Energy efficiency domain for the residential sector		A more balanced mix of policies using demand-pull and technology-push instruments has a greater positive impact on eco-innovation. A more comprehensive policy mix enhances innovation activities

No	References	Definitions of EI	Research questions	Theory	Contexts	Sample	Databases	Main findings
6	Leoncini et al. (2016), pp. 1649–1659	Companies could pursue it through the introduction and/or adoption of eco-innovations1 (EIs) leading to a reduction of their CO_2 footprints (henceforth EICO2)	Influential factor	Taking the dichotomy between radical technological change and outsourcing as a benchmark, we conjecture that EICO2 does not entail (yet) such a substantial degree of novelty and of environmental impact as to require the pursuit of vertically integrated organizational structures	Italy	Photovoltaics and green construction	an original database developed in 2011 by the joint efforts of the Depart- ments of Economics of the Universities of Bologna and Trento (Italy) within the above-mentioned OPENLOC research project	An effect on CO_2-reducing innovations is found for the externalization of tangible activities only, as opposed to intangibles, whose outsourcing even decreases them
7	Albitar et al. (2023), p. 104697	Eco-innovation can improve energy efficiency and consequently reduce energy consumption and carbon emissions in the production process (Kesidou & Demirel, 2012; Lin and Zhu, 2019)	Effect	Resource-based view (RBV)	companies listed on the London Stock Exchange (FTSE-All-Share)		Eikon database;Bloomberg	Eco-innovation is positively associated with climate change commitment
8	Costantini et al. (2015), pp. 577–595	Eco-innovation consists of new or modified processes, techniques, systems and products for avoiding or reducing environmental damage	Drivers		OECD members and some non-OECD countries	Biofuels sector	BioPat	Technological capabilities and environmental regulation spur innovative activities in the biofuels sector

No	References	Definitions of EI	Research questions	Theory	Contexts	Sample	Databases	Main findings
9	Horbach (2008), pp. 163–173	"Environmental innovation consists of new or modified processes, techniques, systems and products to avoid or reduce environmental damage" (Kemp, 2010). environmental innovations may lead to a so-called 'win-win' situation characterized by both economic and environmental benefits (Frondel et al., 2008)	Determinants	Supply side; demand side; institutional and political influences	Germany	Environmental sector	Two German panel databases, the establishment panel of the Institute for Employment Research (IAB) and the Mannheim innovation panel (MIP) of the Centre for European Economic Research (ZEW)	The econometric estimations show that the improvement of the technological capabilities ("knowledge capital") by R&D triggers environmental innovations. Environmental regulation, environmental management tools and general organizational changes also encourage environmental innovation
10	Marin (2014), pp. 301–317	The production, assimilation or exploitation of a product, production process, service or management or business method that is novel to the organisation (developing or adopting it) and which results, throughout its life cycle, in a reduction of environmental risk, pollution and other negative impacts of resources use (including energy use) compared to relevant alternatives. (Kemp and Pearson, 2007)	Effect		Italy	Firms with big polluting plants and the most emission-intensive sectors	Based on administrative data (AIDA by Bureau van Dijk and patent data from PATSTAT) of Italian manufacturing firms	Innovation efforts of polluting firms is significantly biased towards environmental innovations and that environmental innovations tend to crowd out other more profitable (at least in the short run) innovations

No	References	Definitions of EI	Research questions	Theory	Contexts	Sample	Databases	Main findings
11	Rogge and Schleich (2018), pp. 1639–1654		Influential factor	Not only policy mix characteristics such as firm-external determinants of innovation(consistency, credibility, comprehensiveness, coherence), but also both technology push and demand pull factors as classical determi- nants of innovation	Germany	German manufacturers of renewable power generation technologies	Compilie a company database and design a questionnaire which draws upon and exends the CIS	Companies' perceptions regarding the consistency and credibility of the policy mix are positively associated with their innovation expenditures for renewable energies, and this positive link intensifies when considering the mutual interdependence of these policy mix characteristics
12	Krieger and Zipperer (2022), p. 104516	Follow the European Community Innovation Survey in defining firm-level environmental innovations as the introduction of new or significantly improved products or processes that create environmental benefits compared to a firm's implemented state of the art	Drivers		Germany	German manufacturing and service industries	Tenders Electronic Daily database and the German Patent and Trademark Office	Winning public procurement awards with environmental selection criteria increases a firm's probability of introducing more environmentally friendly products on average by 20 percentage points. We show that this effect is driven by small and medium-sized firms and is not statistically significant for larger firms

No	References	Definitions of EI	Research questions	Theory	Contexts	Sample	Databases	Main findings
13	De Marchi (2012), pp. 614–623	"New or modified processes, techniques, practices, sys- tems and products to avoid or reduce environmental harms" (Beise and Rennings, 2005)	Influential factor	The complexity and systemicness of environmental innovations and the market and technological uncertainties that characterize many environmental technologies suggest that complementarities between internal R&D and cooperation strategies are especially important	Spanish	Spanish manufacturing firms (PITEC)		Environmental innovative firms cooperate on innovation with external partners to a higher extent than other innovative firms; cooperation with suppliers, KIBS and universities is more relevant than for other innovators rather than with clients
14	Cainelli and Mazzanti (2013), pp. 1595–1604	MEI (Measuring Eco-Innovation) research project defines eco-innovation as the production, assimilation or exploitation of a product, production process, service or management or business method that is novel to the organisation (developing or adopting it) and which results, throughout its life-cycle, in a reduction of envi-ronmental risks, pollution and other negative impacts of resources use (including energy use) compared to relevant alternatives. (Kemp and Pearson, 2007)	Influential factor		Italy	Italian service firms	Community Innovation Survey; Italian Ministry of the Environment, and NAMEA	Drivers of EI in carbon abatement and energy efficiency differ across service industries, with an important role played by cooperation, training, environmental management sys- tems and public funding. A comparison of the Trade and Transport sectors showed that the latter had more negative environmental effect and demonstrated lower level in EI adoption

No	References	Definitions of EI	Research questions	Theory	Contexts	Sample	Databases	Main findings
15	Ziegler and Seijas Nogareda (2009), pp. 885–893	This definition considers three aspects of a technological innovation. It has to be based on new technology knowledge, it must have been already implemented (i.e. new products must have been introduced on the market or new processes must have been introduced in the firm), and it only has to be new for the firm itself, not necessarily for the market (OECD and Eurostat 1997)	Effect	the resource-based view of the firm also implies that unobserved intangible corporate environmen- tal capabilities could simultaneously influence both environmental activities	Germany	Germany manufacturing sector	A questionnaire-based telephone survey at the ZEW in Mannheim, Germany, in summer/ autumn 2003	A significantly positive effect of environmental process innovations on certified EMS
16	Vasileiou et al. (2022), p. 104530	It follows the mixed definition of EI including technological and non-technological innovations, as well as green organizational changes and marketing with environmental benefits	Effect		Italy	Italian firms	Italian Community Innovation Survey (CIS) 2006–2008 dataset	Environmental benefits achieved due to organizational change have a significant effect on the Italian firms' turnover. Synergies between different innovation domains and EI affect financial performance in a different way with a different sign or strength

No	References	Definitions of EI	Research questions	Theory	Contexts	Sample	Databases	Main findings
17	Fabrizi et al. (2018), pp. 1018–1031		Determinants	The Porter hypothesis, in its weak version, states that "properly designed environmental regulation may spur innovation" (Ambec et al., 2013, p. 5)	Europe		OECD PATSTAT database	Both marked-based regulation policies and participation in green European research networks (in particular with universities and public research centres) positively affect environmental innovation
18	Doblinger et al. (2022), p. 104558	Low-carbon innovation promoting radical innovations for meeting net-zero climate goals, rather than only focusing on incremental innovation that delivers small improvements in the performance of existing clean energy technologies	Drivers		Global	358 global specialized wind suppliers	Navigant Consulting, Orbis, Amadeus, or Bloomberg or the sup- pliers' webpages	The wind industry did not suppress long-term innovation during manufacturing shifts, in this case to China
19	Lanjouw and Mody (1996), pp. 549–571				Global			The increasing interest in environmental protection over the 1970s and 1980s led to the development of new pollution control technologies. Relative to innovations protected primarily in developed countries, those patented in developing countries have a larger family size and a higher level of citations. Developing country innovators have shown a propensity to adaptive innovations

No	References	Definitions of EI	Research questions	Theory	Contexts	Sample	Databases	Main findings
20	Valero-Gil et al. (2023), p. 104737	Eco-innovation is defined as "the production, assimilation or exploitation of a product, production process, service or management or business method that is novel to the organization (developing or adopting it) and which results, throughout its life cycle, in a reduction of environmental risk, pollution and other negative impacts of resources use (including energy use) compared to relevant alternatives" (Kemp and Pearson, 2007, p. 7)	Effect	Based on the natural resource-based view and dynamic capabilities arguments, we show that when firms engage in eco-innovation, they improve their environmental performance	Global		EPO-PATSTAT, Sustainalytics ESG Research, Thomson Reuters ASSET4 ESG, Bloomberg ESG, and COMPUSTAT	Adopting EMS, rather than strengthening the positive impact of eco-innovation on environmental performance, generates organizational rigidities that weaken the eco-innovation–environmental performance link

No	References	Definitions of EI	Research questions	Theory	Contexts	Sample	Databases	Main findings
21	Antonioli et al. (2013), pp. 975–988	EI is defined as "the production, assimilation or exploitation of a product, production process, service or management or business method that is novel o the organisation (developing or adopting it) and which results, throughout its life cycle, in a reduction of environmental risk, pollu- tion and other negative impacts of resources use (including energy use) compared to relevant alternatives". (Kemp, 2010, p. 2)	Drivers	Porter Hypothesis (PH) framework	Italy	555 Italian industrial firms		EI adopted by firms located in a densely industrial region of the European Union which is highly exposed to international competition, strict complementarity is rarely present
22	Borghesi et al. (2015), pp. 669–683	Any product, process, organizational, social or institutional innovation that is able to reduce environmen- tal impact and resource use (Kemp, 2010; Rennings, 2000; del Río González, 2009)	Influential factor		Italy	Manufacturing sectors	CIS dataset	Current and future expected regulation is highly correlated to EI

No	References	Definitions of EI	Research questions	Theory	Contexts	Sample	Databases	Main findings
23	García-Granero et al. (2020), p. 104028	EI is defined as "the production, assimilation or exploitation of a product, production process, service or management or business method that is novel to the organization (developing or adopting it) and which results, throughout its life cycle, in a reduction of environmental risk, pollution and other negative impacts of resources use (including energy use) compared to relevant alternatives" (Kemp and Pearson, 2007 p. 7)	Drivers	According to Howard-Grenville and Bertels (2012), environmental corporate culture is what builds EI practices	Spain	Fuit and vegetable farming-marketing companies of southeast Spain	Questionnaire	Organizations with commercial orientation might develop EI according to consumer preferences and changes in market conditions with the aim of pursuing reduction of costs, improvement of company reputation, and operational efficiency increase in terms of an output gained to run a business operation
24	Kesidou and Demirel (2012), pp. 862–870	A reduction of environmental impact. Including innovation in products, processes, marketing methods, organisational methods, social and institutional structures	Determinants	Interactive process integrating technology push and market pull	UK	Industrial sectors	Department for Environment Food and Rural Affairs (DEFRA)	Demand factors affect the decision of the firm to undertake eco-innovations whilst these factors exhibit no impact upon the level of investments in eco-innovations

No	References	Definitions of EI	Research questions	Theory	Contexts	Sample	Databases	Main findings
25	Wagner (2007), pp. 1587–1602	…measures of relevant actors (firms, private house- holds), which: (1) develop new ideas, behaviour, products and processes, apply or introduce them, and; (2) con- tribute to a reduction of environmental burdens or to ecologically specified sustainability targets" (Rennings, 2000, p. 322)	Influential factor	a "soft" positive EMS influence on less tangible factors such as innovative activity or reputation of firms exists	Germany	German manufacturing firms	DEPATISnet	Environmental innovation can be meaningfully identified using patent data; implementation level of environmental management systems has a positive effect exclusively on environmental process innovation
26	Cainelli et al. (2020), p. 103827	It highlights the ecological attributes of specific new processes, products and methods	Drivers	Porter hypothesis: based on the positive potential impact environmental regulation may have in boosting productivity, efficiency and improvements in organisational or product/ process innovations	EU	Service and manufacturing firms	Community Innovation Survey (CIS)	Environmental policy and demand-side factors are both significant in driving the adoption of innovations that promote recycling, reduce waste and decrease the use of materials
27	Orsatti et al. (2020), p. 103919		Influential factor		EU		European Patent Office (EPO) and PatStat	Green technologies are more likely to be generated by teams that creatively recombine previous knowledge. This effect is moderated by teams' previous experience and environmental policy framework

No	References	Definitions of EI	Research questions	Theory	Contexts	Sample	Databases	Main findings
28	Ghisetti et al. (2015), pp. 1080–1093	The production, assimilation or exploitation of a product, pro- duction process, service or management or business methods that is novel to the firm [or organization] and which results, through- out its life cycle, in a reduction of environmental risk, pollution and other negative impacts of resources use (including energy use) compared to relevant alternatives	Influential factor	Open innovation models in which the knowledge boundary between the firm and the external environment becomes permeable	11 EU countries: Bulgaria, Czech Republic, Germany, Estonia, Hungary, Italy, Lithuania, Latvia, Portugal, Romania and Slovakia		Community Innovation Survey (CIS)	Knowledge sourcing has a positive impact on EI-performance. Absorptive capacity increase this effect. Internal innovation capabilities and knowledge socialization mechanisms decrease this effect
29	Kunapatarawong and Martínez-Ros (2016), pp. 1218–1232	[Green] innovations consist of new or modified processes, techniques, practices, systems and products to avoid or reduce environmental damage. [Green] innovations may be developed with or without the explicit aim of reducing environmental damage. They also may be motivated by usual business goals such as reducing costs or enhancing product quality. Many [green] innovations combine environmental benefit with a ben- efit for the establishment or user" (Rennings, 2000; Rennings et al., 2004, p. 376)	Effect	The net effect at the macro-level is therefore uncertain as green inno- vation reduces labor demand in some industries, while increases labor demand in other industries	Spain		Spanish National Statistics Institute (INE), the Spanish Science and Technology Foun- dation (FECYT), and the Foundation for Technological Innovation (COTEC)	A positive relationship between green innovation and employment, and the relationship is stronger for firms in the so-called 'dirty' industries. The relationship is positive for firms that introduce green innovation voluntarily

No	References	Definitions of EI	Research questions	Theory	Contexts	Sample	Databases	Main findings
30	Conti et al. (2018), pp. 1996–2009	Renewable energy sources (RES) innovation	Influential factor		EU		PATSTAT-CRIOS database	EU RES inventors intensified their citations to other member countries and decreased those to domestic inventors. reduction in fragmentation emerged as a result of the EU support for RES taking mainly the form of demand-pull policies
31	Veugelers (2012), pp. 1770–1778	Substantial improvements for the environment.These environmental effects include CO2 emission reduction for climate change, but also involve other types of pollution reduc- tion, waste treatment as well as the environmental gains from a better use of resources	Drivers		EU		Community Innovation Survey (CIS)	Policy interventions are shown to be more powerful to induce the adoption and development of new clean technologies when designed in policy mix and time consistently, affecting future expectations
32	Chen et al. (2006), pp. 331–339	Hardware or software innovation that is related to green products or processes, including the innovation in technologies that are involved in energy-saving, pollution-prevention, waste recycling, green product designs, or corporate environmental management	Effect	increase reseouce productivity, reduce cost; first mover advantages; product differentiation	Taiwan	Information and electronics industries in Taiwan	Likert five-point scale	The performances of the green product innovation and green process innovation were positively correlated to the corporate competitive advantage

No	References	Definitions of EI	Research questions	Theory	Contexts	Sample	Databases	Main findings
33	Chen (2007), pp. 531–543		Drivers		Taiwan	Information and electronics industries in Taiwan	Seven-point Likert scale from 1 to 7	Green core competences of firms were pos- itively correlated to their green innovation performance and green images
34	Dangelico and Pujari (2010), pp. 471–486	'Green product' or 'environmental product' are used com- monly to describe those that strive to protect or enhance the natural environment by conserving energy and/or resources and reducing or eliminating use of toxic agents, pollution, and waste (Ottman et al., 2006)	Influential factor		Italy and Canada	12 small to medium size manufacturing companies based in Italy and Canada	Personal interviews, company records, and published data sources	Propose a conceptual framework that presents three key environmental dimensions of green product innovation such as energy minimization, materials reduction, and pollution prevention as identified in the life cycle phases of products
35	Chang (2011), pp. 361–370		Mediation role	RBV argues that environmental social responsibility can become a key capability that leads to a sustained competitive advantage (Hart, 1995)	Taiwan	Taiwanese manufacturing industry	"Five-point Likert scale from 1 to 5" rating from strongly disagreement to strongly agreement. The ques- tionnaire comprises five parts	Corporate environmental ethics positively affects green product innovation and green process innovation. Green product Innovation mediates the positive relationship between corporate environmental ethics and competitive advantage, but green process innovation does not

No	References	Definitions of EI	Research questions	Theory	Contexts	Sample	Databases	Main findings
36	Bendell (2015), pp. 277–288	Environment-friendly innovations are a special type of new or modified process, product, practice, or system innovations that have a favorable impact on the natural environment irrespective of whether the effect was the main objective of the innovation (Kemp and Pearson, 2007; Rennings, 2000)	Drivers	Prosocial motivation; compatibility	US	Dry cleaning industry		The innovation's ability to satisfy downstream customer demands has the greatest impact on environment-friendly innovation adoption decisions by business owners
37	Huang and Li (2015), pp. 309–324	Green innovation or eco-innovation can be generally defined as innovation that results in a reduction of environmental impact, regardless of whether or not that effect is intended (OECD, 2010; Cai & Zhou, 2014)	Effect	social network theory, dynamic capability	Taiwan	Information and communication technology industry (ICT industry)	Five-point Likert-type scales	Green product and process innovation have positive effects on environmental performance and organizational performance
38	de Medeiros et al. (2015), pp. 327–341		Drivers		Brazil	Brazilian industry		The drivers influencing the green innovation market are systematically occurring and have different contingencies and structures

No	References	Definitions of EI	Research questions	Theory	Contexts	Sample	Databases	Main findings
39	Delmas and Pekovic (2016), pp. 1071–1088	Sustainable innovation is defined as product, process, marketing, and organizational innovations that lead to a noticeable reduction of environmental burdens	Influential factor	Social interactions, pay-level satisfaction; job strain	France	French Ministry of Industry	The Orga- nizational Changes and Computerization's (COI) survey; the community innovation survey (CIS), the annual enterprise survey and the annual statement of social data	The positive impact of intrinsic motivations (through employee social interactions), and the negative impact of job strain (through high imposed work pace) on corporate sustainable innovation
40	Li et al. (2016), pp. 1089–1104	Green innovation is the improvement of products or pro- cesses which reduces environmental burden or achieve sustainability targets (Rennings, 2000)	Influential factor	Legitimacy theory	China		RESSET database, annual reports of all listed companies and the Baiteng patent network	Environmental legitimacy significantly negatively influences the likeli- hood of corporate carbon disclosure
41	Longoni and Cagliano (2016), pp. 1097–1120		Influential factor		Italy		Interviews; annual reports and sustainability reports of the companies interviewed	An organization's time perspective plays a crucial role in explaining the organization's degree of sustainable inno- innovativeness and improvement of triple bottom line out- comes
42	Galbreath (2017), pp. 47–61	Consisting of actions and/ or practices that seek to reduce a firm's environmental footprint	Drivers	Institutional theory and resource-based view: firm actions can result from both external influence and internal determinism	Australia	Wine industry	Company and names from Winetitles database	Export intensity is positively associated with green innovations; Moderators: women in leadership roles and greater levels of absorptive capacity

No	References	Definitions of EI	Research questions	Theory	Contexts	Sample	Databases	Main findings
43	Leyva-de la Hiz et al. (2018), pp. 1215–1227	"measures of relevant actors, which: (i) develop new ideas, behavior, products and processes, apply or introduce them; and (ii) contribute to a reduction of environmental burdens or to ecologically specified sustainability targets" (Rennings 2000)	Influential factor	Agency theory	Global	75 largest companies in the electrical components and equipment industry worldwide	European Patent Office (EPO)	High levels of slack resources reduce the existing positive relationship between focused environmental innovations and a firm's financial performance
44	Cheng (2018), pp. 393–414		Drivers	Resource-based view (RBV), the knowledge-based view, and capability theory	China	technology firms in Taiwan	China Credit Information Service 2013	Using green supplier involvement as a co-cre- ator enables diversifying green entrants to generate greater green innovation performance than green supplier involvement does as a knowledge source
45	Quan et al. (2021), pp. 535–557		Determinants	Learning theories: CEOs' foreign experience increse their accommodation ability and creativity	China	Manufacturing firms	Chinese National Intellectual Property Administration; CSMAR	CEO foreign experience is positively related to green innovation quality and internationalization
46	Arena et al. (2018), pp. 316–336		Influential factor	Upper-echelons theory: Complex strategic decisions are the result of behavioural factors, in particular personality traits, including CEO hubris	UK	oil and gas industries, alcohol, beverage and tobacco, paper products, cement and biotech firms	ThomsonReuters Asset4	CEO hubris effect on environmental innovation increases with the organizational slack, but weakens with the extent of environmental uncertainty

No	References	Definitions of EI	Research questions	Theory	Contexts	Sample	Databases	Main findings
47	Liao and Liu (2021), pp. 1110–1122		Influential factor	Psychological contract violation theory and attribution theory	China			Firms' reactive eco-innovation positively correlates with consumers' propensity to boycott consumer goods
48	Adomako et al. (2022), pp. 299–320	This construct signifies the processes of incorporating pro-environmental decision-making within a firm's product development activities, with respect to environmentally sustainable packaging, materials, and evaluations conducted to improve recyclability, reuse and decomposability	Effect	Stakeholder theory and innovation constraints perspectives	Vietnam and Ghana			The positive effects of stakeholder green pressures on new product performance are serially mediated by environmental sustainability orientation and eco-product innovation
49	Ren et al. (2022), pp. 576–594	Green innovation refers to the invention of new designs and the creation of novel products and processes to reduce environmental pollu- tion (Berrone et al., 2013)	Influential factor	Legitimacy theory	China	Mining, manufacturing and electricity Industries	The State Intellectual Property Office (SIPO) of China database	Mandatory CSR reporting firms show substantially higher green innovation performance than non-CSR reporting firms; Moderators: negative and positive coverage strengthen the relationship

No	References	Definitions of EI	Research questions	Theory	Contexts	Sample	Databases	Main findings
50	Theyel (2000), pp. 249–266		Influential factor		US	Chemical, plastics and resins and ink manufacturing firms		Firms adopting several key practices are outperforming their competitors in implementing innovations for cleaner production and in reducing chemical waste
51	Kam-Sing Wong and Bigliardi (2012), pp. 468–490	Putting emphasis on innovation toward sustainable development	Effect		China	Electrical and electronics industry		Green product and process innovations are positively associated with green product competitive advantage and green new product success
52	Shou et al. (2022), pp. 879–898	Hardware or software innovation that is related to green products or processes, including the innovation in technologies that are involved in energy-saving, pollution-prevention, waste recycling, green product designs, or corporate environmental management	Influential factor	Theory of planned behavior	China	Small and medium-sized manufacture		Both injunctive and descriptive norms are instrumental in stimulating firms to take actions on green innovation; Moderators: flexibility orientation of a firm

No	References	Definitions of EI	Research questions	Theory	Contexts	Sample	Databases	Main findings
53	Seifert et al. (2023)							Sustainable innovation success requires consideration of refugee-specific needs and cultural preferences, adaptation to host government restrictions and data management policies
54	Chen and Hung (2014), pp. 347–363		Influential factor	Social capital theory		Taiwanese manufacturing companies	Questionnaires	Social capital plays an important role in green management and companies use social capital to generate additional competitive advantages through environmental cooperation
55	Shou et al. (2018), pp. 1683–1704	Develops new or modified products, processes and practices to avoid or reduce environmental burdens	Influential factor	Higher complementarity with supply chain partners is more likely to generate idiosyncratic relationship assets	Taiwan			Overall inter-organizational fit level is positively related to firms' EI outcomes
56	Golgeci et al. (2022), pp. 898–929	Innovation that is able to reduce environmental impact and resource use	Influential factor	Technology diffusion theory: an individual's awareness of the need to innovate influences the decision to engage in innovation	Australia	Australian food and beverage industry		Business moral values positively moderate the relationships between time and budget provisions and managers' environmental innovation behavior and between budget and advice provisions and managers' social innovation behavior

No	References	Definitions of EI	Research questions	Theory	Contexts	Sample	Databases	Main findings
57	Hartmann et al. (2022), p. 101327	Refer to new or modified processes, services, or products that allow for the reduction or avoidance of environmental harms	Drivers	Institutional theory	Multi-country	Transportation and logistics business	Refinitiv	Institutional factors, and regulatory factors in particular, impact innovation decisions
58	Darendeli et al. (2022), pp. 986–1037		Effect				Violation tracker and RepRisk; WRDS and US Patents	Firms that increase their Green Score have higher future profitability, generate more green patents, and receive more citations
59	Yang and Yang (2015), pp. 1003–1012	The process of developing or implementing new products, processes, or organizational arrangements that significantly decrease environmental impact but provide increased competitiveness of the users	Effect		China			China had accelerated its process of eco-innovations during 2006–2010 when a series of ESER policies were enforced
60	Konara et al. (2021), p. 101261	Innovation in new or modified processes, techniques, practices, systems and products to avoid or reduce environmental harms	Influential factor	Institutional theory:Foreign affiliates of multinational enterprises face institutional pressures from both home and host countries, and therefore have complex environmental innovation drivers	Spain	MNEs	The Spanish Technological Innovation Panel (PITEC)	Home-institutional effect on subsidiary-level environmental innovation as well as the moderating effects of the subsidiary establishment mode and host experience

No	References	Definitions of EI	Research questions	Theory	Contexts	Sample	Databases	Main findings
61	Eiadat et al. (2008), pp. 131–145	A class of manufacturing practices that include source reduction, pollution prevention, and the adoption of an environmental management system	Effect	EI Improving performance by reducing costs, increasing competition, waste utilisation revenue, reputation and therefore more cash flow	Jordan	Chemical industry		Environmental innovation strategy is associated with improved perceived firms' business performance
62	Bellamy et al. (2020), pp. 895–932	Both internal and external AEIs are complementary forms of proactive environmental actions driven by simi- lar regulatory, cost, competitive, and governance pres- sures from governments, supply chain partners, competitors, consumers, and other stakeholders	Effect	AEI positively influences the intention of individuals within a company to access environmental information through information about the company's implementation of the man-made environment, thus leading to wider environmental disclosure by the company	Global	GICS sub-industrie	Bloomberg's ESG data	AEI implementation is positively associated with the extent of environmental disclosure
63	Watson et al. (2017), pp. 254–279						Review 88 articles	Engaging with stakeholders to drive environmental innovation requires three levels of capabilities: operational capa- bilities, first-order engagement management capabili- ties, and second-order engagement learning capabilities

No	References	Definitions of EI	Research questions	Theory	Contexts	Sample	Databases	Main findings
64	Berrone et al. (2013), pp. 891–909	Emphasizes pollution prevention. It concerns the invention of new designs and the creation of novel products and processes to reduce or eliminate the use and generation of hazardous substances	Influential factor	Institution theory: Institutionalist perspective, where firms actively implement environmental innovations in order to increase legitimacy and reduce departures	US	Polluting industries	COMPUSTAT	Institutional pressures can trigger environmental innovation, especially in those firms polluting relatively more than their industry peers
65	Xing et al. (2021), p. 101838	A strategy or activities intending to improve-ments in emission control, pollution reduction, and cost-saving, whose scope comprises aspects of firms' technology and management	Effect	Ecological modernization theory and dynamic capability theory: green innovation improve environmental performance and is beneficial for corporate long-term development	China	Manufacturing enterprises	CSMAR	Green innovation promotes access to corporate loans
66	Zhang et al. (2022a, b), p. 101562	The development of products, processes, and services aimed at reducing environmental harm by using new methods for treating emissions, recycling or reusing waste, and finding cleaner energy sources	Influential factor	Imprinting theory: military imprint instills a sense of following rules and stewardship for the collective	China	Heavily polluting industries	CSMAR, WIND, IPE, the Baiteng patent network	Executives with military imprint negatively relate to firm pollution and positively relate to firm environmental innovation
67	Zhang (2022), p. 102311		Effect	Porter Hypothesis: "innovation compensation" and "first-mover advantage"	China	Chinese exporters	CSMAR, Bloomberg ESG Database, The Thomson Reuters' database	A positive relationship between green innovation and export product quality; Moderators: environmental regulations have a negative effect on green innovation, but greenwashing suppression effect curbs this effect

No	References	Definitions of EI	Research questions	Theory	Contexts	Sample	Databases	Main findings
68	Zhou et al. (2023), p. 102504	Alternative Energy Production, Energy Conservation, Environmentally Friendly Farming, Environmental Purification, Protection or Remediation, and Regulation, Design or Education	Influential factor	Zero-Sum Hypothesis and Win-Win Hypothesis: turn this pressure into incentives and conduct more environmental innovations	China		The Chinese State Intellectual Property Office6 (SIPO) and the Chinese Annual Survey of Industrial Firm (CASIF)	Environmental regulations promote green innovation
69	Wang et al. (2023), p. 102623		Influential factor	When companies incorporate ESG objectives it can alleviate the information asymmetry between managers and shareholders and help shareholders to monitor the company more effectively, thus promoting green innovation in the company	China		Chinese Research Data Services (CNRDS) database	A positive relationship between ESG ratings and green innovation
70	Banerjee et al. (2020), p. 101337	Refining ESP into three components: emission reduction, product innovation and resource reduction	Effect	Better environmental activities are associated with better stakeholder engagements, reduce information asymmetry and then reduce financial constraints	Global		The Asset4 database	Environmentally sustainable practices are negatively associated with the financial constraints of firms
71	Wang and Li (2022), p. 100961		Influential factor	Altruistic view, strategic view and legitimacy deficiency	China	A-share firms	CRDS	Guideline effectively promotes the development of green technology innovations

No	References	Definitions of EI	Research questions	Theory	Contexts	Sample	Databases	Main findings
72	Kirikkaleli and Adebayo (2022)	Reduce environmental degradation by recycling natural resources, employing purifying methods and monitoring green practices	Effect	Green innovation (GINO), on the other hand, is simply the most efficient technique of improving environmental quality	Brazil		OECD database	A significant and positive association was found between political risk, green finance, green innovation and social globalization environmental quality
73	Zhang and Jin (2021), p. 101918		Influential factor		China		The China National Intellectual Property Administration (CNIPA)	A positive relationship between R&D expenditures and green patents; Moderators: financial constraints discourage green innovation; financial constraints facilitate R&D investment efficiency and enhance the positive effect on green innovation
74	Flammer et al. (2019), pp. 1097–1122		Influential factor	Companies may take actions that reduce the detrimental impact; companies may take actions that are beneficial to the less salient stakeholders	US	All S&P 500 firms during a 10-year period (2004–2013)	The compensation information that companies report in their proxy statements filed with the Securities and Exchange Commission (SEC)	The adoption of CSR contracting leads to an increase in green innovations
75	Jimenez (2005), pp. 723–750	Any process, technique, practice, or product modification that implies a reduction of the environmental impact of production, even when this is not the crucial objective of such change	Influential factor		Chile			Strong market and regulatory stimuli towords the development of more radical environmental innovations

No	References	Definitions of EI	Research questions	Theory	Contexts	Sample	Databases	Main findings
76	Epicoco (2016), pp. 427–441		Effect		US	chemical sector	USPTO	Companies that adopt environmental innovations have a higher potential for timely radicalisation
77	Ning and Guo (2022), p. 104406		Influential factor	Resource-based view	China	High-tech firms	ZSP Administrative Committee	Diversifying firms' green technological relatedness has an inverted U-shaped relationship with invention impact
78	Dangelico et al. (2013), pp. 642–658		Influential factor	Resource-based view	Italy	The textile and upholstered furniture industries		Incorporating environmental issues into green product design has a positive impact on business performance
79	Olson (2013), pp. 782–793		Effect		US	Hybrids		Hybrids are not currently financially attractive for any link of the GIVC
80	Heidenreich et al. (2017), pp. 343–359		Influential factor					Eco-friendly innovations adoption relates positively to consumer innovativeness and that this effect can be intensified by providing external policies such as infrastructure, incentives, and communication policies
81	Juntunen et al. (2018), pp. 331–355	Aimed at improving the environmental, social, and economic performance of the innovated solution	Influential factor		Europe			There are multiple stakeholder integration strategies that influence the performance of sustainable innovation

No	References	Definitions of EI	Research questions	Theory	Contexts	Sample	Databases	Main findings
82	Paparoidamis et al. (2019), pp. 824–847	An effective way to encourage greater consumption of sustainable products, by providing both better functionality and environmental protections	Influential factor		US			Degree of innovativeness, level of eco-friendliness, and detachability significantly affect consumers' adoption in- tentions
83	Bammens and Hünermund (2020), pp. 431–453		Drivers	Institutional theory and the mixed gamble logic	Germany	All manufacturing firms and some service industries related to innovation		Family ownership is positively related to the introduction of eco-innovations by firms, in part because of the stronger emphasis being placed on the company's reputation
84	Zhao et al. (2022), pp. 195–230	Frms adopt green innvoations to mitigate environmental degradation and achieve sustainability by developing green products or processes or optimizing organizational management	Influential factor	Stakeholder theory: transient institutional investors might lack supervisory motivation to regulate managers and promote firms' green innovation	China	Manufacturing firms	The Certification and Accreditation Administration of the People's Republic of China (CNCA); China National Intellectual Property Administration (CNPA)	Dedicated institutional investors with more shareholding independence and higher portfolio concentration are positively associated with green innovation and are the driving force behind it

No	References	Definitions of EI	Research questions	Theory	Contexts	Sample	Databases	Main findings
85	Javed et al. (2023), p. 113515	The process of mitigating the adverse effects of business activities on the natural environment	Influential factor	Upper echelon theory and gender socialization theory: females are more concerned about the environment	China	Chinese non-financial companies	National Intellectual Property Administration (NIPA)	Female CEOs are greener than their male counterparts; Moderators: Women working in state-owned enterprises and enterprises in more developed regions are more likely to promote green innovation. The impact of female CEOs on green innovation is more pronounced in companies in large and environmentally sensitive industries
86	Moreno-Ureba et al. (2022), p. 133871	Kemp and Pearson (2007, p. 7)	Influential factor	critical mass theory: the achievement of a critical mass of female directors improves the environmental behavior of firms, which enhances their environmental dis- closures and actions	UK		Thomson Reuters ASSET4 database	Board gender diversity has a positive impact on environmental innovation, with companies having at least three women on their boards and higher levels of environmental innovation
87	Cheng and Yu (2023), p. 135902	The general term representing technologies, products and processes for reducing pollutant emissions and energy use	Influential factor	Agency theory, externality theory and theory of citizens' environmental rights: Incentives for alignment of interests, internalisation of environmental innovation, confidence in public participation	China	Heavy pollution industries		Green innovations in new energy sources that radically reduce pollution emissions are not significant

No	References	Definitions of EI	Research questions	Theory	Contexts	Sample	Databases	Main findings
88	Chen et al. (2022), p. 131537	Environmentally sound technologies that protect the environment, are less polluting, use all resources in a more sustainable manner, recycle more of their wastes and products, and handle residual waste in a more acceptable manner than the technologies for which they were substitutes	influential factor	Porter Hypothesis: environmental regulations pressured/motivated polluting firms to seek technological innovation for the reduction of pollution	China	Prefecture-level cities		Environmental regulations of carbon emissions and air pollution had a positive effect on the cities' green technology innovation
89	Zhang et al. (2022a, b), p. 131921		Influential factor	Natural resource-based view: The information program may encourage the green innovation of firms by stimulating the environmental efforts of local governments and strengthening public attention	China	Non-financial companies listed on China's A-share market	Chinese Research Data Services–Green Patent Research Database (CNRDS-GPRD)	There is a positive relationship between the improvement of environmental information transparency and firms' green innovation; the green innovation effect performs stronger in state-owned enterprises (SOEs) and firms in heavily polluting industries

No	References	Definitions of EI	Research questions	Theory	Contexts	Sample	Databases	Main findings
90	Kyaw (2022), p. 132645	It involves, among many others, reducing environmental impacts through waste minimization, introducing new products that are environmentally friendly through technologies, incorporating environmental concerns into corporate strategies and decision makings	Influential factor	Uncertainty can delay investment decisions and thus have a negative impact on environmental innovation	US		Thomson Reuters Refinitiv database	Policy uncertainty could have a negative impact on environmental innovation in 5–6 years' time
91	Aftab et al. (2022), p. 134639	The use of eco-friendly technologies in production processes to produce services and goods that have a minimal adverse effect on the environment	Effect		Pakistan	The manufacturing sector		Green innovation mediates the relationship between corporate environmental ethics and sustainable performance (social, economic, and environmental)
92	Flachenecker et al. (2022), p. 133429	A new or significantly improved product, service, process, marketing approach or organisational structure, which results in lower environmental pressures, irrespectively of Whether or not this was an explicit goal	Effect		European Union			Average publicly supported environmental innovation increases firm employment, turnover and market share

No	References	Definitions of EI	Research questions	Theory	Contexts	Sample	Databases	Main findings
93	Ouyang et al. (2022), p. 134933	Reduce pollution emissions and energy consumption in business activities through developing green products and technologies and improving production processes	Influential factor	Compliance cost effect and compensatory effect: green innovation will help firms to obtain long-term competitive advantages and incentive subsidies,and thus improves the green innovation efficiency	China	Industrial firms	China Industrial Statistical Yearbook and China Science and Technology Statistical Yearbook	SSER not only directly improves the firm's green innovation efficiency but also indirectly improves by inhibiting the behavior of industrial firms transferring into other regions
94	Wu et al. (2023), p. 135248	Reducing environmental pollution and reducing energy consumption, while reducing production costs, improving production efficiency, and enhancing product competitiveness, to promote enterprise economic growth	Effect	Strategic management theory, innovation theory, and stakeholder theory	China	Textile manufacturing firms		Eco-innovation showed a complete and partial mediating effect in the indirect relationships between green credit and environmental performance, and economic performance, respectively
95	Abid et al. (2022), p. 133223	A series of innovative activities accelerating environ- mental sustainability	Effect		Global		OECD stats	Green innovation has a substantial impact on environmental sustainability
96	Yang et al. (2022), p. 130858	Define new products or processes with beneficial impact on the ecological environment that also create economic value	Influential factor		China	China's low- carbon city		The impact of pilot policies on the number of urban green invention patent application lags by approximately 2 years, whereas the impact on the number of patent applications regarding green utility models exhibit a longer lag time

No	References	Definitions of EI	Research questions	Theory	Contexts	Sample	Databases	Main findings
97	Holzner and Wagner (2022), p. 134438	Develop new ideas, behavior, products, and processes, apply or intro- duce them and which contribute to a reduction of environmental burdens or to ecologically specified sustainability targets	Effect	Higher costs and a longer ramp- up lead to longer payback periods with an increasing innovation level	Germany	GERMAN manufacturing firms	The German Sustainability Management Barometer (GSMB)	Green products with high levels of innovation initially hurt profitability and later improve it
98	Su et al. (2022), p. 134945	The technology and process firms develop to reduce pollution emissions and energy consumption	Influential factor	The perspective of resource crowding and the "reverse forcing" effect: When green credit is lower than the threshold value, it will inhibit firms' green technology innovation	China	Heavy polluting industries and cleaning industries	World Intellectual Property Organization (WIPO)	A lower level of green credit significantly inhibits green technology innovation; Moderators: Corporate environmental infor- mation disclosure level can effectively alleviate the inhibitory effect of green credit
99	Xu et al. (2022), p. 133789	A new product or process that significantly reduces environmental impacts and can add value to individuals or companies	Influential factor	Porter Hypothesis: environmental regulation stimulates technological innovation to enhance competitiveness	China	79 cities in the Yellow River Basin (YRB)		ERI and GIE exhibited an inverted "N" relationship
100	Ren et al. (2021), pp. 756–774	'Green', 'clean', 'sustainable', 'cycle', 'ecological', 'low carbon', 'saving', 'energy saving', 'environment', 'environmental protection', 'environmental pollution' and 'emission reduction' as green innovation	Drivers	Upper echelons theory: emotional ties to their hometowns inspires them to care more about the environment and implement green innovations	China	Heavily polluting industries	Baiten database	CEO hometown identity has a positive impact on a firm's green innovation performance; Moderators: institutional ownership nefatively moderates; market complexity positive moderates

References

Abid, N., Ceci, F., Ahmad, F., & Aftab, J. (2022). Financial development and green innovation, the ultimate solutions to an environmentally sustainable society: Evidence from leading economies. *Journal of Cleaner Production, 369*, 133223. https://doi.org/10.1016/j.jclepro.2022.133223

Adomako, S., Simms, C., Vazquez-Brust, D., & Nguyen, H. T. T. (2022). Stakeholder Green Pressure and New Product Performance in Emerging Countries: A Cross-country Study. *British Journal of Management, 34*(1), 299–320. https://doi.org/10.1111/1467-8551.12595

Aftab, J., Abid, N., Sarwar, H., & Veneziani, M. (2022). Environmental ethics, green innovation, and sustainable performance: Exploring the role of environmental leadership and environmental strategy. *Journal of Cleaner Production, 378*, 134639. https://doi.org/10.1016/j.jclepro.2022.134639

Albitar, K., Al-Shaer, H., & Liu, Y. S. (2023). Corporate commitment to climate change: The effect of eco-innovation and climate governance. *Research Policy, 52*(2), 104697. https://doi.org/10.1016/j.respol.2022.104697

Ambec, S., Cohen, M. A., Elgie, S., & Lanoie, P. (2013). The Porter hypothesis at 20: Can environmental regulation enhance innovation and competitiveness? *Review of Environmental Economics and Policy, 7*(1), 2–22.

Antonioli, D., Mancinelli, S., & Mazzanti, M. (2013). Is environmental innovation embedded within high-performance organisational changes? The role of human resource management and complementarity in green business strategies. *Research Policy, 42*(4), 975–988. https://doi.org/10.1016/j.respol.2012.12.005

Arena, C., Michelon, G., & Trojanowski, G. (2018). Big Egos Can Be Green: A Study of CEO Hubris and Environmental Innovation. *British Journal of Management, 29*(2), 316–336. https://doi.org/10.1111/1467-8551.12250

Bammens, Y., & Hünermund, P. (2020). Nonfinancial Considerations in Eco-Innovation Decisions: The Role of Family Ownership and Reputation Concerns. *Journal of Product Innovation Management, 37*(5), 431–453. https://doi.org/10.1111/jpim.12550

Banerjee, R., Gupta, K., & Mudalige, P. (2020). Do environmentally sustainable practices lead to financially less constrained firms? International evidence. *International Review of Financial Analysis, 68*, 101337. https://doi.org/10.1016/j.irfa.2019.03.009

Beise, M., & Rennings, K. (2005). Lead markets and regulation: A framework for analyzing the international diffusion of environmental innovations. *Ecological Economics, 52*(1), 5–17.

Bellamy, M. A., Dhanorkar, S., & Subramanian, R. (2020). Administrative environmental innovations, supply network structure, and environmental disclosure. *Journal of Operations Management, 66*(7–8), 895–932. https://doi.org/10.1002/joom.1114

Bendell, B. L. (2015). I don't Want to be Green: Prosocial motivation effects on firm environmental innovation rejection decisions. *Journal of Business Ethics, 143*(2), 277–288. https://doi.org/10.1007/s10551-015-2588-2

Berrone, P., Fosfuri, A., Gelabert, L., & Gomez-Mejia, L. R. (2013). Necessity as the mother of 'green' inventions: Institutional pressures and environmental innovations. *Strategic Management Journal, 34*(8), 891–909. https://doi.org/10.1002/smj.2041

Borghesi, S., Cainelli, G., & Mazzanti, M. (2015). Linking emission trading to environmental innovation: Evidence from the Italian manufacturing industry. *Research Policy, 44*(3), 669–683. https://doi.org/10.1016/j.respol.2014.10.014

Cai, W., & Zhou, X. (2014). On the drivers of eco-innovation: Empirical evidence from China. *Journal of Cleaner Production, 79*, 239–248.

Cainelli, G., D'Amato, A., & Mazzanti, M. (2020). Resource efficient eco-innovations for a circular economy: Evidence from EU firms. *Research Policy, 49*(1), 103827. https://doi.org/10.1016/j.respol.2019.103827

Cainelli, G., & Mazzanti, M. (2013). Environmental innovations in services: Manufacturing–services integration and policy transmissions. *Research Policy, 42*(9), 1595–1604. https://doi.org/10.1016/j.respol.2013.05.010

Chang, C.-H. (2011). The influence of corporate environmental ethics on competitive advantage: The mediation role of green innovation. *Journal of Business Ethics, 104*(3), 361–370. https://doi.org/10.1007/s10551-011-0914-x

Chen, P.-C., & Hung, S.-W. (2014). Collaborative green innovation in emerging countries: a social capital perspective. *International Journal of Operations & Production Management, 34*(3), 347–363. https://doi.org/10.1108/ijopm-06-2012-0222

Chen, Y., Yao, Z., & Zhong, K. (2022). Do environmental regulations of carbon emissions and air pollution foster green technology innovation: Evidence from China's prefecture-level cities. *Journal of Cleaner Production, 350*, 131537. https://doi.org/10.1016/j.jclepro.2022.131537

Chen, Y.-S. (2007). The driver of green innovation and green image—green core competence. *Journal of Business Ethics, 81*(3), 531–543. https://doi.org/10.1007/s10551-007-9522-1

Chen, Y.-S., Lai, S.-B., & Wen, C.-T. (2006). The Influence of Green Innovation Performance on Corporate Advantage in Taiwan. *Journal of Business Ethics, 67*(4), 331–339. https://doi.org/10.1007/s10551-006-9025-5

Cheng, C. C. J. (2018). Sustainability orientation, green supplier involvement, and green innovation performance: Evidence from diversifying green entrants. *Journal of Business Ethics, 161*(2), 393–414. https://doi.org/10.1007/s10551-018-3946-7

Cheng, Z., & Yu, X. (2023). Can central environmental protection inspection induce corporate green technology innovation? *Journal of Cleaner Production, 387*, 135902. https://doi.org/10.1016/j.jclepro.2023.135902

Conti, C., Mancusi, M. L., Sanna-Randaccio, F., Sestini, R., & Verdolini, E. (2018). Transition towards a green economy in Europe: Innovation and knowledge integration in the renewable energy sector. *Research Policy, 47*(10), 1996–2009. https://doi.org/10.1016/j.respol.2018.07.007

Costantini, V., Crespi, F., Martini, C., & Pennacchio, L. (2015). Demand-pull and technology-push public support for eco-innovation: The case of the biofuels sector. *Research Policy, 44*(3), 577–595. https://doi.org/10.1016/j.respol.2014.12.011

Costantini, V., Crespi, F., & Palma, A. (2017). Characterizing the policy mix and its impact on eco-innovation: A patent analysis of energy-efficient technologies. *Research Policy, 46*(4), 799–819. https://doi.org/10.1016/j.respol.2017.02.004

Dangelico, R. M., Pontrandolfo, P., & Pujari, D. (2013). Developing sustainable new products in the textile and upholstered furniture industries: Role of external integrative capabilities. *Journal of Product Innovation Management, 30*(4), 642–658. https://doi.org/10.1111/jpim.12013

Dangelico, R. M., & Pujari, D. (2010). Mainstreaming green product innovation: Why and how companies integrate environmental sustainability. *Journal of Business Ethics, 95*(3), 471–486. https://doi.org/10.1007/s10551-010-0434-0

Darendeli, A., Law, K. K. F., & Shen, M. (2022). Green new hiring. *Review of Accounting Studies, 27*(3), 986–1037. https://doi.org/10.1007/s11142-022-09696-y

De Marchi, V. (2012). Environmental innovation and R&D cooperation: Empirical evidence from Spanish manufacturing firms. *Research Policy, 41*(3), 614–623. https://doi.org/10.1016/j.respol.2011.10.002

de Medeiros, J. F., Vidor, G., & Ribeiro, J. L. D. (2015). Driving factors for the success of the green innovation market: A relationship system proposal. *Journal of Business Ethics, 147*(2), 327–341. https://doi.org/10.1007/s10551-015-2927-3

Delmas, M. A., & Pekovic, S. (2016). Corporate sustainable innovation and employee behavior. *Journal of Business Ethics, 150*(4), 1071–1088. https://doi.org/10.1007/s10551-016-3163-1

del Río González, P. (2009). The empirical analysis of the determinants for environmental technological change: A research agenda. *Ecological Economics, 68*(3), 861–878.

Doblinger, C., Surana, K., Li, D., Hultman, N., & Anadón, L. D. (2022). How do global manufacturing shifts affect long-term clean energy innovation? A study of wind energy suppliers. *Research Policy, 51*(7), 104558. https://doi.org/10.1016/j.respol.2022.104558

Eiadat, Y., Kelly, A., Roche, F., & Eyadat, H. (2008). Green and competitive? An empirical test of the mediating role of environmental innovation strategy. *Journal of World Business, 43*(2), 131–145. https://doi.org/10.1016/j.jwb.2007.11.012

Epicoco, M. (2016). Patterns of innovation and organizational demography in emerging sustainable fields: An analysis of the chemical sector. *Research Policy, 45*(2), 427–441. https://doi.org/10.1016/j.respol.2015.10.013

Fabrizi, A., Guarini, G., & Meliciani, V. (2018). Green patents, regulatory policies and research network policies. *Research Policy, 47*(6), 1018–1031. https://doi.org/10.1016/j.respol.2018.03.005

Flachenecker, F., Kornejew, M., & Janiri, M. L. (2022). The effects of publicly supported environmental innovations on firm growth in the European Union. *Journal of Cleaner Production, 372*, 133429. https://doi.org/10.1016/j.jclepro.2022.133429

Flammer, C., Hong, B., & Minor, D. (2019). Corporate governance and the rise of integrating corporate social responsibility criteria in executive compensation: Effectiveness and implications for firm outcomes. *Strategic Management Journal, 40*(7), 1097–1122. https://doi.org/10.1002/smj.3018

Frondel, M., Horbach, J., & Rennings, K. (2008). What triggers environmental management and innovation? *Empirical evidence for Germany. Ecological Economics, 66*(1), 153–160.

Galbreath, J. (2017). Drivers of green innovations: The impact of export intensity, women leaders, and absorptive capacity. *Journal of Business Ethics, 158*(1), 47–61. https://doi.org/10.1007/s10551-017-3715-z

García-Granero, E. M., Piedra-Muñoz, L., & Galdeano-Gómez, E. (2020). Measuring eco-innovation dimensions: The role of environmental corporate culture and commercial orientation. *Research Policy, 49*(8), 104028. https://doi.org/10.1016/j.respol.2020.104028

Geffen, C. A., & Rothenberg, S. (2000). Suppliers and environmental innovation: the automotive paint process. *International Journal of Operations & Production Management, 20*(2), 166–186.

Ghisetti, C., Marzucchi, A., & Montresor, S. (2015). The open eco-innovation mode. An empirical investigation of eleven European countries. *Research Policy, 44*(5), 1080–1093. https://doi.org/10.1016/j.respol.2014.12.001

Golgeci, I., Ali, I., Bozkurt, S., Gligor, D. M., & Arslan, A. (2022). The impact of corporate support programs on environmental and social innovation: Empirical insights from the food and beverage industry. *International Journal of Operations & Production Management, 42*(7), 898–929. https://doi.org/10.1108/ijopm-10-2021-0640

Hart, S. (1995). A natural-resource-based view of the firm. *Academy of Management Review, 20*(4), 986–1014.

Hartmann, J., Inkpen, A., & Ramaswamy, K. (2022). An FsQCA exploration of multiple paths to ecological innovation adoption in European transportation. *Journal of World Business, 57*(5), 101327. https://doi.org/10.1016/j.jwb.2022.101327

Heidenreich, S., Spieth, P., & Petschnig, M. (2017). Ready, steady, green: Examining the effectiveness of external policies to enhance the adoption of eco-friendly innovations. *Journal of Product Innovation Management, 34*(3), 343–359. https://doi.org/10.1111/jpim.12364

Holzner, B., & Wagner, M. (2022). Linking levels of green innovation with profitability under environmental uncertainty: An empirical study. *Journal of Cleaner Production, 378*, 134438. https://doi.org/10.1016/j.jclepro.2022.134438

Horbach, J. (2008). Determinants of environmental innovation—New evidence from German panel data sources. *Research Policy, 37*(1), 163–173. https://doi.org/10.1016/j.respol.2007.08.006

Howard-Grenville, J., & Bertels, S. (2012). Organizational culture and environmental action. In T. Bansal & A. Hoffman (Eds.), *The oxford handbook of business and the natural environment* (pp. 194–210). Oxford University Press.

Huang, J.-W., & Li, Y.-H. (2015). Green innovation and performance: The view of organizational capability and social reciprocity. *Journal of Business Ethics, 145*(2), 309–324. https://doi.org/10.1007/s10551-015-2903-y

Javed, M., Wang, F., Usman, M., Ali Gull, A., & Uz Zaman, Q. (2023). Female CEOs and green innovation. *Journal of Business Research, 157*, 113515. https://doi.org/10.1016/j.jbusres.2022.113515

Jimenez, O. (2005). Innovation-oriented environmental regulations: direct versus indirect regulations; An empirical analysis of small and medium-sized enterprises in Chile. *Environment and Planning A, 37*(4), 723–750.

Juntunen, J. K., Halme, M., Korsunova, A., & Rajala, R. (2018). Strategies for integrating stakeholders into sustainability innovation: A configurational perspective. *Journal of Product Innovation Management, 36*(3), 331–355. https://doi.org/10.1111/jpim.12481

Kam-Sing Wong, S., & Bigliardi, B. (2012). The influence of green product competitiveness on the success of green product innovation. *European Journal of Innovation Management, 15*(4), 468–490. https://doi.org/10.1108/14601061211272385

Kemp, R. (2010). Eco-innovation: Definition, measurement and open research issues. *Economia Politica, 27*(3), 397–420.

Kemp, R., & Pearson, P. (2007). Final report MEI project about measuring eco-innovation. *UM Merit, Maastricht, 10*(2), 1–120.

Kesidou, E., & Demirel, P. (2012). On the drivers of eco-innovations: Empirical evidence from the UK. *Research Policy, 41*(5), 862–870. https://doi.org/10.1016/j.respol.2012.01.005

Kim, I., Pantzalis, C., & Zhang, Z. (2021). Multinationality and the value of green innovation. *Journal of Corporate Finance, 69*, 101996. https://doi.org/10.1016/j.jcorpfin.2021.101996

Kim, I., Ryou, J. W., & Yang, R. (2020). The color of shareholders' money: Institutional shareholders' political values and corporate environmental disclosure. *Journal of Corporate Finance, 64*, 101704. https://doi.org/10.1016/j.jcorpfin.2020.101704

Kirikkaleli, D., & Adebayo, T. S. (2022). Political risk and environmental quality in Brazil: Role of green finance and green innovation. *International Journal of Finance & Economics*. https://doi.org/10.1002/ijfe.2732

Konara, P., Lopez, C., & Shirodkar, V. (2021). Environmental innovation in foreign subsidiaries: The role of home-ecological institutions, subsidiary establishment mode and post-establishment experience. *Journal of World Business, 56*(6), 101261. https://doi.org/10.1016/j.jwb.2021.101261

Krieger, B., & Zipperer, V. (2022). Does green public procurement trigger environmental innovations? *Research Policy, 51*(6), 104516. https://doi.org/10.1016/j.respol.2022.104516

Kunapatarawong, R., & Martínez-Ros, E. (2016). Towards green growth: How does green innovation affect employment? *Research Policy, 45*(6), 1218–1232. https://doi.org/10.1016/j.respol.2016.03.013

Kyaw, K. (2022). Effect of policy uncertainty on environmental innovation. *Journal of Cleaner Production, 363*, 132645. https://doi.org/10.1016/j.jclepro.2022.132645

Lanjouw, J. O., & Mody, A. (1996). Innovation and the international diffusion of environmentally responsive technology. *Research Policy, 25*(4), 549–571.

Leoncini, R., Montresor, S., & Rentocchini, F. (2016). CO2-reducing innovations and outsourcing: Evidence from photovoltaics and green construction in North-East Italy. *Research Policy, 45*(8), 1649–1659. https://doi.org/10.1016/j.respol.2016.04.010

Leyva-de la Hiz, D. I., Ferron-Vilchez, V., & Aragon-Correa, J. A. (2018). Do firms' slack resources influence the relationship between focused environmental innovations and financial performance? More is not always better. *Journal of Business Ethics, 159*(4), 1215–1227. https://doi.org/10.1007/s10551-017-3772-3

Li, D., Huang, M., Ren, S., Chen, X., & Ning, L. (2016). Environmental legitimacy, green innovation, and corporate carbon disclosure: Evidence from CDP China 100. *Journal of Business Ethics, 150*(4), 1089–1104. https://doi.org/10.1007/s10551-016-3187-6

Liao, Z., & Liu, Y. (2021). Why firm's reactive eco-innovation may lead to consumers' Boycott. *British Journal of Management, 33*(2), 1110–1122. https://doi.org/10.1111/1467-8551.12483

Longoni, A., & Cagliano, R. (2016). Sustainable innovativeness and the triple bottom line: The role of organizational time perspective. *Journal of Business Ethics, 151*(4), 1097–1120. https://doi.org/10.1007/s10551-016-3239-y

Marin, G. (2014). Do eco-innovations harm productivity growth through crowding out? Results of an extended CDM model for Italy. *Research Policy, 43*(2), 301–317. https://doi.org/10.1016/j.respol.2013.10.015

Moreno-Ureba, E., Bravo-Urquiza, F., & Reguera-Alvarado, N. (2022). An analysis of the influence of female directors on environmental innovation: When are women greener? *Journal of Cleaner Production, 374*. https://doi.org/10.1016/j.jclepro.2022.133871

Nameroff, T. J., Garant, R. J., & Albert, M. B. (2004). Adoption of green chemistry: an analysis based on US patents. *Research Policy, 33*(6–7), 959–974. https://doi.org/10.1016/j.respol.2004.03.001

Ning, L., & Guo, R. (2022). Technological diversification to green domains: Technological relatedness, invention impact and knowledge integration capabilities. *Research Policy, 51*(1), 104406. https://doi.org/10.1016/j.respol.2021.104406

OECD. (2010). *Eco-innovation in industry: Enabling green growth*. OECD Publishing.

OECD & Eurostat. (1997). *Oslo manual: Proposed guidelines for collecting and interpreting technological innovation data*. Organization for Economic Co-Operation and Development.

Olson, E. L. (2013). Perspective: The green innovation value chain: A tool for evaluating the diffusion prospects of green products. *Journal of Product Innovation Management, 30*(4), 782–793. https://doi.org/10.1111/jpim.12022

Orsatti, G., Quatraro, F., & Pezzoni, M. (2020). The antecedents of green technologies: The role of team-level recombinant capabilities. *Research Policy, 49*(3), 103919. https://doi.org/10.1016/j.respol.2019.103919

Ottman, J., Stafford, E., & Hartman, C. (2006). Avoiding green marketing myopia: Ways to improve consumer appeal for environmentally preferable products. *Environment: Science and Policy for Sustainable Development, 48*(5), 22–36.

Ouyang, Y., Ye, F., & Tan, K. (2022). The effect of strategic synergy between local and neighborhood environmental regulations on green innovation efficiency: The perspective of industrial transfer. *Journal of Cleaner Production, 380*, 134933. https://doi.org/10.1016/j.jclepro.2022.134933

Paparoidamis, N. G., Tran, T. T. H., Leonidou, L. C., & Zeriti, A. (2019). Being innovative while being green: An experimental inquiry into how consumers respond to eco-innovative product designs. *Journal of Product Innovation Management, 36*(6), 824–847. https://doi.org/10.1111/jpim.12509

Quan, X., Ke, Y., Qian, Y., & Zhang, Y. (2021). CEO foreign experience and green innovation: Evidence from China. *Journal of Business Ethics, 182*(2), 535–557. https://doi.org/10.1007/s10551-021-04977-z

Ren, S., Huang, M., Liu, D., & Yan, J. (2022). Understanding the impact of mandatory CSR disclosure on green innovation: Evidence from Chinese listed firms. *British Journal of Management, 34*(2), 576–594. https://doi.org/10.1111/1467-8551.12609

Ren, S., Wang, Y., Hu, Y., & Yan, J. (2021). CEO hometown identity and firm green innovation. *Business Strategy and the Environment, 30*(2), 756–774. https://doi.org/10.1002/bse.2652

Rennings, K. (2000). Redefining innovation - eco-innovation research and the contribution from ecological economics. *Ecological Economics, 32*(2), 319–332.

Rennings, K., Ziegler, A., & Zwick, T. (2004). The effect of environmental innovations on employment changes: An econometric analysis. *Business Strategy and the Environment, 13*(6), 374–387.

Rogge, K. S., & Schleich, J. (2018). Do policy mix characteristics matter for low-carbon innovation? A survey-based exploration of renewable power generation technologies in Germany. *Research Policy, 47*(9), 1639–1654. https://doi.org/10.1016/j.respol.2018.05.011

Seifert, L., Kunz, N., & Gold, S. (2023). Sustainable innovations for humanitarian operations in refugee camps. *International Journal of Operations & Production Management*. https://doi.org/10.1108/ijopm-05-2022-0302

Shou, Y., Che, W., Dai, J., & Jia, F. (2018). Inter-organizational fit and environmental innovation in supply chains. *International Journal of Operations & Production Management, 38*(8), 1683–1704. https://doi.org/10.1108/ijopm-08-2017-0470

Shou, Y., Shan, X., Dai, J., Xu, D., & Che, W. (2022). Actions speak louder than words? The impact of subjective norms in the supply chain on green innovation. *International Journal of Operations & Production Management, 43*(6), 879–898. https://doi.org/10.1108/ijopm-04-2022-0265

Su, X., Pan, C., Zhou, S., & Zhong, X. (2022). Threshold effect of green credit on firms' green technology innovation: Is environmental information disclosure important? *Journal of Cleaner Production, 380*, 134945. https://doi.org/10.1016/j.jclepro.2022.134945

Theyel, G. (2000). Management practices for environmental innovation and performance. *International Journal of Operations & Production Management, 20*(2), 249–266.

Valero-Gil, J., Surroca, J. A., Tribo, J. A., Gutierrez, L., & Montiel, I. (2023). Innovation vs. standardization: The conjoint effects of eco-innovation and environmental management systems on environmental performance. *Research Policy, 52*(4), 104737. https://doi.org/10.1016/j.respol.2023.104737

Vasileiou, E., Georgantzis, N., Attanasi, G., & Llerena, P. (2022). Green innovation and financial performance: A study on Italian firms. *Research Policy, 51*(6), 104530. https://doi.org/10.1016/j.respol.2022.104530

Veugelers, R. (2012). Which policy instruments to induce clean innovating? *Research Policy, 41*(10), 1770–1778. https://doi.org/10.1016/j.respol.2012.06.012

Wagner, M. (2007). On the relationship between environmental management, environmental innovation and patenting: Evidence from German manufacturing firms. *Research Policy, 36*(10), 1587–1602. https://doi.org/10.1016/j.respol.2007.08.004

Wang, J., Ma, M., Dong, T., & Zhang, Z. (2023). Do ESG ratings promote corporate green innovation? A quasi-natural experiment based on SynTao Green Finance's ESG ratings. *International Review of Financial Analysis, 87*, 102623. https://doi.org/10.1016/j.irfa.2023.102623

Wang, Y., & Li, M. (2022). Credit policy and its heterogeneous effects on green innovations. *Journal of Financial Stability, 58*, 100961. https://doi.org/10.1016/j.jfs.2021.100961

Watson, R., Wilson, H. N., Smart, P., & Macdonald, E. K. (2017). Harnessing difference: A capability-based framework for stakeholder engagement in environmental innovation. *Journal of Product Innovation Management, 35*(2), 254–279. https://doi.org/10.1111/jpim.12394

Wu, S., Zhou, X., & Zhu, Q. (2023). Green credit and enterprise environmental and economic performance: The mediating role of eco-innovation. *Journal of Cleaner Production, 382*, 135248. https://doi.org/10.1016/j.jclepro.2022.135248

Xing, C., Zhang, Y., & Tripe, D. (2021). Green credit policy and corporate access to bank loans in China: The role of environmental disclosure and green innovation. *International Review of Financial Analysis, 77*, 101838. https://doi.org/10.1016/j.irfa.2021.101838

Xu, Y., Liu, S., & Wang, J. (2022). Impact of environmental regulation intensity on green innovation efficiency in the Yellow River Basin, China. *Journal of Cleaner Production, 373*, 133789. https://doi.org/10.1016/j.jclepro.2022.133789

Yang, F., & Yang, M. (2015). Analysis on China's eco-innovations: Regulation context, intertemporal change and regional differences. *European Journal of Operational Research, 247*(3), 1003–1012. https://doi.org/10.1016/j.ejor.2015.07.029

Yang, S., Wang, W., Feng, D., & Lu, J. (2022). Impact of pilot environmental policy on urban eco-innovation. *Journal of Cleaner Production, 341*, 130858. https://doi.org/10.1016/j.jclepro.2022.130858

Zhang, D. (2022). Environmental regulation, green innovation, and export product quality: What is the role of greenwashing? *International Review of Financial Analysis, 83*, 102311. https://doi.org/10.1016/j.irfa.2022.102311

Zhang, D., & Jin, Y. (2021). R&D and environmentally induced innovation: Does financial constraint play a facilitating role? *International Review of Financial Analysis, 78*, 101918. https://doi.org/10.1016/j.irfa.2021.101918

Zhang, S., Zhang, M.-A., Qiao, Y., Li, X., & Li, S. (2022a). Does improvement of environmental information transparency boost firms' green innovation? Evidence from the air quality monitoring and disclosure program in China. *Journal of Cleaner Production, 357*. https://doi.org/10.1016/j.jclepro.2022.131921

Zhang, Z., Zhang, B., & Jia, M. (2022b). The military imprint: The effect of executives' military experience on firm pollution and environmental innovation. *The Leadership Quarterly, 33*(2). https://doi.org/10.1016/j.leaqua.2021.101562

Zhao, J., Qu, J., Wei, J., Yin, H., & Xi, X. (2022). The effects of institutional investors on firms' green innovation. *Journal of Product Innovation Management, 40*(2), 195–230. https://doi.org/10.1111/jpim.12652

Zhou, P., Song, F. M., & Huang, X. (2023). Environmental regulations and firms' green innovations: Transforming pressure into incentives. *International Review of Financial Analysis, 86*, 102504. https://doi.org/10.1016/j.irfa.2023.102504

Ziegler, A., & Seijas Nogareda, J. (2009). Environmental management systems and technological environmental innovations: Exploring the causal relationship. *Research Policy, 38*(5), 885–893. https://doi.org/10.1016/j.respol.2009.01.020

Yudian Chen is a Doctoral Researcher at Newcastle University Business School, Newcastle University (UK). She obtained an MSc in Accounting and Finance (Distinction) from Cardiff University. Her current research is focused on corporate eco-innovation and financial stability in the banking sector.

Teng Li is an Associate Professor in Accounting at the Essex Business School within the University of Essex (UK). His research interests lie in Social and Environmental Accounting, Corporate Social Responsibility (CSR)/ESG Reporting, Sustainable Corporate Governance, and Climate Finance. His publications have appeared in leading academic journals, including the British Journal of Management; Accounting, Auditing and Accountability Journal; Accounting and Business Research; Accounting Forum; Review of Quantitative Finance and Accounting, and Journal of International Financial Markets, Institutions and Money.

Navigating the Green Path: The Role of Climate Incentives in Shaping Eco-innovation and Firm Policies

Phuong Le, Thao Ngoc Nguyen, and Chau Le

Abstract This chapter overviews the dynamic connection between climate incentives and eco-innovation. It explores how financial and non-financial climate incentives affect the trajectory of eco-innovation within firms. By tracing the historical evolution of climate incentives, this research elucidates their transformative impact on firm policies. This chapter employs bibliometric analysis to shed light on various aspects of the current research landscape concerning climate incentives and eco-innovation. Despite the evident potential of climate incentives, their implementation faces significant challenges. This chapter critically examines these challenges, offering insights into the complexities of design, global coordination, and equity concerns. In addition, the research critiques the effectiveness and fairness of these incentives, fostering a holistic understanding of the subject. Further, this research underscores the promising future research directions for climate incentives and emphasizes their pivotal role in steering the next wave of eco-innovations.

P. Le (✉)
Ethifinance Analytics, Ethifinance, Paris, France

RITM, University of Paris-Saclay, Sceaux, France

Faculty of Banking, Ho Chi Minh University of Banking, Ho Chi Minh City, Vietnam

T. N. Nguyen
Department of Accounting and Finance, Nottingham Trent Business School, Nottingham Trent University, Nottingham, UK
e-mail: thao.nguyen@ntu.ac.uk

C. Le
Lincoln International Business School, University of Lincoln, Lincoln, UK
e-mail: cle@lincoln.ac.uk

V. Q. Trinh (ed.), *Climate Governance and Corporate Eco-innovation*, Sustainable Finance, https://doi.org/10.1007/978-3-031-56423-9_2

1 Introduction

IN AN ERA characterized by the growing challenges posed by climate change, the corporate sector is crucial in directing the goal of environmental sustainability. Within this evolving context, climate incentives and eco-innovation have emerged as essential concepts affecting firm strategies and governance practices (Ambec et al., 2013; Horbach, 2008). These paradigms demonstrate the complex relationship between environmental preservation and economic considerations, setting the stage for a detailed discussion in the current business environment.

Climate incentives refer to stimuli or inducements, either monetary or non-monetary, used to encourage environmentally friendly practices or technologies. These incentives can include tax breaks, grants, subsidies, or intangible benefits such as certifications and awards. Ambec et al. (2013) note that climate incentives offset initial green transition costs and provide a competitive advantage. Climate incentives encourage actions to reduce climate change, aligning economic, social, and environmental (ESG) goals for a more sustainable and low-carbon environment. On the other hand, eco-innovation involves new or improved products and methods that result in significant reductions in environmental footprints or increased ecological efficiency in corporate offerings. According to Horbach (2008), eco-innovation highlights the synergistic relationship between economic growth and environmental stewardship. It enables firms to explore new market areas, reduce operational costs, and improve their value propositions.

Firm policies, influenced by numerous external and internal factors, are critical in directing corporate practices. Among these external influences, climate incentives have become influential drivers in shaping firms' environmental strategies. Environmental regulations can stimulate innovation in clean technologies, though these benefits may not completely offset the regulation costs for the affected entities. When a firm's reputation is closely tied to its environmental responsibility, recognitions like certifications can significantly influence a firm's marketing and corporate responsibility policies (Dechezleprêtre & Sato, 2017). As firms compete for the 'green' label, they adapt their policies to include and highlight sustainable practices, primarily motivated by the appeal of reputational benefits (Darnall et al., 2009).

The role of climate incentives in promoting eco-innovation is a significant topic that requires more scholarly attention. These incentives, both financial and non-financial, aim to encourage environmentally responsible practices. Eco-innovation involves creating sustainable products, processes, or solutions. This not only supports environmental stewardship but also promotes economic growth. Together, these tools address climate change and environmental degradation while enhancing market competitiveness and influencing policies (Ambec et al., 2013; Horbach, 2008; Rennings, 2000).

Box 1
Climate incentives (monetary or non-monetary) encourage environmentally friendly practices or technologies. These incentives include tax breaks, grants, subsidies, carbon pricing, or intangible benefits such as awards, certifications, market access, and information dissemination.

Our research provides an in-depth investigation of the interactions between climate incentives, eco-innovation, and firm policies by examining historical developments, categorizing various types of incentives, and analyzing real-world case studies. We reveal persuasive evidence that climate incentives significantly impact eco-innovation and firm policies, which is consistent with previous findings (Darnall et al., 2009; Dechezleprêtre & Sato, 2017). This study also covers critiques and challenges involved with the implementation of these incentives. As a result, the chapter adds both academic scholarship and practical applications by reviewing and proposing practical recommendations for businesses and policymakers.

This chapter is organized as follows. Section 2 provides the historical development of climate incentives, laying the groundwork for their current significance. Climate incentive categories (financial and non-financial) are discussed in Sect. 3 while Sect. 4 demonstrates climate incentive's effects on eco-innovation and firm policies. Section 5 presents the current state of analysis on climate incentives and eco-innovation. Challenges and critiques associated with climate incentives are examined in Sect. 6. Finally, Sect. 7 concludes by summarizing key findings and suggesting future directions for research and policy interventions.

2 The Evolution of Climate Incentives

The growth of public concern about environmental degradation has triggered the surge in climate incentives to tackle climate change and environmental issues. Climate incentives have experienced a transformative wave in both their design and implementation. This section will explain the history and development of climate incentives.

2.1 Historical Context of Climate Incentives

The origin of climate incentives can be traced back to the latter half of the twentieth century when the global community started to be confronted with the severity of environmental degradation raising the urgency for sustainability practices (Vig & Kraft, 2013). Concerns about air and water pollution began to arise in the 1970s and

1980s, resulting in the implementation of environmental laws and regulations in many nations. Early projects tried to incentivize environmental protection, but the focus was not on climate change particularly. Initial environmental regulations primarily adopted a command-and-control approach, setting standards and penalties for non-compliance (Stavins, 2003). However, as the limitations of these regulatory frameworks became apparent, especially in terms of economic efficiency, the discourse shifted towards more market-based instruments.

The late 1980s and 1990s marked a turning point by introducing the concept of 'tradable permits' under the Clean Air Act in the United States (Ellerman et al., 2000). This innovative mechanism allows firms to buy and sell emission permits, providing a clear economic incentive to mitigate emissions and paving the way for many other market-based environmental instruments. However, deliberations within policy spheres have witnessed a notable surge in partisanship and polarization. This trend has reached the point where amendments to existing legislative frameworks or the enaction of novel legislation to address the emergent challenge of climate change become an impractical endeavour (Schamalensee & Stavins, 2019).

The United Nations Climate Change Convention, established during the Earth Summit in Rio de Janeiro in 1992, initiated the institutional framework for international climate policy[1] which subsequently garnered ratification from most of the world's states. The Kyoto Protocol, formulated during the Third Conference of the Parties to the United Nations Framework Convention on Climate Change in 1997, mandates industrialized nations to restrict emissions of greenhouse gases, with a particular focus on carbon dioxide stemming from fossil fuel combustion. Initially conceived to bring about a substantial reduction in business-as-usual emissions for the developed world, the Kyoto Protocol was evaluated as a critical achievement in international efforts for climate protection (Bohringer & Vogt, 2004).

As concerns about climate change plummeted in the 2000s, governments worldwide began to develop laws to promote renewable energy sources. The Paris Agreement (COP21), agreed at the 21st United Nations Climate Change Conference in December 2015 established an international goal of keeping global average temperatures well below 2 °C over the pre-industrial levels, with efforts to limit temperature increase further to 1.5 °C (Lee et al., 2023). To achieve these ambitious goals, climate incentives have been introduced, along with the development of new technological frameworks and enhanced capacity-building.[2]

Rising public awareness and concern over climate change also drive increasing demands for sustainable goods and services, ethical investing, green finance and corporate sustainability practices. These contribute to promoting the proliferation of climate incentives, especially market-based incentive instruments.

[1] See United Nations: https://www.un.org/en/conferences/environment/rio1992.

[2] See "Key aspects of the Paris Agreement accessed via: https://unfccc.int/most-requested/key-aspects-of-the-paris-agreement#:~:text=The%20Paris%20Agreement's%20central%20aim,further%20to%201.5%20degrees%20Celsius.

2.2 The Role of Climate Incentives in Encouraging Eco-innovation

Over time, the range and diversity of climate incentives have significantly broadened. Various forms of financial incentives such as tax credits, subsidies, and grants… have been introduced across jurisdictions to encourage the adoption of eco-friendly technologies and practices (Jaffe et al., 2002). These financial levers have proven to be particularly effective in sectors like renewable energy, where upfront costs of technologies like solar panels and wind turbines can be prohibitive. In addition to financial incentives, non-financial incentives have also gained traction. Eco-certifications, eco-labels, and awards have provided companies with reputational benefits, making them more appealing to environmentally-conscious consumers and stakeholders (Delmas & Burbano, 2011). This has not only encouraged firms to adopt greener practices but also driven innovation as companies strive to outperform rivals in their environmental initiatives.

The confluence of these incentives has played a critical role in fostering the proliferation of eco-innovation, involving the development of products and processes that reduce environmental impact, pollution, and other negative impacts of resource use. Eco-innovation has become a strategic imperative for many firms, rather than not just an operational nicety (Kemp & Pearson, 2007). Climate incentives, by reducing the financial risk and increasing the potential rewards of eco-innovations, have significantly accelerated their adoption and development. The evolution of climate incentives reflects a broader shift in the global approach to environmental challenges. From rigid regulations to flexible, market-driven incentives, the journey underscores the realization that the fight against climate change requires both innovation and collaboration. As these incentives continue to evolve, they will undoubtedly play an even more critical role in shaping the future of sustainable business practices.

3 Types of Climate Incentives

Climate incentives, in their various forms, play a pivotal role in motivating firms to adopt sustainable practices. These incentives can be broadly categorized into financial and non-financial types, each offering unique advantages and addressing different aspects of corporate behaviour (see Fig. 1).

3.1 Financial Incentives

Financial incentives (or monetary incentives) serve as direct economic benefits to alleviate the cost burden of transitioning to sustainable practices. One of the most prevalent forms is *tax breaks or reductions*, wherein governments offer companies

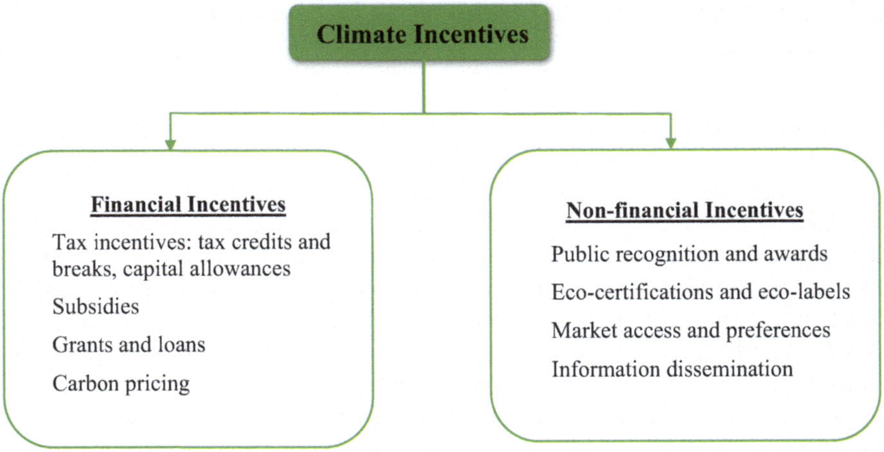

Fig. 1 Financial versus non-financial incentives to promote the transition to a net-zero economy. *Source: Authors' own creation*

reduced tax rates or deductions for adopting eco-friendly technologies or practices (Goulder & Parry, 2008). For instance, the UK government allows firms to claim tax allowances on energy-efficient or zero-carbon technology for their businesses. In March 2021, the UK government announced solar power tax breaks, which were part of the most extensive two-year business tax cuts in recent British history. Another noteworthy example of tax incentives is found in the Plan RePowerEU, proposed by the European Commission in May 2022.[3] This plan envisages the possibility for member states to implement fiscal policies aimed at promoting energy conservation and reducing reliance on fossil fuels. Such tax incentives not only make green technologies more economically viable but also enhance their competitiveness compared to conventional alternatives.

Subsidies are another form of government financial support for environmentally friendly business engagement. These supports are often provided to nascent industries or technologies to boost their market presence. For instance, the renewable energy sectors, particularly solar and wind, have benefitted immensely from subsidies, helping to offset their initial high costs and fostering rapid market penetration (Johnstone et al., 2010). While subsidies provide inducements for emission reduction akin to tax incentives, they concurrently foster market participation in pursuit of subsidy eligibility. Simultaneously, environmentally harmful subsidies have been gradually phased out, as seen in Nigeria's decision to end subsidies for fossil fuel consumption.

[3] More about RePowerEU from European Commission's website: https://commission.europa.eu/strategy-and-policy/priorities-2019-2024/european-green-deal/repowereu-affordable-secure-and-sustainable-energy-europe_en.

The third type of financial incentive is in the form of *grants* and *low-interest loans* offered by several government agencies for green investments, including sustainable agriculture, renewable or low-carbon energy sources, energy-efficient buildings, and electric vehicle infrastructure. Grants are typically non-repayable funds provided to firms or research institutions to foster innovation in areas of strategic environmental importance. By reducing the financial risk associated with research and development, grants have been critical in driving breakthroughs in green technologies and practices (Popp, 2002).

Carbon pricing has become a widely adopted policy mechanism to reduce greenhouse gas (GHG) emissions by imposing fees on emissions and/or providing incentives for emission reductions. The Collaborative Instruments for Ambitious Climate Action (CiACC) classifies carbon pricing instruments into three categories, which include (1) Emission Trading System (ETS), a tradable permit for GHG emissions; (2) Emission Reduction Funds, taxpayer-funded schemes in which a government purchases credits generated by emission reduction projects; and (3) Carbon tax on fossil fuel usage.

Box 2

A case study for the U.K. context:

- The UK government allows firms to claim tax allowances on energy-efficient or zero-carbon technology for their businesses.
- In March 2021, the UK government announced solar power tax breaks, which were part of the most extensive two-year business tax cuts in recent British history.

3.2 *Non-financial Incentives*

While financial incentives target the monetary benefits of corporate decision-making, non-financial incentives appeal to a firm's reputational and strategic considerations. *Recognition,* in the form of accolades or positive publicity for sustainable practices, can enhance a company's brand value and appeal to environmentally conscious consumers (Delmas & Burbano, 2011). Such recognition not only offers firms a competitive edge but also fosters a culture of sustainability within the industry. Furthermore, awards for environmental excellence serve as both a recognition and a benchmark for firms. They not only celebrate a company's achievements but also set industry standards, pushing other firms to elevate their environmental practices (Busch & Hoffmann, 2011).

Eco-certifications and eco-labels have emerged as powerful tools to signify a product's or firm's environmental credentials. These labels, backed by rigorous standards, provide a clear and credible signal to consumers about a product's environmental impact, making them more appealing to a growing segment of eco-conscious shoppers (Dauvergne & Lister, 2013). Governments can create markets for sustainable products by establishing sustainability criteria for public procurement. Edler and

Georghiou (2007) emphasize that when public demand is oriented towards innovative solutions and products, it has the potential to enhance the delivery of public policy and services. For instance, Denmark has implemented progressive policies, legislation, and incentives to promote the adoption of electric vehicles, intending to phase out the sale of new fossil fuel vehicles by 2030.

Box 3

While financial incentives provide the economic rationale for firms to adopt sustainable practices, non-financial incentives appeal to a firm's reputational and strategic considerations:

- Recognition can enhance a company's brand value and appeal to environmentally conscious consumers. It not only offers firms a competitive edge but also fosters a culture of sustainability within the industry.
- Eco-certifications and eco-labels have become powerful tools to signify a product's or firm's environmental credentials. These labels, backed by rigorous standards, provide a clear and credible signal to consumers about a product's environmental impact, making them more appealing to a growing segment of eco-conscious shoppers.

Information disclosure programmes are developed to shape corporate behavior by disseminating information relating to production processes, labor standards, and pollution levels to the state and local government agencies or the public (EPA, 2023). By engaging business owners, employees, shareholders, and customers in the regulatory process, all stakeholders are motivated to adopt socially responsible behavior. In the US, there exist both mandatory and voluntary reporting programmes. As an illustration, the 1969 National Environmental Policy Act (NEPA) serves as an instance of a mandatory programme, requiring federal agencies to prepare environmental impact statements for any activities with potentially significant environmental impact. Conversely, labelling schemes represent a voluntary reporting programme, permitting companies whose products meet environmentally sustainable standards to affix label seals to their products. In the UK, the Task Force on Climate-related Financial Disclosure encourages companies to disclose climate-related financial risks. While financial incentives provide the economic rationale for firms to adopt sustainable practices, non-financial incentives shape the broader business landscape, fostering competition, innovation, and excellence in environmental sustainability.

4 Climate Incentive's Effects on Eco-innovation and Firm Policies

Modern sustainable company strategies emphasize the dynamic interaction between climate incentives and eco-innovation. With expanding environmental challenges, there is a growing demand for innovative solutions. Financial and non-financial climate incentives encourage businesses to embrace innovation and think outside the box. Firm policies guide the overall patterns within corporate strategy and governance. Climate incentives have emerged as powerful forces transforming these strategies in response to the growing emphasis on sustainability and environmental responsibility. These efforts contribute to moving businesses in a more sustainable and environmentally friendly direction.

4.1 Eco-innovation

Eco-innovation is identified by its ability to transform environmental challenges into opportunities. Financial incentives such as tax breaks or subsidies, can significantly reduce the financial risks associated with research and development (R&D) investments in green technologies. This motivates firms to invest more and makes it economically feasible to commercialize these innovations (Johnstone et al., 2010; Popp et al., 2010). Financial incentives provide a vital push for firms to investigate and implement innovative concepts by changing the cost-benefit dynamics.

On the other hand, non-financial incentives address the reputational and strategic dimensions of firm behavior. Eco-certifications and eco-labels, for example, can provide a competitive advantage in the marketplace. The lure of such recognition can inspire firms to innovate, ensuring their products meet and exceed the stringent environmental criteria required for certification (Delmas & Grant, 2014). Moreover, as companies compete for awards and recognition in sustainability, they are often pushed to think outside the box, seeking groundbreaking solutions that not only address environmental concerns but also set them apart in the industry.

We present two case studies, one from Tesla Inc., US and the other from Vestas Wind Systems, Danmark demonstrating how both businesses benefit from climate incentives incorporating the eco-innovation components.

- Tesla, Inc.: *Perhaps one of the most iconic examples of a company benefiting from climate incentives is Tesla. In its early years, Tesla leveraged various federal and state incentives,*[4] *including tax credits for electric vehicle buyers,*[5] *to boost sales and build its brand. These incentives not only made Tesla vehicles more affordable for consumers but also provided the company with the financial breathing space needed to innovate and refine its technologies. As a result, Tesla has revolutionized the electric vehicle industry, setting new standards for performance, efficiency, and innovation.*[6]

---

[4] *Tesla, Inc. (2009, June 23). Tesla gets loan approval from US Department of Energy. Retrieved from* https://www.tesla.com/blog/tesla-gets-loan-approval-us-department-energy.

[5] *Tesla, Inc. (n.d.). Electric vehicle & energy incentives. Retrieved from* https://www.tesla.com/support/incentives.

[6] *Harvard Business School. (n.d.). Tesla and the electric vehicle revolution. Retrieved from* https://d3.harvard.edu/platform-rctom/submission/tesla-and-the-electric-vehicle-revolution/.

- Vestas Wind Systems: *A leading wind turbine manufacturer, Vestas has significantly benefited from subsidies*[7] *and incentives promoting renewable energy and sustainability.*[8] *These financial incentives, coupled with the company's commitment to innovation, have enabled Vestas to develop some of the most efficient and high-performance wind turbines in the industry.*[9] *The ascendancy of the company within the wind energy sector highlights the transformative influence of climate incentives when harmonized with an organization's innovative ethos.*

These case studies exemplify the symbiotic relationship between climate incentives and eco-innovation. While incentives provide the initial impetus, it is the spirit of innovation and the vision of a sustainable future that drive companies to transform these incentives into ground-breaking solutions.

Box 4
Eco-innovation transforms environmental challenges into opportunities:

- Financial incentives can significantly reduce the financial risks associated with investing in research and development of green technologies. This not only encourages firms to channel more resources into eco-innovation but also makes it economically viable to commercialize these innovations. By altering the cost-benefit dynamics, financial incentives provide the necessary push for firms to explore and adopt novel solutions.
- Non-financial incentives tap into the reputational and strategic dimensions of corporate behavior. They can drive firms to innovate, ensuring their products meet and exceed the stringent environmental standards required for certification.

4.2 Firm Policies

The economic and strategic implications of these incentives highlight the connection between climate incentives and firm policies. Financial climate incentives often provide a direct stimulus for firms to alter their operational, investment, and research policies. For instance, there are statistically and economically significant effects of tax incentives on both research and development (R&D) and patenting (Dechezleprêtre et al., 2016). Beyond immediate financial considerations, these

[7] *Financial Time (2022, August 10). Vestas hails US clean energy subsidies as breakthrough. Retrieved from* https://www.ft.com/content/aafd2ffe-bd13-4979-9ff6-852da9ab99c1.

[8] *Vestas Wind Systems (n.d.). Sustainable strategy. Retrieved from* https://www.vestas.com/en/sustainability/sustainability-strategy.

[9] *Financial Time (2023, August 10). Vestas: the wind turns for turbine manufacturer. Retrieved from* https://www.ft.com/content/9989f8a4-e8b0-44b1-9313-6cef1cab4c86.

incentives have the potential to result in long-term strategic shifts. For example, government subsidies are the primary force driving the development of medium-, small-, and micro-sized renewable energy firms (Yang et al., 2019). Subsidies for renewable energy sources can make it more economically advantageous for energy firms to switch from fossil fuels to renewable alternatives. This may result in a full reconsideration of their business models and investment strategies.

Box 5
Financial climate incentives provide a direct stimulus for firms to change their operational, investment, and research policies and they can also result in long-term strategic alterations.

Additionally, stakeholders (i.e., shareholders, customers, regulators, and the general public) are crucial in determining how climate incentives are positioned. Their demands, expectations, and preferences frequently act as both a reward and a punishment, influencing corporate policy in covert and overt ways.

Firstly, shareholders, especially institutional investors, are increasingly emphasizing ESG (Environmental, Social, and Governance) considerations. Their influence is evident in the growing trend of shareholder resolutions focused on environmental responsibility and sustainability. By tying executive compensations or bonuses to environmental targets, shareholders can create powerful incentives for firms to embed sustainability into their core policies (Churchville, 2022).

Secondly, consumers, empowered by information and driven by environmental consciousness, can influence firm policies by showing a preference for sustainable products and practices. Eco-certifications, eco-labels, and other non-financial incentives gain their potency largely from consumer recognition and demand, driving firms to adapt their product development, marketing, and operational policies to meet these preferences (Delmas & Lessem, 2017).

Thirdly, regulators and policymakers, through both mandatory regulations and voluntary incentives, set the broader framework within which firms operate. Their influence on firm policies is direct, shaping compliance, reporting, and operational standards that firms must adhere to (Eccles et al., 2014). In essence, stakeholders, through their expectations and the climate incentives they endorse or demand, play a pivotal role in steering firm policies towards a path of sustainability and environmental responsibility.

Table 1 summarizes the related literature review on the climate incentives on eco-innovation and firm policies.

Table 1 A brief of related literature on the impacts of climate incentives on eco-innovation and firm policies

			Dependent variables			Independent variables		
Studies	Data	Period	Variables	Sources	Relation	Variables	Sources	Key findings
Panel A: Eco-innovation								
Popp et al. (2010)	26 OECD countries	1991–2004	Renewable energy	Renewables information database	+	Knowledge stocks	PATSTAT	Technological advances lead to greater investment, but the effect is small. Investments in other carbon-free energy sources, such as hydropower and nuclear power, serve as substitutes for renewable energy
Delmas and Grant (2014)	13,426 wines	1998–2005	California wine prices	Wine spectator web database	+	Eco-certification	CCOF DCS	Eco-certification leads to a price premium while the use of the eco-label does not
Panel B: Firm policies								
Eccles et al. (2014)	180 US companies	1993–2009	Corporate sustainability	Sustainable asset management	+	Performance	Thompson	High sustainability companies are more likely to have established processes for stakeholder engagement, to be more long-term oriented, and to exhibit higher measurement and disclosure of nonfinancial information
Dechezleprêtre et al. (2016)	UK firms	2006–2011	R&D tax incentives	HRMC, FAME	+	Innovation	PATSTAT	Aggregate business R&D would be around 10% lower in the absence of the tax relief scheme. The R&D generated by the tax policy creates positive spillovers on the innovations of technologically related firms
Delmas and Lessem (2017)	883 responses in US		Eco-labels	Survey	+	Consumers who are more environmentally minded	Survey	Respondents preferred both eco-labelled wines over otherwise identical conventional counterparts when the price was lower, and the wine was from a lower quality region

(+) Positively significant. PATSTAT Worldwide Patent Statistical Database, *CCOF* California Certified Organic Farmers, *DCS* Demeter Certification Services, *HRMC* HM Revenues and Customs, *FAME* Financial Analysis Made Easy

5 Current State of Analysis on Climate Incentives and Eco-innovation

To gain a thorough understanding of the prevailing research concerning climate incentives and eco-innovation, a systematic literature review was conducted. This review aimed to identify and consolidate relevant academic contributions that could provide insights into the intricate dynamics between these two realms.

5.1 Literature Search and Selection

Initiating this academic endeavor, the Web of Science database was employed as the primary source of scholarly articles. Armed with a specific set of keywords, the search was structured as Table 2.

As a result, we gathered a pool of 138 papers from the Web of Sciences using the specified keywords and search strings. Prioritizing quality, we filtered these results to include only those from the SSCI ranking, reducing our sample to 101 papers (Appendix 1).

Table 2 Search strings relating to climate incentives and eco-innovation

No.	Keyword climate incentives	Keyword term eco-innovation
1	Climate incentives	Eco-innovation
2	Climate policy incentives	Sustainable innovation
3	Environmental tax credits	Green technology
4	Carbon pricing	Environmental innovation
5	Renewable energy incentives	Circular economy
6	Emissions trading systems	Eco-efficiency
7	Environmental subsidies	Resource-efficient innovation
8	Green financing	Clean technology
9	Sustainability grants	Eco-design
10	Cap and trade	Sustainability-oriented innovation
11	Corporate sustainability incentives	Renewable energy innovation

Search string:
("Climate Incentives" OR "Climate Policy Incentives" OR "Environmental Tax Credits" OR "Carbon Pricing" OR "Renewable Energy Incentives" OR "Emissions Trading Systems" OR "Environmental Subsidies" OR "Green Financing" OR "Sustainability Grants" OR "Cap and Trade" OR "Corporate Sustainability Incentives")
AND
("Eco-Innovation" OR "Sustainable Innovation" OR "Green Technology" OR "Environmental Innovation" OR "Circular Economy" OR "Eco-efficiency" OR "Resource-efficient Innovation" OR "Clean Technology" OR "Eco-design" OR "Sustainability-oriented Innovation" OR "Renewable Energy Innovation")

5.2 The Distribution of Publications

The authors' subsequent analysis paints a persuasive picture. We investigate many factors related to the distribution of publications, including publication year, journal distribution, top authors, and research areas.

Publication Year Analysis In the first chart, we observe a growing interest in the topics of "Climate Incentives" and "Eco-Innovation" over the years. This trend indicates that these subjects have gained increasing attention in the research community, especially in recent years (Fig. 2).

Journal Distribution The second chart demonstrates the top journals that frequently publish articles related to topics of interest. This information is beneficial for researchers looking to target specific journals for their works or to identify where the primary discussions on these topics are taking place. The dataset indicates that "SUSTAINABILITY" is the predominant journal for this line of inquiry, housing 15 out of the 101 papers. This is followed by "JOURNAL OF CLEANER PRODUCTION" and "ENERGY ECONOMICS" with 7 and 5 papers, respectivel (Fig. 3).

Top Authors The third chart highlights authors who have contributed significantly to the topics. These authors can be considered as influential figures or experts in the domain. Identifying and reviewing their works can offer valuable insights and a deeper understanding of the subject matter. In terms of individual contributions, "Fischer, C" stands out as significant figures, with five publications. Other notable contributors include "Pan, YC", "Ma, JH" and "Lin, JH," further delineating the academic contours of the research (Fig. 4).

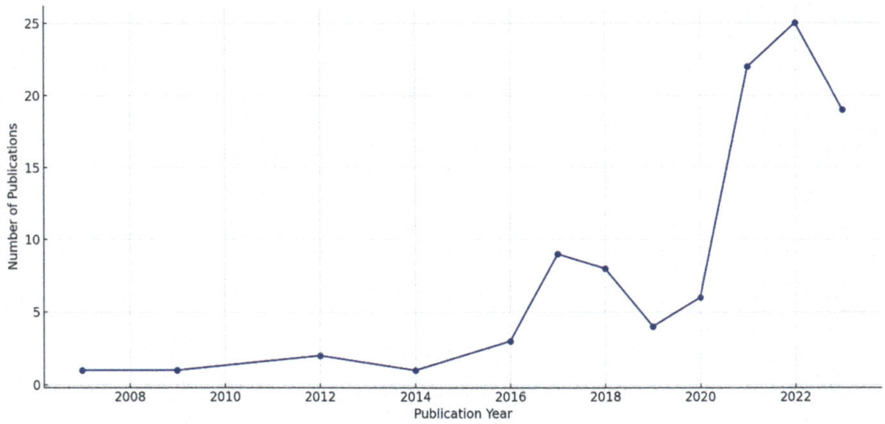

Fig. 2 Number of publications over the years. *Based on 101 papers from the Social Sciences Citation Index (SSCI) on the Web of Science platform, this figure traces the evolution of publications on the topics of interest over time*

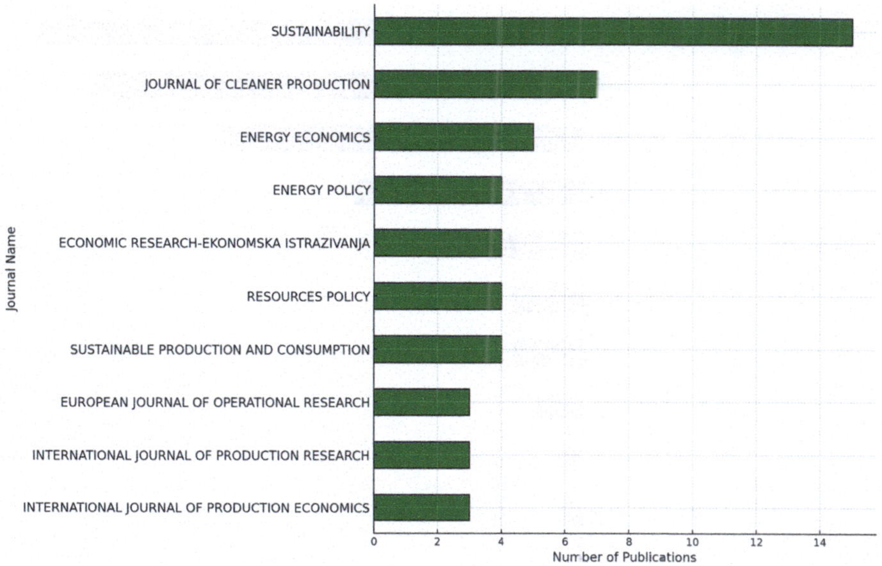

Fig. 3 Top 10 Journals with the most publications. *This figure, grounded in data from the Web of Science's SSCI, showcases the top 10 journals that frequently feature research on "Climate Incentives" and "Eco-Innovation"*

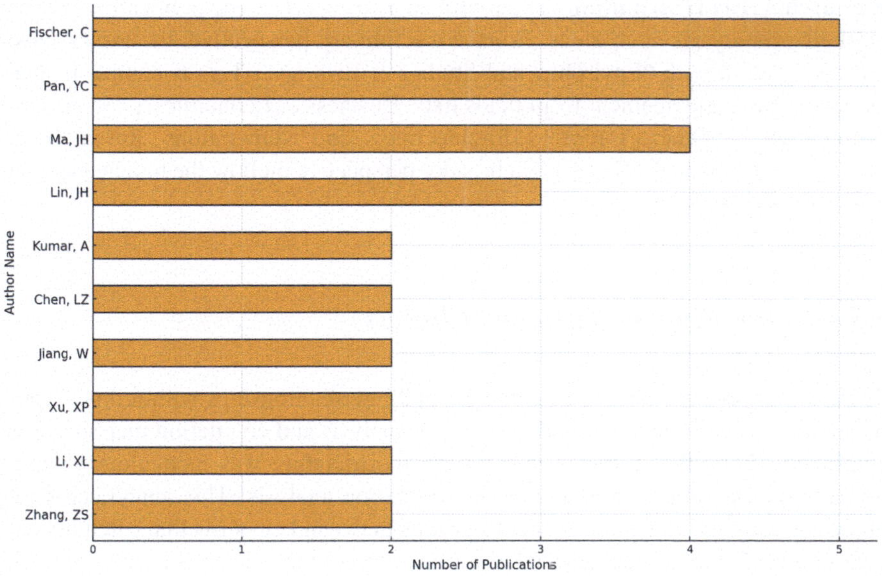

Fig. 4 Top 10 Authors with Most Publications. *Representing data from the SSCI on the Web of Science platform, this chart features the scholars actively contributing and shaping the discourse on "Climate Incentives" and "Eco-Innovation"*

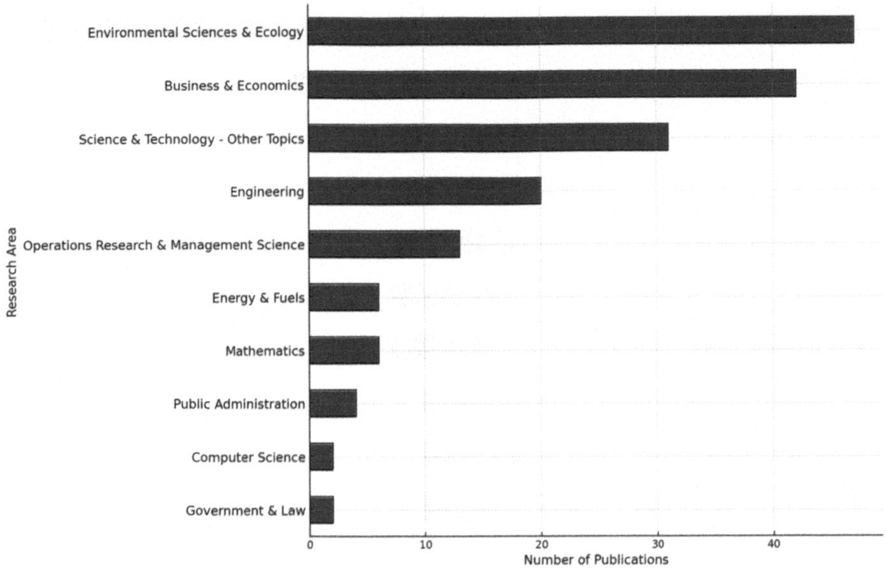

Fig. 5 Top 10 Research Areas. *Sourced from the SSCI on the Web of Science, this figure elucidates the diverse academic fields engaging with the themes of "Climate Incentives" and "Eco-Innovation"*

Research Areas Distribution The fourth chart categorizes the publications based on their primary research areas. From a disciplinary perspective, the topics most intimately align with "Environmental Studies & Ecology". This is complemented by a substantial engagement from fields like "Business & Economics", "Science & Technology – Other Topics", "Engineering" and "Operations Research & Management Science". This gives a broader perspective on how the topics intersect with various disciplines (Fig. 5).

5.3 Unravelling the Thematic Clusters

To delve deeper into the thematic content and interrelationships within this corpus of literature, a combined method of network analysis and co-citation mapping was employed. Using the VOSviewer software, the literature was meticulously organized based on subject matter through co-citation analysis. This analytical technique discerns and maps out the relationships between keywords that often appear conjointly either in the abstracts or keyword listings of the articles. Such an approach offers a granular view of the interconnected themes and concepts within the domain (Fig. 6). For a detailed methodology, please refer to Appendix 2.

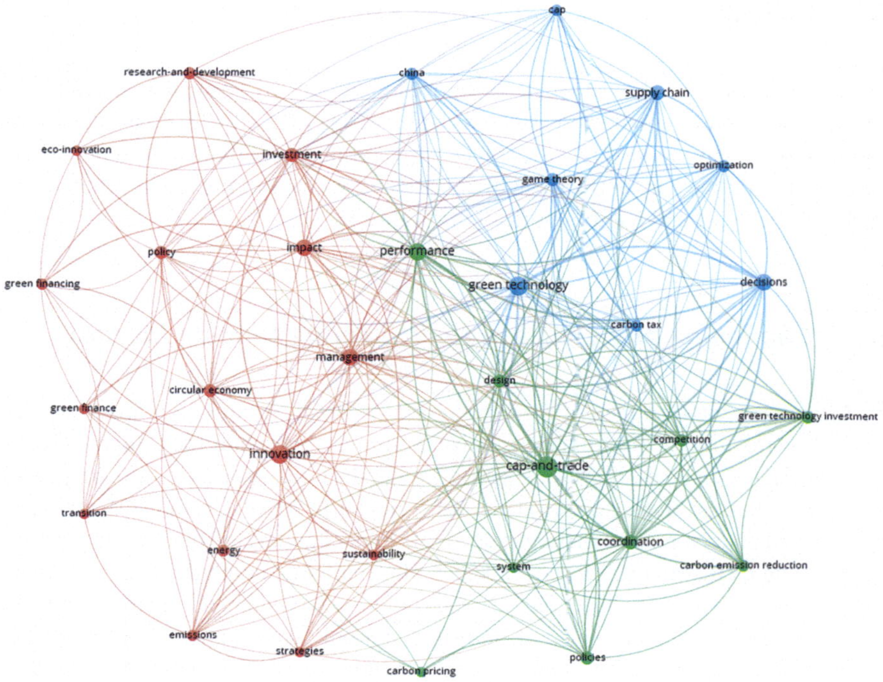

Fig. 6 Thematic clusters of keywords in climate incentives and eco-innovation research. *Derived from a co-citation analysis using VOS viewer, this visualization classifies keywords into three thematic clusters. They capture the essence of sustainability transitions, policy-tech interactions, and decision-making in green tech adoption within the SSCI literature*

The subsequent analysis identified three distinct thematic clusters:

- *A Strategic Transition towards Sustainability (red color)*: This cluster underscores the strategic endeavors firms undertake, emphasizing sustainable practices, green financing, and research-driven sustainability strategies.
- *The Interplay of Policy Instruments and Technological Investments (green color)*: Highlighting the interaction between policy tools and green technology investments, this cluster elucidates the competitive edge firms can acquire through a harmonized approach to policy design and performance.
- *Decision-making Dynamics in Green Technology Adoption (blue color)*: Focusing on decision-making processes, this cluster explores the strategies and regulatory influences that underpin the optimization and adoption of green technologies.

These clusters encapsulate the multifaceted interplay of climate incentives, eco-innovations, and firm policies, reflecting the core tenets of our research.

6 Challenges, Critics, and Future Research

As the momentum behind climate incentives continues to grow, it is essential to understand and address the multifaceted challenges associated with their implementation and effectiveness. While these incentives promise a path towards a more sustainable future, they are not without their critiques, with concerns arising about their real-world impact and equity implications (Table 3).

6.1 Challenges and Critics in Implementing Climate Incentives

- *Complexity of Design and Effectiveness Concerns*: Some critics question the real-world impact of climate incentives, arguing that while they might lead to incremental changes, they fall short of driving the transformative shifts needed to address climate change comprehensively (Hepburn, 2010). Crafting effective climate incentives requires a comprehensive understanding of the targeted industries and technologies. Moreover, successful implementation demands seamless coordination among different agencies and stakeholders. Climate incentives need to be designed in a way that ensures not only environmental effectiveness but also equity and fairness in their distribution. Research shows that economic incentives are more likely to increase social inequality and harm growth (Wang et al., 2018) as these incentives might disproportionately benefit certain socio-economic groups or regions. For instance, financial climate incentives can some-

Table 3 Overview of challenges, critiques, and future research directions

Challenges and critiques	Suggested solutions and future research
Complexity of design	Investigate adaptable frameworks across industries and technologies to ensure robustness
Mismatches and uncertainties	Develop mechanisms to bridge the temporal benefits gap and provide immediate rewards for long-term sustainable practices
Information asymmetry leading to "greenwashing"	Explore transparent reporting standards and monitoring mechanisms for accurate environmental impact reporting
Climate governance and global coordination	Enhance international collaboration and policy harmonization to combat inefficiencies like "carbon leakage" Develop educational initiatives and capacity-building programmes
Concerns about effectiveness	Delve into how climate incentives can catalyze transformative industry shifts beyond just incremental changes
Equity implications favoring large corporations	Design inclusive climate incentives ensuring equitable benefits across large and small firms.
Distributional concerns (regressive nature)	Understand the societal distribution of benefits and design equitable financial incentives
Over-reliance on market mechanisms	Explore integrative frameworks that combine market-based incentives with societal shifts and behavioral nudges

times favour larger corporations with the resources to navigate complex regulatory landscapes, leaving smaller firms disadvantaged. This can exacerbate industry concentration and reduce competition (Georgieva et al., 2021). In addition, tax breaks and subsidies, e.g., subsidies for electric vehicles, might disproportionately benefit wealthier individuals who can afford such vehicles and innovative technologies, raising concerns about the regressive nature of some incentives (Borenstein & Davis, 2015). Poorly designed incentives can lead to unintended consequences, such as promoting suboptimal technologies or practices, undermining the overall goal of fostering sustainable environmental practices (Bennear & Stavins, 2007).

- *Potential Mismatches and Uncertainties*: Potential mismatches may arise between (1) the immediately incurred costs and delayed benefits, (2) the renewable energy industry and the established ones reliant on fossil fuel, and (3) political landscapes and climate policies. First, the benefits of eco-innovations might not be immediately apparent, while the costs, especially for nascent industries or technologies, can be immediate and substantial and are anticipated to increase steeply yearly. This temporal mismatch can deter firms from capitalizing on climate incentives (Acemoglu et al., 2012). Second, specific climate incentives, especially those that promote renewable energy sources, encounter resistance from established industries that rely on fossil fuels. These industries perceive policies favouring renewable energies as threats to their existing business models; then, they may engage in lobbying activities against such transformative policies. Third, shifting political landscapes can lead to changes in climate policies. Zawadzki et al. (2020) prove that climate-skeptical leaders significantly influence public climate beliefs and actions. For example, after Donald Trump took office in 2017, his administration slowed and deprioritized climate action, rolling back policies that aimed to mitigate warming and pollution. Inconsistent policies due to political changes may result in uncertainty for businesses and investors, making it difficult to plan and implement long-term sustainable initiatives.
- *Information Asymmetry*: Information asymmetry arises when businesses, policy authorities, and the general public may not have a complete picture of the environmental impact, cost-effectiveness, and future benefits of green technologies and practices. As a result, climate incentives may give rise to adverse selection and moral hazard. Specifically, if the criteria for green energy subsidies are not well-defined, lower-quality and less environmentally impactful projects may apply and benefit from these incentives. The moral hazards occur when the development of green markets is associated with the growing phenomenon of greenwashing. While companies invest in green marketing communications to achieve better purchase intentions and brand attitudes and benefit from these climate incentives, they make minimal efforts and contribute to the improved environment (De Freitas Netto et al., 2020; Lyon & Montgomery, 2013). Information asymmetry may also distort the functions of carbon markets, a significant climate incentive. Incomplete information and knowledge about carbon markets increase challenges in setting appropriate carbon prices. Additionally,

consumers might lack accurate information about the environmental impacts of products and services, resulting in suboptimal choices. For example, according to MIT Climate,[10] although electric cars are widely agreed to be more environmentally friendly and carry "zero emission" badges, some emissions are created while building and charging vehicles. If the electricity comes from coal-fired power plants, the overall carbon footprint might not be significantly lower than that of fuel-efficient gasoline cars. Another example is the tendency toward paper bags as a replacement for plastic bags; however, producing paper bags is resource-intensive.[11] Therefore, reusable bags from other durable materials may be a better environmental choice.

- *Climate Governance and Global Coordination Challenges*: UNICEF defines multilevel climate governance as "a continuous process of discussion and negotiations involving a diverse group of national and local governments, international organizations, and the private sector, NGOs and other social actors to promote opportunities and prompt action to address climate changes" (Gonzales & Numer, 2020). Climate change is a global issue, but climate incentives are often implemented at a national or regional level. This lack of international coordination can lead to inefficiencies, with firms relocating activities to regions with less stringent regulations, a phenomenon known as "carbon leakage" (Fankhauser et al., 2016). Implementing effective climate incentives requires collaboration between countries sharing knowledge, technology, and resources. Negotiating and maintaining these international agreements can be complex and time-consuming. Different countries have varying degrees of economic development, industrial capacities, and access to resources. While developed countries advocate ESG standards, developing nations might prioritize economic growth over environmental concerns. The Paris Agreement (COP21) represents global agreements to address climate change collectively; however, enforcement mechanisms are weak. Countries may not face significant consequences or punishment for non-compliance, reducing their motivation to meet their commitments.

6.2 Avenues for Future Research

Given the outlined challenges and critiques surrounding climate incentives, it becomes evident that several avenues are yet to be explored in depth. Delving into these areas cannot only address current concerns but also enhance the overall efficacy and fairness of climate incentives.

---

[10] *MIT Climate Portal* https://climate.mit.edu/ask-mit/are-electric-vehicles-definitely-better-climate-gas-powered-cars. *Accessed on 15th October 2023.*

[11] *See: "Sustainable Shopping—Which Bag Is Best?" Accessed on 15th October 2023* via: https://education.nationalgeographic.org/resource/sustainable-shoppingwhich-bag-best/.

- *Policy Evaluation and Design:* Recognizing the intricacies involved in designing effective climate incentives, future research should conduct in-depth analyses of existing climate incentive schemes to identify successful strategies and areas of improvement. Studies should emphasize the social and economic impacts of climate incentives, focusing on their distributional effects across various socioeconomic groups. These may help develop adaptable frameworks across industries and technologies, exploring innovative instruments such as performance-based incentives, green finance mechanisms, and market-based instruments. How can we ensure that incentives are robust enough to promote the best environmental practices while avoiding unintended consequences? Case studies and comparative analyses across industries can offer valuable insights.
- *Mitigating Mismatches and Uncertainties:* With the delayed benefits of eco-innovations posing challenges, it is crucial to explore mechanisms that can bridge the temporal gap. How can we design incentives that provide immediate rewards, thus encouraging firms to invest in long-term sustainable practices? Analytical models capturing the temporal dynamics of costs and benefits could be instrumental. Behaviour economists may consider psychological and sociological factors that affect individual and businesses' responses to different incentive structures, investigating strategies that enhance public awareness, acceptance, and participation in climate incentive schemes.
- *Addressing Information Asymmetry:* To combat the potential pitfalls of "greenwashing", research should delve into transparent reporting standards and monitoring mechanisms. What tools and technologies can be employed to ensure accurate reporting of environmental impacts by firms? Investigating best practices across sectors can shed light on effective strategies.
- *Fostering Climate Governance and Global Coordination:* Given the global nature of climate change, exploring ways to enhance international collaboration becomes paramount. How can nations collectively design and implement climate incentives to prevent inefficiencies like "carbon leakage"? Comparative policy studies and international relation theories can offer a roadmap. Addressing climate and environmental problems is a fundamental human entitlement. Every individual has the right to participate in climate-making processes, and it is the responsibility of national governments and international organizations to guarantee the exercise of this right. Climate governance includes educational initiatives and capacity-building programmes to enhance awareness and understanding of climate change. Research institutions and businesses collaborate to create new technologies for renewable energies and climate adaptation, fostering the development of climate-resilient solutions.
- *Effectiveness and Transformational Impact:* Beyond the incremental changes, there is a pressing need to understand how climate incentives can catalyse transformative shifts. Can these incentives be designed to bring about systemic changes in industries? Experimental designs and longitudinal studies can provide a deeper understanding of their long-term impact.

- *Equity, Competition, and Distribution:* Future research should emphasize designing climate incentives that foster a level playing field. How can we ensure that both large corporations and smaller firms benefit equally? Additionally, understanding the societal distribution of benefits, especially in the context of financial incentives, becomes crucial to addressing equity concerns.
- *Holistic Approaches Beyond Market Mechanisms:* Exploring integrative frameworks that combine market-based incentives with behavioural nudges and societal shifts can be promising. How can we design comprehensive climate action strategies that leverage both market mechanisms and societal transformations? Interdisciplinary studies combining economics, sociology, and environmental sciences can provide a holistic view.

As the world stands at the cusp of a green revolution, it becomes imperative to delve deeper into the complexities surrounding the design, effectiveness, and fairness of climate incentives. The complex nature of corporate responses, policy harmonization, equity considerations, and broader market dynamics require a thorough investigation. The directions outlined above offer a roadmap for future research, promising to deepen our understanding of the challenges and opportunities.

7 Conclusion

The connection between climate incentives and eco-innovation represents environmental care and economic reasoning. As the rise in global environmental awareness, the importance of these incentives in forming firm strategies and policies becomes more apparent. These incentives will be critical in driving innovations to environmentally friendly paths and promoting the widespread use of green technologies.

Firms need to proactively respond to climate incentives, incorporating them into their operational frameworks to demonstrate a long-term commitment to eco-innovation. This aligns corporate environmental efforts with stakeholders' expectations, maximising the value obtained from such incentives. Furthermore, committed investment resources to research and development (R&D) efforts also place firms at the forefront of environmental innovation, providing not only solutions to global challenges but also competitive advantages in the marketplace.

Policy formulation should design climate incentives that balance environmental and economic issues, while encouraging significant eco-innovations. Due to the global nature of environmental challenges, international cooperation and coordination become increasingly vital. Policymakers are encouraged to harmonize climate incentive frameworks across jurisdictions, avoiding potential inefficiencies and fostering the spread of international best practices. Furthermore, the ever-evolving and dynamic nature of the eco-innovation landscape necessitates periodic evaluation and adaptation of these incentives to maintain their ongoing relevance and efficacy. The intersection of climate incentives and eco-innovation holds substantial promise for the future. By adopting a visionary and collaborative stance, both corporate entities and policymakers stand to harness this latent potential, thus ushering in an era characterized by sustainability and prosperity.

Declaration of Generative AI and AI-Assisted Technologies in the Writing Process for This Chapter from Authors The authors of this chapter have used ChatGPT and Grammarly to proofread certain parts of the chapter. However, they declared that they did not use AI to create or write original and new manuscript content.

List of 101 Papers Relating to "Climate Incentives" and "Eco-innovation" in SSCI Web of Sciences

	Article
1	Albitar, K, Al -Shaer, H, & Liu, YS (2023). Corporate commitment to climate change: The effect of eco-innovation and climate governance. Research Policy
2	Alizadeh-Basban, N, & Taleizadeh, AA (2020). A hybrid circular economy – Game theoretical approach in a dual-channel green supply chain considering sale's effort, delivery time, and hybrid remanufacturing. Journal Of Cleaner Production
3	Anser, MK, Godil, DI, Khan, MA, Nassani, AA, Zaman, K, & Abro, MMQ (2021). The impact of coal combustion, nitrous oxide emissions, and traffic emissions on COVID-19 cases: a Markov-switching approach. Environmental Science and Pollution Research
4	Bai, Y, Hua, CC, Jiao, JL, Yang, M, & Li, FY (2018). Green efficiency and environmental subsidy: Evidence from thermal power firms in China. Journal of Cleaner Production
5	Bakhtiari, S (2018). Coming out clean: Australian carbon pricing and clean technology adoption. Ecological Economics
6	Ben Belgacem, S, Khatoon, G, & Alzuman, A (2023). Role of renewable energy and financial innovation in environmental protection: Empirical evidence from UAE and Saudi Arabia. Sustainability
7	Bertini, M, Buehler, S, Halbheer, D, & Lehmann, DR (2022). Carbon Foot printing and Pricing Under Climate Concerns. Journal of Marketing
8	Bi, GB, Jin, MY, Ling, LY, & Yang, F (2017). Environmental subsidy and the choice of green technology in the presence of green consumers. Annals of Operations Research
9	Bian, JS, Zhang, GQ, & Zhou, GH (2020). Manufacturer vs. Consumer Subsidy with Green Technology Investment and Environmental Concern. European Journal of Operational Research
10	Boamah, V, Tang, DC, Zhang, Q, & Zhang, JQ (2023). Do FDI Inflows into African Countries Impact Their CO2 Emission Levels? Sustainability
11	Bompard, EF, Corgnati, SP, Grosso, D, Huang, T, Mietti, G, & Profumo, F (2022). Multidimensional assessment of the energy sustainability and carbon pricing impacts along the belt and road initiative. Renewable & Sustainable Energy Reviews

(continued)

	Article
12	Cao, KY, Xu, XP, Wu, Q, & Zhang, QP (2017). Optimal production and carbon emission reduction level under cap-and-trade and low carbon subsidy policies. Journal of Cleaner Production
13	Chen, K, & Bian, R (2023). Green financing and renewable resources for China's sustainable growth: Assessing macroeconomic industry impact. Resources Policy
14	Chen, S, Huang, FW, & Lin, JH (2023). Green technology choices under the cap-and-trade mechanism with insurer green finance in a dragon-king environment. Energy Economics
15	Chen, W, Ma, YK, & Bai, CG (2021). The Impact of Carbon Emission Quota Allocation Regulations on the Investment of Low-Carbon Technology in Electric Power Industry Under Peak-Valley Price Policy. IEEE Transactions On Engineering Management
16	Chen, WJ (2022). Toward Sustainability: Dynamics of Total Carbon Dioxide Emissions, Aggregate Income, Non-Renewable Energy, and Renewable Power. Sustainability
17	Chen, X, Wang, XJ, Kumar, V, & Kumar, N (2016). Low carbon warehouse management under cap-and-trade policy. Journal of Cleaner Production
18	Chen, Y, & Jin, S (2023). Corporate social responsibility and green technology innovation: The moderating role of stakeholders. Sustainability
19	Cheng, PY, Ji, GX, Zhang, GT, & Shi, YY (2022). A closed-loop supply chain network considering consumer's low carbon preference and carbon tax under the cap-and-trade regulation. Sustainable Production And Consumption
20	Cheng, PY, Zhang, GT, & Sun, H (2022). The sustainable supply chain network competition based on non-cooperative equilibrium under carbon emission permits. Mathematics
21	Coleman, JW (2014). Unilateral Climate Regulation. Harvard Environmental Law Review
22	Corsini, F, & Frey, M (2023). Exploring the development of environmentally sustainable products through reward-based crowdfunding. Electronic Commerce Research
23	Cui, JB (2017). Induced clean technology adoption and international trade with heterogeneous firms. Journal of International Trade & Economic Development
24	Da, BW, Liu, CZ, Liu, NN, & Fan, SD (2021). Strategies of Two-Level Green Technology Investments for Coal Supply Chain under Different Dominant Modes. Sustainability
25	Dou, GW, & Choi, TM (2021). Does implementing trade-in and green technology together benefit the environment? European Journal of Operational Research
26	Drake, DF, Kleindorfer, PR, & Van Wassenhove, LN (2016). Technology Choice and Capacity Portfolios under Emissions Regulation. Production and Operations Management
27	Fan, XS, Chen, KL, & Chen, YJ (2022). Is Price Commitment a Better Solution to Control Carbon Emissions and Promote Technology Investment? Management Science
28	Fischer, C, & Pizer, WA (2019). Horizontal Equity Effects in Energy Regulation. Journal of the Association of Environmental and Resource Economists
29	Fischer, C, & Salant, SW (2017). Balancing the carbon budget for oil: The distributive effects of alternative policies. European Economic Review

(continued)

	Article
30	Fischer, C, Mao, B, & Shawhan, D (2018). Trade between mass- and rate-based regulatory regimes: Bad for emissions? Energy Economics
31	Fischer, C, Preonas, L, & Newell, RG (2017). Environmental and Technology Policy Options in the Electricity Sector: Are We Deploying Too Many? Journal of the Association Of Environmental AND Resource Economists
32	Fischer, C, Torvanger, A, Shrivastava, MK, Sterner, T, & Stigson, P (2012). How should support for climate-friendly technologies be designed? Ambio
33	Fu, WW, & Irfan, M (2022). Does green financing develop a Cleaner environment for environmental sustainability: Empirical Insights from Association of Southeast Asian Nations Economies. Frontiers in Psychology
34	Golpira, H, & Javanmardan, A (2022). Robust optimization of SUSTAINABLE closed-loop supply chain considering carbon emission schemes. Sustainable Production and Consumption
35	Gong, QY, Ying, LM, & Dai, JP (2023). Green finance and energy natural resources nexus with economic performance: A novel evidence from China. Resources Policy
36	Greaker, M, Heggedal, TR, & Rosendahl, KE (2018). Environmental Policy and the Direction of Technical Change. Scandinavian Journal of Economics
37	Guo, Y, Wang, MM, & Yang, F (2022). Joint emission reduction strategy considering channel inconvenience under different recycling structures. Computers & Industrial Engineering
38	Guzman, LI, & Clapp, A (2017). Applying personal carbon trading: a proposed carbon, health and savings System' for British Columbia, Canada. Climate Policy
39	Hasan, MR, Roy, TC, Daryanto, Y, & Wee, HM (2021). Optimizing inventory level and technology investment under a carbon tax, cap-and-trade and strict carbon limit regulations. Sustainable Production and Consumption
40	Hoarau, Q, & Meunier, G (2023). Coordination of sectoral climate policies and life cycle emissions. Resource and Energy Economics
41	Hong, ZF, Chu, CB, Zhang, LDL, & Yu, YG (2017). Optimizing an emission trading scheme for local governments: A Stackelberg game model and hybrid algorithm. International Journal of Production Economics
42	Hussain, J, Pan, YC, Ali, G, & Yue, XF (2020). Pricing behavior of monopoly market with the implementation of green technology decision under emission reduction subsidy policy. Science of the Total Environment
43	Islam, M, Fremeth, A, & Marcus, A (2018). Signaling by early-stage startups: US government research grants and venture capital funding. Journal of Business Venturing
44	Ji, T, Xu, XP, Yan, XM, & Yu, YG (2020). The production decisions and cap setting with wholesale price and revenue sharing contracts under cap-and-trade regulation. International Journal of Production Research
45	Ji, X, Zhang, SQ, & Lu, Y (2023). Does an environmental management system affect green Inno-Vation: The role of green financing in China's tourism sector in a circular economy. Sustainability
46	Jian, X, & Afshan, S (2022). Dynamic effect of green financing and green technology innovation on carbon neutrality in G10 countries: Fresh insights from CS-ARDL approach. Economic Research-Ekonomska Istrazivanja
47	Jiang, W, & Chen, X (2016). Optimal strategies for low carbon supply chain with strategic customer behavior and green technology investment. Discrete Dynamics in Nature and Society

(continued)

	Article
48	Jiang, W, Pu, LQ, Huang, T, yuan, L, & Gan, L (2021). The effect of fairness concern on carbon emission reduction and revenue distribution in construction supply chain: Power structure perspective. Discrete Dynamics in Nature and Society
49	Johnson, KC (2007). Refunded emission taxes: A resolution to the cap-versus-tax dilemma for greenhouse gas regulation. Energy Policy
50	Kar, S, Basu, K, & Sarkar, B (2023). Advertisement policy for dual-channel within emissions-controlled flexible production system. Journal of Retailing and Consumer Services
51	Karslen, R, Papachristos, G, & Rehmatulla, N (2019). An agent-based model of climate-energy policies to promote wind propulsion technology in shipping. Environmental Innovation and Societal Transitions
52	Katariya, D, & Shukla, K (2022). Sustainable economic production quantity (SEPQ) model for inventory having green technology investments - price sensitive demand with expiration dates. Economic Computation and Economic Cybernetics Studies and Research
53	Kumar, L, Nadeem, F, Sloan, M, Restle-Steinert, J, Deitch, MJ, Naqvi, SA, Kumar, A, & Sassanelli, C (2022). Fostering green finance for sustainable development: A focus on textile and leather small medium Enterprises in Pakistan. Sustainability
54	Li, CH, Wang, JL, & Shi, YF (2022). The Impact of Government Intervention and Cap-and-Trade on Green Innovation in Supply Chains: A Social Welfare Perspective. Sustainability
55	Li, CN, Guo, TY, & Chen, Y (2022). Robust emission reduction strategies under cap-and-trade and demand uncertainty. Sustainability
56	Li, J, Lai, KK, & Li, YM (2022). Remanufacturing and low-carbon investment strategies in a closed-loop supply chain under multiple carbon policies. International Journal of Logistics-Research and Applications
57	Li, XL, Chen, LZ, & Lin, JH (2023). Borrowing-firm environmental impact on insurer green finance assessment: Green loan subsidy, regulatory cap, and green technology. Environmental Impact Assessment Review
58	Li, XL, Chen, LZ, & Lin, JH (2023). Cap-and-trade mechanisms, green technology investment, and shadow insurance in a black swan environment. Energy Economics
59	Li, ZM, Pan, YC, Yang, W, Ma, JH, & Zhou, M (2021). Effects of government subsidies on green technology investment and green marketing coordination of supply chain under the cap-and-trade mechanism. Energy Economics
60	Liao, FM, Hu, YY, & Xu, SL (2022). How do environmental subsidies affect the environmental performance of heavily polluting enterprises: evidence from China. Economic Research-Ekonomska Istrazivanja
61	Liao, ZJ, & Zhu, X (2023). The role of different fiscal policies in inducing environmental innovation and enhancing firm competitiveness. Emerging Markets Finance and Trade
62	Lin, XG, Chen, DN, Zhou, YW, & Lin, Q (2022). Horizontal mergers in low carbon manufacturing. European Journal of Operational Research
63	Linnenluecke, MK, Han, JL, Pan, ZY, & Smith, T (2019). How markets will drive the transition to a low carbon economy. Economic Modelling
64	Liu, L, Wang, Z, & Zhang, ZS (2021). Matching-game approach for green technology investment strategies in a supply chain under environmental regulations. Sustainable Production and Consumption

(continued)

	Article
65	Liu, L, Zhang, ZS, & Wang, Z (2021). Two-sided matching and game on investing in carbon emission reduction technology under a cap-and-trade system. Journal of Cleaner Production
66	Long, JR, Zhong, CBA, Ahmad, B, Irfan, M, & Nazir, R (2022). How do green financing and green logistics affect the circular economy in the pandemic situation: Key mediating role of sustainable production. Economic Research-Ekonomska Istrazivanja
67	Markey, R, McIvor, J, O'Brien, M, & Wright, CF (2021). Triggering business responses to climate policy in Australia. Australian Journal of Management
68	McGinty, M, & de Vries, FP (2009). Technology Diffusion, Product Differentiation and Environmental Subsidies. B E Journal of Economic Analysis & Policy
69	Mu, YF, & Niu, F (2022). To be or not to be? Strategic analysis of carbon tax guiding manufacturers to choose low-carbon technology. Sustainability
70	Murmu, V, Kumar, D, & Jha, AK (2023). Quality and selling price dependent sustainable perishable inventory policy: Lessons from Covid-19 pandemic. Operations Management Research
71	Ottelin, J, Heinonen, J, & Junnila, S (2018). Carbon and material footprints of a welfare state: Why and how governments should enhance green investments. Environmental Science & Policy
72	Pan, YC, Hussain, J, Liang, XY, & Ma, JH (2021). A duopoly game model for pricing and green technology selection under cap-and-trade scheme. Computers & Industrial Engineering
73	Purdon, M, Witcover, J, Murphy, C, Ziaja, S, Winfield, M, Giuliano, G, Seguin, C, Kaiser, C, Papy, J, & Fulton, L (2021). Climate and transportation policy sequencing in California and Quebec(sic)(sic)(sic)palabras clave. Review of Policy Research
74	Qin, JJ, Fu, HP, Wang, ZP, & Xia, LJ (2021). Financing and carbon emission reduction strategies of capital-constrained manufacturers in E-commerce supply chains. International Journal of Production Economics
75	Qin, JJ, Han, YQ, Wei, GM, & Xia, LJ (2020). The value of advance payment financing to carbon emission reduction and production in a supply chain with game theory analysis. International Journal of Production Research
76	Ranisau, J, Barbouti, M, Trainor, A, Juthani, N, Salkuyeh, YK, Maroufmashat, A, & fowler, M (2017). Power-to-gas implementation for a Polygeneration system in southwestern Ontario. Sustainability
77	Rausch, S, & Yonezawa, H (2023). Green technology policies versus carbon pricing: An intergenerational perspective. European Economic Review
78	Ren, SG, Sun, HL, & Zhang, T (2021). Do environmental subsidies spur environmental innovation? Empirical evidence from Chinese listed firms. Technological Forecasting and Social Change
79	Riedel, F, Gorbach, G, & Kost, C (2021). Barriers to internal carbon pricing in German companies. Energy Policy
80	Saha, T, Sinha, A, & Abbas, S (2022). Green financing of eco-innovations: Is the gender inclusivity taken care of? Economic Research-Ekonomska Istrazivanja
81	Sharif, A, Saqib, N, Dong, KY, & Khan, SAR (2022). Nexus between green technology innovation, green financing, and CO2 emissions in the G7 countries: The moderating role of social globalisation. Sustainable Development

(continued)

	Article
82	Shen, B, Zhu, C, Li, QY, & Wang, XF (2021). Green technology adoption in textiles and apparel supply chains with environmental taxes. International Journal of Production Research
83	Shinwari, R, Wang, YJ, Payab, AH, Kubiczek, J, & Dorduncu, H (2022). What drives investment in renewable energy resources? Evaluating the role of natural resources volatility and economic performance for China. Resources Policy
84	Song, W, Ren, A, Li, XD, & Li, Q (2021). The orchestrating role of carbon subsidies in a capital-constrained supply chain. Mathematical Problems in Engineering
85	Taleizadeh, AA, Shahriari, M, & Sana, SS (2021). Pricing and Coordination Strategies in a Dual Channel Supply Chain with Green Production under Cap-and-Trade Regulation. Sustainability
86	Talha, M (2023). Green financing and sustainable policy for low carbon and energy saving initiatives: Turning educational Institutes of China into green. Inzinerine Ekonomika-Engineering Economics
87	Taylor, MR (2012). Innovation under cap-and-trade programs. Proceedings of the National Academy of Sciences of the United States of America
88	Udayakumar, R, Priyan, S, Mittal, M, Jirawattanapanit, A, Rajchakit, G, & Kaewmesri, P (2022). A sustainable production scheduling with backorders under different forms of rework process and green investment. Sustainability
89	van Langen, SK, & Passaro, R (2021). The Dutch green deals policy and its applicability to circular economy policies. Sustainability
90	Wang, N, Akimoto, K, & Nemet, GF (2021). What went wrong? Learning from three decades of carbon capture, utilization and sequestration (CCUS) pilot and demonstration projects. Energy Policy
91	Wang, Y, Hu, JL, Hu, Y, & Wang, Y (2022). Which is more effective: The carrot or the stick? Environmental policy, green innovation and Enterprise energy efficiency-A quasi-natural experiment from China. Frontiers in Environmental Science
92	Wasan, P, Kumar, A, & Luthra, S (2021). Green finance barriers and solution strategies for Emerging economies: The case of India. IEEE Transactions on Engineering Management
93	Xu, AD, Qian, FB, Ding, HH, & Zhang, X (2023). Digitalization of logistics for transition to a resource-efficient and circular economy. Resources Policy
94	Xu, XP, He, P, Xu, H, & Zhang, QP (2017). Supply chain coordination with green technology under cap-and-trade regulation. International Journal of Production Economics
95	Yang, W, Pan, YC, Ma, JH, Yang, TY, & Ke, X (2020). Effects of allowance allocation rules on green technology investment and product pricing under the cap-and-trade mechanism. Energy Policy
96	Yang, W, Pan, YC, Ma, JH, Zhou, M, Chen, ZM, & Zhu, WH (2018). Optimization on emission permit trading and green technology implementation under cap-and-trade scheme. Journal of Cleaner Production
97	Zhang, DY (2022). Do heterogenous subsides work differently on environmental innovation? A mechanism exploration approach. Energy Economics
98	Zhang, Q, Li, YW, Lin, GH, & Zhu, XD (2023). Operational research models for green technology cross-licensing with known carbon quota trading prices. International Transactions in Operational Research

(continued)

	Article
99	Zhang, SY, Wang, CX, & Yu, C (2019). The evolutionary game analysis and simulation with system dynamics of manufacturer's emissions abatement behavior under cap-and-trade regulation. Applied Mathematics and Computation
100	Zhang, W, Zhang, MY, Wu, SB, & Liu, F (2021). A complex path model for low-carbon sustainable development of enterprise based on system dynamics. Journal of Cleaner Production
101	Zheng, Y, Zhang, GX, & Zhang, WW (2018). A Duopoly Manufacturers' Game Model Considering Green Technology Investment under a Cap-and-Trade System. Sustainability

Approach for Co-citation Analysis Method

In our exploration of climate incentives and eco-innovation, we conducted an exhaustive co-citation assessment to uncover patterns of collaboration and thematic coherence among the academic literature in the domain of climate incentives and eco-innovation.

We utilized fractional counting techniques, as mentioned in Perianes-Rodriguez et al. (2016). The results were then visualized employing mapping and clustering methodologies through the VOS software, in line with the approaches set forth by Van Eck and Waltman (2014). Visualization serves not only as a representation of the data but also as an analytical tool, aiding in discerning trends, relationships, and areas of significance in the research landscape.

To measure the connection strength between two nodes, i and j, we defined it as s_{ij}. This was achieved by assessing the normalized strength of their association. This metric represents the similarity degree between nodes i and j and is computed as:

$$s_{ij} = \frac{2ma_{ij}}{k_i k_j}$$

In this equation, a_{ij} represents the number of shared studies between node i and node j. The variable m stands for the total count of research elements across the whole network. The aggregate count of elements associated with node i or j is represented by k and is calculated as:

$$k = \sum_i a_{ij}$$

After determining the association degree, we visualized the node network using a mapping method derived from the following function:

$$V(x_1,\ldots x_n) = \sum_{i<j} s_{i,j} \left| x_i - x_j \right|^2$$

This function is bound by the condition:

$$\frac{2}{n(n-1)}\sum_{i<j}\left|x_i - x_j\right| = 1$$

To conclude, we organized the nodes into separate clusters (c_1, …, c_n) by optimizing this function:

$$V(x_1,\ldots,x_n) = \sum_{i<j}\delta(c_i,c_j)(s_{i,j} - \gamma)$$

Here, $\delta(c_i, c_j)$ functions as a delta function that takes the value 1 if c_i matches c_j, and 0 otherwise. The variable γ serves as a cut-off parameter, determining the essential similarity level for two nodes to be grouped into the same cluster.

References

Acemoglu, D., Aghion, P., Bursztyn, L., & Hemous, D. (2012). The environment and directed technical change. *American Economic Review, 102*(1), 131–166.

Ambec, S., Cohen, M. A., Elgie, S., & Lanoie, P. (2013). The porter hypothesis at 20: Can environmental regulation enhance innovation and competitiveness? *Review of Environmental Economics and Policy, 7*(1), 2–22.

Bennear, L. S., & Stavins, R. N. (2007). Second-best theory and the use of multiple policy instruments. *Environmental and Resource Economics, 37*(1), 111–129.

Bohringer, C., & Vogt, C. (2004). The dismantling of a breakthrough: The Kyoto Protocal as sympolic policy. *European Journal of Political Economy, 20*(3), 597–617.

Borenstein, S., & Davis, L. W. (2015). The distributional effects of US clean energy tax credits. *Tax Policy and the Economy, 30*(1), 191–234.

Busch, T., & Hoffmann, V. H. (2011). How hot is your bottom line? Linking carbon and financial performance. *Business & Society, 50*(2), 233–265.

Churchville, S. (2022, October). Linking executive compensation to ESG performance-lessons learned and insights for what's ahead. The Conference Board. https://corpgov.law.harvard.edu/2022/11/27/linking-executive-compensation-to-esg-performance/. Accessed 15.10.23.

Darnall, N., Henriques, I., & Sadorsky, P. (2009). Adopting proactive environmental strategy: The influence of stakeholders and firm size. *Journal of Management Studies, 47*(6), 1072–1094.

Dauvergne, P., & Lister, J. (2013). *Eco-business: A big-brand takeover of sustainability*. MIT Press.

De Freitas Netto, S. V., Sobral, M. F. F., Ribeiro, A. R. B., & Soares, G. R. D. L. (2020). Concepts and forms of greenwashing: A systematic review. *Environmental Sciences Europe, 32*(1), 1–12.

Dechezleprêtre, A., Einiö, E., Martin, R., Nguyen, B., & Van Reenen, J. (2016). *Do tax incentives for research increase firm innovation? An RD design for R&D*. NBER Working Paper No. 22405.

Dechezleprêtre, A., & Sato, M. (2017). The impacts of environmental regulations on competitiveness. *Review of Environmental Economics and Policy, 11*(2), 183–206.

Delmas, M. A., & Burbano, V. C. (2011). The drivers of greenwashing. *California Management Review, 54*(1), 64–87.

Delmas, M. A., & Grant, L. E. (2014). Eco-labeling strategies and price-premium: The wine industry puzzle. *Business & Society, 53*(1), 6–44.

Delmas, M. A., & Lessem, N. (2017). Eco-premium or eco-penalty? Eco-labels and quality in the organic wine market. *Business & Society, 56*(2), 318–356.

Eccles, R. G., Ioannou, I., & Serafeim, G. (2014). The impact of corporate sustainability on organizational processes and performance. *Management Science, 60*(11), 2835–2857.
Edler, J., & Georghiou, L. (2007). Public procurement and innovation—Resurrecting the demand side. *Research Policy, 36*(7), 949–963.
Ellerman, A. D., Joskow, P. L., Schmalensee, R., Montero, J. P., & Bailey, E. M. (2000). *Markets for clean air: The US acid rain program*. Cambridge University Press.
EPA. (2023). Economic incentives. https://www.epa.gov/environmental-economics/economic-incentives#info. Access 22.09.23.
Fankhauser, S., Hepburn, C., & Park, J. (2016). Combining multiple climate policy instruments: How not to do it. *Climate Change Economics, 7*(03), 1650014.
Georgieva, K., Díez, F. J., Duval, R., & Schwarz, D. (2021). Rising market power-a threat to the recovery. *IMF Blog, 15*. https://www.imf.org/en/Blogs/Articles/2021/03/15/blog-rising-market-power-a-threat-to-the-recovery, Accessed 20.10.23.
Gonzales, S. C., & Numer, E. (2020). What is climate governance?. United Nations Childrens Funds (UNICEF), Panama. https://www.unicef.org/lac/media/19651/file/what-is-climate-governance.pdf. Accessed 22.09.23.
Goulder, L. H., & Parry, I. W. H. (2008). Instrument choice in environmental policy. *Review of Environmental Economics and Policy, 2*(2), 152–174.
Hepburn, C. (2010). Environmental policy, government, and the market. *Oxford Review of Economic Policy, 26*(2), 117–136.
Horbach, J. (2008). Determinants of environmental innovation—New evidence from German panel data sources. *Research Policy, 37*(1), 163–173.
Jaffe, A. B., Newell, R. G., & Stavins, R. N. (2002). Environmental policy and technological change. *Environmental and Resource Economics, 22*(1–2), 41–70.
Johnstone, N., Haščič, I., & Popp, D. (2010). Renewable energy policies and technological innovation: Evidence based on patent counts. *Environmental and Resource Economics, 45*(1), 133–155.
Kemp, R., & Pearson, P. (2007). *Measuring eco-innovation*. UM Merit, Maastricht Economic Research Institute on Innovation and Technology. https://www.oecd.org/env/consumption-innovation/43960830.pdf. Accessed 15.11.23.
Lee, L., Choudhury, A., & Shubita, M. (2023). Impact of Paris agreement on financing strategy: Evidence from FPSO industry. *Technological Forecasting and Social Change, 188*, 122266.
Lyon, T. P., & Montgomery, A. W. (2013). Tweetjacked: The impact of social media on corporate greenwashes. *Journal of Business Ethics, 118*(4), 747–757.
Perianes-Rodriguez, A., Waltman, L., & Van Eck, N. J. (2016). Constructing bibliometric networks: A comparison between full and fractional counting. *Journal of Informetrics, 10*(4), 1178–1195.
Popp, D. (2002). Induced innovation and energy prices. *American Economic Review, 92*(1), 160–180.
Popp, D., Hascic, I., & Medhi, N. (2010). Technology and the diffusion of renewable energy. *Energy Economics, 33*(4), 648–662.
Rennings, K. (2000). Redefining innovation — eco-innovation research and the contribution from ecological economics. *Ecological Economics, 32*(2), 319–332.
Schamalensee, R., & Stavins, R. N. (2019). Policy evolution under the clean air act. *Journal of Economic Perspectives, 33*(4), 27–55.
Stavins, R. N. (2003). Experience with market-based environmental policy instruments. *Handbook of Environmental Economics, 1*, 355–435.
Van Eck, N. J., & Waltman, L. (2014). Visualizing bibliometric networks. In *Measuring scholarly impact: Methods and practice* (pp. 285–320). Springer International Publishing.
Vig, N. J., & Kraft, M. E. (2013). *Environmental policy: New directions for the twenty-first century* (8th ed.). Sage.
Wang, J., Ellis, S. E., & Rogers, C. L. (2018). Income inequality and economic development incentives in US states: Robin Hood in reverse? *Review of Regional Studies, 48*(1), 93–117.

Yang, X., He, L., Xia, Y., & Chen, Y. (2019). Effect of government subsidies on renewable energy investments: The threshold effect. *Energy Policy, 132*, 156–166.

Zawadzki, S. J., Bouman, T., Steg, L., Bojarskich, V., & Druen, P. B. (2020). Translating climate beliefs into action in a changing political landscape. *Climatic Change, 161*, 21–42.

Phuong LE holds a Ph.D. from the University of Paris Saclay and a Financial Risk Manager certification (FRM) from the Global Association of Risk Professionals. His expertise includes Cross-Border Banking, Financial Intermediation, Bank Risk, Financial Innovation, and Sustainable Finance. He has published in high-ranking journals like Economic Modelling, Finance Research Letters, and International Journal of Finance & Economics. Phuong LE presents at international conferences on banking risks and ESG analysis and serves as a peer reviewer for many academic journals. His work connects academic research with real-world finance. Dr. Le specializes in credit risk modeling and regulatory compliance.

Thao Ngoc Nguyen MSc, PhD, PGCHE, FHEA is Senior Lecturer in Accounting and Finance at Nottingham Trent University. Before joining Nottingham Trent University, Thao had worked 4 years in the banking sector as the Head of International Settlement Department. He completed a PhD in Finance in 2012 in London (Viva without correction). Thao's research focuses on theoretical and empirical issues of bank/firm competition, efficiency, risk management and climate change. He has published in ABS 3* journals. Thao is the Co-Chair for IFMB 2024 conference (Contemporary Issues in Financial Markets and Banking). Thao is a visiting professor at Ipag Business School, Paris, France; Stockholm Business School, Stockholm, Sweden; and Universidad Loyola Andalucia, Seville, Spain.

Chau Le is a Senior Lecturer in Banking and Finance at Lincoln International Business School, University of Lincoln. She received her PhD in Financial Economics from the University of Birmingham, UK. Chau has research interests in the areas of financial economics and business economics, with an emphasis on the complex dynamic network of financial markets and institutions, corporate finance and firm behaviour. Her research has been published in the Journal of Financial Stability, Small Business Economics, Journal of Small Business Management, International Journal of Finance & Economics, Applied Economics.

Climate Governance Practices and the Evolutionary Trends in Corporate Eco-innovation

Kim Nguyen

Abstract This Chapter provides readers with an overview of climate governance practices at global, national, and organizational levels, as well as the evolutionary trends in corporate eco-innovation. This study primarily centers on applying resource-based and institutional theories to clarify the complex connection between corporate governance and eco-innovation. Companies, often constrained by limited resources, operate within the dynamic interaction of social pressures and institutional regulations in sustainable development and green investments. Effectively allocating these resources to align with societal expectations and governmental mandates, particularly in the pursuit of net-zero emissions and carbon neutrality, requires the development of robust climate governance strategies and substantial investments in eco-innovation.

1 Introduction

Net zero and carbon neutrality have emerged as the long-term emission reduction goals for numerous countries in the mid-twenty-first century as part of their efforts to combat climate change. This global commitment to climate change began with the United Nations Framework Convention on Climate Change (UNFCCC) in 1992. It was reinforced by the Paris Climate Agreement in 2015, gaining the support of over 130 countries and regions (Tan et al., 2022).

Many countries have also initiated environmental programs aimed at mitigating the adverse impacts of climate change and ultimately achieving net-zero emissions. For instance, the United Kingdom (UK) established the Department for Energy Security and Net Zero in 2023, with a key mandate to lead the world in transitioning toward a green industry. Similarly, the European Environment Agency has set a target

K. Nguyen (✉)
Department of Accounting, Finance and Economics, Lincoln International Business School, University of Lincoln, Lincoln, UK
e-mail: knguyen@lincoln.ac.uk

V. Q. Trinh (ed.), *Climate Governance and Corporate Eco-innovation*, Sustainable Finance, https://doi.org/10.1007/978-3-031-56423-9_3

to achieve climate neutrality and net-zero emissions by 2050 in accordance with the Paris Agreement.

As global and domestic regulations continue to evolve towards promoting sustainable practices, companies are increasingly forced to reevaluate and adapt their operations to align with these regulations and meet the expectations of stakeholders, which leads to the development of climate governance frameworks at the organizational level. One influential strategy firms adopt to contribute to greener practices is investment in eco-innovation. This concept encompasses improvements in products, processes, organizational changes, or marketing strategies that reduce the consumption of natural resources and minimize the release of harmful substances into the environment (Eco-Innovation Observatory, 2012; García-Granero et al., 2018; Marcon et al., 2017). The Integrated National Energy and Climate Plan for Germany lists innovation as one of the five drivers to achieve greenhouse gas emission targets while mitigating the trade-off between competitiveness and sustainability (Rennings, 2000).

As eco-innovation and climate governance evolve, understanding these concepts and their theory becomes increasingly critical for stakeholders in planning effective corporate strategies at the micro-level. This study offers a comprehensive review of the existing literature on climate governance and eco-innovation (Sect. 2), accompanied by a theoretical framework that sheds light on their relationship (Sect. 3). This paper also introduces the global landscape of climate governance and eco-innovation, limitations, and suggestions for future research (Sect. 4).

Box 1
Eco-innovation encompasses improvements in products, processes, organizational changes, or marketing strategies that reduce the consumption of natural resources and minimize the release of harmful substances into the environment.

2 The Concept of Climate Governance and Corporate Eco-innovation

2.1 Climate Governance

Climate governance refers to the deliberate mechanisms and strategies designed to guide social systems, including organizations, to address and manage the risks associated with climate change (Jagers & Stripple, 2003). It is a multifaced and evolving field requiring collaboration from governments, society, and the private sector (Betsill & Bulkeley, 2006). The Paris Agreement (UNFCCC, 2015) represents a significant milestone in global climate governance, adopted by 196 Parties and officially effective on 4 November 2016, aiming to hold "*the increase in the global average temperature to well below 2°C above pre-industrial levels*" and "*to limit the temperature increase to 1.5°C above pre-industrial levels*". However, the agreement faces numerous challenges in understanding and implementation (Mitchell et al., 2018).

Okereke et al. (2009) argue that the concept of climate governance should be extended beyond the boundaries of the international regime due to the increasing influence of non-nation-state actors in shaping climate politics. However, Jänicke (2015) reveal the potential benefits of multi-level governance. Environmental concerns are no longer within the national government planning; instead, they are formed by decisions made at global and subnational levels. International regimes and global non-governmental organizations pressure national governments to address global environmental challenges like climate change. This aspect is of interest to scholars focused on *multi-level environmental governance*. Leveraging its conceptual and theoretical flexibility, multi-level governance offers a valuable foundation for constructing a theoretical framework exploring the power of climate governance.

Box 2
Climate governance refers to the deliberate mechanisms and strategies designed to guide social systems, including organizations, in their efforts to address and manage the risks associated with climate change.

Within a country, there is also a debate that climate governance should be tackled by local or national actions (Heinen et al., 2022). Five dimensions capture the multi-level of climate governance, including the *governance issue*, *the types of decision-makers contributing to resolving the issues*, *the types of interactions among decision-makers* such as coordination, competition, and conflict resolution, *the rules-in-use through legislative, legal rules or self-regulation*, and *the formal degree of dependency among decision-makers*. Boasson et al. (2023) indicate that public support is the best model to capture the participation complexity of domestic climate governance. According to Tan et al. (2022), over 130 countries and regions have set the target of net-zero and carbon-neutral emissions, in which 119 countries have submitted their nationally determined contributions. The UK is one of the role models in climate governance internationally with the introduction of the Climate Change Act (CCA) in 2008 and the Climate Change Committee (CCC), which is highly innovative (Fankhauser et al., 2018) and demonstrates the substantial impacts on political parties, government, business, and civil society (Averchenkova et al., 2021).

Box 3
There are five dimensions that capture the multi-level of climate governance including:

- the governance issue
- the types of decision-makers contributing to resolving the issues
- the types of interactions among decision-makers such as coordination, competition and conflict resolution
- the rules-in-use through legislative legal rules or self-regulation
- the formal degree of dependency among decision-makers

From the private sector, firms have a responsibility for climate governance as a part of their corporate governance strategy. The increasing attention to the ESG (Environmental, Social, and Governance) aspects from the stakeholders demonstrates a need to provide sufficient planning for climate governance. The pressure is on firms to report their carbon emissions and social impacts (Bui & De Villiers, 2017; Arena et al. 2018a, b). The literature on non-financial reports is extensive (see, e.g., Stolowy & Paugam, 2018), especially for sustainability reporting (Al-Shaer & Zaman, 2018; Bebbington & Larrinaga, 2014; Unerman et al., 2010), which is affected by climate governance. Bozzolan et al. (2015) indicate that sustainability reporting could signal the quality of corporate governance and response to the demands of different stakeholders (Michelon & Parbonetti, 2012).

The concept of climate governance within a firm could be extended by including environmental committees as a part of the board structure. Peters and Romi (2014) and Liao et al. (2015) reveal the positive impacts of having environmental committees on sustainability disclosure. The practical implications of these committees are examining whether carbon emissions and performance are monitored by the boards (Prado-Lorenzo & Garcia-Sanchez, 2010) or whether directors receive any incentives to monitor carbon emissions or be responsible for climate change issues (Ioannou et al., 2016).

Box 4

There are several aspects of climate governance at a firm level:

- the issuance and quality of sustainability reporting,
- the presence of environmental committees as a part of the board structure
- the incentive packages for directors to be responsible for climate change issues

The integration of climate change issues into corporate governance results in positive impacts on carbon disclosure and provides a strong signal to the markets (Qian & Schaltegger, 2017). With strong climate governance, firms could avoid the possibility of personal acclaim for positive carbon performance (Alrazi et al., 2016) or accountability for poor performance (De Villiers & Van Staden, 2006), which facilitates truthful disclosure for stakeholders. Also, strong climate governance could reduce greenwashing (Ntim & Soobaroyen, 2013), which narrows the gaps between carbon disclosure and carbon performance (Bui et al., 2020). Elsayih et al.

(2023) also confirm that efficient internal governance leads to a quality carbon management system.

Box 5
Existing empirical literature has provided evidences that the integration of climate change issues into corporate governance (i.e., climate governance) has positive impacts on:

- carbon disclosure/performance,
- market valuation,
- performance,
- quality carbon management system,
- and others.

2.2 *Corporate Eco-innovation*

There is a close relationship between national climate governance and eco-innovation. Extant literature shows a strong effect of Government Environmental Attention (GEA), which refers to the decision-making behaviour of the government on environmental issues, on green innovation (Fu et al., 2022; Xu et al., 2022a, b) and the efficiency of green innovation (Xu et al., 2022a, b). The improvement of GEA could affect firms' governance of carbon emissions through regulations, fiscal policies, and energy structure strategies.

Corporate eco-innovation is defined as any improvement in products, processes, organisational change, or marketing strategy, the four eco-innovation dimensions, that reduces the use of natural resources and the exposure of harmful substances to the environment (EIO (Eco-Innovation Observatory), 2012[1]; Marcon et al., 2017; García-Granero et al., 2018); or the innovative operation and production process that reduce environmental risk, pollution and negative impacts of resource use (Horbach et al., 2012; Kemp & Pearson, 2007).

Chen (2008) indicates that the product dimension expresses the use of environmentally friendly materials, packaging, labeling, and product recovery and recycling, while the process dimension refers to the innovation process that helps to save resources and reduce pollution. In addition, Marcon et al. (2017) show the organisational dimension is the development of business models, routines, and actions to reduce the negative impacts on the environment, and the marketing dimension is how firms incorporate environmental aspects into marketing activities such as promotion, price strategies, and product communication.

The revolution of eco-innovation in the last decades indicates the increasing demand for climate change fighting and more sustainable development. The

[1] EIO (Eco-Innovation Observatory) (2012).

literature on eco-innovation started with industrial sectors such as the chemical industry (Alkaya & Demirer, 2015; Van Hemel & Cramer, 2002), building, furniture manufacturing, medical equipment, metal processing, and plastic processing industry (Crabbé et al., 2013) and plastic and resin sector (Theyel, 2000). Recently, adopting eco-innovation has become popular in the agri-food sector in the sustainability transition (Barth et al., 2017; García-Granero et al., 2018). The increasing social requirement for more healthy and sustainable food, the environmental concerns, and the convenience and economic incentives lead to such a trend (Lioutas & Charatsari, 2018). Moreover, legislation and socioeconomic values are among the drivers of eco-innovation in this sector (Guerrero Lara et al., 2019).

One of the explanations for the evolution of eco-innovation is the general innovation theory, including the technology push and market pull (De Marchi, 2012; Rehfeld et al., 2007), which is expressed in the regulatory and institutional frameworks (De Marchi, 2012; Horbach, 2008; Porter & Linde, 1995). The government is crucial in promoting firms' eco-innovation, a "win-win" policy to reduce negative environmental impacts and increase firms' competitiveness (Porter hypothesis). The demand and supply sides are also the drivers of eco-innovation through their expectations and demands (Horbach, 2008). As far as quality is concerned, consumers and suppliers are looking for more environmentally friendly manufacturing methods (Carpentier & Ervin, 2002; Galdeano-Gómez et al., 2013). Corporate culture is also another driver of eco-innovation (Rkein & Andrew, 2012).

Box 6
Some key drivers of eco-innovation:

- legislation and socioeconomic values
- technology push and market pull
- the governments
- the demand and supply sides
- corporate culture
- and others.

3 Theoretical Framework Behind the Relationship Between Eco-innovation and Climate Governance

3.1 Resource-Based Theory (RBT)

To explain the correlation between climate governance and eco-innovation, the first theory that could be applied is Resource-Based Theory (RBT). The RBT was originally introduced by Penrose in 2009, presenting a model for effectively managing a firm's resources. Accordingly, firms coordinate a bundle of resources to achieve their objectives and strategic behaviour. RBT offers a framework for identifying and predicting the core elements of organizational performance and competitive advantage. This approach contrasts with externally driven methods for understanding the success or failure of organisational activities (Kozlenkova et al., 2014). RBT explores the notion of firm resources that are difficult to replicate and could serve as the foundation for sustained competitive advantage (Barney, 1991).

RBT is developed based on two fundamental assumptions regarding how firm-specific resources contribute to competitive development and why certain firms outperform others (Helfat & Peteraf, 2003). While the sets of resources held by different firms are distinct from one another, the assumption of resource immobility prevents firms from trading resources due to its nature of complexity. Resources could be categorised as either internal or external. Internal resources include elements such as research and development capabilities, logistics, brand management, and cost-efficient processes (Kozlenkova et al., 2014), while external resources include factors like the influence of suppliers (Lewis et al., 2010), customer demand, and technological advancements (Li & Calantone, 1998).

Box 7

The RBT presents a model for effectively managing a firm's resources. Accordingly, firms coordinate a bundle of resources to achieve their objectives and strategic behaviour. Resources could be categorised as either internal or external.

- *Internal resources: research and development capabilities, logistics, brand management, and cost-efficient processes*
- *External resources: the influence of suppliers, customer demand, and technological advancements*

According to RBT, with sufficient resources, firms equipped with robust climate change governance and eco-innovation strategies have the capacity to proactively identify and adapt to the evolving demands of climate change, placing them at an advantage over their competitors. Albitar et al. (2023) indicate that eco-innovation and climate governance represent the outcomes of firms' commitment to developing their green competence with all aspects of their business. They serve as inputs that translate corporate climate engagement into obtainable initiatives. Companies employing climate governance and eco-innovation strategies are better positioned to leverage their existing resources and expertise to make meaningful contributions to combat climate change ahead of their peers. Conversely, companies lacking a well-established governance framework and a history of eco-innovation may struggle to address the mounting pressure related to climate change and may be limited to responses.

RBT approach could be used to explain the engagement of large and more profitable firms in eco-innovation due to the significant investment requirements (Qiu et al., 2016), which require both internal and external resources (Marzucchi &

Montresor, 2017). It is confirmed by Gallo and Christensen (2011) and Schreck and Raithel (2018) that larger firms are more likely to issue sustainability reports.

Box 8
According to RBT, with sufficient resources, firms equipped with robust climate change governance and eco-innovation strategies have the capacity to proactively identify and adapt to the evolving demands of climate change, placing them at an advantage over their competitors.

- Companies employing climate governance and eco-innovation strategies are better positioned to leverage their existing resources and expertise to make meaningful contributions to combat climate change ahead of their peers.
- Companies lacking a well-established governance framework and a history of eco-innovation may struggle to address the mounting pressure related to climate change and may be limited to responses

3.2 Institutional Theory

Institutional theory is among the most popular explanation of the relationship between eco-innovation and climate governance. DiMaggio and Powell (1983) indicate that organisations implement business practices to enhance their legitimacy. As a part of the economy, firms need to follow the social contract between businesses and society and follow social expectations to be accepted and survive. Sheng et al. (2011) reveal that better social legitimacy leads to a stronger brand. In addition, firms must conform to regulations and rules to maintain their legitimacy, survival, and resource access (Lin & Sheu, 2012). This is also necessary to gain the support of their stakeholders (Govindan et al., 2014). The theory could be used to explain how technology improvement and legislation influence sustainable activities and environmental management (Tate et al., 2010). With the evolution of climate governance at different levels, firms need to invest in their green innovation to meet society's expectations. Therefore, the institutional theory gained prominence support in the eco-innovation literature (e.g., Shu et al., 2016). Institutional pressure is also discussed in the literature, where firms must engage in climate governance to meet the social norms and governmental regulations, which are the two crucial aspects of environmental management (Brammer et al., 2012; Colwell & Joshi, 2013).

Box 9
With the evolution of climate governance at different levels, firms need to invest in their green innovation to meet the expectations of society. Therefore, the institutional theory gained prominence support in the eco-innovation literature. Institutional pressure is also discussed in the literature where firms must engage in climate governance to meet the social norms and governmental regulations, which are the two crucial aspects of environmental management.

Adomako and Nguyen (2023) examine the impacts of climate management on the relationship between eco-innovation and social legitimacy and confirm that climate governance stimulates the relationship. In countries with high levels of green management, firms must address environmental issues to meet regulators' expectations. For example, ESG disclosure has become compulsory in many developed countries such as the UK, the US, Hong Kong, and Singapore. To meet the new requirements, firms must develop a climate governance strategy to be listed as green companies. Many institutional investors explicitly advertise their interest in green investments or positive ESG investments. Therefore, firms need to develop a strategy to become greener, and one of the solutions is investing in green innovation. Institutional theory clearly explains the relationship between eco-innovation and climate governance at different levels. Under such pressure, firms must follow governmental policies, customer concerns, and public interest in climate governance and eco-innovation (Mont & Plepys, 2008). The knowledge gained from this process is beneficial for firms to improve their social legitimacy and invest in green innovation.

3.3 *Other Related Theories*

As previously discussed, one of the explanations for climate governance and eco-innovation is meeting stakeholders' expectations. Therefore, stakeholder theory is also relevant in this context. Stakeholder theory was developed by Freeman in the 1970s, stating that firms need to maintain their relationship with traditional groups such as employees, customers, and suppliers and non-traditional groups such as the government and other interested parties to achieve their objectives. The previous section emphasizes the role of external stakeholders, including government regulators, shareholders, and customers in stimulating climate governance and eco-innovation. Besides, internal stakeholders such as employees and managers and non-governmental organisations such as NGOs also play an essential part in supporting the relationship (Oxborrow & Brindley, 2013; Tang & Tang, 2012). Sarkis et al. (2010) indicate that stakeholders put pressure on the firms to reduce adverse impacts on the environment.

Box 10
Stakeholder theory implies that firms need to maintain their relationship with different stakeholders, who put pressure on the firms to reduce adverse impacts on the environment.

The theory of planned behaviour (Ajzen, 1985) is also relevant in this context. The intention and behaviour to develop corporate governance and eco-innovation are originated from the attitude, subjective norm, and perceived behavioural control. This intention-led eco-innovation development is found in the petrochemical industry (Freire, 2018) and several polluting industries (Long et al., 2021). Given the cost involved in the process, the intention of the management team is critical to start with the initiatives. Studies confirm the firm-level determinants, including board gender diversity (Garcia-Sanchez et al., 2021; Nadeem et al., 2020); managerial environmental awareness (Peng & Liu, 2016); CEO hubris (Arena et al., 2018a, b); organisational internal capabilities (Salim et al., 2019); firms' sustainability strategy (Tsai & Liao, 2017), and corporate social responsibility practices (Pan et al., 2021).

Box 11
The theory of planned behaviour implies that the intention and behaviour to develop corporate governance and eco-innovation are originated from the attitude, subjective norm and perceived behavioural control.

The innovation theory is relevant to the development of green innovation due to the technology push and market pull (De Marchi, 2012). More particularly, the evolution of net-zero objectives requires firms to advance their manufacturing processes to be more sustainable while customers look forward to greener products. Horbach (2008) even enlarged the concept of innovation theory to environmental innovation theory to accommodate the demand side, supply side, and institutional and political factors in stimulating eco-innovation. This approach was developed by Horbach et al. (2012) and Triguero et al. (2013) to evaluate the drivers of green innovation.

Box 12
The innovation theory implies that the evolution of net-zero objectives requires firms to advance their manufacturing processes to be more sustainable while customers look forward to greener products.

Ecological moderation theory also emphasizes the demand for industrial development and technology breakthroughs so that eco-innovation becomes a norm (York & Rosa, 2003). Accordingly, collaborations between firms are needed to boost green development by reducing the consumption of resources and energy, which in turn requires a thorough climate governance strategy and investment in eco-innovation.

Box 13
Ecological moderation theory emphasizes the demand for industrial development and technology breakthroughs so that eco-innovation becomes a norm.

4 Limitations and Suggestions for Future Research

Although climate governance and eco-innovation are the key contributors to achieving net zero and carbon emissions neutrality, there are limited studies examining the causal effects of this relationship at different levels of governance. Success case studies could be beneficial to firms and countries in the process of developing sufficient governance strategies and investing in green innovation. From the theoretical perspective, although numerous theories are used to explain the determinants of eco-innovation, limited theory explains the relation of the two concepts.

Declaration of Generative AI and AI-Assisted Technologies in the Writing Process for This Chapter The editor only used Grammarly to proof-read and check for typos and inconsistencies. There is no further declaration from the authors.

References

Adomako, S., & Nguyen, N. P. (2023). Eco-innovation in the extractive industry: Combinative effects of social legitimacy, green management, and institutional pressures. *Resources Policy, 80*, 103184.

Ajzen, I. (1985). From intentions to actions: A theory of planned behavior. In *Action control: From Cognition to Behavior* (pp. 11–39). Berlin, Springer.

Albitar, K., Al-Shaer, H., & Liu, Y. S. (2023). Corporate commitment to climate change: The effect of eco-innovation and climate governance. *Research Policy, 52*(2), 104697.

Alkaya, E., & Demirer, G. N. (2015). Water recycling and reuse in soft drink/beverage industry: A case study for sustainable industrial water management in Turkey. *Resources, Conservation and Recycling, 104*, 172–180.

Alrazi, B., De Villiers, C., & Van Staden, C. J. (2016). The environmental disclosures of the electricity generation industry: a global perspective. *Accounting and Business Research, 46*(6), 665–701.

Al-Shaer, H., & Zaman, M. (2018). Credibility of sustainability reports: The contribution of audit committees. *Business Strategy and the Environment, 27*(7), 973–986.

Arena, C., Michelon, G., & Trojanowski, G. (2018a). Big egos can be green: A study of CEO hubris and environmental innovation. *British Journal of Management, 29*(2), 316–336.

Arena, M., Azzone, G., & Mapelli, F. (2018b). What drives the evolution of Corporate Social Responsibility strategies? An institutional logics perspective. *Journal of Cleaner Production, 171*, 345–355.

Averchenkova, A., Fankhauser, S., & Finnegan, J. J. (2021). The impact of strategic climate legislation: evidence from expert interviews on the UK Climate Change Act. *Climate Policy, 21*(2), 251–263.

Barney, J. (1991). Firm resources and sustained competitive advantage. *Journal of Management, 17*(1), 99–120.

Barth, M. E., Cahan, S. F., Chen, L., & Venter, E. R. (2017). The economic consequences associated with integrated report quality: Capital market and real effects. *Accounting, Organizations and Society, 62*, 43–64.

Bebbington, J., & Larrinaga, C. (2014). Accounting and sustainable development: An exploration. *Accounting, Organizations and Society, 39*(6), 395–413.

Betsill, M. M., & Bulkeley, H. (2006). Cities and the multilevel governance of global climate change. *Global Governance, 12*, 141.

Boasson, E. L., Burns, C., & Pulver, S. (2023). The politics of domestic climate governance: making sense of complex participation patterns. *Journal of European Public Policy, 30*(3), 513–536.

Bozzolan, S., Fabrizi, M., Mallin, C. A., & Michelon, G. (2015). Corporate social responsibility and earnings quality: International evidence. *The International Journal of Accounting, 50*(4), 361–396.

Brammer, S., Jackson, G., & Matten, D. (2012). Corporate social responsibility and institutional theory: New perspectives on private governance. *Socio-Economic Review, 10*(1), 3–28.

Bui, B., & De Villiers, C. (2017). Business strategies and management accounting in response to climate change risk exposure and regulatory uncertainty. *The British Accounting Review, 49*(1), 4–24.

Bui, B., Houqe, M. N., & Zaman, M. (2020). Climate governance effects on carbon disclosure and performance. *The British Accounting Review, 52*(2), 100880.

Carpentier, C. L., & Ervin, D. (2002). In F. Brouwer & D. Ervin (Eds.), *The United States in public concerns, environmental standards and agricultural trade*. CABI Publishing.

Chen, Y. S. (2008). The driver of green innovation and green image–green core competence. *Journal of Business Ethics, 81*, 531–543.

Colwell, S. R., & Joshi, A. W. (2013). Corporate ecological responsiveness: Antecedent effects of institutional pressure and top management commitment and their impact on organizational performance. *Business Strategy and the Environment, 22*(2), 73–91.

Crabbé, A., Jacobs, R., Van Hoof, V., Bergmans, A., & Van Acker, K. (2013). Transition towards sustainable material innovation: evidence and evaluation of the Flemish case. *Journal of Cleaner Production, 56*, 63–72.

De Marchi, V. (2012). Environmental innovation and R&D cooperation: Empirical evidence from Spanish manufacturing firms. *Research Policy, 41*(3), 614–623.

De Villiers, C., & Van Staden, C. J. (2006). Can less environmental disclosure have a legitimising effect? Evidence from Africa. *Accounting, Organizations and Society, 31*(8), 763–781.

DiMaggio, P. J., & Powell, W. W. (1983). The iron cage revisited: Institutional isomorphism and collective rationality in organizational fields. *American Sociological Review*, 147–160.

EIO (Eco-Innovation Observatory). (2012). *Methodological Report. Eco-Innovation Observatory. Funded by the European Commission*. DG, Environment.

Elsayih, J., Datt, R., Tang, Q., Hamid, A., & Varua, M. E. (2023). Exploring the determinants of carbon management system quality: The role of corporate governance and climate risks and opportunities. *Accounting & Finance, 63*(4), 4065–4091.

Freire, P. A. (2018). Enhancing innovation through behavioral stimulation: The use of behavioral determinants of innovation in the implementation of eco-innovation processes in industrial sectors and companies. *Journal of Cleaner Production, 170*, 1677–1687.
Fu, Q., Abdul Rahman, A. A., Jiang, H., Abbas, J., & Comite, U. (2022). Sustainable supply chain and business performance: The impact of strategy, network design, information systems, and organizational structure. *Sustainability, 14*(3), 1080.
Galdeano-Gómez, E., Aznar-Sánchez, J. A., & Pérez-Mesa, J. C. (2013). Sustainability dimensions related to agricultural-based development: the experience of 50 years of intensive farming in Almería (Spain). *International Journal of Agricultural Sustainability, 11*(2), 125–143.
Gallo, P. J., & Christensen, L. J. (2011). Firm size matters: An empirical investigation of organizational size and ownership on sustainability-related behaviors. *Business & Society, 50*(2), 315–349.
García-Granero, E. M., Piedra-Muñoz, L., & Galdeano-Gómez, E. (2018). Eco-innovation measurement: A review of firm performance indicators. *Journal of Cleaner Production, 191*, 304–317.
Garcia-Sanchez, I. M., Raimo, N., & Vitolla, F. (2021). CEO power and integrated reporting. *Meditari Accountancy Research, 29*(4), 908–942.
Govindan, K., Kannan, D., & Shankar, K. M. (2014). Evaluating the drivers of corporate social responsibility in the mining industry with multi-criteria approach: A multi-stakeholder perspective. *Journal of Cleaner Production, 84*, 214–232.
Guerrero Lara, L., Pereira, L. M., Ravera, F., & Jiménez-Aceituno, A. (2019). Flipping the Tortilla: Social-ecological innovations and traditional ecological knowledge for more sustainable agri-food systems in Spain. *Sustainability, 11*(5), 1222.
Heinen, D., Arlati, A., & Knieling, J. (2022). Five dimensions of climate governance: a framework for empirical research based on polycentric and multi-level governance perspectives. *Environmental Policy and Governance, 32*(1), 56–68.
Helfat, C. E., & Peteraf, M. A. (2003). The dynamic resource-based view: Capability lifecycles. *Strategic Management Journal, 24*(10), 997–1010.
Horbach, J. (2008). Determinants of environmental innovation—New evidence from German panel data sources. *Research Policy, 37*(1), 163–173.
Horbach, J., Rammer, C., & Rennings, K. (2012). Determinants of eco-innovations by type of environmental impact—The role of regulatory push/pull, technology push and market pull. *Ecological Economics, 78*, 112–122.
Ioannou, I., Li, S. X., & Serafeim, G. (2016). The effect of target difficulty on target completion: The case of reducing carbon emissions. *The Accounting Review, 91*(5), 1467–1492.
Jagers, S. C., & Stripple, J. (2003). Climate govenance beyond the state. *Global Governance, 9*, 385.
Jänicke, M. (2015). Horizontal and vertical reinforcement in global climate governance. *Energies, 8*(6), 5782–5799.
Kemp, R., & Pearson, P. (2007). Final report MEI project about measuring eco-innovation. *UM Merit, Maastricht, 10*(2), 1–120.
Kozlenkova, I. V., Samaha, S. A., & Palmatier, R. W. (2014). Resource-based theory in marketing. *Journal of the Academy of Marketing Science, 42*, 1–21.
Lewis, M., Brandon-Jones, A., Slack, N., & Howard, M. (2010). Competing through operations and supply: The role of classic and extended resource-based advantage. *International Journal of Operations & Production Management, 30*(10), 1032–1058.
Li, T., & Calantone, R. J. (1998). The impact of market knowledge competence on new product advantage: conceptualization and empirical examination. *Journal of Marketing, 62*(4), 13–29.
Liao, L., Luo, L., & Tang, Q. (2015). Gender diversity, board independence, environmental committee and greenhouse gas disclosure. *The British Accounting Review, 47*(4), 409–424.
Lin, R. J., & Sheu, C. (2012). Why do firms adopt/implement green practices?–an institutional theory perspective. *Procedia-Social and Behavioral Sciences, 57*, 533–540.
Lioutas, E. D., & Charatsari, C. (2018). Green innovativeness in farm enterprises: what makes farmers think green? *Sustainable Development, 26*(4), 337–349.

Long, Z., Huang, Y., Zhang, W., Shi, Z., Yu, D., Chen, Y., et al. (2021). Effect of different industrial activities on soil heavy metal pollution, ecological risk, and health risk. *Environmental Monitoring and Assessment, 193*, 1–12.

Marcon, A., de Medeiros, J. F., & Ribeiro, J. L. D. (2017). Innovation and environmentally sustainable economy: Identifying the best practices developed by multinationals in Brazil. *Journal of Cleaner Production, 160*, 83–97.

Marzucchi, A., & Montresor, S. (2017). Forms of knowledge and eco-innovation modes: Evidence from Spanish manufacturing firms. *Ecological Economics, 131*, 208–221.

Michelon, G., & Parbonetti, A. (2012). The effect of corporate governance on sustainability disclosure. *Journal of Management & Governance, 16*, 477–509.

Mitchell, D., Heaviside, C., Schaller, N., Allen, M., Ebi, K. L., Fischer, E. M., et al. (2018). Extreme heat-related mortality avoided under Paris Agreement goals. *Nature Climate Change, 8*(7), 551–553.

Mont, O., & Plepys, A. (2008). Sustainable consumption progress: should we be proud or alarmed? *Journal of Cleaner Production, 16*(4), 531–537.

Nadeem, M., Bahadar, S., Gull, A. A., & Iqbal, U. (2020). Are women eco-friendly? Board gender diversity and environmental innovation. *Business Strategy and the Environment, 29*(8), 3146–3161.

Ntim, C. G., & Soobaroyen, T. (2013). Corporate governance and performance in socially responsible corporations: New empirical insights from a Neo-Institutional framework. *Corporate Governance: An International Review, 21*(5), 468–494.

Okereke, C., Bulkeley, H., & Schroeder, H. (2009). Conceptualizing climate governance beyond the international regime. *Global Environmental Politics, 9*(1), 58–78.

Oxborrow, L., & Brindley, C. (2013). Adoption of "eco-advantage" by SMEs: emerging opportunities and constraints. *European Journal of Innovation Management, 16*(3), 355–375.

Pan, X., Sinha, P., & Chen, X. (2021). Corporate social responsibility and eco-innovation: The triple bottom line perspective. *Corporate Social Responsibility and Environmental Management, 28*(1), 214–228.

Peng, X., & Liu, Y. (2016). Behind eco-innovation: Managerial environmental awareness and external resource acquisition. *Journal of Cleaner Production, 139*, 347–360.

Peters, G. F., & Romi, A. M. (2014). Does the voluntary adoption of corporate governance mechanisms improve environmental risk disclosures? Evidence from greenhouse gas emission accounting. *Journal of Business Ethics, 125*, 637–666.

Porter, M. E., & Linde, C. V. D. (1995). Toward a new conception of the environment-competitiveness relationship. *Journal of Economic Perspectives, 9*(4), 97–118.

Prado-Lorenzo, J. M., & Garcia-Sanchez, I. M. (2010). The role of the board of directors in disseminating relevant information on greenhouse gases. *Journal of Business Ethics, 97*, 391–424.

Qian, W., & Schaltegger, S. (2017). Revisiting carbon disclosure and performance: Legitimacy and management views. *The British Accounting Review, 49*(4), 365–379.

Qiu, Y., Shaukat, A., & Tharyan, R. (2016). Environmental and social disclosures: Link with corporate financial performance. *The British Accounting Review, 48*(1), 102–116.

Rehfeld, K. M., Rennings, K., & Ziegler, A. (2007). Integrated product policy and environmental product innovations: An empirical analysis. *Ecological Economics, 61*(1), 91–100.

Rennings, K. (2000). Redefining innovation—eco-innovation research and the contribution from ecological economics. *Ecological Economics, 32*(2), 319–332.

Rkein, A., & Andrew, B. (2012). Public sector commercial orientation and the social contract: A study of performance management in a non-competitive environment. *Pacific Accounting Review, 24*(3), 292–313.

Salim, N., Ab Rahman, M. N., & Abd Wahab, D. (2019). A systematic literature review of internal capabilities for enhancing eco-innovation performance of manufacturing firms. *Journal of Cleaner Production, 209*, 1445–1460.

Sarkis, J., Gonzalez-Torre, P., & Adenso-Diaz, B. (2010). Stakeholder pressure and the adoption of environmental practices: The mediating effect of training. *Journal of Operations Management, 28*(2), 163–176.
Schreck, P., & Raithel, S. (2018). Corporate social performance, firm size, and organizational visibility: Distinct and joint effects on voluntary sustainability reporting. *Business & Society, 57*(4), 742–778.
Sheng, S., Zhou, K. Z., & Li, J. J. (2011). The effects of business and political ties on firm performance: Evidence from China. *Journal of Marketing, 75*(1), 1–15.
Shu, C., Zhou, K. Z., Xiao, Y., & Gao, S. (2016). How green management influences product innovation in China: The role of institutional benefits. *Journal of Business Ethics, 133*, 471–485.
Stolowy, H., & Paugam, L. (2018). The expansion of non-financial reporting: an exploratory study. *Accounting and Business Research, 48*(5), 525–548.
Tan, X. C., Wang, Y., Gu, B. H., Kong, L. S., & Zeng, A. (2022). Research on the national climate governance system toward carbon neutrality—A critical literature review. *Fundamental Research, 2*(3), 384–391.
Tang, Z., & Tang, J. (2012). Stakeholder–firm power difference, stakeholders' CSR orientation, and SMEs' environmental performance in China. *Journal of Business Venturing, 27*(4), 436–455.
Tate, W. L., Ellram, L. M., & Kirchoff, J. F. (2010). Corporate social responsibility reports: a thematic analysis related to supply chain management. *Journal of Supply Chain Management, 46*(1), 19–44.
Theyel, G. (2000). Management practices for environmental innovation and performance. *International Journal of Operations & Production Management, 20*(2), 249–266.
Triguero, A., Moreno-Mondéjar, L., & Davia, M. A. (2013). Drivers of different types of eco-innovation in European SMEs. *Ecological Economics, 92*, 25–33.
Tsai, K. H., & Liao, Y. C. (2017). Sustainability strategy and eco-innovation: A moderation model. *Business Strategy and the Environment, 26*(4), 426–437.
Unerman, J., Bebbington, J., & O'Dwyer, B. (2010). Introduction to sustainability accounting and accountability. In *Sustainability Accounting and Accountability* (pp. 20–35). Routledge.
United Nations Framework Convention on Climate Change (UNFCCC). (2015). Historic Paris Agreement on Climate Change: 195 Nations Set Path to Keep Temperature Rise Well Below 2 Degrees Celsius.
Van Hemel, C., & Cramer, J. (2002). Barriers and stimuli for ecodesign in SMEs. *Journal of Cleaner Production, 10*(5), 439–453.
Xu, T., Kang, C., & Zhang, H. (2022a). China's efforts towards carbon neutrality: Does energy-saving and emission-reduction policy mitigate carbon emissions? *Journal of Environmental Management, 316*, 115286.
Xu, Y., Liu, S., & Wang, J. (2022b). Impact of environmental regulation intensity on green innovation efficiency in the Yellow River Basin, China. *Journal of Cleaner Production, 373*, 133789.
York, R., & Rosa, E. A. (2003). Key challenges to ecological modernization theory: Institutional efficacy, case study evidence, units of analysis, and the pace of eco-efficiency. *Organization & Environment, 16*(3), 273–288.

Dr. Kim Nguyen is a Senior Lecturer in Accountancy and Finance at Lincoln International Business School (LIBS), University of Lincoln. Her research interests lie in the area of behavioural economics and finance, where she is dedicated to exploring three compelling themes: heuristics, sustainability, and innovation.

Power Dynamics in Climate Governance and Eco-innovation

Monika Malik and Shelley Oberoi

Abstract This Chapter overviews the importance of eco-innovation and the involvement of business actors in climate governance. The study highlights significant disparities in the Power and influence of various business organisations within climate governance structures, operating at the levels of nation-states, supranational entities, and individual actors. These disparities are categorised into two key concepts of Power: Structural Power and Discourse Power. Structural Power pertains to the capacity of business entities to shape agendas and establish regulations within the global climate governance framework, thereby showcasing their influential capabilities. Discourse Power explores how individual consumers exert influence by shaping their perceptions of climate change and influencing the decision-making processes of business actors. Business entities can use different forms of Power to influence climate-related matters.

1 Introduction

Many uncertainties exist in the societal problem of climate change, a pervasive global external factor. Addressing this issue requires international collaboration due to a lack of a governing body with authority beyond individual nation-states. A global framework for climate governance has been established, commencing with the United Nations Framework Convention on Climate Change (UNFCCC) and reaching its pinnacle with the Paris Agreement. This system involves

M. Malik
Department of Applied Sciences and Humanities, Galgotias College of Engineering and Technology, Greater Noida, Uttar Pradesh, India
e-mail: m.malik@galgotiacollege.edu

S. Oberoi (✉)
Department of Humanities and Applied Sciences, K.C. College of Engineering and Management Studies and Research, Thane, Maharashtra, India
e-mail: shelly.oberoi@kccemsr.edu.in

V. Q. Trinh (ed.), *Climate Governance and Corporate Eco-innovation*, Sustainable Finance, https://doi.org/10.1007/978-3-031-56423-9_4

intergovernmental negotiations involving sovereign states as central actors. Nevertheless, the constraints of a governance structure centred around the state have become increasingly apparent. The worldwide governance of climate has transitioned into a new phase, with the central objective being the effective implementation of the Paris Agreement (Jiang & Li, 2020).

The UNFCCC was established in 1992 during the Earth Summit (United Nations Framework on Climate Change). Its primary objective is to facilitate the implementation of a climate governance mechanism through intergovernmental negotiations, specifically involving sovereign states. Parties were categorised based on their respective responsibilities and capacities, clearly delineating their duties in addressing climate change. In 1997, the UNFCCC adopted the Kyoto Protocol (KP), which implemented mandatory targets for reducing greenhouse gas emissions during the initial commitment period, spanning from 2008 to 2012 (Kyoto Protocol; Jiang & Li, 2020). Developed nations bear a moral responsibility to provide financial, technical, and capacity-building support to developing nations while developing nations are not compelled to undertake legally binding emissions reduction obligations (Developed countries debate, 2022).

Box 1

A global framework for climate governance has been established, commencing with the United Nations Framework Convention on Climate Change (UNFCCC) and reaching its pinnacle with the Paris Agreement. This system involves intergovernmental negotiations involving sovereign states as central actors. Nevertheless, the constraints of a governance structure centred around the state have become increasingly apparent.

Nonetheless, the distinction between developed and developing nations has become increasingly ambiguous due to the growing impact of growing economies and their concurrent rise in greenhouse gas (GHG) emissions levels. A loose coalition, referred to as the Umbrella Group, formed, consisting of multiple developed nations outside of the European Union, with the United States assuming a leadership role. The primary objective of this coalition was to critically examine the scientific basis of climate change and emphasise the significance of developing nations taking on their fair share of responsibilities in reducing emissions. The small island states and least-developed countries further underscored their need for protection and little ability to adapt while also highlighting the need for exerting pressure to ensure emission reductions in larger developing nations.

Box 2
A loose coalition, referred to as the Umbrella Group, formed, consisting of multiple developed nations outside of the European Union, with the United States assuming a leadership role. The primary objective of this coalition was to critically examine the scientific basis of climate change and emphasise the significance of developing nations taking on their fair share of responsibilities in reducing emissions.

The decision by the United States and Canada to withdraw from the Kyoto Protocol resulted in a stagnation of global climate negotiations. In 2007, there was a breakthrough in implementing the Bali Roadmap, introducing a new negotiation strategy known as the "dual-track" model. This strategy included emerging economies in the "from the top-down" climate regulation mechanism, a significant milestone. However, the rise in carbon emissions from developing economies exacerbated the divide between developed and developing nations, categorising sovereign stakeholders into four distinct groups (Jiang & Li, 2020).

The Copenhagen Conference in 2009 failed to achieve an updated agreement but marked the beginning of a fragmented and decentralised climate policy framework. The Convention framework gave way to a system where countries submit voluntary carbon reduction pledges, replacing previously negotiated binding emission targets and timetables. After 6 years of negotiations, the international community finally reached the Paris Agreement in 2015 (Van Asselt & Zelli, 2013).

The Paris Agreement recognises the climate system's complex nature and individual states' challenges in implementing climate action. Article 6.8 emphasises the need for parties to cooperate and involve public and private entities in executing the Nationally Determined Contributions (NDCs). In a polycentric context, various actors can assume leadership roles (Jordan et al., 2018). Therefore, this study underscores the importance of going beyond the governance protocols outlined by the UNFCCC and focusing on the essential involvement of technological innovation and business entities in implementing the Paris Agreement (Sustainable Development Goals, 2022).

Box 3
In 2007, there was a breakthrough in implementing the Bali Roadmap, introducing a new negotiation strategy known as the "dual-track" model. This strategy included emerging economies in the "from the top-down" climate regulation mechanism, a significant milestone. However, the rise in carbon emissions from developing economies exacerbated the divide between developed and developing nations, categorising sovereign stakeholders into four distinct groups.

2 Technological Innovation Emerged As a Critical Component in the Efforts to Address Climate Change

Climate change is a significant environmental concern closely tied to human progress and carbon dioxide (CO2) released into the atmosphere (Gielen et al., 2019). Current atmospheric CO2 levels exceed those recorded on Earth approximately 800,000 years ago, and this concentration is expected to persistently increase due to our reliance on fossil fuels (Jiang & Li, 2020). The energy sector, including production, transformation, and utilisation, is responsible for approximately 66% of greenhouse gas (GHG) emissions and 90% of carbon dioxide (CO2) emissions (Jiang & Li, 2020). This underscores the central role of the energy sector in addressing environmental challenges.

The successful transition to a low-carbon economy hinges on technological advancements and innovation. The Two-Degree Scenario (2DS) outlined in the Paris Agreement emphasises the need for targeted measures to adopt low-carbon technologies and facilitate cost-efficient transitions. Supporting low-carbon technologies can result in a 30% decrease in primary energy demand and a 70% decrease in carbon emissions by 2050. Key contributors to emissions reduction include electricity efficiency at 38%, renewable energy at 32%, carbon capture and storage at 12%, and nuclear energy at 7% of the overall energy mix (Global Energy Transformation, 2019).

The Intergovernmental Panel on Climate Change (IPCC) has stressed the urgent need for a comprehensive transformation of the global energy system, including increased adoption of renewable energy sources and enhanced energy efficiency. Integrating renewable energy, deep electrification, and energy efficiency strategies offers the potential to achieve over 90% of the required emissions reductions by 2050 to limit global warming to below 2 °C.

Renewable energy is crucial in shifting toward low-carbon energy systems and mitigating climate change (Special report: Global warming). Chevalier and Geoffron (2013) have observed a growing trend in the twenty-first century towards the long-term use of renewable energy as a viable alternative to fossil fuels. Renewable energy is experiencing significant growth and is expected to contribute substantially to around 50% of global energy supply growth. By 2040, renewable energy is projected to become the dominant source of power generation, surpassing all other forms of energy.

Box 4

The Intergovernmental Panel on Climate Change (IPCC) has stressed the urgent need for a comprehensive transformation of the global energy system, including increased adoption of renewable energy sources and enhanced energy efficiency. Renewable energy is crucial in shifting toward low-carbon energy systems and mitigating climate change.

Religious education plays a crucial role in achieving the objectives set by public administration. The submission of 152 Nationally Determined Contributions (NDCs) during the initial round demonstrates a significant commitment to renewable energy. Energy efficiency is widely recognised as a critical factor in transitioning toward a more environmentally conscious, secure, and sustainable future. Improved energy efficiency has the potential to reduce global energy demand and increase the proportion of renewable energy in final energy consumption by approximately 25%.

On a global scale, energy efficiency has become a significant strategy to meet rising energy demands while reducing consumption. Technological innovation offers inherent benefits, including the potential to surpass projected cost reductions through learning curves and economies of scale. Consequently, the integration of technical innovation has become essential in public administration.

Advancements in technology have played a substantial role in enhancing climate governance, with technical feasibility serving as a critical foundation for climate negotiations. Since the 1973 energy crisis, there has been a notable increase in the utilisation of non-fossil fuel energy technologies. This includes significant investments, such as the allocation of US$10 billion for novel energy sources, France's ambitious nuclear power strategies, and Japan's initiatives known as the "Sunshine Plan" and "Moonlight Plan" (Brugger et al., 2021).

Box 5

On a global scale, energy efficiency has become a significant strategy to meet rising energy demands while reducing consumption. Technological innovation offers inherent benefits, including the potential to surpass projected cost reductions through learning curves and economies of scale. Consequently, the integration of technical innovation has become essential in public administration.

This chapter suggests that integrating low-carbon technologies has significantly influenced countries' recognition of their capacity to mitigate climate change, thereby fostering increased support for the UNFCCC (Zhou, 2019). However, many environmentally sustainable technologies initially faced high costs, which hindered their widespread adoption on a global scale. This cost barrier contributed to the limited success of the Kyoto Protocol, as developed nations showed reluctance to assume the substantial financial responsibility associated with implementing environmentally sustainable technologies. Notably, the cost of technological advancements has significantly decreased, with a remarkable 99.5% reduction in the price of solar photovoltaic modules from 1976 to 2016 (Jiang & Li, 2020). With increasing capacity, there is a corresponding 20% decrease in costs. From 2010 to 2017, there was a notable 23% reduction in the worldwide weighted average cost of electricity generated from onshore wind, reaching an estimated value of US$0.06 per kilowatt-hour (kWh) (Ricaurte-Quijano & Carli-Álvarez, 2016a, b). The continuous decrease in technology costs has enhanced the likelihood of countries successfully transitioning to low-carbon systems, providing a solid foundation for the effectiveness of the Paris Agreement. In contemporary times, there has been a noticeable increase in the establishment of global initiatives to address climate change through technological solutions. In summary, the importance of technological innovation in climate governance is expected to increase due to its facilitation of climate-friendly technological advancements and subsequent cost reductions (Fuchs, 2007).

Box 6
Many environmentally sustainable technologies initially faced high costs, which hindered their widespread adoption on a global scale. This cost barrier contributed to the limited success of the Kyoto Protocol, as developed nations showed reluctance to assume the substantial financial responsibility associated with implementing environmentally sustainable technologies.

3 Role of Business Actors in Global Climate Governance

3.1 Instrumentalist Perspective

The instrumentalist perspective on power emphasises the impact of individual deliberate actions and the immediate consequences that one actor has on another. The present analytical approach provides a theoretical framework for assessing the immediate influence of political interests by considering an actor's accessible resources from a pragmatic power standpoint. Business entities can influence political decisions through collective action within a closely interconnected network of political relationships. Specifically, lobbying and political engagement are the primary ways business corporations exercise their instrumental power (Newell & Paterson, 1998).

Box 7
The instrumentalist perspective on power emphasises the impact of individual deliberate actions and the immediate consequences that one actor has on another. Lobbying and political engagement are the primary ways business corporations exercise their instrumental power.

3.1.1 Lobbying

Lobbying plays a crucial role in the exertion of political influence by business entities, and fossil fuel corporations are actively engaged in extensive lobbying efforts at various levels of governance, including national, regional, and global spheres.

This phenomenon has been documented since the 1980s and is widely recognised as a significant factor influencing climate legislation outcomes, particularly in the United States (Newell & Paterson, 1998).

Major corporations and industry alliances often enlist the assistance of lobbying firms, which leverage their networks to cultivate connections with government officials, creating an 'iron triangle' dynamic among these entities. In 2009, approximately 100 business stakeholders sought the assistance of ten lobbying firms with significant affiliations with Capitol Hill. Their goal was to engage in legislative disputes to address global warming by implementing a cap-and-trade system (Newell et al., 2012).

The Global Climate Coalition and the Climate Council are two prominent organisations that serve as representative bodies for business interests in climate change. The Gulf Cooperation Council (GCC), comprising over 50 members, is widely recognised as the primary representative body for business interests in climate change. The success of the GCC can be mainly attributed to its director, John Schlaes, who effectively leveraged his personal connections and prior high-ranking positions in the White House's executive office, along with his influential role in shaping Republican climate policies within Congress (Ricaurte-Quijano & Carli-Álvarez, 2016a, b).

Box 8
Lobbying plays a crucial role in the exertion of political influence by business entities, and fossil fuel corporations are actively engaged in extensive lobbying efforts at various levels of governance, including national, regional, and global spheres.

3.1.2 Political Engagement

Political engagement primarily involves financial support provided by interest groups representing businesses to electoral campaigns or candidates to influence the development of policies aligned with their interests. In the 1995–1996 election cycle, the U.S. oil industry collectively committed $15.5 million in campaign donations, with approximately 80% of these funds going to Republican candidates. The 2008 election campaign saw climate change become a subject of intense debate and controversy. Notably, various business interest groups engaged in significant financial contributions, aiming to encourage candidates to promote policies aligned with their interests (Jiang & Li, 2020).

Box 9
Political engagement primarily involves financial support provided by interest groups representing businesses to electoral campaigns or candidates to influence the development of policies aligned with their interests.

3.2 Structuralist Approaches

The structuralist perspective emphasises the organisation of constituent components, particularly the intrinsic and internal linkages among structural positions contributing to the formation of individuals as societal entities. This concept represents an inherent relationship, where the presence of structural position A depends on its connection with position B. To assess power distribution and exercise thoroughly, it is imperative to examine the material structures underpinning behavioural choices and delegating indirect and direct decision-making legitimacy. Actor's behavioural choices are influenced by predetermined material structures, which, in turn, grant certain actors the authority to set agendas and establish rules. Scholars in international political economy have noted that structural power can reshape the state and market dynamics. This concept can lead to the state becoming dependent on the private sector due to businesses' capacity to create job opportunities, generate tax revenue, and provide financial support for government initiatives (Jiang & Li, 2020).

The structural power of business actors in global governance arises from their ability to influence agenda-setting processes by capitalising on the state's dependence on the private sector. Additionally, they can exert direct influence over regulations in non-governmental sectors through mechanisms for self-regulation and public-private partnerships (PPPs) (Newell et al., 2012).

Mitigating emissions relies on economic activities, granting business entrepreneurs the capacity to exert structural influence on policymakers due to the implications of climate change. Emission reduction is closely intertwined with economic activities in prominent industries, significantly affecting sectors associated with fossil fuels and causing changes in the cost of fossil energy. The General Circulation Model is commonly linked to the economic consequences of emission reduction efforts and their impact on production and employment. According to Newell and Paterson (1998), businesses can influence and potentially hinder international efforts to mitigate global warming (Newell et al., 2012).

Box 10

The structuralist perspective emphasises the organisation of constituent components, particularly the intrinsic and internal linkages among structural positions contributing to the formation of individuals as societal entities. This concept represents an inherent relationship, where the presence of structural position A depends on its connection with position B.

The structural power of business actors in global governance arises from their ability to influence agenda-setting processes by capitalising on the state's dependence on the private sector. Additionally, they can exert direct influence over regulations in non-governmental sectors through mechanisms for self-regulation and public-private partnerships.

From the international political economy perspective, the significant role that business actors have played in various aspects of economic growth, including investment, job creation, tax revenue, and innovation, has led to a structural reliance on these actors by states. In the Netherlands, prominent large manufacturing industries and oil corporations have indicated their intention to relocate and redirect new investments abroad if the government implements a unilateral energy levy. Consequently, governmental authorities have temporarily suspended the implementation of the levy bill's resolution until the proposal at the European Union level reaches its finalisation stage.

Technological innovation is facilitated by widespread knowledge about technological possibilities and constraints, equipping business entities with enhanced technological capabilities (Modes of Governance). Lawmakers may also seek to establish regulatory mechanisms that promote technological advancement to reduce emissions or modify industrial processes. Business entities can employ their technological capabilities to influence regulatory discussions, primarily because they possess technological knowledge and expertise, which governments often rely on when crafting regulations (Falkner, 2008). Within the domain of carbon capture and storage (CCS), notable entities in the European and American oil and gas industries have successfully adopted and institutionalised CCS as a recognised approach to addressing climate change (Carbon capture and storage – Wikipedia, 2022).

Box 11

From the international political economy perspective, the significant role that business actors have played in various aspects of economic growth, including investment, job creation, tax revenue, and innovation, has led to a structural reliance on these actors by states.

Technological innovation is facilitated by widespread knowledge about technological possibilities and constraints, equipping business entities with enhanced technological capabilities (Modes of Governance). Lawmakers may also seek to establish regulatory mechanisms that promote technological advancement to reduce emissions or modify industrial processes. Business entities can employ their technological capabilities to influence regulatory discussions, primarily because they possess technological knowledge and expertise, which governments often rely on when crafting regulations.

Self-regulation is another mechanism through which business entities exert their structural power within climate governance. Self-regulation encompasses a range of practices, which may involve affiliations with international organisations and voluntary participation in business collectives established by non-governmental organisations, trade associations, government agencies, or independent entities. In climate governance, business entities self-regulate through two distinct avenues: non-binding regulations and, environmental management systems (EMSs) and market certification schemes. The latter demonstrates more external oversight than codes, principles, disclosure schemes, and other non-binding regulations. Self-regulation plays a pivotal role in enabling business entities to wield their structural power within climate governance. This entails establishing connections with international organisations and participating voluntarily in business collectives formed by non-governmental organizations, trade associations, government agencies, or independent entities. Business entities engage in self-regulation using two distinct methods: non-binding regulations, which encompass principles, codes of conduct, reporting and disclosure schemes, voluntary environmental management standards, as well as hybrid models of co-regulation (Kolk & Pinkse, 2007; Thistlethwaite, 2011).

Prominent retailers like Target demonstrate a strong commitment to an ambitious environmental agenda due to their significant influence within the global supply chain. Advocates within these companies push for improvements in supplier production and transportation procedures, aiming to maximise the use of clean energy, optimize fleet efficiency, and minimize solid waste generation (Van der Ven, 2014). BP and Shell are notable corporations that pioneered internal emissions trading systems, setting a precedent for corporate reporting and verifying greenhouse gas emissions. Furthermore, they actively participate in the Greenhouse Gas Protocol Initiative, a global effort to establish universally recognized guidelines for quantifying and disclosing greenhouse gas emissions by corporate entities (Stokke et al., 2005).

The second channel emphasises EMSs and market certification schemes, representing increased external oversight compared to non-binding regulations. Corporations play a pivotal role in formulating these specific requirements and regulations. Market reorganizations are commonly overseen exclusively by industry stakeholders, although they may also involve non-state actors, including non-governmental organisations (NGOs) and third-party auditors. EMSs, such as those in the ISO 14,000 series, exhibit characteristics commonly associated with private and public sectors and are governed by independently certified standards (Clapp & Meckling, 2013).

Box 12

Self-regulation is another mechanism through which business entities exert their structural power within climate governance. Self-regulation encompasses a range of practices, which may involve affiliations with international organisations and voluntary participation in business collectives established by non-governmental organisations, trade associations, government agencies, or independent entities.

In climate governance, business entities self-regulate through two distinct avenues: non-binding regulations and, environmental management systems (EMSs) and market certification schemes. The latter demonstrates more external oversight than codes, principles, disclosure schemes, and other non-binding regulations.

3.3 *Discursive Perspective*

The discursive perspective is a theoretical framework that analyses the influence of language and discourse on the formation of social reality and the construction of meaning. The language is used to construct and shape perceptions and identities, facilitating societal understanding of matters requiring consideration. This phenomenon significantly influences policy challenges and the formulation of corresponding remedies in politics. Within environmental studies, discursive power is closely associated with the possession of 'specialized knowledge' essential for recognising ecological concerns and devising technological solutions. Business entities' acquisition of discursive power is attributed to their central role in driving technological innovation (Jiang & Li, 2020).

In environmental leadership, business entities rely on scientific knowledge and data through marketing, education, and financial support for organisations that challenge the principles of climate science. These entities utilise various resources to construct discourses to influence public opinion, governmental legislation, and fellow business leaders. The fossil fuel manufacturing sectors in the United States strategically employed public relations campaigns to highlight the scientific challenges surrounding global climate change and the potential economic challenges associated with reducing emissions (Bieler et al., 2000).

Industrial associations have been identified as having a primary goal of influencing public discourses through advertising and education. In 1991, Western Fuels, an American utility association and member of the Global Climate Coalition, produced a documentary entitled 'The Greening of Planet Earth.' Additionally, in 1993, they released an advertisement named 'Repeal Rio.' These media productions aimed to portray climate change as a controversial theory lacking empirical evidence. The extent to which their actions and offerings align with market and consumer preferences increasingly determines the effectiveness of their discursive authority in climate governance (Jiang & Li, 2020).

In an era characterised by limited access to information and a lack of comprehensive scientific understanding, individuals involved in business endeavours can employ specialised knowledge to manipulate public sentiment, shape unfavourable narratives related to climate change, and influence consumer decision-making. However, the effectiveness of shaping discourse will decrease as consumer demand evolves. With the growing recognition of the risks associated with global warming, there is a rising trend among individuals to choose environmentally sustainable and low-carbon products. This consumer behaviour has compelled businesses to embrace technological innovations and implement low-carbon practices. Therefore, business entities must seize the opportunities arising from low-carbon development, actively pursue technological innovations, and produce environmentally sustainable products. This empowers individuals to achieve, maintain, and enhance their ability for efficient communication, playing a constructive role in climate governance (Jiang & Li, 2020).

Box 13
The discursive perspective is a theoretical framework that analyses the influence of language and discourse on the formation of social reality and the construction of meaning.

4 A Sustainable Development Approach Through Innovation

The quality of life on Earth and its long-term survival are in jeopardy due to various sustainability concerns that the global civilisation is grappling with. These issues are no longer confined to a single region of the world. Thanks to decades of globalisation and the ongoing intermingling of economies, industries, and cultures, they now affect our entire civilisation. For this reason, they are sometimes referred to as the "Grand Challenges" (GCs) (George et al. 2016). To comprehend the significance of eco-innovation, it is essential first to establish the notion of sustainable development.

Sustainable development was first proposed in The Brundtland Report in 1987. It is defined as the "*development that meets the needs of the present without compromising the ability of future generations to meet their own needs*" (World Commission on Environment and Development, 1987, p. 41). Two core concepts underpin this definition: (1) the recognition that the basic requirements of the world's impoverished populations should take precedence and (2) the understanding that the environment has finite resources, which can support both current and future needs only if technology and social organisation are managed carefully. Consequently, in all nations, whether developing or developed and regardless of whether they have centrally planned or market-based economies, the objectives of social and economic progress must be framed within a sustainable perspective (World Commission on Environment and Development, 1987, p. 41).

The primary objective of development is to meet human needs and aspirations. In many impoverished countries, access to necessities such as food, clothing, shelter, and employment remains elusive, and these individuals harbour legitimate hopes for an improved quality of life beyond their fundamental requirements. The potential for environmental and other catastrophes looms large in a world marked by pervasive poverty and inequality. Achieving sustainable development necessitates meeting the basic needs of all and providing everyone with the opportunity to pursue a better life.

Box 14
Two core concepts underpin the definition of sustainable development: (1) the recognition that the basic requirements of the world's impoverished populations should take precedence and (2) the understanding that the environment has finite resources, which can support both current and future needs only if technology and social organisation are managed carefully.

Since the international community agreed to uphold the ideals of sustainable development in 1992 in Rio, it has become increasingly evident that achieving sustainability necessitates substantial, long-term reforms in institutions, infrastructure, lifestyles, and technologies. There are several compelling reasons for understanding how innovation processes work.

First, there is a pressing need for significant reductions in environmental burdens, including greenhouse gas emissions. This underscores the inadequacy of technological adaptation within current frameworks, calling for "technological regime shifts" and/or "technology-forcing" regulatory strategies.

Second, innovation is anticipated to alleviate the costs and burdens associated with environmental regulations. Benefits such as enhanced competitiveness, reduced expenses, the emergence of new markets for environmentally preferable goods and services, and corresponding employment opportunities are frequently observed when environmental policies encourage innovation. Although Porter and Van der Linde (1995) made similar arguments, the Porter hypothesis, which suggests "innovation offsets" for stringent environmental regulations, is met with skepticism by most economists (Jaffe & Palmer, 1997; Ulph, 1996).

Furthermore, inventing, adapting, and disseminating new technologies for areas such as renewable energy systems or transportation infrastructure often takes a decade or longer. Consequently, we can reasonably anticipate that substantial changes in critical social and economic subsystems, akin to technological transitions in transportation and energy systems, will unfold over 50 years or more. Therefore, it is essential to understand the workings of transition and learning processes, particularly when conditions are far from the desired equilibrium.

Many scenarios also recognise that advancements in environmental technology alone cannot achieve long-term sustainability goals. They necessitate corresponding lifestyle changes, such as reducing energy consumption or altering travel habits, alongside institutional changes from local networks to international organisations.

For most businesses, developing or modifying environmentally friendly processes or products has become routine and the subject of scientific inquiry. Research by Cleff and Rennings (1998) based on the German industry reveals that approximately 80% of all innovative enterprises engaged in environmentally friendly innovation initiatives over the past 3 years. Even small or medium-sized companies, regardless of their industry, are actively involved in producing and utilising environmentally friendly goods, conserving energy, and reducing waste and emissions. For many businesses, managing eco-innovation is of growing importance.

Finally, numerous sustainability initiatives and programs have been launched to promote innovative policy responses and associated scientific research, enhancing our understanding of the global impact of climate change and its effects on social and economic structures. Given longer time horizons, a thorough examination of past experiences is warranted to identify the essential elements and variables in sustainable innovation processes.

Box 15
Many scenarios recognise that advancements in environmental technology alone cannot achieve long-term sustainability goals. They necessitate corresponding lifestyle changes, such as reducing energy consumption or altering travel habits, alongside institutional changes from local networks to international organisations.

4.1 Innovation

The term 'innovation' is employed in various ways within socio-political and scientific discussions. A narrower definition of innovation characterises it as technological novelties. However, it can also have a broader connotation, encompassing the first-time application of a new skill, technique, or product. Moreover, the term can extend beyond technology to encompass non-technological creativity, such as modifying a product's design or a company's organisational structure. The Oslo Manual of the OECD (1997) clearly distinguishes between three types of innovation: process, product, and organisational innovation, which aligns with the traditional understanding of innovation.

- *Process innovation* refers to the ability to generate a certain quantity of outputs (services or goods) with fewer inputs, resulting in increased efficiency.
- *Product innovation* involves the creation of new products or enhancements to existing ones (or services). Interestingly, product innovation in one company often leads to process innovation in another.
- *Organisational innovation* encompasses the adoption of novel management approaches, like total quality management.

4.2 Eco-innovation

The term "eco-innovation" is used in socio-political and scientific discussions to describe various innovative activities. Initially coined in earlier studies like Angelo et al. (2012) and Schiederig et al. (2012), the term encompasses ecological, environmental, green, and sustainable innovation. While these terms share the common goal of reducing environmental impact, eco-innovation represents a broader concept.

According to Carrillo-Hermosilla et al. (2010) and Angelo et al. (2012), eco-innovation plays a pivotal role in achieving sustainability, particularly in the manufacturing sector, as noted by Sezen and Çankaya (2013). The European Union's

Eco-innovation Action Plan (European Commission, 2011) defines eco-innovation as "inventions that promote environmentally friendly growth by minimizing environmental impacts, enhancing adaptability to ecological challenges, or using natural resources more efficiently and responsibly." When evaluated within this framework, innovations can be categorized into environmental and non-environmental groups, underscoring the growing importance of ecological advancements in pursuing sustainable development.

Horbach et al. (2011) provide an alternative perspective, defining eco-innovation as a set of process, product, marketing, and organisational improvements that significantly reduce adverse environmental impacts. This definition emphasises the potential positive effects of a clearly defined goal and an innovation's externalities on the environment, whether within a company's operations or through consumer interactions.

Numerous studies (Cainelli et al., 2020; Chen et al., 2006; Krieger & Zipperer, 2022) have highlighted how eco-innovation, as a technological improvement, enables companies to adopt new procedures, techniques, and products to mitigate environmental harm, promote recycling, and conserve energy. What sets eco-innovation apart from conventional innovation is its strong focus on sustainable development and its environmentally-driven impetus. The primary objective of eco-innovation is to enhance environmental sustainability, whether by reducing environmental costs or meeting environmentally-mandated standards.

The concept of eco-innovation can be understood from two distinct angles: first, by assessing its impact on the environment, and second, by considering the innovator's intention to minimise the environmental footprint of methods or products. This characteristic may even apply to innovations not initially designed to be environmentally friendly. For instance, improvements in fuel efficiency within the automotive industry, while primarily driven by performance or cost considerations, can also lead to positive environmental outcomes. According to Kemp and Pearson (2007), most eco-innovations are incremental improvements or adaptations of existing technologies due to limited economic incentives to exceed regulatory requirements, low taxes, a regulatory preference for quick results, and industry demand for non-disruptive solutions.

Eco-innovation is a helpful gauge for assessing the effectiveness of "smart" regulations, which are crucial in steering industries towards competitiveness and sustainability. Regulatory frameworks have evolved accordingly as innovation trends align with sustainable technology or eco-innovation. With the emergence of "smart regulation," regulators have become innovative, emphasising the importance of evaluating the impact of eco-innovation. Given its significance in the transition to a more sustainable future, studying the effects of past and current policies that influence eco-innovation and its diffusion is imperative, as Horbach (2008) noted.

Regulation often acts as a catalyst for innovation, especially when corporations may not always make the best decisions on their own. The dynamics of progressive competition are characterised by shifting technical opportunities, incomplete information, organizational inertia, and coordination challenges, making it difficult to align the motivations of individuals, groups, and corporations. However, as several observations suggest (Jaenicke & Jacob, 2002; Kemp et al., 2001), stringent environmental standards can encourage innovation in multiple ways. Both for-profit and nonprofit organisations can develop eco-innovations, whether they are traded on markets or not, and regardless of their nature—whether institutional, organisational, social, or technological (Rennings, 2000). There is no universal method for categorising eco-innovation in the literature, but it is generally agreed that eco-innovation can encompass organisational, marketing, or technical innovations as long as they enhance a company's environmental competitiveness, as indicated by various scholars on the subject (Andersen, 2004, 2008). Some authors categorise innovations into environmentally friendly and non-environmentally friendly types within the broader category of eco-innovation (Jakobsen & Clausen, 2014; Montresor et al., 2013).

Another taxonomy of eco-innovation highlights subcategories, including technological, organisational, social, and business park-related innovations. The latter may be associated with changes in consumer behaviour and promoting a sustainable lifestyle (Esders, 2008). However, some scholars argue that eco-innovation primarily focuses on the environmental aspects of the market economy rather than social innovation. Vollenbroek (2002) contends that eco-innovation requires technological solutions closely linked to social values and lifestyles that advance society.

Box 16
Eco-innovation is a helpful gauge for assessing the effectiveness of "smart" regulations, which are crucial in steering industries towards competitiveness and sustainability. Regulatory frameworks have evolved accordingly as innovation trends align with sustainable technology or eco-innovation. With the emergence of "smart regulation," regulators have become innovative, emphasising the importance of evaluating the impact of eco-innovation.

4.3 Features of Eco-innovation

The critical element of eco-innovation is a lifecycle perspective, emphasising consideration of the entire lifecycle rather than solely focusing on environmental issues at various stages. Eco-innovation involves reducing the environmental impact throughout the development, production, consumption, reuse, and recycling stages. This extends beyond creating new products and offering new services. It encompasses resource extraction, manufacturing, distribution, consumption, and end-of-life phases (EIO and CfSD, 2013).

The second attribute of eco-innovation is its efficient resource utilisation (EIO and CfSD, 2013; Kemp & Foxon, 2007). Eco-innovation encompasses environmentally improved products, services, and organisational adjustments. In other words, entirely new processes that minimise resource usage are considered eco-innovations (Kemp & Foxon, 2007).

The third characteristic of eco-innovation is its focus on environmental impact (Rennings, 2000; Kemp & Foxon, 2007; Eco-Innovation Observatory (EIO), 2011;

Angelo et al., 2012). According to the literature, eco-innovation introduces new or significantly enhanced products, processes, organisational changes, or marketing strategies while remaining ecologically friendly or benefiting the environment. Therefore, eco-innovation encompasses both the "unintended reduction of environmental impact" and environmentally-oriented inventions (Kemp & Foxon, 2007; Machiba, 2010).

Fourthly, eco-innovations can be implemented in various business sectors, including agriculture, organisations, manufacturing, managerial approaches, services, rural and urban design and planning, and many more (Antonioli et al., 2013; Cainelli & Mazzanti, 2013). One crucial aspect of eco-innovation is its independence from specific industries or technologies, making it applicable to any economic activity.

In conclusion, it is evident that eco-innovation extends beyond creating novelties in the "eco/environmental" domain; it involves enhancing existing goods, services, organisations, technologies, and marketing strategies to utilise natural resources and products more effectively while reducing or mitigating negative environmental impacts.

Box 17

Characteristics and attributes of eco-innovation:

- Lifecycle perspective: emphasises consideration of the entire lifecycle rather than solely focusing on environmental issues at various stages.
- Efficient resource utilisation: eco-innovation encompasses environmentally improved products, services, and organisational adjustments. Therefore, entirely new processes that minimise resource usage are considered eco-innovations.
- Environmental impact: eco-innovation introduces new or significantly enhanced products, processes, organisational changes, or marketing strategies while remaining ecologically friendly or benefiting the environment. Therefore, eco-innovation encompasses both the "unintended reduction of environmental impact" and environmentally-oriented inventions.
- Implemented in various business sectors: eco-innovations can be implemented in various business sectors, including agriculture, organisations, manufacturing, managerial approaches, services, rural and urban design and planning, and many more. One crucial aspect of eco-innovation is its independence from specific industries or technologies, making it applicable to any economic activity.

4.4 Types of Eco-innovation

The eco-innovation subcategories presented here are sourced from Eco-Innovation Observatory (EIO) (2013) due to the inconsistency in categorisation found across various research studies. Eco-Innovation Observatory (EIO) (2013) outlines the following eco-innovation categories: product, process, organisational, marketing, social, and system eco-innovation.

4.4.1 Product Eco-innovation

According to Eco-Innovation Observatory (EIO) (2013), product innovation encompasses both goods and services aimed at reducing the overall environmental impact of their production, with a strong emphasis on eco-design principles. Eco-design integrates resource constraints into product innovation, resulting in products with a reduced ecological footprint, lower resource consumption during use, and options for repair, remanufacturing, or reuse (Eco-Innovation Observatory (EIO), 2013).

Product innovation can also be defined as developing a service or product that is either entirely new or significantly improved concerning its properties or intended applications. This includes significant advancements in technical specifications, materials and components, software integration, accessibility, and other functional qualities (OECD, 2005).

Additionally, it involves the creation of new eco-products using advanced techniques that optimise material sourcing, construction, and packaging to simplify recycling and minimise resource depletion. This is followed by the development of fresh eco-products using cutting-edge methods that avoid using chemically processed components and instead rely on natural resources to reduce waste and minimize the environmental impact, focusing on minimizing energy consumption (Cheng & Shiu, 2012).

4.4.2 Process Eco-innovation

Reduced material consumption, lower risk, and cost savings are the primary criteria that define process innovations (Eco-Innovation Observatory (EIO), 2013). The OECD (2005) also characterises process innovation as adopting entirely new or significantly improved production or delivery techniques. This can include material modifications to methods, tools, and/or software (OECD, 2005).

4.4.3 Technological Eco-innovation

According to Tseng et al. (2012), technology and eco-innovations are the main drivers of information provision that encompass material-saving strategies and the management of information and documents. They argue that adopting state-of-the-art green production technology and investing in environmentally friendly equipment are critical factors driving innovation (Tseng et al., 2012).

4.4.4 Organisational Eco-innovation

Organisational innovation, as defined by the OECD (2005), requires a fresh approach to a company's operations, workplace structure, or external interactions. As explained by Dong et al. (2014), organisational eco-innovation aims to enhance environmental performance, resource efficiency, and social responsibility in alignment with the company's environmental vision.

4.4.5 Marketing Eco-innovation

As the OECD (2005) and Eco-Innovation Observatory (EIO) (2013) defined, marketing innovation involves significant changes to product positioning, promotion, pricing, design, or packaging. When these adjustments incorporate environmental considerations, they fall under eco-innovation (OECD, 2005). Eco-innovation in marketing encompasses alterations or advancements in product design, packaging, positioning, promotion, pricing, and eco-labelling, among other strategies to encourage consumers to adopt eco-friendly products (Eco-Innovation Observatory (EIO), 2013).

4.4.6 Socio-Eco-innovation

Socio-eco-innovation includes the human element in any discussion of resource utilisation and focuses on assuring the demand for eco-friendly products and services by incorporating market-based behavioural and lifestyle change aspects. Some businesses attempt to adopt and put into practice so-called user-led innovation, which involves collaborating with stakeholders to design new products' functionality and reducing the likelihood of unnecessary product features. Product sharing is another crucial factor that reduces material consumption without lowering the quality of services offered to the consumer (Eco-Innovation Observatory (EIO), 2013).

4.4.7 System Eco-innovation

System eco-innovation is the name given to a collection of interconnected inventions that improve existing systems or build brand-new ones, delivering certain functionalities with a diminished overall adverse effect on the environment (Eco-Innovation Observatory (EIO), 2013). Its distinguishing characteristic is a group of intentional alterations. Systemic eco-innovations are complete solutions built on cutting-edge business models (such as smart cities), sustainable transportation, and industrial ecology (European Commission, 2012).

4.5 Drivers of Eco-innovation

Businesses may be driven to implement eco-innovation by various factors, including ethical, public relations, financial, or legal considerations (Johnson, 2009). Eco-innovation exhibits unique characteristics that necessitate a different approach than conventional innovations, primarily due to the influence of regulatory forces and competitive pressures (De Marchi, 2012; Horbach, 2008).

According to Khanna et al. (2009), regulatory pressures resulting from existing and forthcoming environmental regulations significantly encourage voluntary eco-innovation. These regulations can reshape the competitive landscape for businesses (Kammerer Daniel, 2009; Doran & Ryan, 2012). Stricter environmental requirements are associated with an increase in environmentally friendly product offerings, although the correlation between stringent regulations and the uniqueness of eco-innovations is only marginally positive (Kammerer Daniel, 2009). Weng and Lin (2011) observed that regulatory pressure and government support impact the adoption of green technologies. Governments can act as regulators and provide small and medium-sized enterprises (SMEs) with the necessary financial, technical, and instructional resources to facilitate the implementation of eco-innovations.

Competitiveness is another crucial driver of eco-innovation, as businesses seek a green competitive edge through product differentiation in highly competitive markets (Lin et al., 2013). Environmental advertising strategies can favourably influence competitive advantage, especially in less competitive environments, while becoming more critical in highly competitive settings (Leonidou et al., 2013). Consumer demand for environmentally friendly products is rising globally, with customers willing to pay more for eco-friendly choices (Chen, 2013). This heightened environmental awareness pressures businesses to reduce their ecological impact (Kemp & Foxon, 2007). Consumer opinion is a significant catalyst for eco-innovation (Doran & Ryan, 2012).

Society, including community expectations, environmental affiliations, and media exposure, also influences businesses' decisions to invest in eco-innovation or adopt eco-friendly practices (Zeng et al., 2011). Public perception of a company's environmental performance affects its operations and strategies across industries (Qi et al., 2010). Public and media pressure can drive businesses to adopt more environmentally friendly practices (Bansal & Roth, 2000) and is a crucial driver of eco-innovation (Horbach, 2008; Lee, 2009). However, small businesses may face challenges in implementing eco-innovations due to competition with larger companies and the need to provide excellent offerings while considering limited financial and human resources (Triguero et al., 2013). Investing in eco-innovation often depends on a company's size and the resources at its disposal.

Box 18

Businesses may be driven to implement eco-innovation by various factors, including ethical, public relations, financial, or legal considerations. Eco-innovation exhibits unique characteristics that necessitate a different approach than conventional innovations, primarily due to the influence of regulatory forces and competitive pressures.

4.6 Consequences of Eco-innovation Adoption

In the early stages, businesses were initially reluctant to embrace eco-innovations and adopt eco-conscious practices. Eco-innovation is often seen as a response to regulatory requirements, primarily aimed at compliance. It is also viewed as burdensome and potentially detrimental to a company's performance, particularly in terms of profitability, while attempting to improve environmental conditions. It is worth noting that eco-innovations' impact on growth and employment can vary depending on the specific innovation and its application context (Arundel & Kemp, 2009).

Nevertheless, eco-innovations can be financially beneficial for the business sector. Porter and van der Linde (1995) emphasise that well-designed environmental regulations can stimulate innovations that either reduce the overall cost of a product or increase its value. These innovations not only lower the costs associated with environmental impact reduction but also enhance the productivity of various inputs, including labour, raw materials, and energy.

Eco-innovations also contribute to environmental goals by promoting more efficient resource use during manufacturing, minimising the release of hazardous substances, and achieving other ecological objectives. Sarkar (2013) categorise the direct and indirect benefits of eco-innovation. Direct benefits include reduced expenses and improved resource and administrative task efficiency, leading to increased sales from marketing efforts (Sarkar, 2013). Indirect benefits encompass an enhanced reputation, improved stakeholder relationships, safety and health advantages, higher employee satisfaction, and increased innovation potential. Businesses increasingly recognise that adopting environmentally friendly practices can enhance their short- and long-term competitiveness and open up new markets.

Introducing environmentally friendly or significantly improved products that require fewer inputs in production can boost productivity, achieve cost savings, and reduce environmental impact (Triguero et al., 2013). Innovative products can penetrate new markets, gain a competitive advantage, and improve profit margins (Ramanathan et al., 2010).

From an economic perspective, eco-innovation aims to lower energy and supply costs while creating new goods, services, markets, and customer segments. It also seeks to enhance people's quality of life and create sustainable jobs on a social level. On the environmental front, eco-innovation promotes reduced environmental impact, responsible use of ecological resources, and innovative approaches to addressing climate change (Dogaru, 2017). It strives to preserve biodiversity and maintain ecological balance. The complex eco-innovation process requires the development of business models that consider environmental sustainability and sustainable development as part of a new growth strategy. Eco-innovation encompasses various fields, including food security, bioresources, biotechnology, energy conservation, water supply, and waste management. Successful eco-innovation depends on factors such as the mindset of enterprises, effective political and legal systems, support services, and access to funding (Pansera & Owen, 2018).

5 Conclusion

5.1 Power Dynamics in Climate Governance

The chapter highlights significant disparities in the power and influence of various business organisations within climate governance structures, operating at the levels of nation-states, supranational entities, and individual actors. These disparities are categorised into two key concepts of power:

1. *Structural Power*: This concept pertains to the capacity of business entities to shape agendas and establish regulations within the global climate governance framework, thereby showcasing their influential capabilities.
2. *Discourse Power*: This explores how individual consumers exert influence by shaping their perceptions of climate change and influencing the decision-making processes of business actors.

Business entities can use different forms of power to influence climate-related matters.

5.2 Changing Roles in the Fossil Energy Sector

Stakeholders within the fossil energy sector have significantly shifted their positions concerning climate change. For instance:

- *Collaborative Lobbying*: Prior to the withdrawal of the Trump administration from the Paris Agreement, American fossil energy corporations engaged in collaborative lobbying efforts to advocate for the United States' participation in the agreement.
- *Transition to Low-Carbon Energy*: Contemporary fossil fuel corporations have undergone restructuring efforts to prioritise low-carbon energy solutions. Oil corporations, for example, invest in security measures and allocate resources to research and develop low-carbon technology while divesting from high-carbon-emission assets.
- *Coal Industry Adaptation*: The coal industry has shifted its perspective to embrace environmentally friendly approaches such as carbon capture and storage (CCS) and high-efficiency, low-emission coal technologies.

5.3 Eco-innovation and Climate Governance

Eco-innovation plays a crucial role in addressing escalating environmental issues and resource constraints. The growing demand for ecological ideas, products, and services is anticipated to encourage the growth of environmentally friendly businesses. Eco-innovations offer financial benefits, support small businesses, foster job creation, enhance economic competitiveness, facilitate the transition toward ecological economic development, and contribute significantly to environmental conservation.

In summary, the evolving landscape of climate governance and the changing roles of businesses, particularly in the fossil energy sector, are essential elements in pursuing environmental sustainability and economic growth.

Declaration of Generative AI and AI-Assisted Technologies in the Writing Process for This Chapter from Authors The authors of this chapter have used Quilbot as a writing tool to frame their own sentences in a more creative way and for grammar checking. They declared that did not use AI to produce any original content.

References

Andersen, M. M. (2004). An innovation system approaches to eco-innovation - aligning policy rationales, The Greening of Policies – Inter-linkages and Policy Integration Conference, Berlin, Germany, 3–4 December 2004.

Andersen, M. M. (2008). Eco-innovation - theoretical and methodological considerations. In *DIME WP 2.5 workshop on empirical analyses of environmental innovations*. Fraunhofer Institute for Systems and Innovation Research ISI. 17-18 January 2008.

Angelo, F. D., Jabbour, C. J. C., & Galina, S. V. (2012). Environmental innovation: In search of a meaning. *World Journal of Entrepreneurship, Management and Sustainable Development, 8*(2/3), 113–121.

Antonioli, D., Mancinelli, S., & Mazzanti, M. (2013). Is environmental innovation embedded within high-performance organisational changes? The role of human resource management and complementarity in Green business strategies. *Research Policy, 42*(4), 975–988.

Arundel, A., & Kemp, R. (2009). *Measuring eco-innovation*. UNU-MERIT.

Asselt, H., & Zelli, F. (2013). Connect the dots: Managing the fragmentation of global climate governance. *Environmental Economics and Policy Studies, 16*(2), 137–155.

Bansal, P., & Roth, K. (2000). Why companies go green: A model of ecological responsiveness. *The Academy of Management Journal, 43*(4), 717–736.

Bieler, A., Higgott, R., & Underhill, G. (Eds.). (2000). *Corporate political action in the global polity: National and transnational strategies in the climate change negotiations. Non-state Actors and Authority in the Global System*. Routledge.

Brugger, H., Eichhammer, W., Mikova, N., & Dönitz, E. (2021). Energy efficiency vision 2050: How will new societal trends influence future energy demand in the European countries? *Energy Policy, 152*, 112216.

Cainelli, G., D'Amato, A., & Mazzanti, M. (2020). Resource efficient eco-innovations for a circular economy: Evidence from EU firms. *Research Policy, 49*(1), 103827.

Cainelli, G., & Mazzanti, M. (2013). Environmental innovations in services: Manufacturing–services integration and policy transmissions. *Research Policy, 42*(9), 1595–1604.

Carbon capture and storage – Wikipedia. (2022). In: Carbon capture and storage - Wikipedia. https://wikipedia.org/wiki/Carbon_capture_and_storage

Carrillo-Hermosilla, J., Del Río, P., & Könnölä, T. (2010). Diversity of eco-innovations: Reflections from selected case studies. *Journal of Cleaner Production 18*(10–11), 1073–1083.

Chen, Y.-S. (2013). The positive effect of Green capital on competitive intellectual of firms. *Journal of Business Ethics, 77*(3), 271–286.
Chen, Y.-S., Lai, S.-B., & Wen, C.-T. (2006). The influence of green innovation performance on corporate advantage in Taiwan. *Journal of Business Ethics, 67*(4), 331–339.
Cheng, C. C., & Shiu, E. (2012). Validation of a proposed instrument for measuring eco-innovation: An implementation perspective. *Technovation, 32*(6), 329–344. https://doi.org/10.1016/j.technovation.2012.02.001
Chevalier, J. M., & Geoffron, P. (2013). The new energy crisis. *The New Energy Crisis*, 1–52.
Clapp, J., & Meckling, J. (2013). Business as a global actor. The handbook of global climate and environment policy. 286–303.
Cleff, T., & Rennings, K. (1998). Determinants of eco-innovation behavior at the firm level and the role of environmental policy instruments - New empirical evidence from the Mannheim Innovation Panel and an additional Telephone Survey. Paper prepared for the 7th International Conference of the Greening of Industry Network in Rome, Italy, 15–18 November 1998.
Daniel, K. (2009). The effects of customer benefit and regulation on environmental product innovation. *Ecological Economics, 68*(8–9), 2285–2295.
De Marchi, V. (2012). Environmental innovation and R&D cooperation: Empirical evidence from Spanish manufacturing firms. *Research Policy, 41*(3), 614–623.
Developed Countries Must Deliver on Climate Change. (2022). Finance commitments, delegates stress, as second committee continues its general debate. https://press.un.org/en/2022/gaef3566.doc.htm. Accessed 31.08.23.
Dogaru, L. (2017). Environmental change and its effects. *Curent Juridical, 69*(2), 38–43.
Dong, Y., Wang, X., Jin, J., et al. (2014). Effects of eco-innovation typology on its performance: Empirical evidence from Chinese enterprises. *Journal of Engineering and Technology Management, 34*, 78–98.
Doran, J., & Ryan, G. (2012). Regulation and firm perception, eco-innovation and firm performance. *European Journal of Innovation Management, 15*(4), 421–441.
Eco-Innovation Observatory (EIO). (2011). *The eco-innovation challenge: Pathways to a resource-efficient Europe, eco-innovation observatory, funded by the European Commission.* DG Environment.
Eco-Innovation Observatory (EIO). (2013). *Europe in transition: Paving the way to a green economy through eco-innovation, eco-innovation observatory, funded by the European commission.* DG Environment.
EIO and CfSD. (2013). *Eco-innovate! A guide to eco-innovation for SMEs and business coaches. Eco-innovation observatory. Funded by the European Commission.* DG Environment. http://cfsd.org.uk/site-pdfs/eco-innovate-sme-guide.pdf. Accessed 28 July 2023
Esders, M. (2008). *Conceptualizing the assessment of eco-innovation performance: A theory based framework for deriving eco-innovation key performance indicators and drivers (EI-KPIs).* Centre for Sustainability Management (CSM).
European Commission. (2011). Communication from the Commission to the European Parliament, the Council, the European Economic and Social Committee and the Committee of the Regions: Innovation for a Sustainable Future - The Eco-innovation Action Plan (Eco-AP). COM (2011) 899 final. Brussels, pp. 2.
European Commission. (2012). *Connecting smart and sustainable growth through smart specialisation a practical guide for ERDF managing authorities.* Publications Office of the European Union.
Fuchs, D. (2007). Business power in global governance. https://doi.org/10.1515/9781685853716.
George, G., Howard-Grenville, J., Joshi, A., & Tihanyi, L. (2016). Understanding and tackling societal grand challenges through management research. *Academy of Management Journal, 59*(6), 1880–1895.
Gielen, D., Boshell, F., & Saygin, D. (2019). The role of renewable energy in the global energy transformation. *Energy Strategy Reviews, 24*, 38–50.

Global energy transformation: A roadmap to 2050. (2019 edition). https://www.irena.org/publications/2019/Apr/Global-energy-transformation-A-roadmap-to-2050-2019Edition

Horbach, J. (2008). Determinants of environmental innovation - New evidence from German panel data sources. *Research Policy, 37*, 163–173.

Horbach, J., Rammer, C., & Rennings, K. (2011). Determinants of eco-innovations by type of environmental impact: The role of regulatory push/pull, technology push and market pull. ZEW-Centre for European Economic Research Discussion paper no. 11–027. http://ftp.zew.de/pub/zew-docs/dp/dp11027.pdf

Jaenicke, M., & Jacob, K. (2002). *Ecological modernisation and the creation of lead markets. FFU-report 03–2002 Forschungstelle fuer Umweltpolitik*. Freie Universitaet. https://doi.org/10.17169/refubium-23288

Jaffe, A. B., & Palmer, K. (1997). Environmental regulation and innovation: a panel data study. *Review of Economics and Statistics, 79*(4), 610–619.

Jakobsen, S., & Clausen, T. H. (2014). Innovating for a greener future: The direct and indirect effects of firms' environmental objectives on the innovation process. *Journal of Cleaner Production, 128*, 131–141. https://doi.org/10.1016/j.jclepro.2015.06.023

Jiang, S., & Li, J. (2020). Global climate governance in the new era: Potential of business actors and technological innovation. *Chinese Journal of Population, Resources and Environment, 18*, 165–171.

Johnson, R. L. (2009). Organizational motivations for going Green or profitability versus sustainability. *The Business Review, 13*, 22–28.

Jordan, A., Huitema, D., van Asselt, H., & Forster, J. (Eds.). (2018). *National Governance the state's role in steering polycentric action. Governing climate change: Polycentricity in action*. Cambridge University Press.

Kemp, R., Arundel, A., & Smith, K. (2001). Survey indicators for environmental innovation (paper presented to conference, Towards Environmental Innovation Systems in Garmisch-Partenkirchen).

Kemp, R., & Foxon, T. (2007). Typology of eco-innovation. Project paper: Measuring Eco-innovation. http://www.merit.unu.edu/MEI/deliverables/MEI%20D2%20Typology%20of%20eco-innovation.pdf

Kemp, R., & Pearson, P. (2007). *Final report MEI project about measuring eco-innovation*. UM Merit. http://www.oecd.org/env/consumption-innovation/43960830.pdf

Khanna, M., Deltas, G., & Harrington, D. R. (2009). Adoption of pollution prevention techniques: The role of management systems and regulatory pressures. *Environmental and Resource Economics, 44*(1), 85–106.

Kolk, A., & Pinkse, J. (2007). Towards strategic stakeholder management? Integrating perspectives on sustainability challenges such as corporate responses to climate change. *Corporate Governance: The International Journal of Business in Society, 7*, 370–378. https://doi.org/10.1108/14720700710820452

Krieger, B., & Zipperer, V. (2022). Does green public procurement trigger environmental innovations? *Research Policy, 51*(6), 104516.

Kyoto Protocol to the United Nations Framework Convention On Climate Change. (1998). https://unfccc.int/resource/docs/convkp/kpeng.pdf. Accessed 01.08 23.

Lee, K. H. (2009). Why and how to adopt Green management into business organizations? The case study of Korean SMEs in manufacturing industry. *Management Decision, 47*(7), 1101–1121.

Leonidou, L. C., Leonidou, C. N., Fotiadis, T. A., et al. (2013). Resources and capabilities as drivers of hotel e2nvironmental marketing strategy: Implications for competitive advantage and performance. *Tourism Management, 35*, 94–110.

Lin, R. J., Tan, K. H., & Geng, Y. (2013). Market demand, green product innovation, and firm performance: Evidence from Vietnam motorcycle industry. *Journal of Cleaner Production, 40*, 101–107.

Machiba, T. (2010). Eco-innovation for enabling resource efficiency and green growth: Development of an analytical framework and preliminary analysis of industry and policy practices. *International Economics and Economic Policy, 7*(2–3), 357–370.
Modes of Governance: A Note Towards Conceptual Clarification - CORE Reader. In: Modes of Governance: A Note Towards Conceptual Clarification - CORE Reader. https://core.ac.uk/reader/71735030.
Montresor, S., Ghisetti, C., & Marzucchi, A. (2013). *The "green-impact" of the open innovation mode. Bridging knowledge sourcing and absorptive capacity for environmental innovations*. Publication Office of the European Union.
Newell, P., & Paterson, M. (1998). A climate for business: Global warming, the state and capital. *Review of International Political Economy, 5*, 679–703.
Newell, P., Pattberg, P., & Schroeder, H. (2012). Multiactor governance and the environment. *Annual Review of Environment and Resources, 37*, 365–387.
OECD. (1997). *Proposed guidelines for collecting and interpreting technological innovation data: Oslo manual, the measurement of scientific and technological activities*. OECD Publishing. https://doi.org/10.1787/9789264192263-en
OECD. (2005). Oslo manual: Guidelines for collecting and interpreting innovation data. In *The measurement of scientific and technological activities* (3rd ed.). OECD Publishing. https://doi.org/10.1787/9789264013100-en
Pansera, M., & Owen, R. (2018). *Innovation and development: The politics at the bottom of the pyramid*. Wiley-ISTE.
Porter, M. E., & Van der Linde, C. (1995). Green and competitive: Ending the stalemate. *Harvard Business Review, 73*(September–October), 120–134.
Qi, G. Y., Shen, L. Y., Zeng, S. X., et al. (2010). The drivers for contractors' green innovation: An industry perspective. *Journal of Cleaner Production, 18*(14), 1358–1365.
Ramanathan, R., Black, A., Nath, P., et al. (2010). Impact of environmental regulations on innovation and performance in the UK industrial sector. *Management Decision, 48*(10), 1493–1513.
Rennings, K. (2000). Redefining innovation - eco-innovation research and the contribution from ecological economics. *Ecological Economics, 32*(2), 319–332.
Ricaurte-Quijano, P., & Carli-Álvarez, A. (2016a). The wiki learning project: Wikipedia as an open learning environment. *Comunicar, 24*, 61–69. https://doi.org/10.3916/c49-2016-020.an
Ricaurte-Quijano, P., & Carli-Álvarez, A. (2016b). The wiki learning project: Wikipedia as an open learning environment. *Comunicar, 24*, 61–69. https://doi.org/10.3916/c49-2016-06
Sarkar, A. N. (2013). Promoting eco-innovations to leverage sustainable development of eco-industry and green growth. *European Journal of Sustainable Development, 2*(1), 171–224.
Schiederig, T., Tietze, F., & Herstatt, C. (2012). Green innovation in technology and innovation management - an exploratory literature review. *R&D Management, 42*(2), 180–192.
Sezen, B., & Çankaya, S. Y. (2013). Effects of green manufacturing and eco-innovation on sustainability performance. *Procedia-Social and Behavioural Sciences, 99*, 154–163.
Special report: Global warming of 1.5-degree C. Summary for Policy makers. https://www.ipcc.ch/sr15/chapter/spm.
Sustainable development goals. (2022). https://www.un.org/sustainabledevelopment/climate-change/
Thistlethwaite, J. (2011). Counting the environment: The environmental implications of international accounting standards. *Global Environmental Politics, 11*, 75–97.
Triguero, A., Moreno-Mondéjar, L., & Davia, M. A. (2013). Drivers of different types of eco-innovation in European SMEs. *Ecological Economics, 92*, 25–33.
Tseng, M.-L., Huang, F.-H., & Chiu, A. S. F. (2012). Performance drivers of green innovation under incomplete information. *Procedia - Social and Behavioral Sciences, 40*, 234–250.
Ulph, A. (1996). Environmental policy and international trade when governments and producers act strategically. *Journal of Environmental Economics and Management, 30*(3), 265–281.

United Nations Framework Convention on Climate Change. https://unfccc.int/resource/ccsites/zimbab/conven/text/intro.htm#:~:text=They%20adopted%20the%20United%20Nations,the%20Convention%20received%20155%20signatures. Accessed 01.08 23.

Stokke, et al. (2005). Implementing the Climate Regime: International Compliance. London: Earthscan.

Van der Ven, H. (2014). Socializing the C-suite: Why some big-box retailers are "greener" than others. *Business and Politics, 16*, 31–63.

Vollenbroek, F. A. (2002). Sustainable development and the challenge of innovation. *Journal of Cleaner Production, 10*(3), 215–223.

Weng, M.-H., & Lin, C. Y. (2011). Determinants of green innovation adoption for small and medium-size enterprises (SMES). *African Journal of Business Management, 5*(22), 9154–9163.

What is the United Nations Framework convention on climate change?. United Nations Climate Change. https://unfccc.int/process-and-meetings/what-is-the-united-nations-framework-convention-on-climate-change. Accessed on 31.07.23.

World Commission on Environment and Development. (1987). *Our common future*. Oxford University Press. https://sustainabledevelopment.un.org/content/documents/5987our-common-future.pdf. Accessed 27.07.23

Zeng, S. X., Meng, X. H., Zeng, R. C., et al. (2011). How environmental management driving forces affect environmental and economic performance of SMEs: A study in the northern China district. *Journal of Cleaner Production, 19*(13), 1426–1437.

Zhou, C. (2019). Can intellectual property rights within climate technology transfer work for the UNFCCC and the Paris agreement? *International Environmental Agreements: Politics, Law and Economics, 19*, 107–122.

Dr. Monika Malik obtained her Ph.D. in chemistry and is currently Associate Professor and Deputy-Head of the Department of Applied Sciences and Humanities, Galgotias College of Engineering and Technology Greater Noida, Uttar Pradesh (India). She has been in the teaching profession for more than 21 years. Dr. Monika Malik has authored textbooks with Cengage Learning, a book chapter and published several research papers in peer-reviewed international journals.

Dr. Shelley Oberoi is a competent, seasoned educationist with 21 years of comprehensive experience in degree and engineering colleges in the field of chemistry. She is presently working with the K.C. College of Engineering and Management Studies and Research, Thane, Maharashtra (India) as an Associate Professor and Head of the Department for Humanities and Applied Sciences Department. She has authored books with Cengage Learning, has two patents, and has authored and presented many research papers in the field of chemistry at national and international conferences.

Climate Governance in the Digital Era

Linh Thi My Nguyen, Devmali Perera, and Dao Le Trang Anh

Abstract This Chapter provides insights into climate governance and the implications of emerging technologies such as Artificial Intelligence (AI) and Blockchain in influencing corporate environmental outcomes. We first offer an overview of the traditional corporate governance mechanisms in the context of increasing environmental challenges worldwide. We next define climate governance and discuss various mechanisms and prior findings on their effectiveness. We finally review the roles of the two cutting-edge technologies (AI and Blockchain) in climate governance. Potential applications are also discussed in this chapter.

1 Corporate Governance and Environmental Challenges

1.1 Overview of Corporate Governance Mechanisms

1.1.1 What Is Corporate Governance?

Effective Corporate Governance is critical for the success of any business. Research has found significant impacts of strong corporate governance on various corporate outcomes globally (e.g., Bhagat & Bolton, 2019; Khanchel El Mehdi, 2007; Ozkan, 2011). For example, Bhagat and Bolton (2019) show that directors' stock ownership drives a firm's future financial performance as such ownership can incentivize board members to perform their monitoring tasks better. Similarly, CEO and board characteristics are found to be significantly associated with non-financial performance (Environmental Social and Governance -ESG and Corporate Social Responsibility—CSR activities) (Gillan et al., 2021). So, what is the corporate governance? There is no universal definition of corporate governance, even though this concept has been

L. T. M. Nguyen (✉) · D. Perera · D. L. T. Anh
Department of Economics and Finance, The Business School, RMIT University Vietnam, Hanoi, Vietnam
e-mail: linh.nguyenthimy2@rmit.edu.vn; devmali.perera@rmit.edu.vn; anh.dao28@rmit.edu.vn

V. Q. Trinh (ed.), *Climate Governance and Corporate Eco-innovation*, Sustainable Finance, https://doi.org/10.1007/978-3-031-56423-9_5

widely studied. Many scholars primarily emphasize the control of executives to ensure they work for the best interests of shareholders (Daily et al., 2003). This is to tackle the well-known agency conflicts between shareholders and managers (Jensen & Meckling, 1976). However, corporate governance is also about how firms govern their resources to create value for their shareholders and stakeholders. We follow Daily et al. (2003, p. 371) to define corporate governance as "*the determination of the broad uses to which organizational resources will be deployed and the resolution of conflicts among the myriad participants in organizations*". We believe this definition provides a comprehensive understanding of corporate governance activities in a firm beyond the traditional view of executive management.

1.1.2 Corporate Governance Mechanisms

In this section, we discuss various traditional corporate governance mechanisms, which are mainly guided by the agency theory (Jensen & Meckling, 1976) and resource dependence theory (Pfeffer & Salancik, 2003) to oversee the behavior of executives and provide critical resources for firms. Drawing on the rich literature on strategic management and finance, scholars classify corporate governance mechanisms into three main groups: monitoring, incentives, and ownership (Coles et al., 2001).

First, firms/executives can be monitored internally and externally. Internal monitoring is mainly (but not limited to) about the board of directors and its composition to ensure the top executive team works for the shareholders' best interests. The board of directors represents the interests of shareholders. The top executive team reports directly to the board, and the board has the right to appoint and dismiss executives. Moreover, the board can provide resources based on board members' relevant knowledge and skills. Extant research has shown that the composition of the board matters. For instance, independent directors with different views and values can monitor better (Coles et al., 2001). Research also documents the relationship between busy directors—those who are appointed to multiple boards—and firm performance. For example, reducing the workload of directors, that is, less busy directors, is associated with better performance (Hauser, 2018). Directors from different cultures (board cultural diversity) are shown to add significant value to the board and firm (Dodd et al., 2022; Luo et al., 2021). However, there is also contradicting evidence that board cultural diversity worsens firm performance (Frijns et al., 2016). With external monitoring mechanisms, influential shareholders such as institutional investors who own a large portion of equity also play a significant role. Such blockholders can help reduce managerial myopia, which in turn improves the firm's economic outcomes (i.e., innovation) (Helling et al., 2020).

Second, providing appropriate incentives is another effective governance mechanism. According to the agency theory, managers can prioritize their interests over those of shareholders (agency conflicts), thus making sub-optimal decisions. As a result, in addition to having the board or other mechanisms to oversee the managers, one of the potential solutions is giving managers incentives to motivate them to work for the best interests of shareholders. Various incentive mechanisms align the interests of managers with those of shareholders, including bonuses that link to performance, stock options, and share ownership (Chari et al., 2019).

Last, share ownership is also a commonly used governance mechanism. This mechanism is related to the incentives mechanism, as executives owning shares are more motivated to contribute to the firm's success, which translates to their benefits. The ownership mechanism is applied to other stakeholders. For example, research has shown that stock options for directors can improve a firm's research and development (R&D) activities (Deutsch, 2007). It is also related to the monitoring mechanism, as holding a large portion of shares is associated with more power in monitoring the executive team.

These governance mechanisms are widely employed to better utilize organizational resources and oversee the management team. However, are such mechanisms still effective in governing firms in the context of increasing environmental risks? These mechanisms were originally designed to help firms accomplish financial outcomes that are theoretically different from social and environmental performance. In the next section, we will further discuss our context of interest: climate change, which is considered a grand challenge for human beings and its associated risks. We argue that increasing concerns about climate change risks challenge the traditional corporate governance model.

Box 1
Drawing on the rich literature on strategic management and finance, scholars classify corporate governance mechanisms into three main groups: Monitoring, incentives, and ownership.

1.2 Climate Change and Corporate Governance Challenges

1.2.1 Climate Change Risks

What is climate change? The United Nations defines climate change as "*long-term shifts in temperatures and weather patterns*",[1] which can happen naturally but is also due to human activity, such as burning fossil fuels. Climate change brings huge risks to almost all areas, including economic activities. According to the International Monetary Fund (IMF),[2] climate change is considered a "*global externality*" that can lead to substantial economic harm to all countries, especially the lower-income ones. Scholars have identified potential consequences of climate change, including sea level rise, tropical cyclones, extreme heat impacts, severe floods and droughts, oceanic and atmospheric circulation disruption, and even the collapse of ecosystems (DeFries et al., 2019).

---

[1] https://www.un.org/en/climatechange/what-is-climate-change.

[2] https://www.imf.org/en/Topics/climate-change/climate-and-the-economy.

For example, according to the National Oceanic and Atmospheric Administration (NOAA),[3] the global temperature has risen around 1 °C from 1901 to 2020. Temperature increase causing the destabilization and melting of ice sheets in West Antarctica and Greenland has contributed to global sea level rise. This can lead to flooding and threaten the lives of 600 million people along the coastlines (DeFries et al., 2019). Climate change already adversely influences human health, especially the most vulnerable groups, including children or those with preexisting health conditions (NOAA). In addition, according to the NOAA, severe climate conditions such as cyclones and floods can cause significant damage to the current infrastructures, such as roads, buildings, electrical grids, and internet systems. More importantly, these impacts co-occur, leading to even more severe consequences (DeFries et al., 2019).

1.2.2 Corporate Governance Challenges

The significant impacts of climate change on various aspects mentioned above pose significant risks to people, communities, and firms. However, from an economic perspective, up to date, we are unclear about the full range of economic risks from climate change (DeFries et al., 2019; Rising et al., 2022). According to Rising et al. (2022), there can be two main reasons: (1) time delay between physical climate change and economic impacts and (2) high uncertainty and incomplete understanding of such climate change processes. In particular, it can take considerable time to understand the physical changes caused by climate change and assess their economic impacts. Some changes may not show the impact clearly on a large scale in a short time. Incorporating such impacts into economic analyses also requires much time (Rising et al., 2022). Moreover, climate change is considered a grand challenge. Thus, the changing process is complicated and may not be fully understood by scientists over the short run. As a result, scientists may be more conservative in reporting and assessing the risks, thus leading to a poor understanding of their economic consequences (Rising et al., 2022).

Difficulty in understanding and quantifying the economic impacts of climate change can create more challenges for companies and business leaders in governing firms to tackle and manage the risk, and improve their environmental performance. While traditional corporate governance mechanisms are designed to focus more on maximizing shareholders' best interests, can such mechanisms also effectively address environmental risks and bring long-term value for firms and their stakeholders? Moreover, the potential differences between the expectations of shareholders who may prioritize maximizing stock value versus other stakeholders who may emphasize different social and environmental outcomes can pose challenges to the firm's existing corporate governance structure and mechanisms. Prior studies show that independent board members are found to undertake environmental initiatives

[3] https://www.noaa.gov/education/resource-collections/climate/climate-change-impacts.

just to show their legitimacy and regulation compliance rather than make actual improvements in the firm environmental performance (Haque & Ntim, 2018). Such challenges and evidence pose an urgent need for governance mechanisms that go beyond the traditional corporate governance mechanisms to particularly focus on climate risks (Albitar et al., 2023; Bui et al., 2020). We will discuss climate governance in our next section.

2 Climate Governance

2.1 *Global Definitions and Mechanisms of Climate Governance*

2.1.1 What Is Climate Governance?

The conventional perception of climate governance is that local actions are influenced by international agreements, national policies, the preferences of financial supporters, and the concepts promoted by non-governmental organizations and transnational networks (Anguelovski & Carmin, 2011). Hare et al. (2010) find that a legally enforceable international agreement is crucial for attaining the most substantial reductions in greenhouse gas emissions, aligning to restrain global warming below 2 °C or below 1.5 °C. Countries require well-defined, legally binding obligations within a mutually accepted framework with robust legal and institutional attributes. This is essential to ensure that nations' economic interests are subject to equitable and unbiased treatment.

The first global agreement to tackle climate change was the United Nations Framework Convention on Climate Change (UNFCCC) in 1992, which aimed to address climate change by controlling the greenhouse gas concentration in the atmosphere. In 1995, nations initiated negotiations to enhance the global response to climate change and, 2 years later, ratified the Kyoto Protocol. This Protocol legally obliges developed countries to meet specific emission reduction targets. The initial commitment period of the Protocol ran from 2008 to 2012, and the second commitment period started from 2013 to 2020. There are 197 Parties to the Convention and 192 Parties to the Kyoto Protocol.

The Paris Agreement, established on December 12, 2015, in Paris, represents the latest advancement in the UN climate change framework, building upon the groundwork laid by the Convention. The Paris Agreement marks a new direction in the global campaign against climate change. Following the COVID-19 crisis, Obergassel et al. (2021) show that the UNFCCC process, in conjunction with other international institutions, can facilitate a sustainable recovery in various ways.

The Intergovernmental Panel on Climate Change (IPCC) has emphasized governance's significance in enhancing climate mitigation and adaptation efforts (Intergovernmental Panel on Climate Change (IPCC), 2014). IPCC (2022) indicates that climate governance facilitates mitigation efforts through various channels, including offering a clear direction, establishing goals, integrating climate actions into different policy areas, bolstering regulatory certainty, establishing specialized organizations, and creating an environment conducive to financial mobilization.

As the Paris Agreement is being implemented, more countries are presenting plans to achieve carbon neutrality as their primary way of reducing emissions in the middle of the twenty-first century. Up until now, more than 130 countries and regions have committed to goals of either achieving net-zero emissions or carbon neutrality. Additionally, 119 countries have submitted new or updated plans for what they will do to fight climate change. This is taking global climate governance into a period focused on achieving carbon neutrality (Tan et al., 2022). The Paris Agreement acknowledges the importance of each country determining its climate goals, highlighting the central role of domestic politics in addressing climate change. Consequently, there has been a growing focus on domestic climate governance. It differs from global climate governance because it centers on the national government's significant authority in areas such as local administration, legislation, and the judicial system (Dubash, 2021).

2.1.2 Climate Governance Mechanisms

Researchers have conducted analyses about how climate governance is implemented in specific nations. According to Mildenberger (2021), nations have reorganized existing government agencies or established fresh institutions that supervise climate-related reforms. For instance, Teng and Wang (2021) examine China's climate governance evolution over the past three decades and find that the combination of climate change, energy conservation, and environmental quality promoted the establishment of a specialized climate agency. This agency became a central component of China's Five-Year Plan and was pivotal in climate policy communities. In India, Pillai and Dubash (2021) investigate the emergence and subsequent decline of climate-related institutions in India over three decades. Pillai and Dubash (2021) demonstrate that climate institutions have been added to pre-existing governmental structures and processes to support the bottom-up development of policies that simultaneously align with developmental goals and support mitigation efforts. Lockwood (2021) explores the interplay between politics and climate institutions. The author then emphasizes the importance of placing U.K. climate governance within a broader political and institutional framework. In the U.S., however, relatively few notable transformations have been in restructuring government agencies for climate reforms. Instead, climate institutions in the U.S. have evolved by introducing new mandates and policymaking processes within the framework of existing political institutions.

Box 2
Countries worldwide have reorganized existing government agencies or established fresh institutions that supervise climate-related reforms.

Corporations are also placing a greater emphasis on enhanced climate change practices in their strategic decision-making processes. Under governmental authorities' regulations, investors' expectations, and various stakeholders' attention, large corporations worldwide have adopted diverse carbon and energy management approaches. Sullivan and Gouldson (2017) indicate that external governance pressures can significantly influence corporations' internal governance processes, strategies, and actions. Nevertheless, the external governance pressures confronting these firms depend on geographical locations of operation, market positions, and primary stakeholders. With corporate cultures and typical characteristics, companies have different decisions regarding the significance of climate change in their business operations.

Box 3
Corporations are placing a greater emphasis on enhanced climate change practices in their strategic decision-making processes. Under governmental authorities' regulations, investors' expectations, and various stakeholders' attention, large corporations worldwide have adopted diverse carbon and energy management approaches.

Climate change disclosure is essential for governmental authorities and other stakeholders to investigate the firms' climate governance. The disclosure or reporting on carbon emissions offers insights into a company's activities concerning its environmental impact. This includes details about emission reduction strategies and the associated risks and opportunities. Such disclosures present a complex task for firm managers, managing risks and opportunities concurrently (Abbas et al., 2023). Since climate change disclosure can be regarded as societal pressure for firms, more and more studies have focused on different factors that influence corporate climate change disclosures. The prior research concludes that firms tend to provide more extensive climate change disclosures when they possess robust climate governance structures (Bui et al., 2020), environmental committees (Liao et al., 2015), larger and independent boards (Abbas et al., 2023), and more capable managerial boards (Daradkeh et al., 2023).

Box 4
Firms tend to provide more extensive climate change disclosures when they possess robust climate governance structures.

Climate governance is a dynamic and evolving field encompassing many entities and strategies. The current literature reflects the growing importance of addressing climate change at the global, national, and corporate levels. While the mechanisms of each climate change management level have been developing and improving, the researchers also focus on evaluating the effectiveness of current climate governance worldwide.

2.2 *Effectiveness of Climate Governance*

According to IPCC (2022), efficient climate institutions at the national level manage the coordination among various sectors, scales, and stakeholders, foster agreement for actions among a wide range of interests, and contribute to formulating strategies. Typically, these roles are fulfilled by independent national expert bodies and overall coordination entities that go beyond the scope of specific government departments. Meanwhile, supplementary institutions customize mitigation efforts at the sub-national level to suit local conditions and facilitate experimentation. However, they may face challenges related to fairness and limitations in resources and capacity. It is crucial to emphasize that effective governance necessitates sufficient institutional capabilities at all tiers of governance.

The degree of involvement of civil society groups, policymakers, businesses, and communities has a significant impact on garnering political backing for climate change mitigation efforts and, ultimately, on the outcomes of climate policies. The structural factors within a nation's circumstances and capabilities, such as economic resources, natural assets, political systems, cultural factors, and considerations related to gender, shape the extent and effectiveness of climate governance. Notably, climate-related legal actions are increasing. Some developed countries have witnessed many such cases while developing countries have seen fewer. In certain instances, these legal actions have influenced the direction and ambition of climate governance.

Box 5

The structural factors within a nation's circumstances and capabilities, such as economic resources, natural assets, political systems, cultural factors, and considerations related to gender, shape the extent and effectiveness of climate governance.

In governing climate change mitigation, existing research has predominantly conducted qualitative analyses of the mitigation policies adopted by countries, industries, and corporations (Tan et al., 2022). Government incentives and firms' reactions to climate governance policy vary across countries. According to Sullivan and Gouldson (2017), the incentives for U.S. corporations to address climate change are limited. This absence of robust regulatory or economic motivations to tackle climate change is evident in the approaches adopted by U.S. retailers in managing their greenhouse gas emissions. The predominant emphasis in U.S. energy-related investments remains on achieving short-term financial gains. On the contrary,

Japanese businesses are more attached to business legitimacy and the perception of adhering to ethical practices. Considering Japan's influential role in global climate change negotiations, Japanese firms must visibly exhibit their commitment to addressing climate change.

Regarding climate governance at the firm level, Bui et al. (2020) confirm the positive relationship between climate governance and carbon disclosure. Some other studies have identified a favorable connection between environmental disclosure and environmental performance. For instance, Al-Tuwaijri et al. (2004) observe that robust environmental performance is linked to more extensive disclosure of quantifiable pollution-related metrics. Similarly, findings from Clarkson et al. (2008) and Iatridis (2013) indicate a positive correlation between discretionary disclosure and environmental performance. Luo and Tang (2014) propose that a company's voluntary carbon disclosure reflects its inherent carbon performance, a viewpoint supported by Qian and Schaltegger (2017), who note a positive association between changes in carbon disclosure and subsequent improvements in performance, suggesting an external influence where disclosure motivates firms to enhance their carbon performance. Previous studies have also demonstrated that companies that provide more comprehensive carbon disclosures experience favorable financial outcomes, such as increased market valuation and reduced capital costs (Clarkson et al., 2008; Luo & Tang, 2014).

Box 6
There is academic evidence of the positive relationship between firm-level climate governance and corporate indicators (e.g., financial outcomes, carbon disclosure, carbon performance, environmental performance).

Nevertheless, companies are criticized for greenwashing issues when firms superficially comply with regulatory policies and respond to stakeholder pressure without demonstrating a true dedication to reducing carbon emissions (Haque & Ntim, 2018; Michelon et al., 2019). Highly emissions-intensive companies may persist in emitting high levels of carbon due to the inherent nature of their primary business activities. However, to convey a sense of responsibility to their stakeholders, these firms might enhance the disclosure of qualitative and non-measurable information to elucidate their carbon reduction, even without concrete metrics reflecting actual carbon reduction efforts. By doing so, these companies can project an image of environmental responsibility while maintaining their emissions-intensive operations (Bui et al., 2020).

Box 7
Companies are criticized for greenwashing issues when firms superficially comply with regulatory policies and respond to stakeholder pressure without demonstrating a true dedication to reducing carbon emissions.

In summary, effective climate governance at both national and sub-national levels relies on the coordination among various sectors, scales, and stakeholders. At the corporate level, climate governance may positively influence carbon disclosure, environmental performance, and firm financial performance. However, corporations should avoid greenwashing that "cheats" the stakeholders and conflicts with business ethics. Therefore, the effectiveness of climate governance depends on multifaceted factors, including institutional capabilities, stakeholder involvement, and corporations' dedication to achieving climate governance targets.

3 The Role of Emerging Technologies in Climate Governance

3.1 Challenges of Climate Governance

As highlighted in the previous sections, it is evident that climate change and climate governance currently rank as one of the most critical issues across all different levels, including global, regional, national, firm-level, and individual levels (Jänicke, 2017). Climate change risk is a risk that has no borders. The greenhouse gas emissions of one country can have negative consequences for all the nearby countries and even a country located far away. Hence, collaborative efforts to curtail climate change and introduce a proper and effective climate governance system encompassing all participants is the best way to mitigate the climate change risk (Jänicke, 2017).

Given the complexities and urgency of taking actions to mitigate climate risk, the active involvement of the governments in the climate adaptation process and developing public policies related to climate adaptation are vital now. Bauer et al. (2012) analyze information from ten countries in the Organization for Economic Co-operation and Development (OECD) and identify four key challenges in developing a climate adaptation policy for a country. First, climate adaptation policy requires aligning all other policies of a country, such as tourism, agriculture, healthcare, infrastructure development, etc., to achieve a country's sustainable development. Second, it is challenging to reach a consensus among these levels in the climate governance process (Jänicke, 2017). The differences in the political views, political objectives, level of economic development, and institutional structures of countries lead to this diversity in policies and diversity in commitment to implementing such policies among countries. Third, the high level of uncertainties related to climate scenarios makes it difficult to predict and develop better climate adaptation policies (Deser et al., 2012; Deser, 2020). Fourth, there is a challenge in obtaining the involvement and commitment from non-state stakeholders in the governance of adaptation. Participation and commitment of all stakeholders are required to achieve the effectiveness of climate governance policy.

In addition, the World Development Report (2010) also highlights the funding gap for climate finance in developed and developing countries. According to this report, the climate change mitigation process in developing countries requires approximately 140–175 US dollars billion per annum, which is linked with a financing need of 265–565 US dollars billion per annum as per their estimates in 2010. The UNFCCC report (2022) estimates that developing countries now require approximately six trillion US dollars by 2030 to meet their national commitments to reduce carbon emissions. Until now, developed countries have not been able to collate USD 100 billion targets for funding climate finance for developing countries as planned. Hence, collating adequate funds to support climate mitigation and adaptation is a significant challenge, particularly for developing countries, given their higher demand for funds to finance their developmental activities.

Box 8

There are five main challenges in developing a climate adaptation policy for a country:

- Climate adaptation policy requires aligning all other policies to achieve a country's sustainable development.
- It is challenging to reach a consensus among these multi-levels in the climate governance process due to the differences in the political views and objectives, levels of economic development, and institutional structures.
- The high level of uncertainties related to climate scenarios makes it difficult to predict and develop better climate adaptation policies.
- There is a challenge in obtaining non-state stakeholders' involvement and commitment in the adaptation governance.
- Collating adequate funds to support the climate mitigation and adaptation process is a significant challenge, particularly for developing countries, given their higher demand for funds to finance their developmental activities.

Finally, technology also plays a significant role in climate governance, presenting challenges and remarkable opportunities for stakeholders in this system. Technological developments have paved the way to reduce carbon emissions and developed potential opportunities for low-carbon solutions. Li et al. (2017) discuss the trade-off faced by China between economic growth and environmental protection. Given the constraints in human capital, fixed capital, fossil energy, and non-fossil energy in the country, technological development drives economic development while reducing carbon emissions. Multiple evidence from different countries proves that technological advancement positively impacts carbon emission efficiency (Chen & Lee, 2020; Ferreira et al., 2020; Li & Jiang, 2020).

We live in a digital era where every facet of our lives and business landscape is undergoing paradigm shifts introduced by disruptive technologies such as blockchain and artificial intelligence (AI). These developments in technology create several challenges concerning climate governance. First, when technology advances rapidly, it also requires continuous changes to the methods we use to measure carbon emissions at different levels. At the same time, it requires ongoing changes to the policies and regulations that govern the climate environments to align with these new developments. Another issue is the need for adequate data on carbon emissions and proper data management systems to collect, process, and analyze data required in this multi-level climate governance system. Finally, these technological advancements further widen the disparity between developed and developing countries. Bridging this technological gap between developed and developing countries is essential to achieve well-coordinated climate actions for all countries.

Box 9

Technology plays a significant role in climate governance, presenting both opportunities and challenges:

- Technological development is the driving force to achieve economic development while reducing carbon emissions. There is empirical evidence that technological advancement positively impacts carbon emission efficiency.
- These developments in technology create several challenges concerning climate governance.
- When technology is advancing rapidly, it also requires continuous changes to the methods we use to measure carbon emissions at different levels. At the same time, it requires ongoing changes to the policies and regulations that govern the climate environments to align with these new developments.
- There is a lack of adequate data on carbon emissions and proper data management systems to collect, process, and analyze data required in this multi-level climate governance system.
- Technological advancements widen the disparity between developed and developing countries.

In the next section, we discuss the role of the two most powerful technologies developed in this era, i.e., blockchain and AI, in shaping and reshaping traditional corporate governance and climate governance practices at different levels. We will also discuss some potential use cases of these technologies in governance and the challenges or limitations of the technologies.

3.2 Applications on Emerging Technologies in Climate Related Industries

3.2.1 Role of Blockchain

This section first explains blockchain and then describes some possible applications of this innovative technology in the climate action processes at different levels. Blockchain is an innovative technology providing a platform to share information securely. Transactions are recorded in a distributed ledger, meaning the authority to update the information in the blockchain is given to the participants or the nodes in the blockchain network. Cryptography and consensus mechanisms improve the security of data in this network. The blockchain technology gained its rising popularity with the emergence of Bitcoin in 2008 (Nakamoto & Bitcoin, 2008).

Box 10
Blockchain provides a platform to share information more securely.

- Transactions are recorded in a distributed ledger, meaning the authority to update the information in the blockchain is given to the participants or the nodes in the blockchain network.
- Cryptography and consensus mechanisms improve the security of data in this network.

The energy sector, regrettably, is one of the leading contributors to global greenhouse gas emissions. According to the IEA (2022) report on CO2 emissions, electricity and heat generation sector emissions increased to 14.6 Gt (Gigatons) in 2022 and, that was a 1.8% increase compared to the previous year. The driving factor of this increase was the shift from natural gas to coal to generate electricity due to the shortage of fossil fuels and natural gas supply in 2022. The ongoing conflict between Russia and Ukraine created a turbulent environment for the energy markets, given that Russia is the world's largest exporter of fossil fuels and natural gas. Hence, there is an increased urgency to promote renewable energy sources, adopt innovative technological solutions to enhance energy efficiency, and reduce emission levels in the energy sector (IEA, 2022). In this context, we will explore the potential of blockchain technology in introducing innovative solutions for this sector.

Box 11
There is an increased urgency to promote renewable energy sources, adopt innovative technological solutions to enhance energy efficiency and reduce emission levels in the energy sector.

There is a strand of literature examining the application of blockchain in the energy industry (Soto et al., 2021; Wang & Su, 2020). One potential blockchain application is to create a distributed energy system instead of traditional, centralized energy systems. Distributed energy system connects producers and users and allows peer-to-peer trading of electricity. This system also provides more traceability of the transactions, and reduces the cost of electricity due to the absence of intermediaries in the supply chain (Soto et al., 2021; Wang & Su, 2020). Brooklyn Microgrid in the US is a prominent example of a peer-to-peer electricity market where participants sell their excess solar energy, and consumers purchase it via an auction.[4] It lowers the cost of energy for the consumers and prosumers and reduces carbon emissions. Another example is Powerledger, a distributed energy system launched in Australia in 2017.[5] Powerledger owns its public blockchain for energy and provides peer-to-peer energy trading and tracking.

Box 12
One potential blockchain application is to create a distributed energy system instead of traditional, centralized energy systems. Distributed energy system connects producers and users, allows peer-to-peer trading of electricity, provide more traceability of the transactions, and reduces the cost of electricity due to the absence of intermediaries in the supply chain. Examples: Brooklyn microgrid (US) and Powerledger (Australia).

Another application of blockchain is in the electric vehicle (EV) market. China is the largest market for electric vehicles and then the US. According to IEA's Global Outlook report (2018), the estimated number of EVs on the road is 220 million by 2030. The growth of EVs in the future is inevitable due to their immense contribution to lowering carbon emissions and improving sustainability practices in the transport sector. However, a proper infrastructure system for charging batteries is still needed, along with uniform payment method and ability to accurately measure the cost of charging and with real-time data (IEA, 2018). By combining new energy companies and EV users, a blockchain technology-based charging ecosystem can solve these issues (Fu et al., 2020). This technology is currently adopted in Germany through their '*Share and Charge*' project. This project connects renewable energy sources into a power grid that runs on the Ethereum blockchain and allows EV owners to charge their batteries in private and public charging stations. This project is a winner as it improves the infrastructure for EV users while reducing the carbon emissions of the transport sector by promoting the use of EVs and renewable energy (Wang & Su, 2020).

Box 13
Another application of blockchain is in the electric vehicle (EV) market. However, a proper infrastructure system for charging batteries is still needed, along with uniform payment method ability to accurately measure the cost of charging and with real-time data. A blockchain technology-based charging ecosystem can solve these issues by combining new energy companies and EV users. Example: 'Share and charge' project (Germany).

[4] https://www.brooklyn.energy/about.

[5] https://www.powerledger.io/company/about.

World Economic Forum (2023) report on "*Blockchain for scaling climate action*" provides a detailed analysis of the relationship between blockchain and climate actions, discusses some real-world applications, and offers some recommendations for further development of blockchain usage in climate markets. According to this report, the main benefits of applying blockchain-based infrastructure are enhancing carbon data's trust, transparency, and credibility and reducing the intermediaries in the carbon value chain. In addition, the tokenization of carbon credits for individuals such as farmers and small firms allows them to participate in the digital carbon market and generate climate finance. This is not possible in the traditional carbon markets, as those markets are only accessible by large institutions with significant carbon credit.

Box 14
The main benefits of applying blockchain-based infrastructure are enhancing the trust, transparency, and credibility of carbon data and reducing the intermediaries in the carbon value chain.

Finally, the traditional economic systems measure the growth of a country through the GDP growth rate while overlooking the externalities arising during that economic development process. The world requires an economic system that prioritizes the sustainable use of resources and the enhancement of regenerative practices. The way forward for climate ecosystems will be Regenerative Finance (ReFi) ecosystems, which is much broader than just blockchain, to solve environmental and social issues. Ethereum Organization defines ReFi as "*a set of tools and ideas built on top of blockchains, that aim to create economies which are regenerative, rather than extractive or exploitative*".[6] The development of Web3 technology paved the way for the emergence of digital carbon markets that integrate blockchains, decentralized data storage systems, non-fungible tokens, decentralized organizations, decentralized finance systems and Refi systems (World Economic Forum, 2023). ReFi systems extend beyond the realms of green finance and green fintech. They encompass a decentralized finance system that focuses on reducing the impact on the environment while regenerating the natural resources that have been impacted by the activities of humans (Shih et al., 2023). Examples of such ReFi ecosystems include carbon market infrastructure projects (Toucan), blockchain marketplaces (Senken, Thallo), open MRV for forestation data (Open Forest protocol), and regenerative agriculture and lending for smallholder farmers (ReSeed, Ethic Hub).[7]

Box 15
The world requires an economic system that prioritizes the sustainable use of resources and the enhancement of regenerative practices. The way forward for climate ecosystems will be regenerative finance (ReFi) ecosystems, which is much broader than just blockchain, to solve environmental and social issues.

In summary, climate governance systems are exposed to drastic technological changes to mitigate carbon emissions better and manage climate-related activities at all levels. Leveraging green finance, green fintech, and ReFi systems would accelerate the achievement of sustainable development goals of the world. However, these technological changes also introduce another new challenge: the need for continuous updates to the regulations and policy frameworks related to these markets.

3.2.2 Role of Artificial Intelligence

Artificial intelligence (AI) emerges as a transformative technology evolving in every aspect of the economy, including climate governance. The applications of AI are still in its infancy and continuously evolving. This section explains AI and its current and potential applications in climate governance systems at different levels.

Let's first learn some terms. According to McKinsey & Company (2023), AI is "*a machine's ability to perform the cognitive functions we usually associate with human minds such as perceiving, reasoning, learning, interacting with an environment, problem-solving and even exercising creativity*". Generative AI is "*an AI model that generates content in response to a prompt. It's clear that generative AI tools like ChatGPT and DALL-E have the potential to change how a range of jobs are performed*" (McKinsey & Company, 2023).

The idea of AI dates back to the 1950s, when Alan Turing raised the question, "*can machines think*?" and introduced the Turing Test to ascertain if a computer can think like a human (Epstein et al., 2008). Research on AI has been ongoing, but the introduction of generative AI models such as ChatGPT is presently transforming the world. This section reviews the existing evidence on the AI application in corporate governance, climate governance, and climate change mitigation processes.

Box 16

- AI is "a machine's ability to perform the cognitive functions we usually associate with human minds such as perceiving, reasoning, learning, interacting with an environment, problem-solving and even exercising creativity".
- Generative AI is "an AI model that generates content in response to a prompt. It's clear that generative AI tools like ChatGPT and DALL-E have the potential to change how a range of jobs are performed".

The primary benefit of AI is its ability to collect, analyze, and interpret a complex and vast data set. The board of directors can efficiently utilize AI to improve their decision-making process with more accurate data and analysis (Di Prisco, 2019; McBride et al., 2022). AI can play an advisory role for the board of directors, and a well-developed AI-based information system can improve information transparency. However, there is a severe concern about the ethical and legal issues when delegating governance decisions to an AI-based system. The need for proper regulations, policy frameworks, or even guidelines aggravates this issue. Hickman and Petrin (2021) highlight that AI systems need to be created by considering the human agency and taking into account its technical capabilities, ability to protect the privacy of data, transparency, diversity, and equity, and AI systems should be able to contribute to the societal wellbeing at the end.

Box 17
The major benefit of AI is its ability to collect, analyze, and interpret complex and vast data sets. Its application to corporate governance could be (examples):

- The board of directors can efficiently utilize AI to improve their decision-making process with more accurate data and analysis.
- AI can play an advisory role for the board of directors.
- A well-developed AI-based information system can improve information transparency.

AI can offer significant benefits to energy and climate-related markets. AI can be utilized to solve the issues of lack of data and interoperability between data from different actors in climate governance systems and improve the data analytic capabilities for making informed decisions (McBride et al., 2022). One prominent example of an application is the Future of Sustainable Data Alliance (FoSDA)[8] launched in 2020 as a collaborative effort between Refinitiv and the World Economic Forum. The main objectives of this initiative are to promote standardization of data collection and provide relevant data for the appropriate parties to support achieving shared sustainable development goals. AI can also enhance the accuracy of weather forecasts (which is vital in extreme weather events such as floods, cyclones, hurricanes, earthquakes, etc.) and provide reliable early warning alerts (Nordgren, 2022). Ahmad et al. (2021) find that AI can contribute to the energy industry by improving the forecasting ability of demand and supply of electricity, thereby improving the efficiency in grid management, enhancing the integration between sustainable energy sources, data privacy, and improving data analysis by combining high-quality data sets.

Box 18
AI can potentially offer significant benefits to energy and climate-related markets:

- AI can be utilized to solve the issues of lack of data and interoperability between data from different actors in climate governance systems and improve the data analytic capabilities for making informed decisions.
- One prominent example of an application is the future of sustainable data Alliance (FoSDA).
- AI can improve the forecasting ability of demand and supply of electricity.

On a separate note, another noteworthy strand of emerging literature argues that AI plays a dual role in supporting climate change adaptation and increasing carbon emissions (Dhar, 2020; Nordgren, 2022). AI models require a large amount of computing power, and currently, most of this energy is generated using fossil fuels. Given the rapid expansion of AI across industries, it is vital that we need to prioritize utilizing renewable energy to reduce the carbon emission of AI. Nordgren (2022) also discusses the inequality of access to AI between developed and developing countries. The question is how we ensure developing countries can access these transformative technologies to adapt to their climate change mitigation process. This study also raises another possible dilemma that would arise in the future about who should be responsible for mitigating the climate impact of AI. Should it be the responsibility of the governments, companies who generate AI, or the users of AI, including firms, governments, and individuals?

Box 19
AI plays a dual role in supporting climate change adaptation and increasing carbon emissions.

- Prioritize utilizing renewable energy to reduce the carbon emission of AI.
- The issue of inequality of access to AI between developed and developing countries.
- Who should be responsible for mitigating the climate impact of AI?.

4 Conclusion

Firms (all types of firms, including large multinational companies and small and medium-sized firms) have a solemn responsibility to act to reduce the carbon footprint of their businesses. Research has shown that firms might require more than just traditional corporate governance to effectively tackle on going climate concerns. Instead, scholars have called for governance mechanisms focusing on climate issues. The multi-level climate governance system has a clear sustainable development goal: maintaining global warming levels below 2 °C or below 1.5 °C by reducing carbon emissions. However, due to the complex nature of climate change, it is not the responsibility of only a few actors in this system. Since the consequences of rising temperature and sea levels can be devastating, all countries and organizations should declare a 'climate emergency' situation and take necessary actions to meet their contributions to carbon reduction. These efforts will indeed provide additional benefits for the firms. For example, Saka and Oshika (2014) find that the disclosures of carbon management positively impact the market value of equity. Matsumura et al. (2014) document that the market value of firms disclosing their carbon emissions will be affected adversely, but the firms that do not disclose their carbon footprint will be more adversely affected in the market. Bose et al. (2023) also report an improvement in the climate strategy of a firm has a positive impact on the firm value.

The future of corporate governance and climate governance will face uncertainties due to the rapid advancement of technologies such as blockchain and AI and their applications in firms. Hence, the board of directors and/or senior managers must possess adequate knowledge of these technologies to successfully adopt the technologies to achieve sustainability goals at the firm level. It is essential to fully comprehend these technologies and adapt at the strategic level of the firms by realigning the business models instead of adopting these new technologies on an ad hoc basis. At the same time, firms must be cautious in applying these technologies as lacking a complete understanding of AI and its risks might lead to severe consequences later.

Declaration of Generative AI and AI-Assisted Technologies in the writing process for This Chapter The authors of this chapter have used Grammarly to proofread certain parts of the chapter. However, they declared that they did not use AI to create or write original and new manuscript content.

References

Abbas, A., Zhang, G. B., & Chengang, Y. (2023). Firm governance structures, earnings management, and carbon emission disclosures in Chinese high-polluting firms. *Business Ethics, the Environment & Responsibility*. https://doi.org/10.1111/beer.12582

Ahmad, T., Zhang, D., Huang, C., Zhang, H., Dai, N., Song, Y., & Chen, H. (2021). Artificial intelligence in sustainable energy industry: Status quo, challenges and opportunities. *Journal of Cleaner Production, 289*, 125834.

Albitar, K., Al-Shaer, H., & Liu, Y. S. (2023). Corporate commitment to climate change: The effect of eco-innovation and climate governance. *Research Policy, 52*(2), 104697. https://doi.org/10.1016/j.respol.2022.104697

Al-Tuwaijri, S. A., Christensen, T. E., & Hughes Ii, K. E. (2004). The relations among environmental disclosure, environmental performance, and economic performance: A simultaneous equations approach. *Accounting, Organizations and Society, 29*(5–6), 447–471. https://doi.org/10.1016/S0361-3682(03)00032-1

Anguelovski, I., & Carmin, J. (2011, May). Something borrowed, everything new: Innovation and institutionalization in urban climate governance. *Current Opinion in Environmental Sustainability, 3*(3), 169 – 175. https://doi.org/10.1016/j.cosust.2010.12.017

Bauer, A., Feichtinger, J., & Steurer, R. (2012). The governance of climate change adaptation in 10 OECD countries: Challenges and approaches. *Journal of Environmental Policy & Planning, 14*(3), 279–304. https://doi.org/10.1080/1523908X.2012.707406

Bhagat, S., & Bolton, B. (2019). Corporate governance and firm performance: The sequel. *Journal of Corporate Finance, 58*, 142–168. https://doi.org/10.1016/j.jcorpfin.2019.04.006

Bose, S., Burns, N., Minnick, K., & Shams, S. (2023). Climate-linked compensation, societal values, and climate change impact: International evidence. *Corporate Governance: An International Review, 31*(5), 759–785.

Bui, B., Houqe, M. N., & Zaman, M. (2020). Climate governance effects on carbon disclosure and performance. *The British Accounting Review, 52*(2), 100880. https://doi.org/10.1016/j.bar.2019.100880

Chari, M. D. R., David, P., Duru, A., & Zhao, Y. (2019). Bowman's risk-return paradox: An agency theory perspective. *Journal of Business Research, 95*, 357–375. https://doi.org/10.1016/j.jbusres.2018.08.010

Chen, Y., & Lee, C. C. (2020). Does technological innovation reduce CO2 emissions? Cross-country evidence. *Journal of Cleaner Production, 263*, 121550.

Clarkson, P. M., Li, Y., Richardson, G. D., & Vasvari, F. P. (2008). Revisiting the relation between environmental performance and environmental disclosure: An empirical analysis. *Accounting, Organizations and Society, 33*(4–5), 303–327. https://doi.org/10.1016/j.aos.2007.05.003

Coles, J. W., McWilliams, V. B., & Sen, N. (2001). An examination of the relationship of governance mechanisms to performance. *Journal of Management, 27*(1), 23–50. https://doi.org/10.1016/S0149-2063(00)00085-4

Daily, C. M., Dalton, D. R., & Cannella, A. A. (2003). Corporate governance: Decades of dialogue and data. *Academy of Management Review, 28*(3), 371–382. https://doi.org/10.5465/amr.2003.10196703

Daradkeh, H., Shams, S., Bose, S., & Gunasekarage, A. (2023). Does managerial ability matter for corporate climate change disclosures? *Corporate Governance: An International Review, 31*(1), 83–104. https://doi.org/10.1111/corg.12436

DeFries, R. S., Edenhofer, O., Halliday, A. N., Heal, G. M., Lenton, T., Puma, M., et al. (2019). The missing economic risks in assessments of climate change impacts.

Deser, C. (2020). Certain uncertainty: The role of internal climate variability in projections of regional climate change and risk management. Earth's. *Futures, 8*, e2020EF001854. https://doi.org/10.1029/2020EF001854

Deser, C., Phillips, A., Bourdette, V., & Teng, H. (2012). Uncertainty in climate change projections: The role of internal variability. *Climate Dynamics, 38*, 527–546. https://doi.org/10.1007/s00382-010-0977-x

Deutsch, Y. (2007). The influence of outside Directors' stock-option compensation on Firms' R&D. *Corporate Governance: An International Review, 15*(5), 816–827. https://doi.org/10.1111/j.1467-8683.2007.00611.x

Dhar, P. (2020). The carbon impact of artificial intelligence. *Nature Machine Intelligence, 2*(8), 423–425. https://doi.org/10.1038/s42256-020-0219-9

Di Prisco, D. (2019). Blockchain and AI: The technological revolution's impact on corporate governance relationships. *New Challenges in Corporate Governance: Theory and Practice*, 368–381. https://doi.org/10.22495/ncpr_47

Dodd, O., Frijns, B., & Garel, A. (2022). Cultural diversity among directors and corporate social responsibility. *International Review of Financial Analysis, 83*, 102337. https://doi.org/10.1016/j.irfa.2022.102337

Dubash, N. K. (2021). Varieties of climate governance: The emergence and functioning of climate institutions. *Environmental Politics, 30*(sup1), 301–325. https://doi.org/10.1080/09644016.2021.1979775

Epstein, R., Roberts, G., & Beber, G. (Eds.). (2008). *Parsing the turing test: Philosophical and methodological issues in the quest for the thinking computer*. Springer.

Ferreira, J. J., Fernandes, C. I., & Ferreira, F. A. (2020). Technology transfer, climate change mitigation, and environmental patent impact on sustainability and economic growth: A comparison of European countries. *Technological Forecasting and Social Change, 150*, 119770. https://doi.org/10.1016/j.techfore.2019.119770

Frijns, B., Dodd, O., & Cimerova, H. (2016). The impact of cultural diversity in corporate boards on firm performance. *Journal of Corporate Finance, 41*, 521–541. https://doi.org/10.1016/j.jcorpfin.2016.07.014

Fu, Z., Dong, P., & Ju, Y. (2020). An intelligent electric vehicle charging system for new energy companies based on consortium blockchain. *Journal of Cleaner Production, 261*, 121219.

Gillan, S. L., Koch, A., & Starks, L. T. (2021). Firms and social responsibility: A review of ESG and CSR research in corporate finance. *Journal of Corporate Finance, 66*, 101889. https://doi.org/10.1016/j.jcorpfin.2021.101889

Haque, F., & Ntim, C. G. (2018). Environmental policy, sustainable development, governance mechanisms and environmental performance. *Business Strategy and the Environment, 27*(3), 415–435.

Hare, W., Stockwell, C., Flachsland, C., & Oberthür, S. (2010). The architecture of the global climate regime: A top-down perspective. *Climate Policy, 10*(6), 600–614. https://doi.org/10.3763/cpol.2010.0161

Hauser, R. (2018). Busy directors and firm performance: Evidence from mergers. *Journal of Financial Economics, 128*(1), 16–37. https://doi.org/10.1016/j.jfineco.2018.01.009

Helling, A. R., Maury, B., & Liljeblom, E. (2020). Exit as governance: Do blockholders affect corporate innovation in large US firms? *Accounting & Finance, 60*(2), 1703–1725. https://doi.org/10.1111/acfi.12509

Hickman, E., & Petrin, M. (2021). Trustworthy AI and corporate governance: The EU's ethics guidelines for trustworthy artificial intelligence from a company law perspective. *European Business Organization Law Review, 22*(4), 593–625.

Iatridis, G. E. (2013). Environmental disclosure quality: Evidence on environmental performance, corporate governance and value relevance. *Emerging Markets Review, 14*, 55–75. https://doi.org/10.1016/j.ememar.2012.11.003

IEA. (2018). *Global EV Outlook 2018*. IEA. https://www.iea.org/reports/global-ev-outlook-2018, License: CC BY 4.0

IEA. (2022). *World energy outlook 2022*. IEA. https://www.iea.org/reports/world-energy-outlook-2022, License: CC BY 4.0 (report); CC BY NC SA 4.0

Intergovernmental Panel on Climate Change (IPCC). (2014). *Climate change 2014: Synthesis report. Contribution of working groups I, II and III to the fifth assessment report of the intergovernmental panel on climate change*. Cambridge University Press.

IPCC. (2022). Climate change 2022: Impacts, adaptation and vulnerability. Contribution of working group II to the sixth assessment report of the intergovernmental panel on climate change [H.-O. Pörtner, D.C. Roberts, M. Tignor, E.S. Poloczanska, K. Mintenbeck, A. Alegría, M. Craig, S. Langsdorf, S. Löschke, V. Möller, A. Okem, B. Rama (eds.)]. Cambridge University Press. Cambridge, UK and New York, NY, USA, 3056 pp. https://doi.org/10.1017/9781009325844.

Jänicke, M. (2017). The multi-level system of global climate governance–the model and its current state. *Environmental Policy and Governance, 27*(2), 108–121.

Jensen, M. C., & Meckling, W. H. (1976). Theory of the firm: Managerial behavior, agency costs and ownership structure. *Journal of Financial Economics, 3*(4), 305–360. https://doi.org/10.1016/0304-405X(76)90026-X

Khanchel El Mehdi, I. (2007). Empirical evidence on corporate governance and corporate performance in Tunisia. *Corporate Governance: An International Review, 15*(6), 1429–1441. https://doi.org/10.1111/j.1467-8683.2007.00655.x

Li, R., & Jiang, R. (2020). Investigating effect of R&D investment on decoupling environmental pressure from economic growth in the global top six carbon dioxide emitters. *Science of the Total Environment, 740*, 140053.

Li, Y., Wang, J., & Shi, J. (2017). Can China meet its 2020 economic growth and carbon emissions reduction targets? *Journal of Cleaner Production, 142*. 993–1001. https://doi.org/10.1016/j.jclepro.2016.08.018

Liao, L., Luo, L., & Tang, Q. (2015). Gender diversity, board independence, environmental committee and greenhouse gas disclosure. *The British Accounting Review, 47*(4), 409–424. https://doi.org/10.1016/j.bar.2014.01.002

Lockwood, M. (2021). A hard act to follow? The evolution and performance of UK climate governance. *Environmental Politics, 30*(sup1), 26–48. https://doi.org/10.1080/09644016.2021.1910434

Luo, K., Lim, E. K., Qu, W., & Zhang, X. (2021). Board cultural diversity, government intervention and corporate innovation effectiveness: Evidence from China. *Journal of Contemporary Accounting & Economics, 17*(2), 100256. https://doi.org/10.1016/j.jcae.2021.100256

Luo, L., & Tang, Q. (2014). Does voluntary carbon disclosure reflect underlying carbon performance? *Journal of Contemporary Accounting & Economics, 10*(3), 191–205. https://doi.org/10.1016/j.jcae.2014.08.003

Matsumura, E. M., Prakash, R., & Vera-Munoz, S. C. (2014). Firm-value effects of carbon emissions and carbon disclosures. *The Accounting Review, 89*(2), 695–724.

McBride, R., Dastan, A., & Mehrabinia, P. (2022). How AI affects the future relationship between corporate governance and financial markets: A note on impact capitalism. *Managerial Finance, 48*(8), 1240–1249.

McKinsey & Company. (2023). *What is AI?* McKinsey. https://www.mckinsey.com/featured-insights/mckinseyexplainers/what-is-ai

Michelon, G., Patten, D. M., & Romi, A. M. (2019). Creating legitimacy for sustainability assurance practices: Evidence from sustainability restatements. *European Accounting Review, 28*(2), 395–422. https://doi.org/10.1080/09638180.2018.1469424

Mildenberger, M. (2021). The development of climate institutions in the United States. *Environmental Politics, 30*(sup1), 71–92. https://doi.org/10.1080/09644016.2021.1947445

Nakamoto, S., & Bitcoin, A. (2008). A peer-to-peer electronic cash system. *BIT, 4*(2), 15. https://bitcoin.org/bitcoin.pdf

Nordgren, A. (2022). Artificial intelligence and climate change: Ethical issues. *Journal of Information, Communication and Ethics in Society, 21*(1), 1–15.

Obergassel, W., Hermwille, L., & Oberthür, S. (2021). Harnessing international climate governance to drive a sustainable recovery from the COVID-19 pandemic. *Climate Policy, 21*(10), 1298–1306. https://doi.org/10.1080/14693062.2020.1835603

Ozkan, N. (2011). CEO compensation and firm performance: An empirical investigation of UK panel data. *European Financial Management, 17*(2), 260–285. https://doi.org/10.1111/j.1468-036X.2009.00511.x

Pfeffer, J., & Salancik, G. R. (2003). *The external control of organizations: A resource dependence perspective*. Stanford University Press.

Pillai, A. V., & Dubash, N. K. (2021). The limits of opportunism: The uneven emergence of climate institutions in India. *Environmental Politics, 30*(sup1), 93–117. https://doi.org/10.1080/09644016.2021.1933800

Qian, W., & Schaltegger, S. (2017). Revisiting carbon disclosure and performance: Legitimacy and management views. *The British Accounting Review, 49*(4), 365–379. https://doi.org/10.1016/j.bar.2017.05.005

Rising, J., Tedesco, M., Piontek, F., & Stainforth, D. A. (2022). The missing risks of climate change. *Nature, 610*(7933), 643–651. https://doi.org/10.1038/s41586-022-05243-6

Saka, C., & Oshika, T. (2014). Disclosure effects, carbon emissions and corporate value. *Sustainability Accounting, Management and Policy Journal, 5*(1), 22–45. https://doi.org/10.1108/SAMPJ-09-2012-0030

Shih, C., Gwizdalski, A., & Deng, X. (2023). Building a sustainable future: Exploring green finance, regenerative finance, and green financial technology (May 15, 2023). World scientific annual review of Fintech (Forthcoming), Nanyang Business School Research Paper No. 23–18, Available at SSRN: https://ssrn.com/abstract=4449096 or doi:10.2139/ssrn.4449096

Soto, E. A., Bosman, L. B., Wollega, E., & Leon-Salas, W. D. (2021). Peer-to-peer energy trading: A review of the literature. *Applied Energy, 283*, 116268.

Sullivan, R., & Gouldson, A. (2017). The governance of corporate responses to climate change: An international comparison. *Business Strategy and the Environment, 26*(4), 413–425. https://doi.org/10.1002/bse.1925

Tan, X. C., Wang, Y., Gu, B. H., Kong, L. S., & Zeng, A. (2022). Research on the national climate governance system toward carbon neutrality—A critical literature review. *Fundamental Research, 2*(3), 384–391. https://doi.org/10.1016/j.fmre.2022.03.010

Teng, F., & Wang, P. (2021). The evolution of climate governance in China: Drivers, features, and effectiveness. *Environmental Politics, 30*(sup1), 141–161. https://doi.org/10.1080/09644016.2021.1985221

UNFCCC. (2022). *Summary and recommendations by the standing committee on finance: Fifth biennial assessment and overview of climate finance flows*. UNFCCC.

Wang, Q., & Su, M. (2020). Integrating blockchain technology into the energy sector—from theory of blockchain to research and application of energy blockchain. *Computer Science Review, 37*, 100275.

World development report. (2010). *Development and climate change*. World Bank. http://documents.worldbank.org/curated/en/201001468159913657/World-development-report-2010-development-and-climate-change

World Economic Forum. (2023). *Blockchain for scaling climate action*. World Economic Forum. https://www.weforum.org/whitepapers/blockchain-for-scaling-climate-action/

Dr. Linh Nguyen is a Lecturer and Senior Program Manager (Finance) at RMIT University, Vietnam. She is also a CFA charterholder, regular member of CFA Institute, and CFA Society Melbourne. Linh holds a PhD degree at QUT Business School, Queensland University of Technology, Australia. Her work has been published in journals like: Technological Forecasting and Social Change, Journal of International Financial Markets, Institutions and Money, Accounting and Finance, Finance Research Letters. Linh also serves as an editorial board member of Review of Behavioral Finance journal. Her research interests include sustainable finance, behavioral finance, corporate governance, and innovation.

Dr. Devmali Perera is a Lecturer in Finance at RMIT University Vietnam, holds PhD in Finance and MCOM in Finance from the University of Canterbury, New Zealand and MBA in Finance from the University of Colombo, Sri Lanka. She holds prior academic roles in University of Canterbury, New Zealand and the University of Sri Jayewardenepura, Sri Lanka. Her research expertise encompasses a broad spectrum, including agricultural commodity markets, international finance, financial technology, and meta-analysis.

Dr. Dao Le Trang Anh is a lecturer in Finance at The Business School, RMIT University, Hanoi, Vietnam and a visiting lecturer at Lincoln University, New Zealand. She earned her MSc. Financial Forecasting and Investment at the University of Glasgow, the UK, and her PhD in Accounting and Finance (with Dean's List) at Lincoln University, New Zealand. She is awarded "Literati Award Winners 2022" for Outstanding Paper of Journal of Economic Studies. Dr. Anh is Associate Editor for International Journal of Social Economics. Dr. Anh's research expertise spans across corporate finance, financial economics, and Asian studies.

Part II
Case Studies and Research on Climate Governance and Eco-innovation

Achieving the Impossible: Perils of Eco-innovation and Transformational Impact of Charismatic Leadership

Tabish Zaman, Ngan Duong Cao, and Thi Tuong Giang Trinh

Abstract This Chapter provides an overview of the role of charismatic leadership in corporate eco-innovation. In our pursuit of elucidating the concept of eco-innovation, we explore how charismatic leadership can catalyse corporate strategies in the realm of sustainability and contribute to establishing a robust framework for eco-innovation. The exploration is rooted in a theoretical discourse. It aims to illuminate the theoretical linkage between charismatic leadership attributes and their hypothesized impact on fostering sustainability-oriented initiatives within organizational structures, as well as elucidating the potential pathways through which charismatic leadership might facilitate and encourage eco-innovation strategies. Through systematically exploring this subject, we aim to provide a more insightful and professionally grounded perspective on the intersection of charismatic leadership, sustainability, and eco-innovation.

1 Introduction

Sustainability, often hailed as one of the most pressing global challenges, has posed a significant dilemma for policymakers, politicians, and the wider public (Proctor et al., 2015). Despite the exponential growth in sustainability literature, there remains a glaring gap between theory and practical implementation (Hysa et al., 2020; Purvis et al., 2019). Sustainability, in its essence, refers to the capacity of

T. Zaman
Anglia Ruskin University Faculty of Business and Law, Cambridge campus, Cambridge, UK
e-mail: tabish.zaman@aru.ac.uk

N. D. Cao (✉)
University of Bath School of Management, Bath, UK
e-mail: n.d.cao@bath.ac.uk

T. T. G. Trinh
Durham University International Study Centre, Durham University, Durham, UK
e-mail: tuong.g.trinh@durham.ac.uk

V. Q. Trinh (ed.), *Climate Governance and Corporate Eco-innovation*, Sustainable Finance, https://doi.org/10.1007/978-3-031-56423-9_6

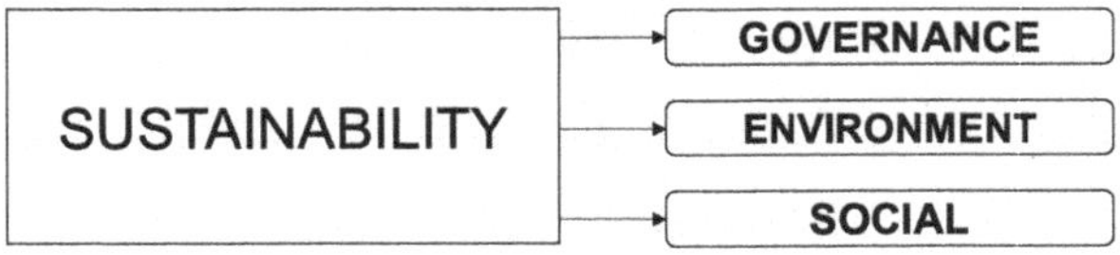

Fig. 1 The three pillars of sustainability. *Source:* Purvis et al. (2019)

systems and processes to endure over an extended period, ensuring a long-term future. It encompasses the idea of persistence and endurance, not only in environmental terms but also in social and economic contexts. Sustainability is not merely an abstract concept; it embodies the tangible and intangible facets that shape our world (Giovannoni & Fabietti, 2013). It is about finding the delicate balance between economic growth, environmental protection, and social equity (Barrier, 2017). One of the seminal frameworks in sustainability is the three pillars model, consisting of environmental, social, and governance (ESG) aspects. These pillars are interconnected and interdependent, forming the foundation of sustainable practices (Fig. 1):

A) *Environmental Sustainability*: This pillar focuses on minimizing negative impacts on the environment, conserving natural resources, reducing pollution, and mitigating climate change. Businesses play a pivotal role in adopting eco-friendly practices, such as reducing greenhouse gas emissions, optimizing resource use, and adopting renewable energy sources.
B) *Social Sustainability*: Social sustainability pertains to fostering equitable and inclusive societies (Wamsler, 2020). This involves fair labor practices, diversity and inclusion, community engagement, and ensuring the well-being of employees, customers, and local communities (Desiderio et al., 2022). Companies are expected to demonstrate social responsibility by addressing issues like labor rights, human rights, and social justice (Panapanaan et al., 2003).
C) *Governance Sustainability*: Governance sustainability centers around effective corporate governance, transparency, and accountability (Solomon, 2020). It encompasses ethical decision-making, regulatory compliance, and responsible management practices (Naciti, 2019). Maintaining high governance standards builds trust with stakeholders and reduces the risk of financial and reputational crises (Gangi et al., 2019).

2 Background

2.1 Integration of Sustainability in Corporate Strategies

Integrating sustainability into corporate strategies represents a pivotal paradigm shift in contemporary business operations (Calabrese et al., 2019). Historically, sustainability has often occupied a peripheral role in corporate agendas, with businesses resorting to fragmented and ad-hoc initiatives primarily aimed at bolstering their environmental and social credentials (Ahlström & Monciardini, 2021; Golgeci et al., 2021). However, in recent years, a noticeable transformation has begun to take shape as corporations increasingly recognize sustainability as an ethical obligation and a strategic imperative.

Motivated by a confluence of factors, including resource constraints, tightening regulatory frameworks, growing consumer demand for sustainable products and services, the necessity for efficient corporate governance, and the call for greater social responsibility, companies are departing from reactive approaches toward sustainability integration (Sana, 2020; Zhan & Tang, 2013). One key driver of this shift is the realization that sustainability is inexorably linked to long-term business success (Avery & Bergsteiner, 2011; Lloret, 2016). Beyond the moral obligation to operate responsibly, firms are recognizing that sustainable practices can drive financial performance, enhance brand reputation, and fortify resilience in a rapidly changing business landscape (Sroufe & Gopalakrishna-Remani, 2019).

The first facet of this transformation involves embedding sustainability principles into the core of corporate strategies (Lozano, 2012). To achieve this, businesses are recalibrating their goals, aligning them with Environmental, Social, and Governance (ESG) criteria, and enshrining sustainability as a fundamental driver of their operations. A prime example is the integration of sustainability metrics into performance evaluations, tying executive compensation to ESG targets, and explicitly incorporating sustainability objectives into corporate mission statements and strategic plans (Büyüközkan & Karabulut, 2018; Zhou et al., 2012). Furthermore, successful companies are extending their sustainability commitments beyond mere compliance with regulations (Aureli et al., 2020; Boström et al., 2015).

Box 1
Businesses are recalibrating their goals, aligning them with environmental, social, and governance (ESG) criteria, and enshrining sustainability as a fundamental driver of their operations.

They proactively seek innovative solutions to minimize environmental impacts, address social inequalities, and uphold strong governance practices. This proactivity is driven by a more profound understanding that sustainability challenges are not merely ethical or regulatory concerns but core business risks and opportunities (Haldar, 2019). A notable aspect of sustainability integration is the shift away from a narrow focus on short-term profitability (Stubbs, 2019). While it is crucial for businesses to remain financially viable, sustainability demands a broader perspective that acknowledges the interconnectedness of environmental, social, and economic dimensions. This perspective has given rise to the triple bottom line concept, emphasizing that businesses should account for their social and environmental impacts alongside financial performance (Lopez-Cabrales & Valle-Cabrera, 2020).

Moreover, adopting sustainability principles necessitates an organizational culture that fosters continuous improvement and embraces responsible practices as a core value. Leading firms are implementing employee sustainability training programs, fostering cross-functional collaboration to address sustainability challenges, and ensuring that sustainability considerations are embedded in decision-making processes at all levels. A telling example of this shift is the growing prominence of Chief Sustainability Officers (CSOs) within corporate leadership structures. These executives are tasked with championing sustainability strategies, overseeing ESG reporting, and driving innovation in sustainable business practices. Their presence underscores the elevation of sustainability from a peripheral concern to a central aspect of corporate governance.

Box 2

Chief sustainability officers (CSOs) within corporate leadership structures are tasked with championing sustainability strategies, overseeing ESG reporting, and driving innovation in sustainable business practices.

Case studies and real-world examples further illustrate the significance of sustainability integration (Chatty et al., 2022).

Take, for instance, *Unilever*, a global consumer goods company. Unilever's Sustainable Living Plan not only commits the company to reducing its environmental footprint but also aims to enhance the well-being of over a billion people worldwide by 2020 (Lawrence et al., 2018). This initiative has not only garnered accolades for Unilever's commitment to sustainability but has also delivered tangible benefits, including cost savings, brand loyalty, and market competitiveness (Aust et al., 2018).

Similarly, *Patagonia*, an outdoor apparel company, has made sustainability a cornerstone of its business strategy (Rattalino, 2018). It has embraced transparency, sustainability certifications, and ethical sourcing, all of which resonate strongly with its customer base. Patagonia's commitment to sustainability has not only bolstered its reputation as a socially responsible brand but has also translated into robust financial performance, demonstrating that sustainability can be a source of competitive advantage (O'Rourke & Strand, 2017).

These examples underscore the idea that sustainability integration is not merely an altruistic endeavour but a pragmatic business decision (Engert et al., 2016). Companies that effectively integrate sustainability principles into their strategies are better positioned to thrive in the evolving business landscape (Asif et al., 2011). The path to sustainability integration is, however, fraught with challenges. One persistent hurdle is the perception that sustainability initiatives come at a high cost (Sodiq et al., 2019). While there may be upfront investments required, these are increasingly seen as wise expenditures that yield long-term returns in terms of cost savings, risk mitigation, and market competitiveness. In many cases, sustainability initiatives have demonstrated a positive return on investment (Chernysheva et al., 2019).

Another challenge arises from the dynamic nature of sustainability itself (Pascual et al., 2023). Environmental and social issues evolve continuously, requiring businesses to remain adaptable and responsive (Velenturf & Purnell, 2021). Staying attuned to emerging sustainability trends, such as climate change mitigation, circular economy practices, and ethical supply chain management, is imperative for companies committed to long-term sustainability (Barauskaite & Streimikiene, 2021).

Box 3
Sustainability integration is not merely an altruistic Endeavour but a pragmatic business decision. Companies that effectively integrate sustainability principles into their strategies are better positioned to thrive in the evolving business landscape.

2.2 *Theoretical Framework*

The intersection of leadership, sustainability, and corporate performance has garnered significant attention in recent years (Nguyen et al., 2021; Pinto, 2019). Charismatic leadership, characterized by visionary and inspirational qualities, has been recognized as a potent force in shaping organizational culture and driving performance (Ly, 2020). Within the context of sustainability, charismatic leaders have the potential to inspire organizational commitment to eco-innovation and ESG practices (Dan, 2023; DuBrin, 2022) Research has indicated that charismatic leadership is positively associated with corporate social responsibility (CSR) initiatives and sustainability efforts (Jamal & Abu Bakar, 2017; Le Blanc et al., 2021). However, it is crucial to consider the cultural dimension, as the endorsement and expectation of charismatic leadership vary across countries.

In an era defined by the imperative of sustainability, the dynamic interplay between leadership, cultural values, and corporate performance has taken center stage in academic research and practical corporate strategy (Eisenbeiss et al., 2015). Central to this discourse is the concept of charismatic leadership and its influence on eco-innovation and ESG performance. This research context explores the intricate relationships between culturally endorsed charismatic leadership, sustainability, and corporate outcomes, elucidating how the endorsement of charismatic leadership within different cultural contexts can drive eco-innovation and foster enhanced ESG performance.

At the heart of this context lies the notion that charismatic leadership, characterized by visionary, inspirational, and transformational qualities, serves as a potent catalyst for sustainability efforts within organizations (Dalati, 2015; Ytterstad & Olaisen, 2023). Research suggests that charismatic leaders have the unique ability to articulate a compelling vision of a sustainable future, igniting a sense of purpose and passion among employees. Leaders' own behaviours and actions energise the environment within to achieve higher goals and objectives, resulting in individuals being intrinsically motivated and engaging in innovative behaviour (Amabile et al., 1996).

While Arthur Schlesinger underlined the importance of charismatic leadership, sociologist Mark Weber defined 'charismatic organisation' as one that comes into being due to the personal magnetism of the person leading it (McCulloch, 2016). Weber or Schlesinger—the importance of charisma in leaders or firms has forever piqued scholarly interest, leading to the development of a range of theoretical arguments in the realm of executive leadership and its impact on firms (Javidan and Waldman, 2003; Meslec et al., 2020; Wivel and Grøn, 2021). The diverse effect of charismatic leadership, also referred to as transformational in its effect, has been fully established in the literature, highlighting its impetus in generating radical changes (Fiol et al., 1999).

Box 4
Charismatic leaders, characterized by visionary, inspirational, and transformational qualities, can play a pivotal role in fostering a commitment to sustainability and innovation within their organizations. Research suggests that charismatic leaders have the unique ability to articulate a compelling vision of a sustainable future, igniting a sense of purpose and passion among employees.

One emerging area of research explores the influence of culturally endorsed charismatic leadership on firms' eco-innovation and ESG performance. This theoretical work offers an overview of this evolving domain, focusing on a key proposition:

2.2.1 Firms Operating in Countries That Emphasize Charismatic Leadership Tend to Achieve Stronger Eco-innovation and ESG Performance

The impact of culturally endorsed charismatic leadership on firms' eco-innovation and ESG performance is a dynamic area of study within the realm of leadership and sustainability (Al-Najjar & Salama, 2022). The proposition posits that firms operating in countries where charismatic leadership is strongly endorsed or desired, influenced by cultural norms, tend to exhibit stronger eco-innovation and ESG performance. This assertion underscores the influence of cultural contexts in shaping leadership preferences and behaviors. Charismatic leaders, known for their visionary and inspirational qualities, can play a pivotal role in fostering a commitment to sustainability and innovation within their organizations (McClean & Collins, 2019). Research has shown that the cultural endorsement of charismatic leadership varies significantly across countries, impacting the extent to which charismatic leaders are able to drive eco-innovative practices and ESG performance (Mittal, 2015; Stephan & Pathak, 2016). As some cultures place a higher emphasis on charismatic leadership styles, others prioritize different leadership attributes, creating a dynamic interplay between cultural norms and leadership dynamics (Dimitrov, 2015).

However, the cultural context in which organizations operate plays a pivotal role in determining the degree of influence that charismatic leaders can exert on sustainability initiatives (Warrick, 2017). Cultural values and norms shape leadership preferences and behaviors. Some cultures place a pronounced emphasis on charismatic leadership, valuing leaders who possess visionary qualities and inspire organizational commitment to sustainability (Tortola & Pansardi, 2019). In contrast, other cultures may prioritize different leadership attributes, potentially limiting the impact of charismatic leadership in driving eco-innovation and ESG performance (Visser, 2017). Thus, the endorsement and expectation of charismatic leadership vary significantly across countries, underscoring the dynamic and culturally contingent nature of this leadership style (Stephan & Pathak, 2016). Building on these foundational concepts, an empirical framework emerges, shedding light on the mechanisms through which culturally endorsed charismatic leadership shapes sustainability governance and cultivates a stakeholder-centered culture (Papagiannakis & Lioukas, 2018). This framework posits that firms operating in countries where charismatic leadership is culturally valued are more likely to encourage the development of robust sustainability governance structures. Sustainability governance comprises policies, procedures, and mechanisms integrating sustainability principles into organizational decision-making processes and strategies. Charismatic leaders in such cultural contexts are predisposed to advocate for and implement sustainability governance practices, facilitating aligning sustainability goals with the organizational agenda (Tuan, 2019).

Box 5

Some cultures place a pronounced emphasis on charismatic leadership, valuing leaders who possess visionary qualities and inspire organizational commitment to sustainability. In contrast, other cultures may prioritize different leadership attributes, potentially limiting the impact of charismatic leadership in driving eco-innovation and ESG performance. Thus, the endorsement and expectation of charismatic leadership vary significantly across countries, underscoring the dynamic and culturally contingent nature of this leadership style.

Overall, charismatic leadership brings a transformative dimension to organizations, particularly when it comes to sustainability (Ekmekcioglu et al., 2018). Charismatic leaders are visionary, inspiring, and capable of galvanizing teams toward common objectives. They communicate a compelling vision of a sustainable future and instill a sense of purpose and passion among employees (Nikoloski, 2015). Charismatic leaders excel in fostering a culture of innovation, risk-taking, and unwavering commitment to sustainable practices (Nisbett & Walmsley, 2016). One of the critical attributes of charismatic leadership is the ability to envision and communicate a future state where sustainability is at the core of an organization's identity (Skinner et al., 2018). They articulate a clear and motivating sustainability narrative that resonates with employees, stakeholders, and the wider community. This narrative acts as a guiding star, aligning organizational efforts with sustainability goals and creating a shared sense of responsibility (Kantabutra, 2020). Charismatic leaders also excel

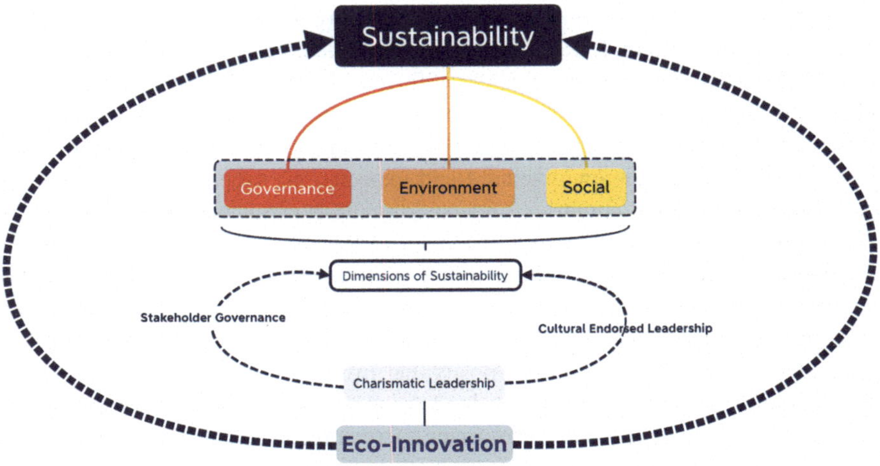

Fig. 2 Theoretical framework linking eco-innovation and sustainability mediated by charismatic leadership

in modelling the behaviors they advocate. Their personal commitment to sustainability serves as a powerful example, inspiring employees to embrace eco-friendly practices and align their actions with the organization's sustainability objectives. In essence, charismatic leadership elevates sustainability from a mere organizational goal to a collective mission that transcends individual roles and responsibilities (Luu et al., 2019; Shamir & Howell, 1999). See Fig. 2.

2.3 *Discussion: Sustainability-Driven Leadership Through Eco-innovation*

Eco-innovation represents a paradigm shift in how organizations approach sustainability (Pichlak & Szromek, 2022). It encompasses the creative integration of environmentally responsible solutions into the core of a firm's operations (Mady et al., 2023). Eco-innovative initiatives span diverse sectors, from energy-efficient technologies and sustainable materials to waste reduction strategies and circular business models (Karttunen et al., 2021). What sets eco-innovation apart is its ability to align environmental and business objectives seamlessly (Zhang et al., 2023). Rather than viewing sustainability as a constraint, eco-innovation reframes it as an opportunity for growth, competitive advantage, and long-term resilience (Peyravi et al., 2023). Eco-innovation is not confined to product development; it extends to operational practices and the adoption of sustainable supply chain management (Nagano & Iacono, 2019). This holistic approach considers the entire lifecycle of products and services, from conception and design to production, consumption, and disposal. As a result, eco-innovation contributes to reduced resource consumption, minimized environmental impact, and the creation of products that resonate with eco-conscious consumers. The magic happens in the synergy between eco-innovation and charismatic leadership (Bucea-Manea-Ţoniş et al., 2021). Charismatic leaders, with their visionary outlook, are instrumental in championing eco-innovative initiatives within their organizations. They create an environment where employees are not only encouraged but excited to explore sustainable solutions to environmental challenges. The culture they cultivate values creativity, risk-taking, and a relentless pursuit of sustainable practices.

One of the critical roles of charismatic leaders in the realm of eco-innovation is the *transformation of mindset* (Visser, 2017). They inspire employees to perceive sustainability not as a limitation but as an opportunity for growth and differentiation in the market. This shift in perspective is pivotal in motivating individuals to explore novel ideas, experiment with sustainable technologies, and integrate eco-friendly practices into their daily work. The visionary guidance of charismatic leaders helps employees understand that sustainability is not merely a compliance requirement but a strategic imperative that aligns with both ecological and business objectives. Moreover, charismatic leaders serve as custodians of organizational purpose (Carroll et al., 2008). Their unwavering commitment to sustainability ensures that eco-innovation remains at the forefront of the organizational agenda (Munodawafa & Johl, 2019). This sustained focus reinforces the integration of sustainable practices into every aspect of the organization, from product development and production to marketing and customer engagement. In turn, eco-innovation bolsters the influence of charismatic leadership.

Box 6

One of the critical roles of charismatic leaders in the realm of eco-innovation is the transformation of mindset. They inspire employees to perceive sustainability not as a limitation but as an opportunity for growth and differentiation in the market. This shift in perspective is pivotal in motivating individuals to explore novel ideas, experiment with sustainable technologies, and integrate eco-friendly practices into their daily work.

The innovative solutions that arise from eco-innovation efforts enhance an organization's environmental credentials and contribute to its reputation as a sustainability leader (Carrillo-Hermosilla et al., 2009; Hojnik & Ruzzier, 2016). This reputation, in turn, reinforces the charismatic leader's position as a driving force behind the organization's sustainability initiatives. The fusion of eco-innovation and charismatic leadership constitutes a powerful mechanism for advancing sustainability within organizations (Pichlak, 2021). Eco-innovation offers a strategic approach to aligning ecological and business objectives, while charismatic leadership provides the vision, inspiration, and cultural transformation needed to drive eco-innovation forward (Harsanto et al., 2022; Yuanyuan et al., 2022). Together, they create a symbiotic relationship that not only reduces environmental footprints but also strengthens corporate sustainability (Wang et al., 2021). In an era where sustainability is a defining criterion for organizational success, this nexus of eco-innovation and charismatic leadership represents a compelling path toward sustainability excellence (Mi et al., 2019).

Box 7
Eco-innovation offers a strategic approach to aligning ecological and business objectives, while charismatic leadership provides the vision, inspiration, and cultural transformation needed to drive eco-innovation forward. Together, they create a symbiotic relationship that not only reduces environmental footprints but also strengthens corporate sustainability. In an era where sustainability is a defining criterion for organizational success, this nexus of eco-innovation and charismatic leadership represents a compelling path toward sustainability excellence.

While the debate continues to evolve from a leadership perspective, an increased number of firms and investors have recognised sustainability as a priority but fraught with risk and opportunities (Charles et al., 2017; Elkington, 2020) It also underlines the lack of organisational structure contained within firms aimed to address sustainability and its dimensions as a critical business issue (Carayannis et al., 2015). It should be noted that organisations pushing for sustainability have mostly focused on investor relations, public relations, and social responsibility (Pompper, 2015). In these contexts, the key commitment for a successful sustainable firm not only involves managing stakeholder communication, target setting or reporting but, more critically, leadership engaging proactively and attempting to create measurable impact. Given the range of issues under sustainability, firms, through their leadership, ought to identify the right fit of sustainability programs within their part of businesses. It allows businesses to carefully align their objectives to the objectivity of sustainable parameters (Epstein & Buhovac, 2014).

Box 8
Organisations pushing for sustainability have mainly focused on investor relations, public relations, and social responsibility. In these contexts, the critical commitment for a successful sustainable firm involves managing stakeholder communication, target setting, or reporting and, more critically, leadership engaging proactively and attempting to create measurable impact.

3 Conclusion

The key takeaways, therefore, for leaders in this regard can be segregated into the following:

A) Charismatic leaders Charismatic leaders ought to take into consideration the micro-issues within the ESG parameters. Sustainability as a dimension is too vast for a firm to focus on its entire design
B) Charismatic leaders, through their culturally endorsed leadership domain, should be seeking to invest in process as opposed to public relations to account for the complexity of sustainable dimensions.
C) Leaders have to delegate and build a central team to create a structure that best aligns with the agenda of the business as a whole and gives the freedom to the team to implement those changes.

In the contemporary business landscape, charismatic leaders are increasingly called upon to navigate the intricate terrain of ESG (Environmental, Social, and Governance) parameters and sustainability. This is no small feat, as the concept of sustainability itself is both vast and multifaceted (Swilling, 2020). These leaders must consider several crucial aspects to lead their organizations in this context effectively.

Firstly, charismatic leaders must acknowledge the sprawling nature of sustainability (Zhang & Wei, 2021). Sustainability is not a singular entity that can be tackled in its entirety by any organization, no matter how charismatic its leadership may be. Instead, it consists of numerous micro-issues, each of which warrants individual attention. These micro-issues span a wide spectrum, encompassing environmental concerns like climate change, resource management, and pollution, as well as social aspects such as diversity and inclusion, labor practices, and community engagement, in addition to governance matters related to ethics, transparency, and regulatory compliance. Attempting to address all these aspects simultaneously is often impractical for any organization. Charismatic leaders, therefore, should employ a discerning approach, homing in on specific micro-issues that are most relevant to their industry, stakeholders, and core values. By understanding that sustainability is not a one-size-fits-all concept, they can tailor their efforts to make a meaningful impact where it matters most. This requires a deep understanding of the organization's unique challenges and opportunities within the ESG framework (Jan et al., 2021).

Secondly, charismatic leaders must leverage their culturally endorsed leadership domain to guide their approach to sustainability (Raelin, 2016). Charismatic leadership is often rooted in values, vision, and authenticity, and these qualities can play a pivotal role in promoting sustainability. Leaders should prioritize investments in internal processes and operations rather than focusing solely on external public relations efforts to enhance their image in the eyes of stakeholders. Sustainability is inherently complex and cannot be reduced to mere public relations exercises (Scherer et al., 2013). It demands substantive organizational changes, affecting everything from supply chains and product design to employee engagement and corporate governance. Charismatic leaders can foster a culture of sustainability by championing these changes from within, aligning them with the organization's core values, and embedding them (Men et al., 2020). By investing in sustainable processes, leaders promote a genuine commitment to sustainability and reap tangible benefits, such as cost savings, improved reputation, and access to new markets. Sustainability becomes a part of the organization's identity rather than a superficial image-enhancing strategy (Chan et al., 2014).

Lastly, charismatic leaders must embrace the importance of delegation and team building in their pursuit of sustainability (Baker, 2013; Germano, 2011). To drive meaningful change, leaders must create a structure that aligns with the broader business agenda. This involves building central teams dedicated to sustainability and ESG objectives (Reis, 2022). These teams can serve as the driving force behind the implementation of sustainable initiatives. Effective delegation allows leaders to provide a clear vision and strategic direction while giving their teams the freedom to innovate and execute. This empowerment not only fosters a sense of ownership among team members but also encourages creative problem-solving and adaptability, which are essential qualities in navigating the evolving landscape of sustainability (Annamalah et al., 2023).

In conclusion, charismatic leaders facing the challenges of ESG and sustainability should approach this complex terrain with a clear understanding of its vastness, the authenticity of their leadership style, and the power of delegation and team building. By focusing on relevant micro-issues, prioritizing sustainable processes, and empowering dedicated teams, they can steer their organizations towards a more sustainable and responsible future while maintaining their charismatic leadership presence. In doing so, they not only fulfil their corporate responsibilities but also inspire others to follow suit, ultimately driving positive change on a global scale.

Declaration of Generative AI and AI-Assisted Technologies in the Writing Process for This Chapter The editor only used Grammarly to proof-read and check for typos and inconsistencies. There is no further declaration from the authors.

References

Ahlström, H., & Monciardini, D. (2021). The regulatory dynamics of sustainable finance: Paradoxical success and limitations of EU reforms. *Journal of Business Ethics*, 1–20.

Al-Najjar, B., & Salama, A. (2022). Mind the gap: Are female directors and executives more sensitive to the environment in high-tech us firms? *Technological Forecasting and Social Change, 184*, 122024.

Amabile, T. M., Conti, R., Coon, H., Lazenby, J., & Herron, M. (1996). Assessing the work environment for creativity. *Academy of Management Journal, 39*(5), 1154–1184.

Annamalah, S., Paraman, P., Ahmed, S., Dass, R., Sentosa, I., Pertheban, T. R., Shamsudin, F., Kadir, B., Aravindan, K. L., & Raman, M. (2023). The role of open innovation and a normalizing mechanism of social capital in the tourism industry. *Journal of Open Innovation: Technology, Market, and Complexity, 9*, 100056.

Asif, M., Searcy, C., Zutshi, A., & Ahmad, N. (2011). An integrated management systems approach to corporate sustainability. *European Business Review, 23*, 353–367.

Aureli, S., Del Baldo, M., Lombardi, R., & Nappo, F. (2020). Nonfinancial reporting regulation and challenges in sustainability disclosure and corporate governance practices. *Business Strategy and the Environment, 29*, 2392–2403.

Aust, I., Muller-Camen, M., & Poutsma, E. (2018). 19. Sustainable HRM: A comparative and international perspective. In *Handbook of research on comparative human resource management* (p. 358). Edward Elgar Publishing Ltd.

Avery, G. C., & Bergsteiner, H. (2011). Sustainable leadership practices for enhancing business resilience and performance. *Strategy & Leadership, 39*, 5–15.

Baker, J. P. (2013). Leadership theories and approaches. *Leadership in psychiatry*, 49–62.

Barauskaite, G., & Streimikiene, D. (2021). Corporate social responsibility and financial performance of companies: The puzzle of concepts, definitions and assessment methods. *Corporate Social Responsibility and Environmental Management, 28*, 278–287.

Barrier, E. B. (2017). *The concept of sustainable economic development*. Routledge.

Boström, M., Jönsson, A. M., Lockie, S., Mol, A. P., & Oosterveer, P. (2015). Sustainable and responsible supply chain governance: Challenges and opportunities. *Journal of Cleaner Production, 107*, 1–7.

Bucea-Manea-Ţoniş, R., Prokop, V., Ilic, D., Gurgu, E., Bucea-Manea-Ţoniş, R., Braicu, C., & Moanţă, A. (2021). The relationship between eco-innovation and smart working as support for sustainable management. *Sustainability, 13*, 1437.

Büyüközkan, G., & Karabulut, Y. (2018). Sustainability performance evaluation: Literature review and future directions. *Journal of Environmental Management, 217*, 253–267.

Calabrese, A., Costa, R., Levialdi, N., & Menichini, T. (2019). Integrating sustainability into strategic decision-making: A fuzzy AHP method for the selection of relevant sustainability issues. *Technological Forecasting and Social Change, 139*, 155–168.

Carayannis, E. G., Sindakis, S., & Walter, C. (2015). Business model innovation as lever of organizational sustainability. *The Journal of Technology Transfer, 40*, 85–104.

Carrillo-Hermosilla, J., del González, P. R., Könnölä, T., Carrillo-Hermosilla, J., del González, P. R., & Könnölä, T. (2009). *What is eco-innovation?* Springer

Carroll, B., Levy, L., & Richmond, D. (2008). Leadership as practice: Challenging the competency paradigm. *Leadership, 4*, 363–379.

Chan, I. Y., Liu, A. M., & Fellows, R. (2014). Role of leadership in fostering an innovation climate in construction firms. *Journal of Management in Engineering, 30*, 06014003.

Charles, J. R., Holliday, C., Schmidheiny, S., & Watts, P. (2017). *Walking the talk: The business case for sustainable development*. Routledge.

Chatty, T., Harrison, W., Ba-Sabaa, H. H., Faludi, J., & Murnane, E. L. (2022). Co-creating a framework to integrate sustainable design into product development practice: Case study at an engineering consultancy firm. *Sustainability, 14*, 9740.

Chernysheva, N. A., Perskaya, V. V., Petrov, A. M., & Bakulina, A. A. (2019). Green energy for belt and road initiative: Economic aspects today and in the future. *International Journal of Energy Economics and Policy, 9*, 178–185.

Dalati, S. (2015). Leadership and sustainable entrepreneurship: Classical approaches and contemporary contexts. *Entrepreneurship and Sustainability issues, 2*, 209.

Dan, T. (2023). Transformational leadership theory in the Chinese context: Relevance and limitations. International journal of Frontiers. *Sociology, 5.*

Desiderio, E., García-Herrero, L., Hall, D., Segrè, A., & Vittuari, M. (2022). Social sustainability tools and indicators for the food supply chain: A systematic literature review. *Sustainable Production and Consumption, 30*, 527–540.

Dimitrov, D. (2015). Leadership in a humane organization. *European Journal of Training and Development, 39*, 122–142.

Dubrin, A. J. (2022). *Leadership: Research findings, practice, and skills*. Cengage Learning.

Eisenbeiss, S. A., Van Knippenberg, D., & Fahrbach, C. M. (2015). Doing well by doing good? Analyzing the relationship between CEO ethical leadership and firm performance. *Journal of Business Ethics, 128*, 635–651.

Ekmekcioglu, E. B., Aydintan, B., & Celebi, M. (2018). The effect of charismatic leadership on coordinated teamwork: A study in Turkey. *Leadership & Organization Development Journal, 39*, 1051–1070.

Elkington, J. (2020). *Green swans: The coming boom in regenerative capitalism*. Greenleaf Book Group.
Engert, S., Rauter, R., & Baumgartner, R. J. (2016). Exploring the integration of corporate sustainability into strategic management: A literature review. *Journal of Cleaner Production, 112*, 2833–2850.
Epstein, M. J., & Buhovac, A. R. (2014). *Making sustainability work: Best practices in managing and measuring corporate social, environmental, and economic impacts*. Berrett-Koehler Publishers.
Fiol, C. M., Harris, D., & House, R. (1999). Charismatic leadership: Strategies for effecting social change. *The Leadership Quarterly, 10*(3), 449–482.
Gangi, F., Meles, A., D'angelo, E., & Daniele, L. M. (2019). Sustainable development and corporate governance in the financial system: Are environmentally friendly banks less risky? *Corporate Social Responsibility and Environmental Management, 26*, 529–547.
Germano, M. (2011). Library leadership that creates and sustains innovation.
Giovannoni, E., & Fabietti, G. (2013). What is sustainability? A review of the concept and its applications. In *Integrated reporting: Concepts and cases that redefine corporate accountability* (pp. 21–40). Springer.
Golgeci, I., Makhmadshoev, D., & Demirbag, M. (2021). Global value chains and the environmental sustainability of emerging market firms: A systematic review of literature and research agenda. *International Business Review, 30*, 101857.
Haldar, S. (2019). Towards a conceptual understanding of sustainability-driven entrepreneurship. *Corporate Social Responsibility and Environmental Management, 26*, 1157–1170.
Harsanto, B., Mulyana, A., Faisal, Y. A., & Shandy, V. M. (2022). Open innovation for sustainability in the social enterprises: An empirical evidence. *Journal of Open Innovation: Technology, Market, and Complexity, 8*, 160.
Hojnik, J., & Ruzzier, M. (2016). The driving forces of process eco-innovation and its impact on performance: Insights from Slovenia. *Journal of Cleaner Production, 133*, 812–825.
Hysa, E., Kruja, A., Rehman, N. U., & Laurenti, R. (2020). Circular economy innovation and environmental sustainability impact on economic growth: An integrated model for sustainable development. *Sustainability, 12*, 4831.
Jamal, J., & Abu Bakar, H. (2017). The mediating role of charismatic leadership communication in a crisis: A Malaysian example. *International Journal of Business Communication, 54*, 369–393.
Jan, A. A., Lai, F. W., & Tahir, M. (2021). Developing an Islamic corporate governance framework to examine sustainability performance in Islamic banks and financial institutions. *Journal of Cleaner Production, 315*, 128099.
Javidan, M., & Waldman, D. A. (2003). Exploring charismatic leadership in the public sector: Measurement and consequences. *Public Administration Review, 63*(2), 229–242.
Kantabutra, S. (2020). Toward an organizational theory of sustainability vision. *Sustainability, 12*, 1125.
Karttunen, E., Tsytsyna, E., Lintukangas, K., Rintala, A., Abdulkareem, M., Havukainen, J., & Nuortila-Jokinen, J. (2021). Toward environmental innovation in the cement industry: A multiple-case study of incumbents and new entrants. *Journal of Cleaner Production, 314*, 127981.
Lawrence, J., Rasche, A., & Kenny, K. (2018). *Sustainability as opportunity: Unilever's sustainable living plan. Managing sustainable business: An executive education case and textbook*. Springer.
Le Blanc, P. M., González-Romá, V., & Wang, H. (2021). Charismatic leadership and work team innovative behavior: The role of team task interdependence and team potency. *Journal of Business and Psychology, 36*, 333–346.
Lloret, A. (2016). Modeling corporate sustainability strategy. *Journal of Business Research, 69*, 418–425.

Lopez-Cabrales, A., & Valle-Cabrera, R. (2020). Sustainable HRM strategies and employment relationships as drivers of the triple bottom line. *Human Resource Management Review, 30*, 100689.

Lozano, R. (2012). Towards better embedding sustainability into companies' systems: An analysis of voluntary corporate initiatives. *Journal of Cleaner Production, 25*, 14–26.

Luu, T. T., Rowley, C., Dinh, C. K., Qian, D., & Le, H. Q. (2019). Team creativity in public healthcare organizations: The roles of charismatic leadership, team job crafting, and collective public service motivation. *Public Performance & Management Review, 42*, 1448–1480.

Ly, N. B. (2020). Cultural influences on leadership: Western-dominated leadership and non-Western conceptualizations of leadership. *Sociology and Anthropology, 8*, 1–12.

Mady, K., Battour, M., Aboelmaged, M., & Abdelkareem, R. S. (2023). Linking internal environmental capabilities to sustainable competitive advantage in manufacturing SMEs: The mediating role of eco-innovation. *Journal of Cleaner Production, 417*, 137928.

McClean, E., & Collins, C. J. (2019). Expanding the concept of fit in strategic human resource management: An examination of the relationship between human resource practices and charismatic leadership on organizational outcomes. *Human Resource Management, 58*, 187–202.

McCulloch, A. D. (2016). *Charisma and Patronage: Reasoning with.* Max Weber. Routledge.

Men, L. R., Yue, C. A., & Liu, Y. (2020). "Vision, passion, and care:" the impact of charismatic executive leadership communication on employee trust and support for organizational change. *Public Relations Review, 46*, 101927.

Meslec, N., Curseu, P. L., Fodor, O. C., & Kenda, R. (2020). Effects of charismatic leadership and rewards on individual performance. *The Leadership Quarterly, 31*(6), 101423.

Mi, L., Gan, X., Xu, T., Long, R., Qiao, L., & Zhu, H. (2019). A new perspective to promote organizational citizenship behaviour for the environment: The role of transformational leadership. *Journal of Cleaner Production, 239*, 118002.

Mittal, R. (2015). Charismatic and transformational leadership styles: A cross-cultural perspective. *International Journal of Business and Management, 10*, 26.

Munodawafa, R. T., & Johl, S. K. (2019). A systematic review of eco-innovation and performance from the resource-based and stakeholder perspectives. *Sustainability, 11*, 6067.

Naciti, V. (2019). Corporate governance and board of directors: The effect of a board composition on firm sustainability performance. *Journal of Cleaner Production, 237*, 117727.

Nagano, M. S., & Iacono, A. (2019). Knowledge management in eco-innovation practice: An analysis of the contribution of eco-innovation tools in the early stages of the product development process. *Journal of Information & Knowledge Management, 18*, 1950047.

Nguyen, N. T. T., Nguyen, N. P., & Hoai, T. T. (2021). Ethical leadership, corporate social responsibility, firm reputation, and firm performance: A serial mediation model. *Heliyon, 7*.

Nikoloski, K. (2015). Charismatic leadership and power: Using the power of charisma for better leadership in the enterprises. *Journal of Process Management and New Technologies, 3*, 18–26.

Nisbett, M., & Walmsley, B. (2016). The romanticization of charismatic leadership in the arts. *The Journal of Arts Management, Law, and Society, 46*, 2–12.

O'Rourke, D., & Strand, R. (2017). Patagonia: Driving sustainable innovation by embracing tensions. *California Management Review, 60*, 102–125.

Panapanaan, V. M., Linnanen, L., Karvonen, M. M., & Phan, V. T. (2003). Roadmapping corporate social responsibility in Finnish companies. *Journal of Business Ethics, 44*, 133–148.

Papagiannakis, G., & Lioukas, S. (2018). Corporate environmental management: Individual-level drivers and the moderating role of charismatic leadership. *European Management Review, 15*, 475–489.

Pascual, U., Balvanera, P., Anderson, C. B., Chaplin-Kramer, R., Christie, M., González-Jiménez, D., & Zent, E. (2023). Diverse values of nature for sustainability. *Nature, 620*(7975), 813–823.

Peyravi, B., Peleckis, K., & Jakubavičius, A. (2023). Eco-innovation performance of Lithuania in the context of European environmental policy: Eco-innovation indicators and efficiency. *Sustainability, 15*, 3139.

Pichlak, M. (2021). The drivers of technological eco-innovation—Dynamic capabilities and leadership. *Sustainability, 13*, 5354.

Pichlak, M., & Szromek, A. R. (2022). Linking eco-innovation and circular economy—A conceptual approach. *Journal of Open Innovation: Technology, Market, and Complexity, 8*, 121.

Pinto, J. (2019). Key to effective organizational performance management lies at the intersection of paradox theory and stakeholder theory. *International Journal of Management Reviews, 21*, 185–208.

Pompper, D. (2015). *Corporate social responsibility, sustainability and public relations: Negotiating multiple complex challenges*. Routledge.

Proctor, E., Luke, D., Calhoun, A., McMillen, C., Brownson, R., McCrary, S., & Padek, M. (2015). Sustainability of evidence-based healthcare: Research agenda, methodological advances, and infrastructure support. *Implementation Science, 10*, 1–13.

Purvis, B., Mao, Y., & Robinson, D. (2019). Three pillars of sustainability: In search of conceptual origins. *Sustainability Science, 14*, 681–695.

Raelin, J. A. (2016). It's not about the leaders: It's about the practice of leadership. *Organizational Dynamics, 45*.

Rattalino, F. (2018). Circular advantage anyone? Sustainability-driven innovation and circularity at Patagonia, Inc. *Thunderbird International Business Review, 60*, 747–755.

Reis, L. (2022). *How can compliance steer companies to deliver on ESG goals?* Springer.

Sana, S. S. (2020). Price competition between green and non green products under corporate social responsible firm. *Journal of Retailing and Consumer Services, 55*, 102118.

Scherer, A. G., Palazzo, G., & Seidl, D. (2013). Managing legitimacy in complex and heterogeneous environments: Sustainable development in a globalized world. *Journal of Management Studies, 50*, 259–284.

Shamir, B., & Howell, J. M. (1999). Organizational and contextual influences on the emergence and effectiveness of charismatic leadership. *The Leadership Quarterly, 10*, 257–283.

Skinner, J., Smith, A. C., Swanson, S., Skinner, J., Smith, A. C., & Swanson, S. (2018). *Creating innovative sporting cultures: Enabling an innovation Enterprise* (pp. 145–176). Fostering Innovative Cultures in Sport.

Sodiq, A., Baloch, A. A., Khan, S. A., Sezer, N., Mahmoud, S., Jama, M., & Abdelaal, A. (2019). Towards modern sustainable cities: Review of sustainability principles and trends. *Journal of Cleaner Production, 227*, 972–1001.

Solomon, J. (2020). *Corporate governance and accountability*. John Wiley & Sons.

Sroufe, R., & Gopalakrishna-Remani, V. (2019). Management, social sustainability, reputation, and financial performance relationships: An empirical examination of US firms. *Organization & Environment, 32*, 331–362.

Stephan, U., & Pathak, S. (2016). Beyond cultural values? Cultural leadership ideals and entrepreneurship. *Journal of Business Venturing, 31*, 505–523.

Stubbs, W. (2019). Strategies, practices, and tensions in managing business model innovation for sustainability: The case of an Australian BCorp. *Corporate Social Responsibility and Environmental Management, 26*, 1063–1072.

Swilling, M. (2020). *The age of sustainability: Just transitions in a complex world*. Taylor & Francis.

Tortola, P. D., & Pansardi, P. (2019). The charismatic leadership of the ECB presidency: A language-based analysis. *European Journal of Political Research, 58*, 96–116.

Tuan, L. T. (2019). Catalyzing employee OCBE in tour companies: Charismatic leadership, organizational justice, and pro-environmental behaviors. *Journal of Hospitality & Tourism Research, 43*, 682–711.

Velenturf, A. P., & Purnell, P. (2021). Principles for a sustainable circular economy. *Sustainable Production and Consumption, 27*, 1437–1457.

Visser, W. (2017). *Sustainable frontiers: Unlocking change through business, leadership and innovation*. Routledge.

Wamsler, C. (2020). Education for sustainability: Fostering a more conscious society and transformation towards sustainability. *International Journal of Sustainability in Higher Education, 21*, 112–130.

Wang, Y. F., Lee, S. K., & Ye, Q. (2021). Opinion leaders in eco-innovation diffusion: Analysis of information networks for waste separation in Shanghai. *Resources, Conservation and Recycling, 174*, 105822.

Warrick, D. D. (2017). What leaders need to know about organizational culture. *Business Horizons, 60*, 395–404.

Wivel, A., & Grøn, C. H. (2021). Charismatic leadership in foreign policy. *International Affairs, 97*(2), 365–383.

Ytterstad, S., & Olaisen, J. (2023). *An overview of perspectives of transformational leadership. Learning transformational leadership: A pedagogical and practical perspective* (pp. 13–33). Springer.

Yuanyuan, C., Yahya, F., Waqas, M., & Hongbo, L. (2022). Do visionary-feedback seeking CEOs enhance firm sustainability through eco-innovation? A moderated mediation model. *Frontiers in Psychology, 12*, 750885.

Zhan, X., & Tang, S. Y. (2013). Political opportunities, resource constraints and policy advocacy of environmental NGOs in China. *Public Administration, 91*, 381–399.

Zhang, M., Abbasi, K. R., Inuwa, N., Sinisi, C. I., Alvarado, R., & Ozturk, I. (2023). Does economic policy uncertainty, energy transition and ecological innovation affect environmental degradation in the United States? *Economic Research-Ekonomska Istraživanja, 36*, 2177698.

Zhang, Y., & Wei, F. (2021). SMEs' charismatic leadership, product life cycle, environmental performance, and financial performance: A mediated moderation model. *Journal of Cleaner Production, 306*, 127147.

Zhou, L., Tokos, H., Krajnc, D., & Yang, Y. (2012). Sustainability performance evaluation in industry by composite sustainability index. *Clean Technologies and Environmental Policy, 14*, 789–803.

Dr. Tabish Zaman is a Senior Lecturer specializing in Innovation and Entrepreneurship at Anglia Ruskin University in Cambridge, UK, holds a faculty position in the interdisciplinary realm of Management & Entrepreneurship. Tabish has been exploring innovation and its adoption within the National Health Service (NHS) UK. His research is at the intersection of socio-cognitive theory, exploring innovation adoption, entrepreneurship, and digital transformation. Integrated within the context of healthcare and public services, his core interest underlines the complexity of team cognition, performance, leadership, and strategy.

Dr. Ngan Duong Cao (Rosie Cao) is an assistant professor in Finance and Accounting at the University of Bath, School of Management, the UK. She specialises in Cultural, Linguistic, Behavioural Finance, governance and Corporate Finance. At the heart of her research agenda is a desire to better understand individuals' and corporations' decision-making under risk and uncertainty and how corporate governance, such as board compositions and CEO's characteristics, plays a role in a firm's strategic decisions: CSR, capital structure, risk-taking, cash holding, dividend pay-out, etc.

Thi Tuong Giang Trinh is a business tutor of the Durham University International Study Centre. She holds her MSc degree in finance and investment from the University of Nottingham. She has some publications in refereed journals and working papers targeting high-ranked ones.

Climate Governance in South Asia

Maryam Eqan and Junfeng Wan

Abstract This Chapter provides readers with an overview of the pressing necessity for strong climate governance in South Asia, analyzing global and local aspects. South Asia nations have taken proactive measures by implementing domestic regulations, engaging in international initiatives, and developing technical solutions to address climate-related concerns. However, enduring political, socioeconomic, and governance barriers necessitate strategic resolutions. Regional cooperation is crucial for successful climate measures, requiring skilled diplomacy. The chapter thus highlights the importance of South Asia in global efforts to reduce climate change, focusing on the transition to renewable energy and active engagement in international advocacy. Enduring endeavours, collaborative initiatives, and fair settlements are the key as they will convert the goal of climate resilience in South Asia from a mere ambition to a binding commitment that surpasses national boundaries and temporal limitations.

1 Introduction

The Climate Change is a pressing global concern that has extensive consequences for the natural environment, economies, and societies worldwide (IPCC, 2023). The impacts of this phenomenon have been progressively more apparent in many geographical areas, such as South Asia (Shaw et al., 2022). This introduction section offers a comprehensive perspective on climate change in South Asia and underscores the significance of climate governance in effectively tackling the regional obstacles presented by this phenomenon.

The region of South Asia is characterised by its rich diversity and high population density. It encompasses several countries like *India, Pakistan, Bangladesh,*

M. Eqan (✉) · J. Wan
School of Ecology and Environment, Zhengzhou University, Zhengzhou, Henan, China

Henan International Joint Laboratory of Environment and Resources, Zhengzhou University, Zhengzhou, People's Republic of China
e-mail: wanjunfeng@zzu.edu.cn

V. Q. Trinh (ed.), *Climate Governance and Corporate Eco-innovation*, Sustainable Finance, https://doi.org/10.1007/978-3-031-56423-9_7

Nepal, Sri Lanka, Bhutan, and *the Maldives* (Akhtar et al., 2018) (see Fig. 1). This region's susceptibility to the consequences of climate change is heightened due to its distinctive geographical and socioeconomic attributes (Mbah et al., 2022).

The increase in average temperatures is a notable consequence of climate change in South Asia (Kim et al., 2023) (see Fig. 2). The region is currently facing heightened occurrences and heightened intensity of heat waves due to the emission of greenhouse gases and several other anthropogenic activities. These heatwaves have increased the prevalence of heat-related illnesses, fatalities, and disruptions in agricultural practices and water supplies (Sharma et al., 2022).

Another significant issue of concern pertains to the alteration of precipitation patterns, which has the potential to result in catastrophic flooding events and extended periods of drought. According to Mondal et al. (2022), these extreme weather events significantly peril the region's food security, infrastructure, and human life.

Furthermore, the Himalayan glacier melting due to escalating temperatures augments the volume of water being channelled into river networks. Although the first consequence of this phenomenon is an increased abundance of water resources, it also gives rise to the potential hazards of glacial lake outburst floods and long-term water scarcity.

Climate change has wide-ranging effects that extend beyond its direct implications. These effects encompass phenomena such as the rise in sea levels, coastal erosion, the decline in biodiversity, and alterations in monsoon patterns.

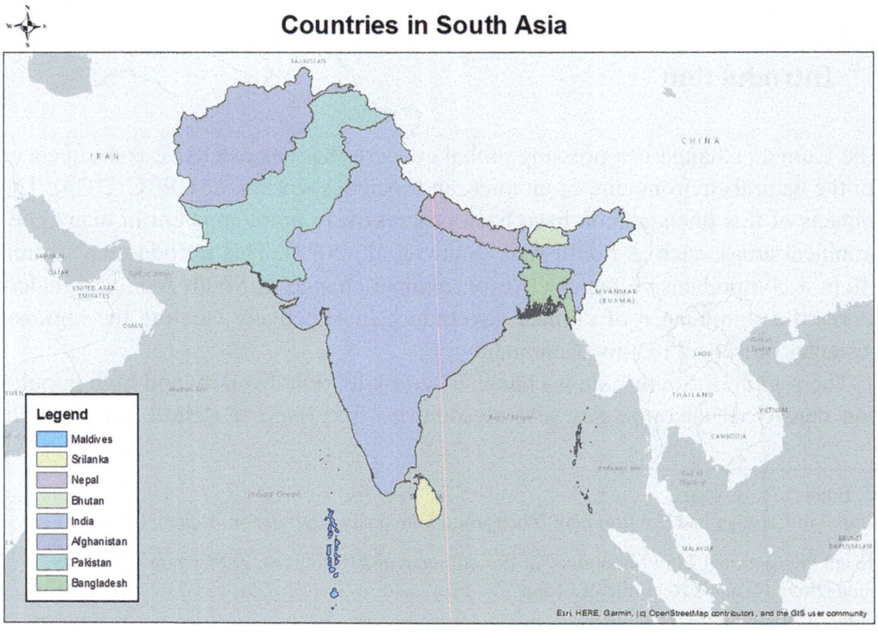

Fig. 1 Countries in South Asia

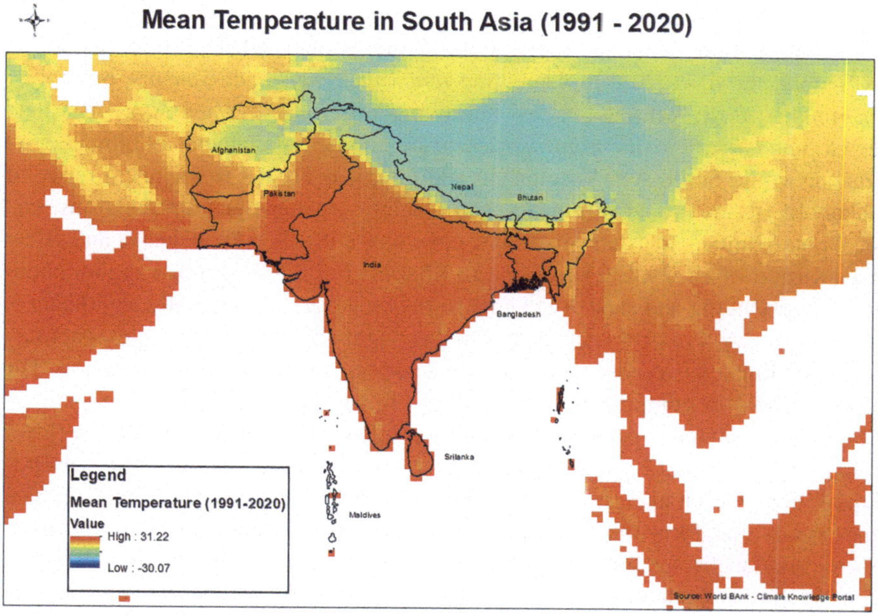

Fig. 2 Mean temperature in South Asia (1991–2020)

Consequently, these changes significantly impact both natural ecosystems and human settlements (Bhatt, 2022).

Given the significant obstacles, the importance of climate governance in South Asia cannot be overstated (Abbass et al., 2022). Climate governance encompasses the range of policies, institutions, and endeavours undertaken by governmental bodies, organisations, and communities to mitigate and adapt to climate change's impacts (World Bank Group, n.d.-a, b). In order to adequately tackle the issue of climate change, nations in South Asia must engage in collaborative efforts about regional initiatives, the exchange of information and resources, and the implementation of coordinated plans (Mbah et al., 2022). Establishing climate governance frameworks ought to be grounded in scientific research, ensuring a fair allocation of responsibilities and adhering to common but differentiated responsibilities. This approach recognises the varying roles developed and developing nations play in addressing the issue of climate change (Craig, 2017).

Box 1

In order to adequately tackle the issue of climate change, nations in South Asia must engage in collaborative efforts about regional initiatives, the exchange of information and resources, and the implementation of coordinated plans. Establishing climate governance frameworks ought to be grounded in scientific research, ensuring a fair allocation of responsibilities and adhering to common but differentiated responsibilities.

Furthermore, it is of utmost importance to integrate climate change considerations into both national and regional development plans (IISD, 2017). According to Neupane et al. (2022), implementing *renewable energy investments*, promoting *sustainable agricultural practices*, improving *water management strategies*, and developing *climate-resilient infrastructure* are all integral elements of climate governance in the South Asian region. In addition, it is crucial to engage a range of stakeholders, such as governments, civil society organisations, corporations, and local communities, to establish climate governance that is both inclusive and effective (Kusters et al., 2020). According to Khatibi et al. (2021), enhancing individuals' understanding and capacity to engage in climate action is equally significant.

The primary aim of this chapter is to thoroughly analyse the complex interplay between climate governance and its diverse aspects in the South Asian region. The chapter seeks to comprehensively analyse climate governance in the region by examining essential aspects such as climate science, policy frameworks, regional collaboration, technology innovation, and societal participation. Through this exploration, the chapter strives to clarify the difficulties, prospects, and optimal approaches that form the foundation of successful regional climate governance. Moreover, the chapter aims to emphasise the significance of continuous endeavours in mitigating and adapting to climate change, pushing for a cohesive and cooperative strategy that surpasses national boundaries and utilises the combined capabilities of the region. By conducting a comprehensive examination of these objectives, the chapter seeks to make a scholarly contribution towards enhancing comprehension of how South Asia may effectively address the intricacies of climate governance to promote a future that is both sustainable and resilient to climate change.

2 Understanding Climate Change in South Asia

2.1 Climate Science and Regional Impacts

The scientific study of climate change highlights the complex network of elements that impact weather patterns and their subsequent effects on the South Asian region (Siddiqui, 2023). The escalation of greenhouse gas emissions, primarily attributed to anthropogenic activity, intensifies the greenhouse effect, resulting in global warming (The United States Environmental Protection Agency (USEPA), 2023a). In South Asia, this gives rise to numerous discernible consequences. The increasing occurrence and severity of heatwaves are readily apparent, posing significant risks to public health, agriculture, and labour productivity (Sharma et al., 2022), see Box 2. The profound connection between climate change and precipitation patterns holds equal importance, as stated by the United States Environmental Protection Agency (The United States Environmental Protection Agency (USEPA), 2023b). The alteration of monsoon dynamics can disturb established agricultural cycles, leading to adverse consequences such as droughts or severe floods (Ishaque et al., 2022). The combination of rising sea levels and coastal erosion presents a significant and concerning risk to densely inhabited coastal regions, hence increasing the susceptibility of both communities and ecosystems to adverse impacts (Azevedo de Almeida & Mostafavi, 2016).

Box 2
Heat waves in Pakistan and India.

In May 2022, a case study was done by an international team of scientists, with World Weather Attribution leading the effort. The study aimed to emphasize the significant influence of the climate crisis on the severe heat wave that affected India and Pakistan during the spring of that year. The peer-reviewed analysis conducted by the researchers indicated that this catastrophic event was around 30 times more probable due to the climate catastrophe. The region was affected by a heat wave that resulted in unprecedented temperatures, leading to India seeing its warmest March in 122 years and Pakistan observing the highest March temperature anomaly worldwide. The prolonged absence of precipitation led to persistently hot and arid conditions during April, impacting a substantial portion of India, approximately 70 percent. The atypical and protracted heat wave, which commenced unusually early, has resulted in a minimum of 90 fatalities, induced glacial floods, exacerbated wildfires, affected agricultural operations, and caused widespread power outages affecting millions of individuals. The report highlights the significant impact experienced by vulnerable populations, including outdoor workers and farmers. It emphasises the pressing need for worldwide efforts to reduce emissions and implement adaptation measures in response to the escalating severity of heat waves. Moreover, it is projected that the occurrence and severity of heat waves will further escalate in a scenario where global temperatures increase by two degrees or more. This underscores the urgent necessity for decisive measures to address climate change (Rosane, 2022; World Weather Attribution, 2022).

2.2 *Historical Climate Trends and Projections*

Examining historical climate changes in South Asia offers valuable insights into the dynamic environmental context, as Casile (2021) highlighted. In the region under consideration, there has been a constant increase in temperatures over the last century. Notably, recent decades have exhibited significant upward trends (Wang et al., 2023). The tendencies above correlate with worldwide patterns; nevertheless, the distinctive geography of South Asia amplifies the consequences. According to Ullah et al. (2022), these patterns are anticipated to continue and become more pronounced. According to The Royal Society (2020), the ongoing increase in greenhouse gas emissions is anticipated to significantly raise average temperatures, intensifying the difficulties associated with heat-related issues. The complexities of monsoons, which serve as a crucial source of sustenance for agriculture and water supplies, are also anticipated to change, perhaps resulting in imbalanced precipitation patterns and presenting substantial challenges in water resource management (Scott et al., 2019). Moreover, the expeditious thawing of Himalayan glaciers is significant, bearing consequences for immediate water accessibility and enduring river flow consistency (Wood et al., 2020).

2.3 Vulnerabilities and Risks Faced By South Asian Nations

South Asian countries face many vulnerabilities and dangers intricately linked to the intricate fabric of climate change (The World Bank Group, n.d.). Agriculturally dependent economies encounter significant challenges as alterations in precipitation patterns and extreme events impact food production (Ali et al., 2017). The region's high population density, particularly in urban areas and along the coast, renders it particularly vulnerable to the detrimental effects of climate change, encompassing a range of consequences such as health hazards and infrastructure degradation (Kugelman, 2020). The depletion of glacier reserves directly correlates with the heightened risk of glacial lake outburst floods (see Box 3), posing a significant threat to communities residing in downstream areas (Taylor et al., 2023). In addition, the combination of restricted availability of resources, insufficient infrastructure, and socioeconomic inequalities exacerbate the difficulties, resulting in marginalised communities being disproportionately vulnerable to the adverse effects of climate change (Islam & Winkel, 2017). As South Asia grapples with these vulnerabilities, it is imperative to prioritise collaborative and adaptable methods to effectively address risks and cultivate resilience in response to the dynamic climate conditions (The World Bank Group, n.d.).

Box 3

Glacial Lake outburst flood in Pakistan.

The spring of 2022 presented Pakistan with exceptional difficulties as temperatures above typical levels, laying the foundation for climate-induced calamities. During March, the nation encountered an intense heatwave characterized by daytime maximum temperatures that surpassed the average by 5–8 °C in multiple places. The increase in temperatures in the northern regions of Gilgit-Baltistan and Khyber Pakhtunkhwa has expedited the process of glacial melting, resulting in the creation of 33 ice-dammed lakes, with a cumulative count exceeding 3000. Alarmingly, 33 lakes have been categorized as high-risk in terms of potential bursting, presenting a significant peril to an estimated population of 7.1 million individuals residing in these susceptible regions. Glacial lake outburst floods (GLOFs) pose a significant and immediate threat, as they have the potential to discharge substantial quantities of water and sediment, resulting in the loss of human lives, damage of assets, and profound disruption to the economic activities of isolated mountain settlements. The events that unfolded in Pakistan in 2022 serve as a poignant reminder of the pressing necessity for climate mitigation and adaptation endeavors to safeguard the ecosystem and the susceptible communities residing within it (UNDP Climate, 2022).

3 Policy and Institutional Framework for Climate Governance

3.1 National Climate Change Policies in South Asia

South Asian governments have acknowledged a pressing need for effective climate governance, leading them to implement comprehensive policies at the national level to address climate change (Gong et al., 2020). According to Moallemi et al. (2020), the policies mentioned above exemplify a customised strategy aimed at tackling the distinctive issues of the region while also being in line with the broader objectives of global climate initiatives. To balance economic growth and environmental sustainability, these governments seek to develop policies that incorporate mitigation and adaptation measures (Dejenie & Kakiso, 2023). The policies discussed in this chapter span various sectors, including energy, agriculture, water management, and urban planning. This comprehensive approach demonstrates a commitment to enhancing climate resilience (Chaudhry, 2017). The successful implementation and monitoring of these policies require efficient coordination across different sectors, active involvement of stakeholders, and the incorporating of climate considerations into broader national development plans (Di Gregorio et al., 2017).

3.2 Multilateral Agreements and South Asian Countries' Commitments

South Asian countries demonstrate their commitment to collective climate action through active engagement in multilateral agreements (Mizo, 2016). The Paris Agreement, a significant global agreement, serves as a forum for participating nations to express their goals for reducing emissions, methods for adapting to climate change, and financial needs (UNFCCC, n.d.). The pledges of South Asian countries under the Paris Agreement, as outlined in their Nationally Determined Contributions (NDCs), demonstrate their determination to participate in global initiatives (Asian Development Bank (ADB), 2020). As mentioned above, the pledges emphasise the ideas of common but differentiated duties, which acknowledge nations' diverse capacities and historical contributions (Chen, 2021). South Asian countries cultivate a sense of collective obligation, collaboration, and reciprocal assistance by participating in these multilateral agreements, recognising the transnational nature of climate change (Butt, 2022).

3.3 Role of International Organizations and Support Mechanisms

International organisations are crucial in facilitating climate governance in South Asia by providing technical knowledge, financial assistance, and capacity-building programmes (Elazari, 2022). Collaborative initiatives with organisations such as the United Nations Development Programme (UNDP), World Bank, and Global Environment Facility (GEF) allow the dissemination of knowledge and the sharing of best practices. These organisations play a crucial role in developing comprehensive climate policies, fostering the harmonisation of national strategies with global objectives, and providing essential assistance to strengthen climate resilience. The organisation's endeavours encompass the facilitation of empowerment within local communities, the cultivation of innovation, and the encouragement of inclusive involvement. By utilising these international alliances, South Asian governments enhance their capacity for climate governance and strengthen their efforts to mitigate climate-related hazards, safeguard susceptible communities, and provide a sustainable future for future generations (Agarwal et al., 2022).

4 Climate Governance at the Regional Level in South Asia

4.1 Collaborative Initiatives Among South Asian Nations

The emergence of collaborative initiatives among South Asian nations has been recognised as a crucial method for effective climate governance, given their shared climate issues (Mbah et al., 2022). According to United Nations Economic Commission for Europe (UNECE) (2015), these initiatives facilitate the exchange of ideas, collaboration, and the consolidation of resources in order to tackle climate-related challenges that transcend national boundaries effectively. Forums and platforms facilitate knowledge exchange, allowing countries to gain insights and adopt best practices from each other's experiences (UNICEF, 2018). South Asian nations demonstrate their ability to address many difficulties, including water shortages, natural resource management, and disaster preparedness, by collaborating. Through this collaborative effort, they aim to find new solutions and enhance the magnitude of their impact (UNESCAP, 2017). These cooperative endeavours establish the groundwork for a cohesive regional strategy toward climate governance, fostering reciprocal assistance and strengthening the recognition that tackling climate change necessitates communal engagement.

4.2 Regional Climate Change Adaptation Strategies

The significance of regional adaptation techniques is emphasised by distinct climatic vulnerabilities common throughout South Asian nations (Agarwal et al., 2022). The primary objective of collaborative efforts in this domain is to enhance the capacity to adapt and withstand the impacts of dynamic climatic circumstances (Carmen et al., 2022). According to Gaudenzi et al. (2023), implementing policies, sharing data, and coordinating activities contribute to improving adaptive skills across international boundaries. Ecosystem-based techniques, such as the restoration of mangroves and the management of watersheds, possess the capacity to extend beyond the confines of individual nations and provide advantages that are shared collectively (Nishi et al., 2023). Moreover, it is worth noting that regional disaster preparedness plans are strategically formulated to facilitate prompt and efficient reaction and restoration efforts following severe meteorological phenomena (Alexander, 2015). By implementing these collaborative adaptation methods, South Asian countries can strengthen their capacity to withstand and recover from the adverse effects of climate change. These strategies aim to mitigate risks and prevent any nation from being marginalised due to climate-related challenges.

4.3 Cross-Border Climate Migration and Displacement Issues

Regional cooperation and governance are crucial in addressing climate-induced cross-border migration and displacement (McAdam, 2012). The phenomenon of communities being compelled to migrate due to shifting climate conditions, frequently crossing international boundaries, necessitates a collective effort among South Asian states to tackle the intricate socioeconomic and humanitarian challenges that ensue (McMichael et al., 2012). According to Blake et al. (2021), the implementation of collective policy coordination plays a crucial role in ensuring that climate migrants have sufficient support, protection, and access to critical services. According to Reimann et al. (2023), sharing data on migration patterns enables governments to anticipate issues and develop proactive policies. The protection of climate migrants' rights, including the preservation of their dignity and well-being, is facilitated by regional legal frameworks and agreements (United Nations Human Rights (UNHR), n.d.). South Asia recognises the mutual reliance among its countries and endeavours to address climate-induced displacement in a manner characterised by empathy, equity, and a collective dedication to upholding human dignity.

5 Mitigation Efforts and Renewable Energy Transition in South Asia

Addressing the negative consequences of climate change is an urgent priority for South Asian nations. A crucial approach to attaining sustainable development and decreasing greenhouse gas emissions is adopting renewable energy sources, which hold significant importance (Asian Development Bank (ADB), 2022). The region's endeavours to mitigate the issue are supported by ambitious objectives, interventions specific to various sectors, and inventive policies (Soergel et al., 2021). According to the United Nations Economic and Social Commission for Asia and the Pacific (UNESCAP, 2018), countries in the South Asian region have established specific goals for reducing emissions that are aligned with their distinct situations and corresponding obligations, span a range of sectors, including energy, industry, agriculture, and transportation, indicating a holistic strategy for addressing emissions (Yang et al., 2023). According to Yu et al. (2023), the countries in question strive to achieve sustainable development trajectories by advocating the adoption of renewable energy technology and implementing energy efficiency measures. Their objective is to separate economic growth from carbon emissions.

According to the International Renewable Energy Agency (IRENA, 2022), adopting renewable energy sources is fundamental to South Asia's efforts to mitigate environmental impacts. The geographical area possesses a substantial capacity for renewable energy, encompassing various sources such as sun, wind, hydropower, and biomass (Haq et al., 2020). Solar energy exhibits significant potential as a result of the ample sunlight that the area receives (Vaka et al., 2020). India has initiated ambitious initiatives to enhance its solar power generation capabilities, focusing on installing solar infrastructure in urban and rural regions, see Box 4 (The World Bank, 2021). According to Olabi et al. (2023), wind energy initiatives, particularly those in coastal areas, significantly use wind resources to generate electricity. Hydropower projects harness the inherent energy of rivers and water bodies, while biomass utilisation presents prospects for generating clean energy and effectively managing waste (Sibtain et al., 2021).

Box 4

Solar power project, India.

In 2015, India embarked on a significant solar energy initiative in partnership with the government of Karnataka, establishing the Karnataka Solar Power Development Corporation Ltd. (K.S.P.D.C.L.). This endeavor's primary objective was to utilise the ample sunlight available in the region effectively. In early 2016, K.S.P.D.C.L. implemented an innovative strategy to address the complex task of acquiring large amounts of property while mitigating the risk of land conflicts. The solar corporation assumed the role of tenants by leasing land from local landowners for 28 years, establishing themselves as landlords. This novel strategy successfully acquired approximately 13,000 acres of property from 1900 landowners, compensating them with a yearly rental fee of 21,000 rupees per acre, subject to incremental adjustments. The K.S.P.D.C.L. organization swiftly altered the physical environment by establishing solar farms, collaborating with multinational enterprises, and successfully attaining its solar capacity objectives before the predetermined timeline. As of 2023, India had achieved a solar capacity of 60,000 megawatts. Nevertheless, the proliferation of solar farms, although crucial in addressing the issue of climate change, also raises ecological concerns (The New Yorker, 2023).

Adopting renewable energy sources in South Asia has implications beyond mere emissions reduction. It also presents notable co-benefits for the region's socioeconomic framework (Shukla et al., 2017). The transformation mentioned above offers significant prospects for the generation of employment, namely in the sectors of manufacture, installation, operation, and maintenance of renewable energy systems (Ram et al., 2022). In addition, it plays a role in bolstering energy security by diminishing reliance on imported fossil fuels, thus strengthening the region's ability to withstand variations in energy prices and supply disruptions (Dahlan et al., 2022). According to Belgacem et al. (2023), the presence of the renewable energy sector in South Asian nations promotes innovation, research, and technological developments. It establishes these nations as frontrunners in the global green economy.

Nevertheless, this change is not devoid of problems. The acquisition of funds necessary for the initial investment in renewable energy infrastructure continues to pose a substantial challenge, especially for nations with limited fiscal resources (Li et al., 2021). According to Ramirez et al. (2021), the intermittent characteristics exhibited by specific renewable sources, such as solar and wind, create a need to advance resilient energy storage technologies and methods for integrating these sources into the grid. According to the World Bank and Energy Charter Secretariat (2023), modifying regulatory frameworks to enable the private sector's participation and enhance foreign direct investment attractiveness is imperative. Moreover, it is essential to emphasise establishing technological capabilities, advancing effective energy markets, and resolving social and environmental issues as indispensable elements for achieving a prosperous transition towards renewable energy in the South Asian region (Babayomi et al., 2022).

6 Adaptation and Resilience Building

The response to the implications of climate change in South Asia necessitates a strong focus on adaptation and resilience development, as highlighted by Abbass et al. (2022). The foundation of these endeavours is the evaluation of susceptibilities and establishing fortitude (United Nations Office for Disaster Risk Reduction, 2023). Vulnerability assessments encompass a thorough examination of the susceptibility of a particular area to climate-related hazards and its ability to effectively manage and rebound from such events (Al-Kalbani et al., 2014). According to Aryal et al. (2020), South Asian countries can prioritise specific adaptation methods by identifying significant vulnerabilities, including water scarcity, coastline erosion, and agricultural disruptions. Developing resilience involves incorporating adaptive strategies into policies and programmes, aiming to enhance the capacity of communities and ecosystems to endure and recuperate from adverse impacts associated with climate change (Carmen et al., 2022). These actions include augmentation of local capabilities, establishing infrastructure that can withstand climate-related challenges, and promoting sustainable resource management practices (Shammin et al., 2022). By effectively addressing vulnerabilities and implementing measures to enhance resilience, South Asian countries can more effectively manage the complex difficulties presented by the impacts of climate change (Daron et al., 2022).

According to Swanson et al. (2021), establishing climate-resilient infrastructure and implementing urban planning strategies are fundamental components of the region's initiatives to adapt to and enhance resilience against climate change. Incorporating climate considerations into infrastructure projects, such as constructing roads, bridges, and energy systems, is crucial to enhancing resilience against severe weather events and evolving environmental circumstances (Markolf et al., 2019). Simultaneously, incorporating climate considerations into urban planning contributes to developing cities that exhibit enhanced resilience against climate-related challenges such as flooding, heat waves, and other stressors generated by climate change (Abdul & Yu, 2020). This encompasses strategies such as implementing green spaces to regulate temperatures, constructing flood-resistant buildings, and establishing efficient public transit systems (Pritipadmaja & Sharma, 2023). In addition, establishing efficient strategies for managing and preparing for climate-induced disasters is crucial for developing resilience (Etinay et al., 2018). The countries of South Asia are currently enacting comprehensive policies for responding to disasters, which include the establishment of early warning systems, the provision of community training, and the facilitation of efficient coordination among government agencies (National Bureau of Asian Research (NBR), 2022). These precautions facilitate prompt evacuation and relief operations in climate-related calamities, mitigating human and economic losses. Integrating climate-resilient infrastructure, urban planning, and disaster management in South Asia is a basis for enhancing adaptability and resilience in response to persistent climate-related difficulties (Abdul & Yu, 2020).

7 Climate Finance and Investment

7.1 Funding Challenges for Climate Projects in South Asia

The region of South Asia encounters notable financial obstacles in implementing essential climate initiatives. The region, known for its susceptibility to climate change, frequently faces financial constraints and conflicting development objectives (Agarwal et al., 2021). The allocation of sufficient financial resources towards climate initiatives might burden national budgets, impeding the effective implementation of crucial adaptation and mitigation measures (Malhi et al., 2021). Furthermore, the presence of intricate administrative and bureaucratic protocols can potentially result in the postponement of project payout and implementation (Masud et al., 2023). Addressing these funding difficulties necessitates implementing creative strategies, strategically allocating resources, and promoting improved collaboration among governmental bodies, international stakeholders, and financial institutions.

7.2 *International Climate Finance and South Asian Nations*

International climate finance plays a crucial role in supporting South Asian governments in their endeavours to mitigate and adapt to the challenges posed by climate change. Developed countries extend financial aid to support the implementation of climate projects in developing nations within the area through mechanisms such as the Green Climate Fund (GCF) (see Box 5) and bilateral partnerships (ADB, 2020). The provision of these funds plays a crucial role in facilitating the uptake of environmentally friendly technology, constructing infrastructure that can withstand the impacts of climate change, and strengthening the ability to adapt to changing environmental conditions (Commonwealth Secretariat, 2022). According to Clark et al. (2018), international climate finance plays a crucial role in addressing funding gaps and promoting transparent and fair distribution of resources. However, to optimise the effectiveness of these funds in supporting climate efforts in South Asia, it is imperative to prioritise their efficient utilisation and establish mechanisms for proper accountability.

Box 5

Recharge Pakistan.

It is anticipated that Pakistan will encounter temperature rises that are 1 °C above the global average by the year 2100. This is projected to result in notable alterations in precipitation distribution and an increased occurrence of extreme weather phenomena. The significant floods in 2023, impacting a population of 33 million individuals, serve as a poignant reminder of Pakistan's pressing need for climate adaptation measures. The primary objective of the Recharge Pakistan effort is to bring about a comprehensive transformation in managing floods and water resources within the Indus Basin river system. The proposed approach involves utilising ecosystems-based adaptation strategies and implementing green infrastructure measures to bolster the resilience of communities against the adverse impacts of droughts and floods. Additionally, it aims to strengthen community-based resource management practices as part of the overall strategy. The primary objective of this program is to enhance water storage and recharge capacities, foster the development of resilient livelihoods to climate change, and establish a model for forthcoming endeavors. Implementing nature-based solutions for climate adaptation in Pakistan necessitates collaboration between government institutions and WWF-Pakistan (Green Climate Fund, 2023).

7.3 *Private Sector Engagement and Climate Investment Opportunities*

According to Lu (2022), the involvement of the private sector in climate investment offers a substantial opportunity to expedite sustainable development in the South Asian region. There is a growing acknowledgment among businesses of the possibility of successful endeavours that are in line with climate objectives (Amini Sedeh et al., 2023). Numerous opportunities are available in renewable energy, energy-efficient technology, sustainable agriculture, and climate-resilient infrastructure, as highlighted by Flores and Peralta (2019). Governments have the potential to encourage private sector investment by creating a conducive climate through the implementation of incentives, legislative frameworks, and systems that share risks (Post et al., 2021). According to Tall et al. (2021), the combination of public and private sector collaboration has the potential to unlock innovation and allocate resources necessary for the advancement of climate initiatives. This collaborative approach cannot only generate employment opportunities but also contribute to the enhancement of the region's ability to withstand climate-related challenges. Additionally, it facilitates economic progress.

8 Role of Civil Society and Public Awareness

According to Mumtaz (2021), civil society in South Asia plays a crucial role in advancing climate action and promoting sustainable development. Civil society, which encompasses non-governmental organisations, community groups, academic institutions, and grassroots activists, is pivotal in driving transformative processes. It achieves this by engaging in activities such as pushing for legislative reforms, enhancing public consciousness, and endorsing ecologically sustainable behaviours (Abiddin et al., 2022). According to Samnuzulsari et al. (2021), the active involvement of individuals guarantees that climate-related matters continue to be prioritised in public discussions and policy frameworks.

The amplification of marginalised communities' voices, which are frequently the most susceptible to the effects of climate change, is a crucial contribution to civil society (Thomas et al., 2019). These organisations employ inclusive and participatory methodologies to include local knowledge and perspectives in climate policies and initiatives (Wamsler et al., 2020). According to Costa et al. (2022), the involvement of communities in decision-making processes empowers civil society and consequently boosts the pertinence and efficacy of climate measures. According to Broeckhoven et al. (2020), the instrumental function of climate governance frameworks is to promote social justice and fairness, ensuring that no individuals are excluded in the endeavour to achieve a sustainable future.

According to Khatibi et al. (2021), public awareness programmes initiated by civil society have a crucial role in influencing individual behaviours and attitudes about climate change. These endeavours facilitate the connection between scientific knowledge and public comprehension through educational efforts, outreach programmes, and the transmission of information (Deisenrieder et al., 2020). According to Montoute et al. (2019), civil society organisations organise workshops, seminars, and public events to disseminate information to individuals regarding the ramifications of climate change, measures for adaptation, and the advantages associated with sustainable practices. According to Shayan et al. (2022), civil society plays a crucial role in promoting a sense of ownership and responsibility among citizens, thereby motivating them to make educated choices, embrace environmentally friendly lifestyles, and ensure that policymakers are held accountable.

Moreover, civil society plays a crucial role as a monitoring entity, overseeing the implementation of climate policies and lobbying for their efficient execution (Espinosa & Rangel, 2022). Civil society organisations have a crucial role in upholding accountability among governments and corporations, hence promoting transparency, integrity, and compliance with environmental legislation (Heuty, 2012). In addition, policymakers benefit from the valuable input provided by individuals directly involved in the field, which aids in developing evidence-based policies and promoting responsive governance (Court et al., 2006).

In contemporary times, civil society organisations utilise various digital technologies such as social media, online platforms, and digital communication tools to enhance the reach and impact of their messages, hence facilitating broader engagement with diverse audiences (Abbas et al., 2019). The endeavours of the individuals involved transcend the confines of their nations, establishing links between civil society in South Asia and international networks and partnerships (Rahman et al., 2012). According to Rahman et al. (2012), civil society plays a crucial role in enhancing the collective representation of South Asian states on the global climate platform through promoting solidarity and knowledge sharing.

9 Technological Innovation and Climate Governance

According to Aparicio and Ofa (2021), technological innovation is crucial in facilitating effective climate governance in the South Asian region, providing diverse solutions to various difficulties related to climate change. By using state-of-the-art technologies, nations within the area may bolster their efforts in mitigating and adapting to climate change, foster sustainable development, and expedite advancements toward a future characterised by reduced carbon emissions (Xue et al., 2021).

Technological innovation is a crucial factor in mitigation as it contributes significantly to reducing greenhouse gas emissions in diverse sectors (Wang et al., 2021). The accessibility and affordability of renewable energy sources, such as solar photovoltaics and wind turbines, have been enhanced due to technological advancements (Koch, 2012). Seetharaman et al. (2019) notes that countries in the South Asian region are actively allocating resources toward research and development endeavours aimed at enhancing the efficacy and expandability of various technologies. This concerted effort is intended to facilitate the seamless integration of these technologies into the energy grids of respective nations. In addition, implementing cutting-edge energy storage technologies, such as advanced battery systems and pumped hydro storage, addresses the inherent intermittency of renewable energy sources. This, in turn, contributes to establishing a more dependable and robust power grid (Worku, 2022). According to Farhangi (2017), innovative grid technologies enable real-time monitoring and management of energy distribution, optimising efficiency and reducing wastage.

Technological innovation bolsters climate resilience and disaster preparedness (Samarakkody et al., 2023). The utilisation of advanced data analytics, remote sensing, and Geographic Information Systems (GIS) facilitates the precise modelling of climate conditions and the assessment of associated risks, hence supporting the formulation of focused adaptation strategies (Jain et al., 2023). According to Shah et al. (2023), flood and drought forecasting systems play a crucial role in issuing advance notifications to susceptible communities, facilitating prompt evacuation and allocation of resources. According to Markolf et al. (2019), climate-resilient infrastructure designs integrate novel materials and engineering methods to endure severe weather occurrences, guaranteeing critical facilities' durability and operational effectiveness. In addition, implementing precision agriculture technologies, such as satellite images and soil sensors, optimises resource utilisation and improves crop yields. This, in turn, plays a crucial role in ensuring food security, particularly in light of the shifting climatic patterns (Sishodia et al., 2020).

According to Homberg and McQuistan (2019), the climate governance field is significantly impacted by technological innovation, particularly in monitoring, reporting, and verification (MRV) systems. The utilisation of high-resolution satellite imagery, remote sensing data, and Internet of Things (IoT) devices facilitates precise monitoring of forest cover, carbon sequestration, and sources of emissions (Singh et al., 2022). According to a press release from PR Newswire (2023), utilising blockchain technology facilitates the establishment of transparent and unalterable documentation about carbon credits and financial transactions. This implementation guarantees the preservation of the credibility and reliability of programmes aimed at reducing emissions. These innovations enhance the level of accountability, improve the process of international cooperation, and foster the development of confidence among governments involved in global climate agreements.

10 Case Studies and Best Practices

10.1 Case Study 1: Aga Khan Rural Support Programme (AKRSP)—Pakistan

One noteworthy case study originating from Pakistan is the Aga Khan Rural Support Programme (AKRSP) and its climate adaptation measures spearheaded by the local population in the Gilgit-Baltistan region. The AKRSP has been crucial in promoting participatory methods for enhancing climate resilience and acknowledging mountain communities' susceptibility to the effects of climate change. The "Water and Energy Security" project was initiated by the Aga Khan Rural Support Programme (AKRSP) in 2011, with funding from the Swiss Agency of Development Cooperation. This project was implemented in the Yarkhun and Laspoor valleys of East Chitral District in Pakistan. This effort consisted of two distinct phases. The first phase focused on establishing hydropower infrastructure and village-owned power utility businesses. The second phase, from 2015 to 2018, aimed to further enhance economic-ecological development by promoting electricity utilisation and reducing the risks associated with natural disasters. The primary goals of the project were to facilitate the provision of clean and sustainable energy, enhance livelihood chances, and mitigate socioeconomic inequalities, all while ensuring resilience against natural disasters caused by climate change. AKRSP's initiatives, consisting of 57 hydro projects and an electricity generation capacity of 8.2 MW, have been acknowledged by the United Nations Framework Convention on Climate Change (UNFCCC) and have gained international acclaim. These efforts are a notable illustration of a sustainable strategy to address water and energy security and promote ecological development and disaster resilience (Aga Khan Rural Support Programme (AKRSP), 2011).

In conjunction with the endeavours of AKRSP, the National Disaster Risk Management Fund (NDRMF) in Pakistan is an illustrative instance of a specialised financial instrument to enhance climate resilience. The National Disaster Risk Management Fund (NDRMF) is a significant non-banking financial intermediary established by the federal government. Its primary objective is to enhance Disaster Risk Reduction (DRR), Disaster Risk Financing (DRF), and Climate Change initiatives across Pakistan, explicitly focusing on the country's most susceptible areas. The NDRMF promotes resilience by providing grant finance to public and private sector organisations. This financial support allows them to carry out activities that aim to decrease Pakistan's population's susceptibility to natural disasters in terms of socioeconomic and fiscal aspects. The prioritisation and allocation of resources towards disaster risk reduction and preparedness programmes are crucial in attaining desired goals with significant effects (NDRMF, n.d.).

The NDRMF is notable for its adaptable financial structures that enable the combination of funds and the utilisation of public resources in conjunction with international, multilateral, and bilateral funding sources. The Fund's ability to mobilise various resources to tackle the complex challenges presented by climate change and natural catastrophes in Pakistan is highlighted by this collaborative approach (NDRMF, n.d.).

10.2 Case Study 2: Enhancing Climate Resilience of India's Coastal Communities—India

The Ministry of Environment, Forest and Climate Change, Government of India, in partnership with the United Nations Development Programme (UNDP), initiated a significant case study, the 'Enhancing Climate Resilience of India's Coastal

Communities' project. This revolutionary endeavour, which commenced in 2019 and is set to conclude in 2024, aims to enhance the ability of India's coastal communities to withstand and adapt to the impacts of climate change. The main aim of this effort was to improve the climate resilience of India's most susceptible populations, particularly women living in coastal areas. A notable transformation occurred throughout project implementation, signifying a deviation from traditional methodologies. The initiative effectively incorporated ecosystem-centered and community-based methodologies into coastal management and planning, engaging the governmental, private, and civil society sectors. A significant allocation of the project's resources was devoted to the development of ecological infrastructure with the capacity to mitigate climate-induced risks, including those that arise from storm surges. Simultaneously, the project encouraged the development of coastal livelihoods resilient to climate change and fostered the implementation of cross-sectoral planning and governance strategies informed by climate risk assessments within the coastal zone. Upon reflection, this project has made a significant contribution to the advancement of India's climate policy. The alignment of this initiative with India's National Action Plan on Climate Change (2008) and the corresponding State Action Plans is evident. Moreover, it significantly contributed to fulfilling India's obligations as delineated in its Nationally Determined Contribution (2015). This case study provides evidence of the efficacy of comprehensive, community-led strategies in bolstering climate resilience in at-risk coastal communities (UNDP, 2023).

10.3 Case Study 3: The Coastal Climate Resilient Infrastructure Project (CCRIP)—Bangladesh

The Coastal Climate Resilient Infrastructure Project (CCRIP) was an influential endeavour that originated from the distinctive obstacles encountered by Bangladesh, a South Asian nation characterised by significant poverty and profound vulnerability to bad climate conditions. In addition to mitigating the impacts of climate change, the CCRIP also aimed to address the urgent needs of rural producers, specifically those impoverished and engaged in small-scale farming. These individuals face two significant challenges: firstly, the lack of proper road and market infrastructure, which hampers their ability to access larger markets and increases transportation expenses, and secondly, the limited availability of dem. The primary objective of this project was to develop climate-resilient road infrastructure and cyclone shelters in the southwestern parts of Bangladesh. High poverty levels and susceptibility to natural disasters characterise these regions.

Additionally, the project aimed to enhance market accessibility in these areas. The objective of the CCRIP was to improve the quality of life, financial stability, and access to food for a population of 3.5 million, focusing on small-scale farmers, small traders, microentrepreneurs, landless individuals, and economically disadvantaged women. This initiative was implemented in 12 coastal districts to promote resilience to climate change and foster socioeconomic progress in the area (IFAD, 2019).

The case above studies, as well as additional ones from the South Asian region, underscore the significance of active involvement at the local level, inventive methods of funding, and the harmonisation of climatic objectives with broader developmental aims. By leveraging these experiences, nations may enhance their climate governance policies, promote inclusive collaborations, and create adaptive solutions, contributing to a more resilient and sustainable future. The global dissemination of these achievements facilitates the interchange of knowledge and emphasises the imperative of collective efforts in addressing the challenges posed by climate change.

11 Challenges and Future Prospects

11.1 Political and Socioeconomic Barriers to Effective Climate Governance

The region of South Asia encounters a multifaceted assortment of obstacles that hinder the achievement of efficient climate governance (Butt, 2023). The development and execution of cohesive climate policies might be impeded by political obstacles, such as divergent national interests and constrained political resolve (Tosun & Peters, 2021). Socioeconomic inequalities and conflicting development agendas frequently divert attention and resources from climate-related projects. In addition, it should be noted that corruption, bureaucratic inefficiencies, and governance weaknesses can result in the improper allocation of money designated for climate programmes (World Bank Group, n.d.-a, b). To surmount these obstacles, it is imperative to possess effective leadership, establish transparent governance, and develop resilient institutional structures that prioritise implementing climate-related measures (Roesch & Nobre, 2021). Ensuring the responsiveness of climate governance initiatives to the needs of vulnerable populations and their alignment with long-term sustainable development goals necessitates effectively addressing political and socioeconomic difficulties.

11.2 Regional Cooperation and Diplomacy for Climate Action

According to Zafarullah and Huque (2018), the significance of regional cooperation and diplomacy cannot be overstated in achieving effective climate governance in South Asia. Collaborative endeavours that surpass national boundaries are crucial in addressing the climatic problems that extend beyond borders (Prabhakar et al., 2021). Nevertheless, the presence of historical tensions and geopolitical rivalries has the potential to impede collective action (Scheffran, 2023). In order to promote consensus on climate goals that are shared, diplomatic discussions must effectively traverse intricate power relations and reconcile competing interests (United Nations Department of Political and Peacebuilding Affairs (UN DPPA), 2022). Organisations such as the South Asian Association for Regional Cooperation (SAARC) serve as forums for exchanging ideas, disseminating information, and collaborative efforts to enhance collective capabilities (European Union, 2021). Through multilateral agreements and regional collaborations, South Asian countries can combine their resources, exchange knowledge on effective strategies, and collaboratively tackle issues such as transboundary pollution, water resource management, and migration caused by climate change (Mukhopadhyay et al., 2018). By cultivating a culture of collaboration, the South Asian region has the potential to enhance its global influence and make a meaningful contribution towards a more cohesive and practical approach to addressing the challenges posed by climate change.

11.3 Looking Ahead: South Asia's Role in Global Climate Change Mitigation

According to Mbah et al. (2022), the significance of South Asia's contribution to global climate change mitigation is expected to grow. According to Raihan et al. (2023), the region's population growth, economic expansion, and urbanisation would be significant factors contributing to the increase in energy demand. Consequently, the importance of sustainable development and emission reduction becomes vital to address these challenges effectively. South Asian nations possess the potential to bypass carbon-intensive growth trajectories and instead adopt clean technologies and green innovation as they progress their economies (UNESCAP, 2017). According to a report by the United Nations Economic and Social Commission for Asia and the Pacific (UNESCAP, 2017), the allocation of resources towards renewable energy, sustainable agriculture, and climate-resilient infrastructure has the potential to establish South Asia as a frontrunner in the shift towards a low-carbon trajectory. In addition, South Asia's combined influence and diplomatic endeavours in the global arena can influence climate discussions worldwide, push for enhanced climate finance, and stimulate a more substantial commitment to reducing emissions (Masud et al., 2023). By assuming this position, South Asia has the potential to make a significant contribution not just to its climate resilience but also to the broader global endeavour of addressing climate change and ensuring the protection of the planet for future generations.

12 Conclusion

In summary, the complex relationship between climate change and governance in the South Asian region underscores the presence of obstacles and prospects in the pursuit of sustainability. The region's susceptibility to climate impacts is emphasised by significant changes in temperature, water availability, and extreme weather events, requiring a comprehensive climate governance framework. Throughout this discourse, considerable discoveries have surfaced, unveiling the intricate and diverse characteristics of endeavours in climate governance.

The legislative and institutional framework for climate governance in South Asia plays a pivotal role in facilitating coordinated action. National climate change policies highlight the dedication of nations to addressing and responding to climate change, whereas multilateral accords and international partnerships emphasise the significance of shared accountability. In addition, the involvement of civil society and advancements in technology have become crucial factors in promoting efficient climate governance. These factors raise public consciousness, ensure transparency, and incorporate state-of-the-art solutions.

Despite the advancements made, obstacles still need to be addressed. Political and economic obstacles and deficiencies in governance highlight the intricate nature of climate governance. The necessity to effectively tackle these difficulties is of utmost importance, as is the imperative for ongoing regional collaboration and diplomatic efforts. Through the transcendence of geopolitical rivalries and the promotion of collaborative projects, states in South Asia have the potential to enhance their influence and formulate a cohesive approach to addressing mutual climate vulnerabilities.

In the future, the contribution of South Asia to global climate change mitigation is expected to be significant and influential. The region's rapidly expanding population and robust economic growth present a favourable prospect for advocating sustainable development, fostering innovation, and showcasing global leadership. The region's significant contribution to building a more sustainable future is highlighted by its capacity to exploit renewable energy, strengthen climate resilience, and influence international climate negotiations.

The significance of persistent endeavours in climate governance cannot be exaggerated. In light of the escalating ramifications of climate change, it is imperative to sustain progress to cultivate climate resilience and protect the welfare of current and future populations. The imperative for action is evident: South Asia should intensify its dedication to effective climate governance, emphasising cooperation, ingenuity, and fair resolutions. Through the strategic utilisation of policy, technology, and active involvement of civil society, South Asia has the potential to establish a trajectory that leads to a future characterised by sustainability and resilience in the face of climatic challenges. Through the collective efforts of governments, communities, and individuals, South Asia has the potential to become a symbol of optimism and an exemplar of proficient climate governance on an international scale.

Declaration of Generative AI and AI-Assisted Technologies in the Writing Process for This Chapter The editor only used Grammarly to proof-read and check for typos and inconsistencies. There is no further declaration from the authors.

References

Abbas, J., Aman, J., Nurunnabi, M., & Bano, S. (2019). The impact of social media on learning behavior for sustainable education: Evidence of students from selected universities in Pakistan. *Sustainability, 11*(6), 1683. https://doi.org/10.3390/su11061683

Abbass, K., Qasim, M. Z., Song, H., et al. (2022a). A review of the global climate change impacts, adaptation, and sustainable mitigation measures. *Environmental Science and Pollution Research, 29*, 42539–42559. https://doi.org/10.1007/s11356-022-19718-6

Abdul, L., & Yu, T. F. (2020). Resilient urbanization: A systematic review on urban discourse in Pakistan. *Urban Science, 4*(4), 76. https://doi.org/10.3390/urbansci4040076

Abiddin, N. Z., Ibrahim, I., & Abdul Aziz, S. A. (2022). Non-governmental organisations (NGOs) and their part towards sustainable community development. *Sustainability, 14*(8), 4386. https://doi.org/10.3390/su14084386

Aga Khan Rural Support Programme (AKRSP). (2011). Renewable energy. Retrieved from http://akrsp.org.pk/index.php/projects/accomplished/renewable-energy/

Agarwal, R., Balasundharam, V., Blagrave, P., Cerutti, E. M., Gudmundsson, R., & Mousa, R. (2021). Climate change in South Asia: Further need for mitigation and adaptation. *IMF Working Papers, 2021*(217), A001. Retrieved Sep 13, 2023, from https://doi.org/10.5089/9781513590677.001.A001

Agarwal, R., Balasundharam, V., Blagrave, P., Cerutti, E. M., Gudmundsson, R., & Moussa, R. (2022). Chapter 7: Climate change: Further need for mitigation and adaptation in South Asia. In *South Asia's path to resilient growth* (pp. 123–137). International Monetary Fund. https://doi.org/10.5089/9781513587219.071.CH007

Akhtar, M. I., Karam, K., & Khan, F. A. (2018). Representation of south Asian countries in five high-impact anesthesia journals. *Saudi Journal of Anaesthesia, 12*(3), 379–383. https://doi.org/10.4103/sja.SJA_635_17

Alexander, D. (2015). Disaster and emergency planning for preparedness, response, and recovery. Oxford research encyclopedias. https://doi.org/10.1093/acrefore/9780199389407.013.12.

Ali, S., Liu, Y., Ishaq, M., Shah, T., Abdullah, I., & A., & Din, I. U. (2017). Climate change and its impact on the yield of major food crops: Evidence from Pakistan. *Food, 6*, 39. https://doi.org/10.3390/foods6060039

Al-Kalbani, M. S., Price, M. F., Abahussain, A., Ahmed, M., & O'Higgins, T. (2014). Vulnerability assessment of environmental and climate change impacts on water resources in Al Jabal Al Akhdar, Sultanate of Oman. *Water, 6*(10), 3118–3135. https://doi.org/10.3390/w6103118

Amini Sedeh, A., Caiazza, R., & Pezeshkan, A. (2023). Unraveling the resource puzzle: Exploring entrepreneurial resource management and the quest for new venture success. *Journal of Technology Transfer*. https://doi.org/10.1007/s10961-023-10024-y

Aparicio, B. C., & 'Ofa, S. V. (2021). Digital technologies for climate change adaptation in Asia and the Pacific. UN ESCAP. Retrieve from https://www.unescap.org/sites/default/d8files/knowledge-products/Digital%20technologies%20for%20climate%20change%20adaptation%20in%20Asia%20and%20the%20Pacific.pdf

Aryal, J. P., Sapkota, T. B., Khurana, R., et al. (2020). Climate change and agriculture in South Asia: Adaptation options in smallholder production systems. *Environment, Development and Sustainability, 22*, 5045–5075. https://doi.org/10.1007/s10668-019-00414-4

Asian Development Bank (ADB). (2020). Global funds. Partnership Report 2020. Retrieved from https://www.adb.org/multimedia/partnership-report2020/modalities/project-specific-cofinancing/global-funds/

Asian Development Bank (ADB). (2022). Climate change mitigation: policies and lessons for Asia. DOI: https://doi.org/10.56506/OJYG4210.

Azevedo de Almeida, B., & Mostafavi, A. (2016). Resilience of infrastructure systems to sea-level rise in coastal areas: Impacts, adaptation measures, and implementation challenges. *Sustainability, 8*(11), 1115. https://doi.org/10.3390/su8111115

Babayomi, O. O., Dahoro, D. A., & Zhang, Z. (2022). Affordable clean energy transition in developing countries: Pathways and technologies. *iScience, 25*(5), 104178. https://doi.org/10.1016/j.isci.2022.104178

Belgacem, S. B., Khatoon, G., & Alzuman, A. (2023). Role of renewable energy and financial innovation in environmental protection: Empirical evidence from UAE and Saudi Arabia. *Sustainability, 15*(11), 8684. https://doi.org/10.3390/su15118684

Bhatt, R. P. (2022). Consequences of climate change impacts and implications on ecosystem and biodiversity; impacts of developmental projects and mitigation strategy in Nepal. In *Climate change in Asia and Africa - examining the biophysical and social consequences, and Society's responses (pp. chapter/page range)*. IntechOpen. https://doi.org/10.5772/intechopen.96455

Blake, J. S., Clark-Ginsberg, A., & Balagna, J. (2021). *Addressing climate migration: A review of national policy approaches*. Rand Corporation. Retrieved from https://www.rand.org/content/dam/rand/pubs/perspectives/PEA1000/PEA1085-1/RAND_PEA1085-1.pdf

Broeckhoven, N., Gidey, D. G., Reda, K. T., Townsend, D., & Verschuuren, J. (2020). CSOs in sustainable development in Ethiopia: Past practices and new trajectories. *African Journal of Legal Studies, 13*(1), 43–72. https://doi.org/10.1163/17087384-12340063

Butt, A. (2022). *It's time for South Asia to talk climate*. United States Institute of Peace. USIP. Retrieved from https://www.usip.org/publications/2022/10/its-time-south-asia-talk-climate

Butt, A. (2023). South Asia's climate challenges are transnational. Its climate solutions must be, too. Atlantic Council. Retrieved from https://www.atlanticcouncil.org/commentary/south-asias-climate-challenges-are-transnational-its-climate-solutions-must-be-too/

Carmen, E., Fazey, I., Ross, H., et al. (2022). Building community resilience in a context of climate change: The role of social capital. *Ambio, 51*, 1371–1387. https://doi.org/10.1007/s13280-021-01678-9

Casile, A. (2021). Climatic variation and Society in Medieval South Asia: Unexplored threads of history and archaeology of Mandu. *The Medieval History Journal, 24*(1–2), 56–91. https://doi.org/10.1177/09719458211056147

Chaudhry, Q. U. Z. (2017). *Climate change profile of Pakistan*. Asian Development Bank. Retrieved from https://www.adb.org/sites/default/files/publication/357876/climate-change-profile-pakistan.pdf

Chen, Y. (2021). Reconciling common but differentiated responsibilities principle and no more favorable treatment principle in regulating greenhouse gas emissions from international shipping. *Marine Policy, 123*, 104317. https://doi.org/10.1016/j.marpol.2020.104317

Clark, R., Reed, J., & Sunderland, T. (2018). Bridging funding gaps for climate and sustainable development: Pitfalls, progress and potential of private finance. *Land Use Policy, 71*, 335–346. https://doi.org/10.1016/j.landusepol.2017.12.013

Commonwealth Secretariat. (2022). Toolkit to enhance access to climate finance: A commonwealth practical guide. Retrieved from https://unfccc.int/sites/default/files/resource/Toolkit_to_Enhance_Access_to_Climate_Finance_UPDF.pdf

Costa, M. J., Salvador Leitão, A., Silva, R., Monteiro, V., & Melo, P. (2022). Climate change prevention through community actions and empowerment: A scoping review. *International Journal of Environmental Research and Public Health, 19*(22), 14645. https://doi.org/10.3390/ijerph192214645

Court, J., Mendizabal, E., Osborne, D., & Young, J. (2006). Policy engagement: How civil society can be more effective. *Overseas Development Institute*. http://cdn-odi-production.s3-website-eu-west-1.amazonaws.com/media/documents/200.pdf

Craig, R. K. (2017). Climate change and common but differentiated responsibilities for the ocean. *Carbon & Climate Law Review, 11*(4), 325–334. https://www.jstor.org/stable/26245381

Dahlan, N. Y., Ahmad, N., Ilham, N. I., & Yusoff, S. H. (2022). Chapter 4 - energy security: Role of renewable and low-carbon technologies. In M. Asif (Ed.), *Handbook of energy and environmental security* (pp. 39–60). Academic Press. https://doi.org/10.1016/B978-0-12-824084-7.00015-1

Daron, J., Soares, M. B., Janes, T., et al. (2022). Advancing climate services in South Asia. *Climate Services, 26*, 100295. https://doi.org/10.1016/j.cliser.2022.100295

Deisenrieder, V., Kubisch, S., Keller, L., & Stötter, J. (2020). Bridging the action gap by democratizing climate change education—The case of k.i.d.Z.21 in the context of Fridays for future. *Sustainability, 12*(5), 1748. https://doi.org/10.3390/su12051748

Dejenie, T., & Kakiso, T. (2023). Development and environmental policies of Ethiopia: Policy review from the viewpoint of development-environment sustainability linkage. *Heliyon, 9*(6), e16608. https://doi.org/10.1016/j.heliyon.2023.e16608

Di Gregorio, M., Nurrochmat, D. R., Paavola, J., Sari, I. M., Fatorelli, L., Pramova, E., et al. (2017). Climate policy integration in the land use sector: Mitigation, adaptation, and sustainable development linkages. *Environmental Science & Policy, 67*, 35–43. https://doi.org/10.1016/j.envsci.2016.11.004

Elazari, E. (2022). *The role of international organizations in climate governance*. Global Risk Insight. https://globalriskinsights.com/2022/04/the-role-of-international-organizations-in-climate-governance/

Espinosa, C., & Rangel, G. (2022). What roles do civil society organizations play in monitoring and reviewing the sustainable development goals? An exploration of cases from Ecuador, Colombia, and Argentina. : Latin American Science, Technology and Society, 5(1), 2143669. doi:https://doi.org/10.1080/25729861.2022.2143669.

Etinay, N., Egbu, C., & Murray, V. (2018). Building urban resilience for disaster risk management and disaster risk reduction. *Procedia Engineering, 212*, 575–582. https://doi.org/10.1016/j.proeng.2018.01.074

European Union. (2021). South Asian Association for Regional Cooperation (SAARC). Retrieved from https://www.eeas.europa.eu/eeas/south-asian-association-regional-cooperation-saarc_en

Farhangi, H. (2017). Smart Grid. In M. A. Abraham (Ed.), *Encyclopedia of sustainable technologies* (pp. 195–203). Elsevier. https://doi.org/10.1016/B978-0-12-409548-9.10135-6

Flores, A., & Peralta, L. (2019). *The enhancement of resilience to disasters and climate change in the Caribbean through the modernization of the energy sector*. United Nations. https://repositorio.cepal.org/server/api/core/bitstreams/ce56ff24-ee7e-4c0e-af46-abae23726186/content

Gaudenzi, B., Pellegrino, R., & Confente, I. (2023). Achieving supply chain resilience in an era of disruptions: A configuration approach of capacities and strategies. *Supply Chain Management, 28*(7), 97–111.

Gong, X., Liu, Y., & Sun, T. (2020). Evaluating climate change governance using the "polity–policy–politics" framework: A comparative study of China and the United States. *Sustainability, 12*(16), 6403. https://doi.org/10.3390/su12166403

Green Climate Fund. (2023). Recharge Pakistan: Building Pakistan's resilience to climate change through ecosystem-based adaptation for integrated flood risk management. https://www.greenclimate.fund/project/fp207

Haq, A. U., Jalal, M., Sindi, H. F., & Ahmad, S. (2020). Energy scenario in South Asia: Analytical assessment and policy implications. *IEEE Access*. https://doi.org/10.1109/ACCESS.2020.3019648

Heuty, A. (2012). Chapter 18. The role of transparency and civil Society in Managing Commodities for inclusive growth and development. In *Commodity Price volatility and inclusive growth in low-income countries*. International Monetary Fund. https://doi.org/10.5089/9781616353797.071.ch018

Homberg, M. V., & McQuistan, C. (2019). Technology for climate justice: A reporting framework for loss and damage as part of key global agreements. In R. Mechler, L. Bouwer, T. Schinko, S. Surminski, & J. Linnerooth-Bayer (Eds.), *Loss and damage from climate change (climate risk management, policy and governance, pp. chapter 22)*. Springer. https://doi.org/10.1007/978-3-319-72026-5_22

IFAD. (2019). Coastal climate resilient infrastructure project. https://www.ifad.org/en/web/operations/-/project/1100001647

IISD. (2017). Integrating climate considerations into National development planning in the spotlight. Retrieved in August 2023 from http://sdg.iisd.org/news/integrating-climate-considerations-into-national-development-planning-in-the-spotlight/

IPCC. (2023). Summary for policymakers. In Core Writing Team, H. Lee, & J. Romero (Eds.), *Climate change 2023: Synthesis report. Contribution of working groups I, II and III to the sixth assessment report of the intergovernmental panel on climate change* (pp. 1–34). IPCC. https://doi.org/10.59327/IPCC/AR6-9789291691647.001

IRENA. (2022). Renewable energy outlook for ASEAN: Towards a regional energy transition. https://www.irena.org/-/media/Files/IRENA/Agency/Publication/2022/Sep/IRENA_Renewable_energy_outlook_ASEAN_2022.pdf?rev=ef7557c64c3b4750be08f9590601634c

Ishaque, W., Tanvir, R., & Mukhtar, M. (2022). Climate change and water crises in Pakistan: Implications on water quality and health risks. *Journal of Environmental Public Health*. https://doi.org/10.1155/2022/5484561

Islam, S. N., & Winkel, J. (2017). *Climate change and social inequality*. Department of Economic & Social Affairs. https://www.un.org/esa/desa/papers/2017/wp152_2017.pdf

Jain, H., Dhupper, R., Shrivastava, A., et al. (2023). AI-enabled strategies for climate change adaptation: Protecting communities, infrastructure, and businesses from the impacts of climate change. *Computational Urban Science, 3*, 25. https://doi.org/10.1007/s43762-023-00100-2

Khatibi, F. S., Dedekorkut-Howes, A., & Howes, M. (2021). Can public awareness, knowledge and engagement improve climate change adaptation policies? *Discovery of Sustainability, 2*, 18. https://doi.org/10.1007/s43621-021-00024-z

Kim, H. L., Li, T., Kalsi, N., et al. (2023). Prehistoric human migration between Sundaland and South Asia was driven by sea-level rise. *Communications Biology, 6*, 150. https://doi.org/10.1038/s42003-023-04510-0

Koch, H. J. (2012). Foreword. In IEA-retd, R. de Vos, & J. Sawin (Eds.), *READy: Renewable energy action on deployment*. Academic Press. https://doi.org/10.1016/B978-0-12-405519-3.06001-1

Kugelman, M. (2020). *Climate-induced displacement: South Asia's clear and present danger*. Wilson Center. https://www.wilsoncenter.org/article/climate-induced-displacement-south-asias-clear-and-present-danger

Kusters, K., De Graaf, M., Buck, L., Galido, K., Maindo, A., Mendoza, H., et al. (2020). Inclusive landscape governance for sustainable development: Assessment methodology and lessons for civil society organizations. *Land, 9*(4), 128. https://doi.org/10.3390/land9040128

Li, M., Hamawandy, N. M., Wahid, F., Rjoub, H., & Bao, Z. (2021). Renewable energy resources investment and green finance: Evidence from China. *Resources Policy, 74*. https://doi.org/10.1016/j.resourpol.2021.102402

Lu, X. (2022). *Accelerating private sector engagement in adaptation in Asia and the Pacific*. Asian Development Bank. https://www.adb.org/sites/default/files/publication/838831/sdwp-084-private-sector-adaptation-asia-pacific.pdf

Malhi, G. S., Kaur, M., & Kaushik, P. (2021). Impact of climate change on agriculture and its mitigation strategies: A review. *Sustainability, 13*(3), 1318. https://doi.org/10.3390/su13031318

Markolf, S. A., Hoehne, C., Fraser, A., Chester, M. V., & Underwood, B. S. (2019a). Transportation resilience to climate change and extreme weather events—Beyond risk and robustness. *Transport Policy, 74*, 174–186. https://doi.org/10.1016/j.tranpol.2018.11.003

Masud, M. A. K., Sahara, J., & Kabir, M. H. (2023). A relationship between climate finance and climate risk: Evidence from the south Asian region. *Climate, 11*(6), 119. https://doi.org/10.3390/cli11060119

Mbah, M. F., Shingruf, A., & Molthan-Hill, P. (2022). Policies and practices of climate change education in South Asia: Towards a support framework for an impactful climate change adaptation. *Climate Action, 1*, 28. https://doi.org/10.1007/s44168-022-00028-z

McAdam, J. (2012). *Climate change, forced migration, and international law*. Oxford University Press. https://www.ohchr.org/sites/default/files/documents/issues/climatechange/cfi-hrc-53-session/submissions/2022-11-28/Jame-McAdam-4.pdf

McMichael, C., Barnett, J., & McMichael, A. J. (2012). An ill wind? Climate change, migration, and health. *Environmental Health Perspectives, 120*(5), 646–654. https://doi.org/10.1289/ehp.1104375

Mizo, R. (2016). India, China, and climate cooperation. *India Quarterly, 72*(4), 375–394. https://www.jstor.org/stable/48505519

Moallemi, E. A., Malekpour, S., Hadjikakou, M., Raven, R., Szetey, K., Ningrum, D., Dhiaulhaq, A., & Bryan, B. A. (2020). Achieving the sustainable development goals requires transdisciplinary innovation at the local scale. *One Earth, 3*(3), 300–313. https://doi.org/10.1016/j.oneear.2020.08.006

Mondal, S. K., Huang, J., Wang, Y., Su, B., Kundzewicz, Z. W., Jiang, S., et al. (2022). Changes in extreme precipitation across South Asia for each 0.5°C of warming from 1.5°C to 3.0°C above pre-industrial levels. *Atmospheric Research, 266*, 105961. https://doi.org/10.1016/j.atmosres.2021.105961

Montoute, A., Mohammed, D., & Francis, J. (2019). Prospects and challenges for civil society and climate change engagement in the Caribbean: The case of Trinidad and Tobago. *Caribbean Studies, 47*(2), 81–109.

Mukhopadhyay, R., Karisiddaiah, S. M., & Mukhopadhyay, J. (2018). Carbon policy of South Asia. In R. Mukhopadhyay, S. M. Karisiddaiah, & J. Mukhopadhyay (Eds.), *Climate change* (pp. 71–98). Elsevier. https://doi.org/10.1016/B978-0-12-812164-1.00004-9

Mumtaz, M. (2021). Role of civil society organizations for promoting green and blue infrastructure to adapting climate change: Evidence from Islamabad city, Pakistan. *Journal of Cleaner Production, 309*, 127296. https://doi.org/10.1016/j.jclepro.2021.127296

National Bureau of Asian Research (NBR). (2022). Strengthening disaster response and cooperation in South Asia. Report from nontraditional security challenges in South Asia. https://www.nbr.org/publication/strengthening-disaster-response-and-cooperation-in-south-asia/

NDRMF. (n.d.). About us. Retrieved from https://ndrmf.pk/about-us/who-we-are/

Neupane, N., Chaudhary, P., Rijal, Y., Ghimire, B., & Bhandari, R. (2022). The role of renewable energy in achieving water, energy, and food security under climate change constraints in South Asia. *Frontiers in Sustainable Food Systems, 6*, 1016093. https://doi.org/10.3389/fsufs.2022.1016093

Nishi, M., Subramanian, S. M., & Melaku, A. (2023). Synthesis: Ecosystem restoration in the context of socio-ecological production landscapes and seascapes (SEPLS). In M. Nishi & S. M. Subramanian (Eds.), *Ecosystem restoration through managing socio-ecological production landscapes and seascapes (SEPLS). (Satoyama initiative thematic review)*. Springer. https://doi.org/10.1007/978-981-99-1292-6_14

Olabi, A. G., Obaideen, K., Abdelkareem, M. A., AlMallahi, M. N., Shehata, N., Alami, A. H., et al. (2023). Wind energy contribution to the sustainable development goals: Case study on London Array. *Sustainability, 15*(5), 4641. https://doi.org/10.3390/su15054641

Post, L., Schmitz, A., Issa, T., & Oehmke, J. (2021). Enabling the environment for private sector investment: Impact on food security and poverty. *Journal of Agricultural & Food Industrial Organization, 19*(1), 25–37. https://doi.org/10.1515/jafio-2021-0013

PR Newswire. (2023). *How green foundation utilizes blockchain technology to help in the fight against deforestation and global warming*. Yahoo Finance. https://finance.yahoo.com/news/green-foundation-utilizes-blockchain-technology-125000812.html

Prabhakar, S. V. R. K., Issar, R., Abu Bakar, A. B., & Yokoo, M. (2021). Mitigating transboundary risks by integrating risk reduction frameworks of health and DRR: A perspective from COVID-19 pandemic. In A. L. Ramanathan, C. Sabarathinam, M. V. Francisco Arriola, P. K. Prasanna, & M. P. Jonathan (Eds.), *Environmental resilience and transformation in times of COVID-19* (pp. 63–76). Elsevier. https://doi.org/10.1016/B978-0-323-85512-9.00014-0

Pritipadmaja, G. R. D., & Sharma, A. K. (2023). Assessing the cooling effect of blue-green spaces: Implications for urban Heat Island mitigation. *Water, 15*(16), 2983. https://doi.org/10.3390/w15162983

Rahman, S. H., Khatri, S., & Brunner, H.-P. (2012). *Regional integration and economic development in South Asia*. Asian Development Bank. https://www.adb.org/sites/default/files/publication/29871/regional-integration-economic-development-south-asia.pdf

Raihan, A., Rashid, M., Voumik, L. C., Akter, S., & Esquivias, M. A. (2023). The dynamic impacts of economic growth, financial globalization, fossil fuel, renewable energy, and urbanization on load capacity factor in Mexico. *Sustainability, 15*(18), 13462. https://doi.org/10.3390/su151813462

Ram, M., Osorio-Aravena, J. C., Aghahosseini, A., Bogdanov, D., & Breyer, C. (2022). Job creation during a climate-compliant global energy transition across the power, heat, transport, and desalination sectors by 2050. *Energy, 238*(Part A), 121690. https://doi.org/10.1016/j.energy.2021.121690

Ramirez, J. M., Hernandez-Tolentino, A., & Marmolejo-Saucedo, J. A. (2021). Chapter 3 - A stochastic robust approach to deal with the generation and transmission expansion planning problem embedding renewable sources. In A. F. Zobaa & S. H. E. Abdel Aleem (Eds.), *Uncertainties in modern power systems* (pp. 57–91). Academic Press. https://doi.org/10.1016/B978-0-12-820491-7.00003-7

Reimann, L., Jones, B., & Bieker, N. (2023). Exploring spatial feedbacks between adaptation policies and internal migration patterns due to sea-level rise. *Nature Communications, 14*, 2630. https://doi.org/10.1038/s41467-023-38278-y

Roesch, L. J., & Nobre, J. A. (2021). *Strengthening the current climate governance system: Mapping leading states and initiatives*. Global Challenges Foundation. https://www.ipinst.org/wp-content/uploads/2021/11/Strengthening-the-Current-Climate-Governance-System.pdf

Rosane, O. (2022). *Deadly heat wave in India and Pakistan was 30x more likely due to climate change, scientists say*. World Economic Forum. https://www.weforum.org/agenda/2022/06/deadly-heat-wave-in-india-and-pakistan-was-30x-more-likely-due-to-climate-change-scientists-say/

Samarakkody, A., Amaratunga, D., & Haigh, R. (2023). Technological innovations for enhancing disaster resilience in smart cities: A comprehensive urban Scholar's analysis. *Sustainability, 15*(15), 12036. https://doi.org/10.3390/su151512036

Samnuzulsari, T., Kristanti, D., Susanto, H., Yudiatmaja, W. E., Yunanto, M. K., & Meilinda, S. D. (2021). The strategic role of civil society organisations in handling climate change: A case of Riau in Indonesia. *IOP Conference Series: Earth and Environmental Science, 824*, 012104. https://doi.org/10.1088/1755-1315/824/1/012104

Scheffran, J. (2023). Limits to the Anthropocene: Geopolitical conflict or cooperative governance? *Frontiers in Political Science, 5*. https://doi.org/10.3389/fpos.2023.1190610

Scott, C. A., Zhang, F., Mukherji, A., Immerzeel, W., Mustafa, D., & Bharati, L. (2019). Water in the Hindu Kush Himalaya. In P. Wester, A. Mishra, A. Mukherji, & A. Shrestha (Eds.), *The Hindu Kush Himalaya assessment* (pp. 169–186). Springer. https://doi.org/10.1007/978-3-319-92288-1_8

Seetharaman, K. M., Patwa, N., Saravanan, & Gupta, Y. (2019). Breaking barriers in deployment of renewable energy. *Heliyon, 5*(1), e01166. https://doi.org/10.1016/j.heliyon.2019.e01166

Shah, A. A., Ullah, A., Khan, N. A., Khan, A., Tariq, M. A. U. R., & Xu, C. (2023). Community social barriers to non-technical aspects of flood early warning systems and NGO-led interventions: The case of Pakistan. *Frontiers in Earth Science, 11*. https://doi.org/10.3389/feart.2023.1068721

Shammin, M. R., Haque, A. K. E., & Faisal, I. M. (2022). A framework for climate resilient community-based adaptation. In A. K. E. Haque, P. Mukhopadhyay, M. Nepal, & M. R. Shammin (Eds.), *Climate change and community resilience* (p. 2). Springer. https://doi.org/10.1007/978-981-16-0680-9_2

Sharma, A., Andhikaputra, G., & Wang, Y.-C. (2022). Heatwaves in South Asia: Characterization, consequences on human health, and adaptation strategies. *Atmosphere, 13*(5), 734. https://doi.org/10.3390/atmos13050734

Shaw, R., Luo, Y., Cheong, T. S., Abdul Halim, S., Chaturvedi, S., Hashizume, M., et al. (2022). Asia. In H.-O. Pörtner, D. C. Roberts, M. Tignor, E. S. Poloczanska, K. Mintenbeck, A. Alegría, & B. Rama (Eds.), *Climate change 2022: Impacts, adaptation and vulnerability. Contribution of working group II to the sixth assessment report of the intergovernmen-*

tal panel on climate change (pp. 1457–1579). Cambridge University Press. https://doi.org/10.1017/9781009325844.012
Shayan, N. F., Mohabbati-Kalejahi, N., Alavi, S., & Zahed, M. A. (2022). Sustainable development goals (SDGs) as a framework for corporate social responsibility (CSR). *Sustainability, 14*(3), 1222.
Shukla, A. K., Sudhakar, K., & Baredar, P. (2017). Renewable energy resources in south Asian countries: Challenges, policy, and recommendations. *Resource-Efficient Technologies, 3*(3), 342–346. https://doi.org/10.1016/j.reffit.2016.12.003
Sibtain, M., Li, X., Bashir, H., & Azam, M. I. (2021). Hydropower exploitation for Pakistan's sustainable development: A SWOT analysis considering current situation, challenges, and prospects. *Energy Strategy Reviews, 38*, 100728. https://doi.org/10.1016/j.esr.2021.100728
Siddiqui,U.(2023).“WhatmakesSouthAsiasovulnerabletoclimatechange?”AlJazeera,8Jul.https://www.aljazeera.com/news/2023/7/8/what-makes-south-asia-so-vulnerable-to-climate-change
Singh, R., Gehlot, A., Akram, S. V., Thakur, A. K., Buddhi, D., & Das, P. K. (2022). Forest 4.0: Digitalization of forest using the internet of things (IoT). *Journal of King Saud University - Computer and Information Sciences, 34*(8), 5587–5601. https://doi.org/10.1016/j.jksuci.2021.02.009
Sishodia, R. P., Ray, R. L., & Singh, S. K. (2020). Applications of remote sensing in precision agriculture: A review. *Remote Sensing, 12*(19), 3136. https://doi.org/10.3390/rs12193136
Soergel, B., Kriegler, E., & Weindl, I. (2021). A sustainable development pathway for climate action within the UN 2030 agenda. *Nature Climate Change, 11*, 656–664. https://doi.org/10.1038/s41558-021-01098-3
Swanson, D., Murphy, D., Temmer, J., & Scaletta, T. (2021). *Advancing the climate resilience of Canadian infrastructure: A review of literature to inform the way forward.* International Institute for Sustainable Development. https://www.iisd.org/system/files/2021-07/climate-resilience-canadian-infrastructure-en.pdf
Tall, A., Lynagh, S., Blanco Vecchi, C., Bardouille, P., Montoya Pino, F., Shabahat, E., et al. (2021). *Enabling private investment in climate adaptation & resilience: Current status, barriers to investment and blueprint for action.* World Bank Group. https://openknowledge.worldbank.org/server/api/core/bitstreams/127de8c7-d367-59ac-9e54-27ee52c744aa/content
Taylor, C., Robinson, T. R., Dunning, S., Carr, J. R., & Westoby, M. (2023). Glacial lake outburst floods threaten millions globally. *Nature Communications, 14*(1), 487. https://doi.org/10.1038/s41467-023-36033-x
The New Yorker. (2023). India's Quest to Build the World's Largest Solar Farms. https://www.newyorker.com/news/dept-of-energy/indias-quest-to-build-the-worlds-largest-solar-farms
The Royal Society. (2020). How does climate change affect the strength and frequency of floods, droughts, hurricanes, and tornadoes? https://royalsociety.org/topics-policy/projects/climate-change-evidence-causes/question-13/
The United States Environmental Protection Agency (USEPA). (2023a). Climate Change Indicators: Greenhouse Gases. https://www.epa.gov/climate-indicators/greenhouse-gases
The United States Environmental Protection Agency (USEPA). (2023b). Climate Change Indicators: U.S. and global precipitation. https://www.epa.gov/climate-indicators/climate-change-indicators-us-and-global-precipitation
The World Bank. (2021). India's solar learning curve inspires action across the World. https://www.worldbank.org/en/news/feature/2021/07/09/india-s-solar-learning-curve-inspires-action-across-the-world
The World Bank Group. (n.d.). Climate and development in South Asia. Retrieved in September 2023 from https://www.worldbank.org/en/region/sar/brief/integrating-climate-and-development-in-south-asia/integrating-climate-and-development-in-south-asia-region
Thomas, K., Hardy, R. D., Lazrus, H., Mendez, M., Orlove, B., Rivera-Collazo, I., et al. (2019). Explaining differential vulnerability to climate change: A social science review. *Wiley Interdisciplinary Reviews: Climate Change, 10*(2), e565. https://doi.org/10.1002/wcc.565

Tosun, J., & Peters, B. G. (2021). The politics of climate change: Domestic and international responses to a global challenge. *International Political Science Review, 42*(1), 3–15. https://doi.org/10.1177/0192512120975659

Ullah, I., Saleem, F., Iyakaremye, V., Yin, J., Ma, X., Syed, S., & Omer, A. (2022). Projected changes in socioeconomic exposure to heatwaves in South Asia under changing climate. *Earth's Future, 10*, e2021EF002240. https://doi.org/10.1029/2021EF002240

UNDP. (2023). Enhancing climate resilience of India's coastal communities. Retrieved from https://www.adaptation-undp.org/projects/enhancing-climate-resilience-india%E2%80%99s-coastal-communities#:~:text=Implemented%20by%20the%20Ministry%20of,in%20the%20coastal%20areas%20of

UNDP Climate. (2022). Melting glaciers, growing lakes and the threat of outburst floods. https://undp-climate.exposure.co/melting-glaciers-growing-lakes-and-the-threat-of-outburst-floods

UNESCAP. (2017). Achieving the sustainable development goals in South Asia: Key policy priorities and implementation challenges. https://www.unescap.org/sites/default/files/publications/UNESCAP%20-%20SRO-SSWA%20SDG%20Report_Sep2018.pdf

UNESCAP. (2018). Integrating South Asia's power grid for a sustainable and low carbon future. https://www.unescap.org/sites/default/files/Integrating%20South%20Asia%E2%80%99s%20Power%20Grid%20for%20a%20Sustainable%20and%20Low%20Carbon%20Future_WEB.pdf

UNFCCC. (n.d.). The Paris Agreement. https://unfccc.int/process-and-meetings/the-paris-agreement

UNICEF. (2018). Using knowledge exchange to support innovations in program monitoring and response for child health. https://www.unicef.org/esa/media/511/file/ESA-2018-Using-Knowledge-Exchange.pdf

United Nations Department of Political and Peacebuilding Affairs (UN DPPA). (2022). The implications of climate change for mediation and peace processes: DPPA Practice Note. https://peacemaker.un.org/sites/peacemaker.un.org/files/DPPAPracticeNote-TheImplicationsofClimateChangeforMediationandPeaceProcesses.pdf

United Nations Economic Commission for Europe (UNECE). (2015). Water and climate change adaptation in transboundary basins: Lessons learned and good practices. https://unece.org/sites/default/files/2021-12/ece.mp_.wat_.45_eng.pdf

United Nations Human Rights (UNHR). (n.d.). Climate change: Protecting the rights of migrants. https://www.ohchr.org/sites/default/files/Documents/Issues/ClimateChange/materials/2PMigrationLight.pdf

United Nations Office for Disaster Risk Reduction. (2023). GAR special report: Measuring resilience for the sustainable development goals. Geneva. Retrieved from https://www.undrr.org/gar/gar2023-special-report

Vaka, M., Walvekar, R., Rasheed, A. K., & Khalid, M. (2020). A review on Malaysia's solar energy pathway towards carbon-neutral Malaysia beyond Covid-19 pandemic. *Journal of Cleaner Production, 273*, 122834. https://doi.org/10.1016/j.jclepro.2020.122834

Wamsler, C., Wickenberg, B., Hanson, H., Alkan Olsson, J., Stålhammar, S., Björn, H., et al. (2020). Environmental and climate policy integration: Targeted strategies for overcoming barriers to nature-based solutions and climate change adaptation. *Journal of Cleaner Production, 247*, 119154. https://doi.org/10.1016/j.jclepro.2019.119154

Wang, F., Harindintwali, J. D., Yuan, Z., Wang, M., Wang, F., Li, S., et al. (2021). Technologies and perspectives for achieving carbon neutrality. *The Innovation, 2*(4), 100180. https://doi.org/10.1016/j.xinn.2021.100180

Wang, L., Wang, L., Li, Y., & Wang, J. (2023). A century-long analysis of global warming and earth temperature using a random walk with drift approach. *Decision Analytics Journal, 7*, 100237. https://doi.org/10.1016/j.dajour.2023.100237

Wood, L. R., Neumann, K., Nicholson, K. N., Bird, B. W., Dowling, C. B., & Sharma, S. (2020). Melting Himalayan glaciers threaten domestic water resources in the Mount Everest region, Nepal. *Frontiers in Earth Science, 8*, 128. https://doi.org/10.3389/feart.2020.00128

Worku, M. Y. (2022). Recent advances in energy storage systems for renewable source grid integration: A comprehensive review. *Sustainability, 14*(10), 5985. https://doi.org/10.3390/su14105985

World Bank and Energy Charter Secretariat. (2023). *Enabling foreign direct Investment in Renewable Energy Sector: Reducing regulatory risks and preventing investor-state conflicts*. World Bank. https://openknowledge.worldbank.org/server/api/core/bitstreams/c8a71ae5-a09b-4f42-8253-b44672c6b914/content

World Bank Group. (n.d.-a). Climate change governance. Retrieved in August 2023 from https://www.worldbank.org/en/programs/climate-change-governance

World Bank Group. (n.d.-b). Social dimensions of climate change. https://www.worldbank.org/en/topic/social-dimensions-of-climate-change

World Weather Attribution. (2022). Climate Change made devastating early heat in India and Pakistan 30 times more likely. https://www.worldweatherattribution.org/climate-change-made-devastating-early-heat-in-india-and-pakistan-30-times-more-likely/

Xue, L., Haseeb, M., Mahmood, H., Alkhateeb, T. T. Y., & Murshed, M. (2021). Renewable energy use and ecological footprints mitigation: Evidence from selected south Asian economies. *Sustainability, 13*(4), 1613. https://doi.org/10.3390/su13041613

Yang, M., Chen, L., & Wang, J. (2023). Circular economy strategies for combating climate change and other environmental issues. *Environmental Chemistry Letters, 21*, 55–80. https://doi.org/10.1007/s10311-022-01499-6

Yu, Y., Xu, Y., & Zhao, X. (2023). Environmental management through examining the technical factors of carbon emissions in south Asian economies. *Journal of Environmental Management, 342*, 118123. https://doi.org/10.1016/j.jenvman.2023.118123

Zafarullah, H., & Huque, A. S. (2018). Climate change, regulatory policies and regional cooperation in South Asia. *Public Administration and Policy: An Asia-Pacific Journal, 21*(1), 22–35. https://doi.org/10.1108/PAP-06-2018-001

Maryam Eqan is an environmental scientist, holding a degree in environmental science. She has authored eight academic papers and book chapters in reputable journals, including "Science of the Total Environment" and Springer Nature. Currently, Maryam serves as an officer in Water Sensitive Cities at WWF-Pakistan, focusing on sustainable water management. Additionally, she is a Fellow for GEO-7 at the United Nations Environment Programme (UNEP), contributing to global environmental management and policy development.

Junfeng Wan is an environmental engineer and academic, earned his BEng from Southeast University in 2000 and a Ph.D. from INSA-Toulouse in 2009. His postdoctoral work at the University of Limoges in France focused on remediation of arsenic-polluted groundwater. He later undertook academic exchanges in Singapore. Currently an associate professor at Zhengzhou University, his research interests include environmental biotechnology and wastewater treatment. Dr. Wan has authored over 50 papers in reputable journals, such as Water Research and Bioresource Technology, and serves as a reviewer for international academic journals.

Promoting Sustainable Development Through Improving Green Banking Behaviour

Sang Tang My

Abstract This chapter provides readers with empirical evidence on green banking behaviour in Vietnam. Green banking has recently emerged as an ideal future model for banks, serving as a foundation for transitioning to a green economy and sustainable development. The study finds that subjective norms, attitudes toward the green bank, perceived behavioural control, and top management support directly affect green banking intention. Subjective norms had the most significant impact of all. All independent variables were found to affect green banking behaviour through the indirect contribution of green banking intention. Furthermore, green banking intention significantly influences green banking behaviour. The research findings imply effective solutions for promoting green banking behaviour in developing countries.

1 Introduction

Due to the insecurity of the development process and the over-exploitation of the natural environment for economic gain, sustainable development has emerged as a new trend in the development concept (Jan et al., 2022). Allowing markets to operate under effective economic instruments and cost management mechanisms is the most effective way to achieve sustainable development (Ambrosio et al., 2022). One of the factors affecting general industrial activity and economic growth is financial institutions, typically the banking sector (Tsindeliani et al., 2022).

Banking operations have significant impacts on economic growth (Lukšić et al., 2022) since the sector provides the primary funding source for firms and organisations (Ozili, 2020). Consequently, it is critical to encourage investments in environmentally sustainable development and community responsibility. While banks may not be direct polluters, they may be involved with current or future polluting

S. T. My (✉)
Faculty of Finance and Accounting, Ho Chi Minh City University of Economics and Finance (UEF), Ho Chi Minh City, Vietnam
e-mail: sangtm@uef.edu.vn

V. Q. Trinh (ed.), *Climate Governance and Corporate Eco-innovation*, Sustainable Finance, https://doi.org/10.1007/978-3-031-56423-9_8

companies or investments (Park & Kim, 2020). The banking sector is generally considered environmentally friendly regarding emissions and pollution (Nath et al., 2014). Energy, paper, and water usage are frequently minimal in the banking sector (Park & Kim, 2020). The environmental impacts of banks are not directly related to banking operations but rather to external activities generated by the bank's customers (Stauropoulou et al., 2023). As a result, while the impact of banks' external activities is significant, estimating it can be challenging (Tan, 2022).

Furthermore, environmental management is very similar to risk management in the banking industry (Ambrosio et al., 2022; Park & Kim, 2020). In other words, green banking[1] is one of the proactive risk management strategies promoting sustainable development (Hasan et al., 2022; Park & Kim, 2020). The success of a green banking strategy is strongly influenced by employee attitudes and behaviours (Hasan et al., 2022; Nath et al., 2014). Bank employees are the people who perform green banking activities daily and have a particular impact on customers' choice of services (Rehman et al., 2021). According to the Theory of Reasoned Action—TRA, behavioural intention influences customer behaviour, which is influenced by subjective norms, attitude, and perceived behaviour control (Madden et al., 1992). When researching the fields of e-banking and sustainable development, these factors are also identified as the primary factors influencing behaviour (Ramayah et al., 2009), (Hasan et al., 2022). Besides, prior research shows that top management support significantly affects bank employees' behavioural intention and behaviour (Hasan et al., 2022; Rodríguez Bolívar et al., 2015). Green banking necessitates a shift in service delivery and an investment in people and capital (Peterson & Jun, 2006). As a result, senior managers must be available and have a decisive influence on performance.

Box 1
Green banking is one of the proactive risk management strategies promoting sustainable development. Employee attitudes and behaviours strongly influence the success of a green banking strategy.

Green banking has been becoming increasingly appealing to credit institutions in Vietnam. However, there is a need for more research on this area, especially the role of top management support in green banking strategy. The existing findings (e.g., Hà & Hà, 2019) show that green banking assists businesses in developing green products through credit granting. Other research on green banking applications focuses primarily on energy conservation, straightforward procedures, time feasibility, cost-effectiveness, and product accessibility. The findings indicate minimal public awareness and understanding (Giao, 2020). To the best of our knowledge,

[1] It was a thriving new banking model in India, but activities increased (Nath et al., 2014). Pakistan is also a country with numerous environmental issues; its central bank has incorporated environmental safety regulations into its regulations (Rehman et al., 2021).

behavioural research on green banking is still scarce. There had been no research on the factors influencing the attitude toward using green banking services, thereby influencing behaviour in Vietnam. In this chapter, we fill the critical void by examining green banking behaviour in this country and the role of senior managers in such behaviour.

2 Literature Review

2.1 *Related Theories*

2.1.1 Theory of Reasoned Action: TRA

Ajzen and Fishbein developed the Theory of Reasoned Action (TRA) in 1967 and expanded it since the early 1970s (Madden et al., 1992). According to the theory model, behavioural intentions lead to behaviour, and intentions are determined by individuals' attitudes toward the behaviour and the influence of subjective norms surrounding the performance of those behaviours. In this case, attitude and subjective norms influence behavioural intention (Blue, 1995). This model predicts and explains the propensity to perform behaviour based on the consumer's attitude toward consumer behaviour rather than the consumer's attitude toward the product or service.

The TRA model includes behaviour, behavioural intention, attitudes, and subjective norms (Madden et al., 1992). Behaviours are observable actions of an object that are determined by behavioural intentions (i.e., measuring a subject's subjective ability to perform a behaviour that is determined by individual attitudes toward behaviours and subjective norms). The attitude expresses an individual's positive or negative perceptions of performing a behaviour and could be measured by the sum of the strength of belief and evaluation of this belief. Subjective norms are defined as an individual's perception, based on critical references, of whether or not a particular behaviour should or should not be performed (Yousafzai et al., 2010). See Fig. 1.

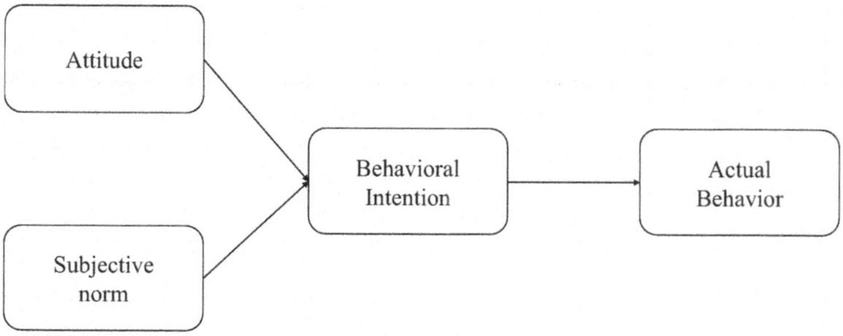

Fig. 1 Theory of reasoned action. Source: Fishbein and Ajzen (1977)

TRA theory is commonly used in several fields, such as services (Tanhan & Young, 2022), food (Rahman et al., 2021), environmentally friendly products (Sharma et al., 2022), and bank (Hasan et al., 2022). It is appropriate for green banking research because subjective norms and attitudes are two premises that could influence green banking attitudes. Also, research using TRA for green banks reveals that attitude affects behaviour toward green banks (Hasan et al., 2022). Based on this theory, a study on credit card use behaviour in Malaysia shows that a better attitude toward behaviour positively impacts behaviour (Amin, 2013).

Box 2
The components of the Theory of Reasoned Action (TRA) model include behaviour, behavioural intention, attitudes, and subjective norms. It can be used in the research on green banking because subjective norms and attitudes are two premises that could potentially influence green banking attitudes.

2.1.2 Theory of Planned Behaviour: TPB

TPB theory evolves from the TRA, which holds that behavioural tendencies to perform a behaviour can be predicted or explained (Yousafzai et al., 2010). Three factors could influence the behavioural intention: *attitudes* (i.e., positive or negative assessments of performance behaviour), *social influence* (i.e., perceived social pressure to perform or refrain from performing the behaviour), and *perceived behavioural control* (in the TRA model) (Conner & Armitage, 1998). The TPB model overcomes the disadvantages of the TRA model by adding *controlling perceived behaviour* (Yousafzai et al., 2010). Perceived behavioural control reflects the ease or difficulty of performing the behaviour, which is determined by the availability of resources and opportunities to serve the behaviour. It is proposed that the behavioural control factors directly affect the tendency to perform the behaviour and that if the person is correct in his perception of the degree of control, behavioural control also predicts the behaviour (Ajzen & Driver, 1992). See Fig. 2.

Box 3
The Theory of Planned Behaviour (TPB) model overcomes the disadvantages of the TRA by adding controlling perceived behaviour. Perceived behavioural control reflects the ease or difficulty of performing the behaviour, which is determined by the availability of resources and opportunities to serve the behaviour.

The TPB model has been widely used in studies on the intent to use and behaviour of online banking and e-banking (Aldammagh et al., 2021; Shih & Fang, 2004).

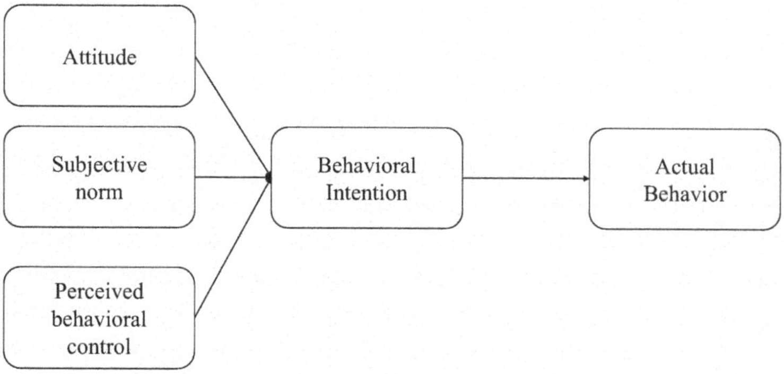

Fig. 2 Theory of Planned Behaviour. Source: Ajzen and Driver (1992)

Some studies have applied the TPB model in various contexts, e.g., for Islamic banking acceptance behaviour in Uganda (Bananuka et al., 2020) and for green banking behaviour in Pakistan. In this latter, the TPB model is used in addition to the TRA model to clarify banking behaviour based on the ease or difficulty of performing the behaviour.

2.2 *Hypotheses Development*

2.2.1 Green Banking

There are two common understandings of green banking. In a broad sense, green banking is a sustainable bank (Sharma & Choubey, 2022). To grow sustainably, the bank's investment decisions must consider the big picture and act in ways that benefit consumers, the economy, society, and the environment. In a narrow sense, green bank refers to the bank's professional activities that encourage environmental activities and reduce carbon emissions (Hasan et al., 2022). These banks promote using green technology in operations and service providers to reduce emissions to the environment and support environmental management (Bose et al., 2018).

Previously, banks were less involved in green activities, but the global popularity of green banking campaigns has drawn more attention to commercial banks in recent years (M. Sharma & Choubey, 2022). The original green banking concept refers to reducing the use of paper to reduce tree destruction and carbon dispersion. It was then broadened to include electronic transactions, such as encouraging the use of ATMs, mobile banking, online banking, and so on (Tara et al., 2015). Besides, green banking could be promoted in various ways, such as by prioritising green credit and mortgages. Furthermore, this activity was promoted within the bank's internal operating process (Furrer et al., 2012). Green banking represents the bank's corporate social responsibility. Integrating social, governance, and environmental criteria into the core business strategy is required.

Box 4
Green banking refers to the bank's professional activities that encourage environmental activities and reduce carbon emissions. Some examples are as follows: reduction of the use of paper; reduction of tree destruction; reduction of carbon dispersion; electronic transactions (e.g., encouraging the use of ATMs, mobile banking, and online banking); green credit and green mortgages; bank's corporate social responsibility (i.e., The integration of social, governance, and environmental criteria into the core business strategy).

Green financial mechanisms and environmentally friendly activities are considered part of the green banking initiative, providing numerous benefits (Bose et al., 2018). Customers tend to trust green banks more than traditional banks because this banking model is considered ethical in business (Alshebami, 2021). Green banking has improved a bank's reputation, allowing it to grow sustainably. As a result, this banking model focuses on creating an environmentally friendly image to attract customers (Sharma & Choubey, 2022).

2.2.2 Green Bank Intention and Green Banking Behaviour

Behavioural intention is a measure of behavioural acceptability. Behaviour is affected by behavioural intention (Montano & Kasprzyk, 2015). According to the TRA and TPB models, behaviour is an object's observable actions determined by behavioural intention (Fishbein & Ajzen, 1977). Green behaviour refers to actions that contribute to or ensure environmental sustainability (Alshebami, 2021), and green banking intention is a measure of green banking acceptability. Ali et al. (2020) refer to green behaviour as employees' proactive efforts to protect the environment while providing customer service. Green behaviour has a positive impact on the environment; it is the behaviour that helps to reduce people's adverse effects on the environment.

Employees must be enthusiastic about a green banking strategy to succeed. Bank employees spend most of their time at work, performing tasks prescribed and imposed by the bank. As a result, many factors, including the bank's rules, regulations, policies, and culture, will influence employees' green banking behaviour (Alshebami, 2021).

Employees' Green banking behaviour has five elements: conservation, work sustainability, avoiding harm, influencing others, and taking initiative (Ali et al., 2020). Conservation, in particular, was the efficient use of energy and waste reduction (Ones & Dilchert, 2013). Work sustainability represents the adaptability of employees. It refers to workplace behaviours implemented to improve the sustainability of the environment and work processes. This adapt process improves product delivery to reduce harmful environmental effects (Ali et al., 2020). Avoiding harm is the avoidance and limitation of harmful ecological behaviours. Influencing others involves spreading sustainable behaviours to other individuals, such as education, mentoring, leading, inspiring, and supporting (Ones & Dilchert, 2013). Taking the initiative is defined as employees' willingness to take action to promote the green behaviour program (Ali et al., 2020). Based on the preceding discussions, the following hypothesis has been developed:

H1: Green banking intention positively affects green banking behaviour

2.2.3 Attitude Toward the Green Banking and Green Banking's Intention

Attitude is defined as an individual's feelings about the intention to perform a specific behaviour, which can be positive or negative (Yousafzai et al., 2010). According to the TRA and TPB models, attitude is formed by solid beliefs about outcomes and performance evaluations (Fishbein & Ajzen, 1977). Accordingly, employees' green attitudes are defined by their beliefs, feelings, and standards regarding green activities (Hasan et al., 2022).

Attitude is important in predicting banking behavioural intentions (Shih & Fang, 2004). The more positive the attitude, the more likely the intention to engage in the behaviour (Afridi et al., 2023). Previous research has shown that current and potential users' behavioural intentions are influenced by their attitudes toward using Islamic financial services (Bananuka et al., 2020). In the field of green banking, research findings in Bangladesh show that attitude influences green banking intention (Hasan et al., 2022). Based on the preceding discussions, the following hypothesis has been developed:

H2: Attitude toward green banking positively affects green banking intention

2.2.4 Subjective Norms and Green Banking Intention

According to the TRA and TPB models, subjective norms are social pressures that motivate individuals to engage in a particular behaviour (Fishbein & Ajzen, 1977). Subjective norms in green banking are social pressures that lead to green behaviour during the implementation of banking activities (Hasan et al., 2022; Wu & Chen, 2005). It is evaluated as one of the critical factors in determining behavioural intentions (Fishbein & Ajzen, 1977), and one of the predictors of user behavioural intention in banking and finance (Hasan et al., 2022; Taneja & Ali, 2021). Furthermore, prior research has shown that it is the most influential factor affecting personal financial behavioural intentions (Taneja & Ali, 2021), behavioural intent to deposit money at a bank (Abduh et al., 2011), and green bank intention when compared to other factors in the TRA and TPB models (Hasan et al., 2022). As a result, the following hypotheses are proposed:

H3: Subjective norms has a positive impact on green banking intention

2.2.5 Perceived Behavioural Control and Green Banking Intention

Perceived behavioural control refers to how difficult it is to perform a behaviour (Aldammagh et al., 2021). Green banking perceived behavioural control demonstrates an understanding of green banking behaviour (Hasan et al., 2022). Processes, finances, and other resources impact this understanding (Bose et al., 2018). According to the TPB model, perceived behavioural control directly influences behaviour intention (Abduh et al., 2011; Aldammagh et al., 2021). When an individual is aided in performing a behaviour, their intention to perform the behaviour increases (Montano & Kasprzyk, 2015). Acceptance of behaviour is limited by obstacles such as a lack of skills or difficulty controlling behaviour (Ali et al., 2021). In Bangladesh, perceived behavioural control has been discovered to affect green banking intention (Hasan et al., 2022). As a result, it is hypothesised that:

H4: Perceived behavioural control has a positive impact on green banking intention

2.2.6 Top Manager Support and Green Banking Intention

When top bank managers focus on green banking, green operations become more convenient (Okyere-Kwakye & Md Nor, 2021). Managerial guidance in organising, designing, innovating, and implementing activities could be provided by top management (Hasan et al., 2022). Ethical principles should be established directly in the bank's operations and widely communicated to employees and customers to gain a competitive advantage and increase sustainability (Alshebami, 2021). Financial and other resources for the transition would also be prioritised (Okyere-Kwakye & Md Nor, 2021).

Top management support is discovered to have a positive and significant impact on green banking intention. Research results in Bangladesh during the COVID-19 pandemic show that top manager support positively influences green banking intention (Hasan et al., 2022). Furthermore, top management support is found to have the most significant impact on green banking intention in India (Tara & Kumar, 2015). We have similar predictions for the context of green banking in Vietnamese commercial banks, and thereby, the following hypothesis is proposed:

H5: Top management support positively influences green banking behaviour

2.2.7 The Mediating Effect of Green Banking Intention

In behavioural research, it is essential to understand the indirect role of intention in shaping behaviour. According to the TRA and TPB models, intention is crucial in predicting behaviour. In these models, intention plays a mediating role in the relationship between attitude and intention. This mediating relationship sheds light on how attitudes and intentions influence behaviour (Conner & Armitage, 1998).

A positive attitude positively affects behaviour, but social pressure from important people may lead to the action not being taken. As a result, these two models incorporate subjective norms to clarify the impact of society and individuals on behaviour. The goal of the intention mediating effect in the relationship between attitude and behaviour is to describe the influence of subjective norms on behaviour under the motivation of behavioural intention (Yousafzai et al., 2010). Prior evidence has demonstrated that the mediating role of intention on attitude and behaviour has varying degrees of impact. While Wicker's study reveals a relatively minor effect (Wicker, 1969), Hasan et al. (2022) find a significant effect.

Furthermore, the TPB model includes the perceived behavioural control factor to account for the full effect of these factors on behaviour. Thus, the influence of intention is indispensable in green banking practice because standards, attitudes, senior management support, and perceived behavioural control all indirectly shape green banking behaviour. Hasan et al. (2022) find this relationship. Then, the hypotheses are formed as follows:

H6: Top management support positively influences green banking behaviour
H7: Perceived behavioural control positively influences green banking behaviour
H8: Subjective norms positively influences green banking behaviour
H9: Attitude toward green banking positively influences green banking behaviour

This research aims to clarify further the green banking behaviour of employees at Vietnamese commercial banks. Figure 3 illustrates the research model.

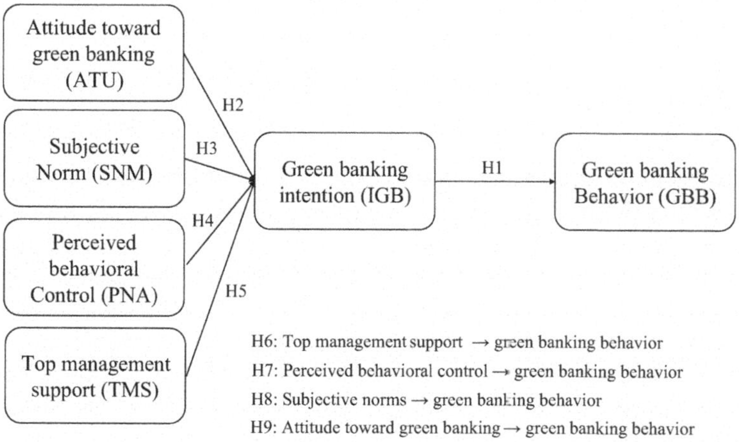

Fig. 3 Proposed research model

3 Methodology

3.1 Research Design

This research aims better to understand green banking practices in Vietnamese commercial banks. The dependent variable is green banking behaviour. The independent variables include subjective norms, attitude toward green banks, perceived behavioural control, and top management support. The intermediate variable is green bank intention. We use the Structural Equation Modelling (SEM) model to achieve the research goal. This method is commonly used to test theories, determine the relationship between variables, and prioritise resources to promote green banking behaviour. The SEM model evaluation process consists of two stages: the model's fit and the structural model.

3.2 Data Collection

The study's survey subjects are bank employees. First, the survey was translated from English into Vietnamese with the assistance of experts with expertise and knowledge of specialised English to ensure that the survey content was not biased. The survey was then pre-tested with a small group of 15 bank employees to ensure the questions were straightforward. The survey was then submitted to Google Forms and converted into a QR code for distribution to respondents. A total of 30 Vietnamese commercial banks were approached. The number of questionnaires sent was 360; 349 samples were obtained, and 344 valid responses were obtained after checking; the valid response rate was approximately 96%. This sample size is adequate, as in SEM studies, a sample size of more than 200 is considered a large sample size.

3.3 Measurements

The variables in the model are assessed using a 5-factor Likert scale, with agreement increasing from 1 to 5. Where 1 means "strongly disagree", and 5 means "strongly agree". The research questions are based on previous literature, mainly the work of Wu and Chen (2005), Cheng et al. (2006), and Al Amin et al. (2022). The research questions are modified to fit the research objectives and subjects.

Subjective Norms (SNM) include three questions based on Wu and Chen's research (Wu & Chen, 2005). Attitude toward green banking (ATU) is based on research by Cheng et al. (2006), including three questions. Green banking behaviour (GBB) is based on Al Amin et al.'s (2022) research and consists of four

Table 1 Survey questionnaire

Subjective Norms (SNM): [Source: (Wu & Chen, 2005)]	
SNM1	People who are important to me would think that I should apply to the green banking.
SNM2	People who influence me would think that I should apply to the green banking.
SNM3	People whose opinions are valued by me would prefer that I should apply for the green banking.
Attitude toward green banking (ATU): [Source:(Cheng et al., 2006)]	
ATU1	I think that green banking is a good idea
ATU2	I think that green banking for financial transactions would be a wise idea
ATU3	I think that applying to the green banking is pleasant
Green banking behaviour (GBB): [Source: (M. Al Amin et al., 2022)]	
GBB1	I intend to apply green banking for my work
GBB2	If I have an opportunity, I will apply green banking
GBB3	I intend to keep apply green banking
GBB4	I intend to continue applying for green banking
Green banking intention (IGB): [Source:(Cheng et al., 2006)]	
IGB1	I would apply green banking
IGB2	Using the green banking for handling my transactions is something I would do
IGB3	I would see myself using the green banking for handling my transactions
Perceived behavioural control (PNA): [Source:(Wu & Chen, 2005)]	
PNA1	I think that I would be able to use the green banking well.
PNA2	I think that using green banking would be entirely within my control.
PNA3	I think that I have the resources, knowledge, and ability to use the green banking.
Top Management Support (TMS): [Source: M. Al Amin et al., 2022)]	
TMS1	The top management allocates resources necessary for green banking activities.
TMS2	The top management supports the green banking.
TMS3	The top management would be enthusiastic about the green banking.
TMS4	The top management is willing to take risks involved in the green banking.

questions. Green banking intention (IGB) is based on Cheng et al.'s (2006) research and consists of three questions. Based on Wu and Chen's research, perceived behavioural control (PNA) consists of three questions (Wu & Chen, 2005). Top management support (TMS) consists of four questions based on Chuah et al.'s research. Table 1 presents the content of the survey questionnaires.

3.4 *Statistical Data Analysis*

The analysis of SEM model data is done in two steps. The measurement model must be evaluated first. The structural model is then evaluated in the next step. Internal consistency reliability assessment, convergence validity assessment, discriminant validity assessment, and the bootstrap method to statistical hypothesis testing must all be completed in the first step. The study then evaluates the VIF coefficient, statistical significance, and magnitude of the regression coefficient in three direct, indirect, and total effects cases. In addition, the adjusted R^2 coefficient and f^2 coefficient are evaluated.

4 Results

4.1 Analysis of the Measurement Model

According to the analysis results in Table 2, both scale and composite reliability meet the research threshold (greater than 0.7). Cronbach Alpha is precisely in the range of 0.712–0.828, indicating adequate internal consistency reliability (DeVellis & Thorpe, 2021). The composite reliability (CR) ranges from 0.838 to 0.897, indicating a high level of convergent validity is confirmed. AVE ranges from 0.634 to 0.743, more significant than the required threshold of 0.5, indicating that the model achieves a discriminant validity. The results also show that rho_A ranges from 0.727 to 0.835, which, compared to the required threshold of 0.70–0.90, indicates that the model has high confidence.

A latent variable indicator must represent a distinct outcome. According to the findings, the outer loading coefficients of all indicators are greater than the other cross-load coefficients. This is the reliability (Table 3).

The results of the HTMT index evaluation show that all of these indexes were less than 0.848, indicating that the accuracy level of discrimination between pairs of scales had been achieved (Table 4).

According to the Fornell and Lacker analysis, GBB's AVE is 0.699 (Table 2), and its square root was 0.836. This result is greater than the correlation value in the GBB column (0.622, 0.513, 0.364, and 0.488) and more significant than the correlation value in the row (0.424). The remaining variables yield similar results, including ATU, IGB, PNA, SNM, and TMS. This result shows that discriminant validity is well established (Table 5).

Table 2 Construct reliability. Source: Analysis results from SmartPLS 4.0

Constructs	Cronbach's Alpha	rho_A	CR	AVE
Subjective norms (SNM)	0.712	0.727	0.838	0.634
Attitude toward green banking (ATU)	0.757	0.779	0.859	0.670
Green banking behaviour (GBB)	0.786	0.792	0.875	0.699
Perceived behavioural control (PNA)	0.752	0.759	0.858	0.668
Top management support (TMS)	0.784	0.796	0.860	0.608
Green banking intention (IGB)	0.828	0.835	0.897	0.743

Table 3 Cross loadings. Source: Analysis results from SmartPLS 4.0

	ATU	GBB	IGB	PNA	SNM	TMS
ATU1	**0.773**	0.330	0.429	0.404	0.388	0.535
ATU2	**0.826**	0.297	0.368	0.409	0.359	0.452
ATU3	**0.854**	0.397	0.544	0.554	0.479	0.587
GBB1	0.380	**0.849**	0.524	0.471	0.348	0.417
GBB2	0.390	**0.839**	0.565	0.450	0.338	0.457
GBB3	0.283	**0.820**	0.461	0.355	0.214	0.337
IGB1	0.530	0.592	**0.880**	0.607	0.531	0.587
IGB2	0.458	0.513	**0.865**	0.481	0.479	0.508
IGB3	0.452	0.495	**0.841**	0.462	0.495	0.514
PNA1	0.535	0.335	0.486	**0.810**	0.371	0.622
PNA2	0.380	0.397	0.443	**0.799**	0.419	0.423
PNA3	0.472	0.514	0.544	**0.841**	0.471	0.582
SNM1	0.461	0.295	0.471	0.441	**0.804**	0.444
SNM2	0.293	0.180	0.389	0.333	**0.740**	0.279
SNM3	0.441	0.371	0.520	0.447	**0.841**	0.495
TMS1	0.557	0.436	0.570	0.655	0.511	**0.788**
TMS2	0.442	0.353	0.418	0.446	0.372	**0.721**
TMS3	0.468	0.330	0.438	0.414	0.353	**0.731**
TMS4	0.542	0.387	0.498	0.531	0.365	**0.870**

Table 4 Heterotrait–Monotrait ratio (HTMT). Source: Analysis results from SmartPLS 4.0

	ATU	GBB	IGB	PNA	SNM	TMS
ATU						
GBB	0.534					
IGB	0.686	0.762				
PNA	0.732	0.655	0.754			
SNM	0.669	0.466	0.750	0.696		
TMS	0.824	0.609	0.763	0.848	0.673	

4.2 Analysis of the Structural Model

The results show that the effect of PNA on IGB is moderate (0.052). We also find that the effect of SNM on IGB is 0.100, the impact of TMS on IGB is 0.055, and the effect of ATU on IGB is 0.050. These effects are moderate. The impact of IGB on GBB is 0.631, which is a strong effect (Table 6).

The model does not exhibit multicollinearity because all VIF coefficients are less than 3. In addition, the analysis results also show that the coefficients of determinations (R2) for IGB and GBB are 0.522 and 0.516, respectively. This is the moderate effect. The p-values of all weights are less than 0.05 in the bootstrap test with a sample size of 5000.

Table 5 Fornell and Lacker criteria. Source: Analysis results from SmartPLS 4.0

	ATU	GBB	IGB	PNA	SNM	TMS
ATU	**0.818**					
GBB	0.424	**0.836**				
IGB	0.560	0.622	**0.862**			
PNA	0.568	0.513	0.604	**0.817**		
SNM	0.508	0.364	0.583	0.516	**0.796**	
TMS	0.650	0.488	0.624	0.669	0.521	**0.780**

Table 6 Strength of effect (f^2). Source: Analysis results from SmartPLS 4.0

	f^2	Effect size
Effect of IGB		
PNA → IGB	0.052	Moderate effect
SNM → IGB	0.100	Moderate effect
TMS → IGB	0.055	Moderate effect
ATU → IGB	0.050	Moderate effect
Effect of GBB		
IGB → GBB	0.631	Strong effect

We further find that subjective norms (SNM), attitude toward green banking (ATU), perceived behavioural control (PNA), and top management support (TMS) have a direct influence on green banking intention (IGB). Furthermore, green banking intention (IGB) directly impacts green banking behaviour (GBB). According to the indirect effect results, all variables affect green banking behaviour (GBB) via the indirect contribution of green banking intention (IGB). See Table 7.

The direct effect of attitude toward green banking (ATU) on green banking intention (IGB) is 0.135 (very small compared to 1), and the average level of this effect from bootstrap samples is 0.137, which is statistically significant (p-value = 0.014 < 0.05). The original sample's indirect impact of attitude toward green banking (ATU) on green banking behaviour (GBB) is 0.084, which is very small compared to 1 and the lowest compared to other variables in the model. This effect is statistically significant (p-value = 0.016 < 0.05) based on the average of the bootstrap samples (0.086). The original sample has a total impact of 0.084, the bootstrap sample has an effect of 0.086, and the p-value is 0.016. This result is consistent with hypotheses H2, H9 and comparable to the studies of Hasan et al. (2022), Afridi et al. (2023, 2024), and Bananuka et al. (2020). The findings support the TRA and TPB models' contention that attitude is the proclivity to respond to a specific behaviour (Yousafzai et al., 2010). Green banking attitudes influence the formation of an intention to perform a behaviour, promoting green banking behaviour among employees of Vietnamese commercial banks. These employees' attitudes determine whether they will participate in the bank's green activities. Positive attitudes among employees increase the likelihood of green behaviour. Furthermore, research at Vietnamese commercial banks indicates that the total effect of green banking intention is the lowest of the factors influencing green banking behaviour.

Table 7 Results of the direct, indirect, and total effect. Source: Analysis results from SmartPLS 4.0

Relationship	Original sample	Sample mean	Standard deviation	T statistics	P-values
Direct effect					
ATU -> IGB	0.135	0.137	0.055	2.460	0.014
IGB -> GBB	0.622	0.624	0.034	18.452	0.000
PNA -> IGB	0.222	0.223	0.059	3.796	0.000
SNM -> IGB	0.271	0.272	0.047	5.729	0.000
TMS -> IGB	0.247	0.246	0.060	4.100	0.000
Indirect effect					
ATU -> IGB -> GBB	0.084	0.086	0.035	2.406	0.016
SNM -> IGB -> GBB	0.169	0.170	0.030	5.614	0.000
PNA -> IGB -> GBB	0.138	0.140	0.039	3.555	0.000
TMS -> IGB -> GBB	0.153	0.153	0.038	3.999	0.000
Total effect					
ATU -> GBB	0.084	0.086	0.035	2.406	0.016
PNA -> GBB	0.138	0.140	0.039	3.555	0.000
SNM -> GBB	0.169	0.170	0.030	5.614	0.000
TMS -> GBB	0.153	0.153	0.038	3.999	0.000

The direct effect of perceived behavioural control (PNA) on green banking intention (IGB) is 0.222 (very small compared to 1); the average of this effect from bootstrap samples is 0.223 and is considered to be statistically significant (p-value = 0.000 < 0.05). The indirect effect of perceived behavioural control (PNA) on green banking behaviour (GBB) from the original sample is 0.138, minimal compared to 1 and lower than the direct effect (0.222). The average impact from the bootstrap samples is 0.140 and is considered statistically significant (p-value = 0.000 < 0.05). According to the original sample, the total effect of PNA on GBB is 0.138, the bootstrap sample is 0.086, and the p-value is 0.000. This result is consistent with hypotheses H4 and H7 and similar to the study of Hasan et al. (2022), Aldammagh et al. (2021), and Abduh et al. (2011). Green behaviour increases as perceived behavioural control increases. Green banking behaviour tends to increase when employees have complete knowledge and skills about green banking. Green banking intentions and behaviour are also influenced by self-assurance about implementing green banking. Furthermore, favourable working conditions are a concern. This result is consistent with the TPB model's arguments (Blue, 1995).

The direct influence of subjective norms (SNM) on green banking intention (IGB) is 0.271 (very small compared to 1), and the average level of this effect from bootstrap samples is 0.272, which is considered statistically significant (p-value = 0.000 < 0.05). The indirect impact of subjective norms (SNM) on green banking behaviour (GBB) in the original sample is 0.169, which is very small in comparison with 1 and less than the direct effect (0.271). This effect's average from the bootstrap samples is 0.170, which is considered statistically significant

(p-value = 0.000 < 0.05). SNM has a total impact of 0.169 on the GBB original sample, 0.170 on the bootstrap sample, and a p-value of 0.000 on the bootstrap sample. This result is consistent with hypotheses H3 and H8 and comparable to the study of Hasan et al. (2022), Wu and Chen (2005), Taneja and Ali (2021), and Abduh et al. (2011). According to psychological research, the opinions of reference groups are essential when behaviour is first practised, and this influence tends to decrease over time. This finding indicates that a person's behaviour is influenced by their social group. As critical people's influence grows, so do bankers' green banking behaviour. Furthermore, subjective norms are discovered to have the most significant impact on green bank behaviour in Vietnamese commercial banks.

The direct influence of top management support (TMS) on green banking intention (IGB) is 0.247 (very small compared to 1), the average level of this impact from bootstrap samples is 0.246, and this effect is statistically significant (p-value = 0.000 < 0.05). The indirect impact of top management support (TMS) on green banking behaviour (GBB) in the original sample is 0.153, which is very small compared to 1 and less than the direct impact. (0.246). This effect is statistically significant (p-value = 0.000 < 0.05) based on the average of the bootstrap samples. TMS has a total impact on GBB of 0.153 in the original sample and 0.153 in the bootstrap sample, with a p-value of 0.000. This result is consistent with the hypotheses H5 and H6 and comparable to the study of Hasan et al. (2022) and Wu and Chen (2005). Green behaviour intention and behaviour increase as top management support increases. As a result, top management support has the second greatest effect on green banking behaviour. As the top manager's support grows, the planning, design, development, and implementation would be more specifically guided and have a more favourable mechanism. Then, top management assists employees in creating an environment in which attitudes, motivations, and attitudes toward green banking can be defined. Furthermore, banks are willing to exchange financial resources to promote green banking behaviour and have better risk management policies.

The level of direct influence of green banking intention (IGB) on green banking behaviour (GBB) is 0.622; this is a significant influence. The average effect from the bootstrap samples is 0.624 and is considered statistically significant (p-value = 0.000 < 0.05). This result is consistent with hypothesis H1 and similar to the study of Ali et al. (2020) and Ones and Dilchert (2013). A person's intention is one of the main predictors of behaviour. Employee intentions would determine green banking behaviour.

Figure 4 presents the results of the structural model analysis. The results show that all outer loadings and p-values meet the required threshold and are explained well for the research model.

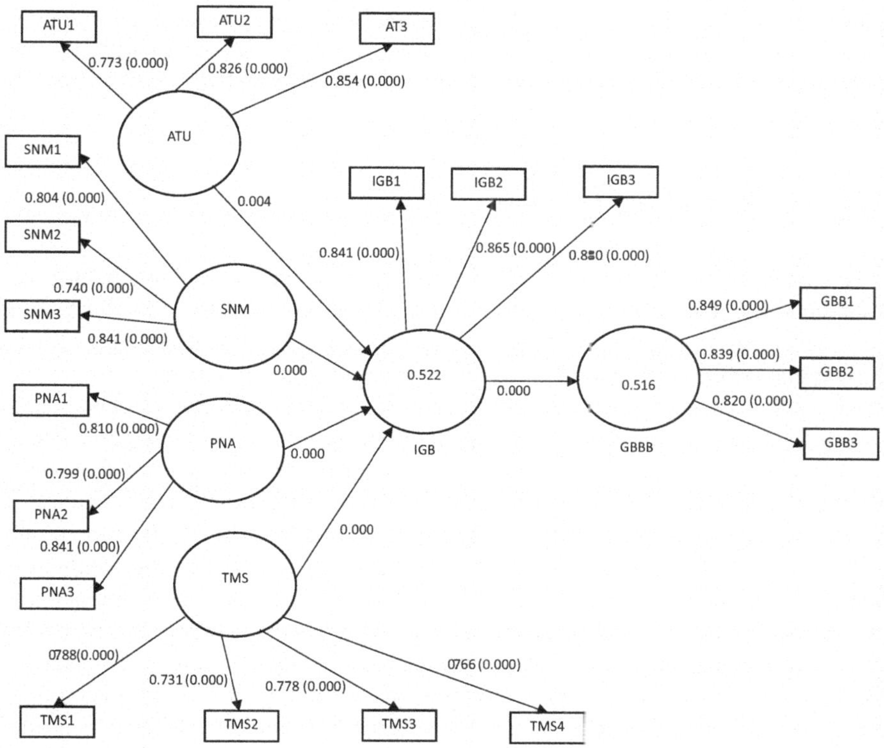

Fig. 4 The structural model assessment. Source: Analysis results from SmartPLS 4.0

5 Conclusions and Managerial Implications

5.1 Conclusions

Subjective norms, attitudes toward green banking, perceived behavioural control, and top management support are found to influence green banking intention directly. Subjective norms have the most influence of all. Subjective norms, attitudes toward green banking, perceived behavioural control, and top management support are also found to impact green banking behaviour through the indirect contribution of green banking intention. Furthermore, green banking intention has a significant impact on green banking behaviour.

Employee banking behaviour in Vietnam is consistent with the arguments in the theoretical models TRA and TPB, according to research findings. The direction of effect results is comparable to previous studies in Bangladesh and Uganda. This study, in particular, demonstrates that subject norms are the most influential factor in behaviour. Furthermore, the results show the decisive influence of top management. Thus, this study has clarified green banking behaviour in a developing country where sustainable development activities are implemented early on. The findings of this study can help bank executives develop green banking strategies.

5.2 Managerial Implications

Green banking intention has a significant effect on green banking behaviour. Following that, banks must promote green banking intentions to create long-term green behaviour change. Previously, Vietnamese commercial banks operated traditionally; however, green banking activities have only recently emerged. To change employee behaviour, banks must create an environment conducive to change and ensure the reason for the change is compelling. The process of evolving green banking behaviour must limit the number of behaviours. Ensure that the plan only includes the behaviours necessary to make a difference. Because green banking is a long-term strategy, the bank must focus on a few critical changes in the short term.

According to the study's findings, subjective norms have the greatest influence on behavioural intention and green banking behaviour. Thus, besides instilling positive motivations and effective green behaviour propaganda in employees, banks must invest in the importance of green behaviour in their relatives and friends. Banks, in particular, must promote programs that encourage the use of green products and clean consumption on a local level. Since then, individuals' responsibility for environmental protection has gradually increased.

The findings also reveal that behavioural intention and green banking behaviour are influenced by attitude toward green banking. Employees would be more likely to adopt green banking behaviour if they see the need for them. As a result, employees must evaluate how effective these behaviours would be in practice. Banks must educate their employees about the benefits of green banking so that they adopt a positive attitude toward the practice until it becomes a habit in the workplace.

Top management support influences behavioural intent and green banking behaviour. Senior management is essential in strengthening and changing employees' green banking behaviour. These managers use systems or processes to reinforce the new behaviour. As a result, bank executives must concentrate on developing long-term operational processes. The culture is also essential in ensuring employee success in implementing green banking practices. Corporate culture has a significant impact on each employee. Like the domino effect, this effect would affect individuals, then a small group, and then spread to the collective, the organisation, and the broader economy. As a result, the bank must create a green working culture. Employees would always be encouraged to voice their opinions, promote creativity in green banking, and improve the quality of cooperation and group work.

Perceived behavioural control also influences behavioural intentions and green banking behaviour. Employees with complete knowledge and understanding of green banking will be more confident in their activities. As a result, the bank must develop a strategy for organising training and seminars to exchange experiences and knowledge on green banking development to strengthen the capacity of its employees. To effectively communicate green banking activities, the bank should improve training for key staff on environmental and social risk management and build a team of knowledgeable trainers.

5.3 Limitations

The research has not yet compared Vietnam's green banking behaviour to other countries in the region. Banking is an international activity; if the study can compare these differences, banks can develop a more effective strategy for establishing a competitive position.

Declaration of Generative AI and AI-Assisted Technologies in the Writing Process for This Chapter The editor only used ChatGPT (Premium GPT4.0) and Grammarly to proof-read and check for typos and inconsistencies. There is no further declaration from the authors.

References

Abduh, M., Duasa, J., & Omar, M. A. (2011). Factors influence depositors-withdrawal behavior in Islamic banks: A theory of reasoned action. *International Journal of Economics and Management Engineering, 5*(12), 1813–1818.

Afridi, S. A., Zahid, R. M., Khan, W., & Anwar, W. (2023). Embracing green banking as a mean of expressing green behavior in a developing economy: Exploring the mediating role of green culture. *Environmental Science and Pollution Research*, 1–11. https://doi.org/10.1007/s11356-023-25449-z

Ajzen, I., & Driver, B. L. (1992). Application of the theory of planned behavior to leisure choice. *Journal of Leisure Research, 24*(3), 207–224. https://doi.org/10.1080/00222216.1992.11969889

Al Amin, M., Razib Alam, M., & Alam, M. Z. (2022). Antecedents of students' e-learning continuance intention during COVID-19: An empirical study. *E-Learning and Digital Media, 513*, 224. https://doi.org/10.1177/20427530221103915

Aldammagh, Z., Abdeljawad, R., & Obaid, T. (2021). Predicting mobile banking adoption: An integration of TAM and TPB with trust and perceived risk. *Financial Internet Quarterly*, 35–46.

Ali, Q., Islam, U., Sharif, S., Parveen, S., Senin, A. A., Zaini, Z., Islam, U., & Sharif, S. (2020). Islamic bankers' green behaviour for the growth of green banking in Malaysia. *International Journal of Environment And Sustainable Development, 19*(4), 393–411. https://doi.org/10.1504/IJESD.2020.110650

Ali, M. A., Nazim, M., Hussain, S., Rehman, J. U., & Rehman, S. U. (2021). Impact of Islamic financial literacy, subjective norms, risk perception and perceived behavioral control on adoption of Islamic banking in Pakistan. *Revista Geintec-Gestao Inovacao E Tecnologias, July, 11*(3), 220–233. https://doi.org/10.47059/revistageintec.v11i3.1929

Alshebami, A. S. (2021). Evaluating the relevance of green banking practices on Saudi banks' green image: The mediating effect of employees' green behaviour. *Journal of Banking Regulation, 22*(4), 275–286. https://doi.org/10.1057/s41261-021-00150-8

Ambrosio, T., Hall, S. G. F., Obydenkova, A., Ambrosio, T., Hall, S. G. F., Obydenkova, A., Ambrosio, T., & Hall, S. G. F. (2022). Sustainable development agendas of regional international organizations: The European Bank of reconstruction and development and the Eurasian development bank. *Problems of Post-Communism, 69*(4–5), 304–316. https://doi.org/10.1080/10758216.2021.1979412

Amin, H. (2013). Factors influencing Malaysian bank customers to choose Islamic credit cards: Empirical evidence from the TRA model. *Journal of Islamic Marketing, 4*(3), 245–263. https://doi.org/10.1108/JIMA-02-2012-0013

Bananuka, J., Kasera, M., Najjemba, G. M., Musimenta, D., Ssekiziyivu, B., & Kimuli, S. N. L. (2020). Attitude: Mediator of subjective norm, religiosity and intention to adopt Islamic banking. *Journal of Islamic Marketing, 11*(1), 81–96. https://doi.org/10.1108/JIMA-02-2018-0025

Blue, C. L. (1995). The predictive capacity of the theory of reasoned action and the theory of planned behavior in exercise research: An integrated literature review. *Research in Nursing & Health, 18*, 105–121. https://doi.org/10.1002/nur.4770180205

Bose, S., Khan, H. Z., Rashid, A., & Islam, S. (2018). What drives green banking disclosure? An institutional and corporate governance perspective. *Asia Pacific Journal of Management, 35*, 501–527. https://doi.org/10.1007/s10490-017-9528-x

Cheng, T. C. E., Lam, D. Y. C., & Yeung, A. C. L. (2006). Adoption of internet banking: An empirical study in Hong Kong. *Decision Support Systems, 42*, 1558–1572. https://doi.org/10.1016/j.dss.2006.01.002

Conner, M., & Armitage, J. (1998). Extending the theory of planned behavior: A review and avenues for further research. *Journal of Applied Social Psychology, 28*, 1429–1464. https://doi.org/10.1111/j.1559-1816.1998.tb01685.x

DeVellis, R. F., & Thorpe, C. T. (2021). *Scale development: Theory and applications*. Sage publications. https://doi.org/10.1016/0886-1633(93)90012-e

Fishbein, M., & Ajzen, I. (1977). Belief, attitude, intention, and behavior: An introduction to theory and research. https://doi.org/10.2307/2065853.

Furrer, B., Hamprecht, J., & Hoffmann, V. H. (2012). Much ado about nothing? How banks respond to climate change. *Business & Society, 51*(1), 62–88. https://doi.org/10.1177/0007650311427428

Giao, H. N. K. (2020). Awareness and awareness of green banking in Vietnam. *Economic – Technical Magazine, June*, 1–10. https://doi.org/10.31219/osf.io/rzx7w

Hà, N. V., & Hà, Đ. N. (2019). Green bank with green tourism: Current status and some recommendations. *Journal of Banking Science & Training*, 74–85.

Hasan, M. M., Al Amin, M., Moon, Z. K., & Afrin, F. (2022). Role of environmental sustainability, psychological and managerial supports for determining bankers' green banking usage behavior: An integrated framework. *Psychology Research and Behavior Management*, 3751–3773. https://doi.org/10.2147/PRBM.S377682

Jan, A. A., Lai, F. W., Asif, M., Akhtar, S., & Ullah, S. (2022). Embedding sustainability into bank strategy: Implications for sustainable development goals reporting. *International Journal of Sustainable Development & World Ecology, 30*, 1–15. https://doi.org/10.1080/13504509.2022.2134230

Lukšić, I., Bošković, B., Novikova, A., & Vrbensky, R. (2022). Innovative financing of the sustainable development goals in the countries of the Western Balkans. *Energy, Sustainability and Society, 12*(1), 15. https://doi.org/10.1186/s13705-022-00340-w

Madden, T. J., Ellen, P. S., & Ajzen, I. (1992). A comparison of the theory of planned behavior and the theory of reasoned action. *Personality and Social Psychology Bulletin, 18*(1), 3–9. https://doi.org/10.1177/0146167292181001

Montano, D. E., & Kasprzyk, D. (2015). Theory of reasoned action, theory of planned behavior, and the integrated behavioral model. *Health Behavior: Theory, Research and Practice, 70*(4), 231.

Nath, V., Nayak, N., & Goel, A. (2014). Green banking practices–A review. *IMPACT: International Journal of Research in Business Management (IMPACT: IJRBM), 2*(4), 45–62. https://citeseerx.ist.psu.edu/document?repid=rep1&type=pdf&doi=575c39d4a9fc41e588e7e251982dc2e18e9ff388

Okyere-Kwakye, E., & Md Nor, K. (2021). The intention of banks to adopt green banking in an emerging market: The employees' perspective. *Economic and Political Studies, 9*(4), 497–504. https://doi.org/10.1080/20954816.2021.1899621

Ones, D. S., & Dilchert, S. (2013). Measuring, understanding, and influencing employee green behaviors. *Green organizations: Driving Change with IO Psychology*, 115–148. https://doi.org/10.4324/9780203142936-19

Ozili, P. K. (2020). Financial inclusion research around the world: A review. In *Forum for social economics* (Vol. 50, No. 4, pp. 457–479). Routledge.

Park, H., & Kim, J. D. (2020). Transition towards green banking Role of financial regulators and financial institutions. *Asian Journal of Sustainability and Social Responsibility, 5*(1), 1–25. https://citeseerx.ist.psu.edu/document?repid=rep1&type=pdf&doi=575c39d4a9fc41e588e7e251982dc2e18e9ff388

Peterson, R. T., & Jun, M. (2006). Small business manager attitudes relating to the significance of social responsibility issues: A longitudinal study. *Journal of Applied Management and Entrepreneurship, 11*(2), 32. https://www.proquest.com/openview/70b5b16b08ad9f18f744144d24051e06/1?pq-origsite=gscholar&cbl=25565

Rahman, R. A., Zahari, M. S. M., Hanafiah, M. H., & Mamat, M. N. (2021). Effect of halal food knowledge and trust on Muslim consumer purchase behavior of Syubhah semi-processed food products. *Journal of Food Products Marketing, 27*(6), 319–330. https://doi.org/10.1080/10454446.2021.1994079

Ramayah, T., Rouibah, K., Gopi, M., & Rangel, G. J. (2009). A decomposed theory of reasoned action to explain intention to use Internet stock trading among Malaysian investors. *Computers in Human Behavior, 25*(6), 1222–1230. https://doi.org/10.1016/j.chb.2009.06.007

Rehman, A., Ullah, I., Afridi, F. E. A., Ullah, Z., Zeeshan, M., Hussain, A., & Rahman, H. U. (2021). Adoption of green banking practices and environmental performance in Pakistan: A demonstration of structural equation modelling. *Environment, Development and Sustainability*, 1–21. https://doi.org/10.1007/s10668-020-01206-x

Rodríguez Bolívar, M. P., Garde Sánchez, R., & López Hernández, A. M. (2015). Managers as drivers of CSR in state-owned enterprises. *Journal of Environmental Planning and Management, 58*(5), 777–801.

Sharma, K., Aswal, C., & Paul, J. (2022). Factors affecting green purchase behavior: A systematic literature review. *Business Strategy and the Environment, 32*(4), 2078–2092. https://doi.org/10.1002/bse.3237

Sharma, M., & Choubey, A. (2022). Green banking initiatives: A qualitative study on Indian banking sector. *Environment, Development and Sustainability, 24*(1), 293–319. https://doi.org/10.1007/s10668-021-01426-9

Shih, Y.-Y., & Fang, K. (2004). The use of a decomposed theory of planned behavior to study internet banking in Taiwan. *Internet Research, 14*(3), 213–223. https://doi.org/10.1108/10662240410542643

Stauropoulou, A., Sardianou, E., Malindretos, G., Evangelinos, K., & Nikolaou, I. (2023). The role of customers' awareness towards the sustainable development goals (SDGs) of banks on their behavior. *Environmental Science and Pollution Research, 30*(5), 13495–13507. https://doi.org/10.1007/s11356-022-23111-8

Tan, C. (2022). Private investments, public goods: Regulating markets for sustainable development. *European Business Organization Law Review, 23*(1), 241–271. https://doi.org/10.1007/s40804-021-00236-w

Taneja, S., & Ali, L. (2021). Determinants of customers' intentions towards environmentally sustainable banking: Testing the structural model. *Journal of Retailing and Consumer Services, 59*, 102418. https://doi.org/10.1016/j.jretconser.2020.102418

Tanhan, A., & Young, J. S. (2022). Muslims and mental health services: A concept map and a theoretical framework. *Journal of Religion and Health*, 1–41. https://doi.org/10.1007/s10943-021-01324-4

Tara, K., & Kumar, R. (2015). Green banking for environmental management: A paradigm shift. *Current World Environment, 10*(3), 1029–1038. https://doi.org/10.12944/CWE.10.3.36

Tara, K., Singh, S., & Kumar, R. (2015). Green banking for environmental management: A paradigm shift. *Current World Environment, 10*(3), 1029–1038. https://doi.org/10.12944/cwe.10.3.36

Tsindeliani, I. A., Proshunin, M. M., Sadovskaya, T. D., Popkova, Z. G., Davydova, M. A., & Babayan, O. A. (2022). Digital transformation of the banking system in the context of sustainable development. *Journal of Money Laundering Control, 25*(1), 165–180. https://doi.org/10.1108/JMLC-02-2021-0011

Wicker, A. W. (1969). Attitudes versus actions: The relationship of verbal and overt behavioral responses to attitude objects. *Journal of Social Issues, XXV*(4), 41–78. https://doi.org/10.1111/j.1540-4560.1969.tb00619.x

Wu, L., & Chen, J. L. (2005). An extension of trust and TAM model with TPB in the initial adoption of on-line tax: An empirical study. *International Journal of Human-Computer Studies, 62*(6), 784–808. https://doi.org/10.1016/j.ijhcs.2005.03.003

Yousafzai, S. Y., Foxall, G. R., & Pallister, J. G. (2010). Explaining internet banking behavior: Theory of reasoned action, theory of planned behavior, or technology acceptance model? *Journal of Applied Social Psychology, 40*(5), 1172–1202. https://doi.org/10.1111/j.1559-1816.2010.00615.x

Dr. Sang Tang My is currently working as a lecturer at Ho Chi Minh City University of Economics and Finance, Vietnam. She has practical as well as theoretical expertise in the field of Finance, management and sustainable development.

Carbon Discourse, Climate Governance, and Audit Fees

Chengruizhi Ma and Yifei Bi

Abstract This chapter provides readers with empirical evidence on whether the audit fees would be affected by the firms' carbon disclosure. The findings show that firms disclosing carbon emission information can significantly reduce audit fees. Further analysis reveals that the state-owned firms' disclosure of carbon emissions has a more significant impact on audit fees than non-state-owned firms. In addition, the following industries drive the primary results: scientific research and technology services and metal, nonmetal, and machinery.

1 Introduction

Many related global climate policies have been promulgated. Among them, the 'United Nations Framework Convention on Climate Change' in 1992 and the 'Kyoto Protocol' in 1997 are significant. In 2015, the Paris Climate Change Conference (COP21) adopted the 'Paris Agreement' (Ares & Hirst, 2016), which aimed to strengthen the global response to tackle climate change, marking a significant change in international climate governance (Liobikienė & Butkus, 2017). In April 2016, more than 170 countries jointly signed the Paris Agreement, committing to keep the global temperature rise within 2 °C. Particularly in September 2016, when the G20 Hangzhou Summit opened, China and the United States officially ratified the Paris Agreement. The two major carbon emitters' ratification of the Paris Agreement marked the beginning of a new historical phase of global carbon emissions control (Bodansky, 2016).

C. Ma (✉)
Faculty of Business and Law, The Department of Accounting and Finance, The Open University, Milton Keynes, UK
e-mail: chengruizhi.ma@open.ac.uk

Y. Bi
School of Economics and Finance, Queen Mary University of London, London, UK
e-mail: y.bi@qmul.ac.uk

V. Q. Trinh (ed.), *Climate Governance and Corporate Eco-innovation*, Sustainable Finance, https://doi.org/10.1007/978-3-031-56423-9_9

China's international climate pledge (its nationally determined contribution, or NDC) promises to peak CO2 emissions 'before 2030' and to reduce the country's carbon intensity—its emissions per unit of GDP—by 'over 65%' in 2030 from 2005 levels. Specifically, on February 7, 2013, the China Banking Regulatory Commission (CBRC) and the State Council jointly established the '*Opinions of Green Credit Work*', aiming to impose the incorporation of green loans into banks' lending activities and ensure green credit allocation from the legislative perspective (CBRC, 2013).

Prior literature has found some key determinants of corporate social responsibility (CSR) disclosure, such as corporate governance (Jizi et al., 2014), market value (Nekhili et al., 2017), and cost of capital (Dhaliwal et al., 2014). However, there needs to be more research examining the carbon disclosure level of Chinese-listed firms and how they minimise the impact of carbon emissions on the environment and climate. We aim to fill this gap in this chapter, and the results of which may help the company better manage carbon emissions.

Also, few empirical studies have examined the relationship between firm-level factors and the number of carbon disclosures, focusing on audit fees in the context of the Chinese stock market. There are two types of enterprises in China: state-owned enterprises (SOEs) and non-state-owned enterprises (Non-SOEs). This research looks at how both SOEs differ from non-SOEs in corporate governance. We extend the existing literature by examining if carbon disclosures convey information about the quantity and quality of risk management activities for companies, which impacts audit fees because of altered perceptions of audit risk. On the one hand, auditors might demand an audit fee premium to compensate for the additional effort required to collect evidence to verify carbon management information. If the audit risk is high, the auditor must collect more evidence, leading to higher fees. On the other hand, greater levels of carbon disclosures might improve the information environment and reduce information asymmetry, leading to lower audit fees. This paper's results can help auditors better understand how carbon management disclosure affects the company's audit risk level and future audit work schedules.

This chapter provides three findings on the relationship between carbon disclosure and audit fees. First, our results show a significant negative relationship between carbon disclosure and audit fees in the Chinese-listed firms from 2017 to 2021. The results suggest that auditors spend less time finding related information for firms disclosing carbon emissions, which helps auditors access the carbon information in the annual report. Second, regarding the sub-samples (state-owned enterprises (SOEs) and non-SOEs) tests, we find that the relationship between carbon disclosure and audit fees is more vital for the former group than the latter. In addition, we find that our primary results (i.e., negative relationship between carbon disclosure and audit fees) are more pronounced in the metal, nonmetal, machinery, and scientific research and technology services industries.

The study makes three contributions to the literature. First, it contributes to studies examining the carbon disclosure level of Chinese-listed firms. Recently, Chinese enterprises have devoted efforts to integrating ESG into their business development strategies (KPMG, 2022). However, most studies focus on studying the ESG disclosures in firms listed on the developed market (e.g., Cormier & Magnan, 1999; Depoers et al., 2016; Garanina & Kim, 2023; Sun et al., 2022). This study extends the literature by investigating the carbon disclosures in Chinese-listed firms. Second, this study contributes to the literature that focuses on audit fees. Prior studies found the determinants of audit fees are Big four auditors, audit hours, audit complexity, and audit risk (Causholli et al., 2011; Hay et al., 2006; Simunic, 1980). We extend the scope of the literature by showing a vital determinant affecting audit fees: carbon information. Third, this study adds to the literature regarding how state ownership and industry factors impact the relationship between carbon information disclosure and audit fees.

The rest of this chapter is organised as follows. Sections 2 and 3 review institutional developments and prior literature. Section 4 presents information about the sample and research methodology. Section 5 provides a descriptive analysis of the percentage of companies disclosing carbon information. Section 6 presents the results of the implications of carbon disclosure on audit fees. Finally, Sect. 7 concludes this chapter by summarising the main findings and providing recommendations for policy-making and future research.

2 Institutional Background

2.1 *Sustainable Developments in International Accounting Standards*

In September 2020, the IFRS Foundation issued a Consultation Paper on Sustainability Reporting (2020 Consultation). Feedback was to be received by 31 December 2020.

In February 2021, the IOSCO Board issued a public statement announcing IOSCO's intention to work with the IFRS Foundation in developing a plan to establish a new board for setting sustainability reporting standards that meet the needs of the capital markets.

In March 2021, the Trustees of the IFRS Foundation met to continue their analysis and discussions of the feedback received from their 2020 Consultation. The feedback indicated an urgent need for global sustainability reporting standards and support for the IFRS Foundation to play a role in their development. Furthermore, the IFRS Foundation Trustees also created the Technical Readiness Working Group (TRWG) to develop a Climate-related disclosure prototype. The TRWG consists of leading organisations with expertise in sustainability and integrated reporting. The TWRG published prototypes for Climate-related Disclosures (Climate Prototype) and General Requirements for Disclosure of Sustainability-related Financial Information (General Requirements Prototype).

In June 2021, the International Integrated Reporting Council (IIRC) and the Sustainability Accounting Standards Board (SASB) merged to form the Value Reporting Foundation (VRF). The purpose of VRF was to help businesses and investors develop a shared understanding of how enterprise value is created, preserved, or eroded over time.

In November 2021, at the COP26 climate conference in Glasgow, the IFRS Foundation stressed that climate change is a critical global issue, and there is an urgent need to develop global standards on climate-related matters. On 3 November 2021, the IFRS Foundation Trustees announced the formation of the International Sustainability (ISSB).

On 31 January 2022, the Climate Disclosure Standards Board (CDSB) was consolidated into the IFRS Foundation (under which the IASB and the ISSB reside).

On 24 March 2022, the IFRS Foundation and the GRI announced a collaboration agreement for their respective standard-setting boards (the ISSB and the GSSB) to coordinate their work programmes and standard-setting activities.

In August 2022, VRF was also consolidated into the IFRS Foundation. These consolidations were aimed to help ISSB build on the work of existing initiatives and become the global standard-setter for sustainability disclosures for the financial markets.

2.1.1 The ISSB and IFRS Sustainability Disclosure Standards

As mentioned above, on 3 November 2021, the IFRS Foundation announced the establishment of the International Sustainability Standards Board (ISSB). The purpose of the ISSB is to develop international standards for sustainability reporting. These standards will provide an international guideline and present an opportunity to reduce the fragmentation of existing and new disclosure requirements. Thus, Sustainability reports will enable investors and other relevant participants in capital markets to make informed financial decisions.

Box 1
The International Sustainability Standards Board (ISSB) (established by the IFRS Foundation) aims to develop international standards for sustainability reporting.

2.1.2 International Sustainability Reporting Standards

Building on the sustainability-related disclosures prototype developed by the TRWG in November 2021, the ISSB issued exposure drafts for two new sustainability standards on 31 March 2022. IFRS S1 *General Requirements for Disclosure of Sustainability-related Financial Information* and IFRS 2 *Climate-related Disclosures*.

IFRS S1 *General Requirements for Disclosure of Sustainability-related Financial Information* outlines the requirements for a reporting entity to disclose all material financial information about its significant sustainability-related risks and opportunities. The aim is to ensure that the reporting entity has provided all financially important sustainability information to the capital market participants to inform their financial decision-making.

Specifically, in terms of core content, the reporting companies should disclose:

- the governance processes, controls, and procedures they used to monitor and manage sustainability-related risks and opportunities;
- the approach and process they used to address these risks and opportunities;
- the information used to assess, manage, and monitor the entity's performance about sustainability-related risks and opportunities over time.

IFRS S2 *Climate-related Disclosures* aims to set overall requirements for a reporting entity regarding disclosure of climate-related opportunities and risks. This standard applies to physical risks from climate change, risks associated with transitioning to a lower-carbon economy, and available climate-related opportunities to firms. The standard's purpose is:

- to enable the investors and other stakeholder groups to evaluate how various climate-related opportunities and threats in an organisation's environment influence its corporate value;
- to assess the effectiveness of an organisation's response to various climate-related threats and opportunities;
- to determine how effectively an organisation has made use of organisational resources to deal with them;
- to examine an organisation's ability to adapt in the face of substantial climate-related opportunities and risks;
- to understand how the entity assesses its climate-related performance, including progress towards the climate-related targets it has set.

An entity shall apply this Standard in preparing and disclosing climate-related disclosures in accordance with IFRS S1 General Requirements for Disclosure of Sustainability-related Financial Information.

The consultation and feedback period on these exposure drafts ended on 29 July 2022. The ISSB will review the feedback received on these drafts, and new sustainability-related standards are expected to be issued by the end of 2022. Once the standards are introduced, it will be on individual jurisdictions to decide whether IFRS Sustainability Disclosure Standards are to be mandated for use, the scope of the companies required for compliance, and the timeframe for implementing these new standards.

The IFRS Foundation also tries to drive synergy between sustainability and financial reporting. The newly appointed chairman of the IASB, Andreas Barckow, has committed to devote IASB and staff time to ensure connectivity between IASB and ISSB. The close connection between the IASB (which sets the IFRS Accounting Standards) and the ISSB (which forms the IFRS Sustainability Disclosure Standards) is necessary to connect sustainability reporting and financial reporting. It can also promote the link between financial information and non-financial information. A firm's non-financial performance can also affect financial performance. Investors can have a better understanding of the firm's performance.

Box 2
The IFRS Foundation is trying to drive synergy between sustainability reporting and financial reporting.

2.2 *Sustainable Reporting Developments in China*

Chinese enterprises are showing considerable improvements in sustainable reporting, possibly due to developments in sustainable reporting requirements in China. Table 1 highlights the timeline of critical corporate sustainable reporting requirements in China from 2003 to 2015. In 2018, a Listed Company Governance Code was issued. Listed firms in China are expected to disclose environmental, social,

Table 1 Timeline of key corporate sustainability Reporting Requirements in China

Year	Name	Disclosure requirement
2003	Environmental Impact Assessment Law	Explains the submission process content requirements and consequence or non-compliance to assessing the environmental impact of projects.
2006	Shenzhen Stock Exchange Social Responsibility Guidelines for Listed Companies	Encourages listed companies to publish annual CSR reports voluntarily.
2008	Measures for the Disclosure of Environmental Information (MDEI)	Denotes nine information items that enterprises should disclose.
2008	Guidelines on China's Industrial Enterprises and Industrial Associations' Social Responsibilities	Encourages industrial enterprises to establish a CSR information release system.
2008	Notice on Strengthening Listed Companies' Assumption of Social Responsibility (SSE Notice)	Requires the corporate governance sector, overseas listed companies, and financial companies to disclose their CSR.
2008	Guidelines on Environmental Information Disclosure by Companies Listed on the Shanghai Stock Exchange (SSE Guideline)	Requires three types of companies to release a corporate social responsibility (CSR) report: • Corporate Governance Index constituent companies • Dual-listed companies (listed in overseas markets) • Financial companies
2011	Chinese CSR Report Preparation Guide 2.0	Provides a basic framework for companies to write their CSR reports.
2015	Environmental Impact Assessment Law (revised)	States procedures for submitting and assessing the environmental impact of projects, environmental impact assessment report content, and legal responsibilities of non-compliance. Revision: States that citizens, legal persons, and other organisations shall have the right to obtain environmental information.

and governance (ESG) information under this code. Two years later, in 2020, China's central bank, the People's Bank of China, issued guidance on environmental disclosure to financial institutions. According to KPMG (2022), the percentage of companies listed on the Chinese mainland and Hong Kong stock exchanges that voluntarily published annual ESG reports increased to 89%.

3 Literature Review and Hypothesis Development

3.1 Theoretical Framework

Voluntary disclosure refers to the provision of information beyond legal requirements, and it can be considered a rational trade-off between costs and benefits of an economic nature (Beattie, 2014). Hence, managers must make strategic decisions on the types and amount of voluntary-based disclosure to the capital market. If the benefits of disclosures outweigh the cost, the managers may disclose such information; otherwise, they may not disclose it (García-Meca & Sanchez-Ballesta, 2010; Healy & Palepu, 2001; Leuz & Wysocki, 2016). Several academic studies in environmental disclosure (Cormier & Magnan, 1999; Depoers et al., 2016), corporate social responsibility [CSR] disclosure (Garanina & Kim, 2023; Sun et al., 2022), and other general voluntary disclosures (Depoers, 2000) have applied the cost-and-benefit theory to their research. The purpose of making voluntary disclosures is to allow managers to increase company transparency in the capital market. If voluntary disclosure is being made, information asymmetry between managers and shareholders or outside investors is likely to decrease. Reducing information asymmetry can bring several benefits to the firm, such as lowering the cost of raising capital, reducing operational or credit risk, and increasing the share price and liquidity (Beyer et al., 2010).

Box 3
Several studies in environmental disclosure (Cormier & Magnan, 1999; Depoers et al., 2016), corporate social responsibility [CSR] disclosure (Garanina & Kim, 2023; Sun et al., 2022), and other general voluntary disclosures (Depoers, 2000) have applied the cost-and-benefit theory to their research.

Managers also need to consider the costs of preparing voluntary disclosures besides these incentives from capital markets. The costs of collecting information, litigation, and proprietary costs are potential costs of voluntary disclosure. Competitors can use some disclosed items, which can hurt the firm. Hence, managers must consider the benefits and costs of disclosing information to the public.

From an agency theory perspective, managers tend to exhibit opportunistic behaviour and hold more information to maximise their economic benefits rather than shareholders' benefit, and hence, information asymmetry increases (e.g., Aboody & Lev, 2000; Eisenhardt, 1989; Li et al., 2008). In this regard, Jensen and Meckling (1976) argued that firms should adopt corporate governance mechanisms to deal with agency problems. Since then, much accounting literature has focused on how to help firms increase information transparency in the financial reporting process and provided evidence on the impact of control mechanisms, including the board of directors, auditors, the ownership structure of a firm, executive compensation, and market-based activities on agency problems (Keasey & Wright, 1993). Companies can hire outside directors, auditors, and sell-side analysts to deal with agency conflicts because they are considered independent parties. More specifically, external independent auditors can provide their opinions on disclosed information, and this can increase its credibility, and shareholders' interests might be better served if disclosed information is being checked by auditors (e.g., Beattie & Thomson, 2007; Bukh et al., 2005; Roos & Roos, 1997).

Box 4
From the agency's perspective, external independent auditors can provide their opinions on disclosed information, increasing its credibility. Shareholders' interests might be better served if auditors are checking disclosed information.

3.2 *Carbon Disclosure and Audit Fee*

Carbon disclosure may cause changes in a firm's financial transparency. Many studies confirm that a higher level of carbon disclosure in a company's CSR report means that the company is more transparent and has less ability to manipulate profits (Kim et al., 2011). This is also supported by Kim et al. (2012) that firms with good CSR performance are more likely to provide more transparent financial information to investors, and it can also constrain earnings management.

Climate-related considerations are relatively new to auditors. Embedding these into the audit process requires knowledge acquisition and a mindset shift. The auditor needs to spend time acquiring knowledge of carbon emissions and management and its impact on the climate. Auditors need to understand how climate-related issues could impact the entity's annual report and how this needs to be incorporated into the audit work being performed. Specifically, auditors need to identify the climate-related risks the business is exposed to that could affect the audit approach and annual report.

Moreover, auditors need to understand management's process for identifying and responding to climate-related issues, and they need to test financial statement figures regarding climate-related risks. Lastly, auditors must test management's financial statement disclosures and review the disclosed information on climate-related matters. The demand for audits is assumed to be the efficient solution to costly contracting problems where the company's accounting technology, risk management systems, and corporate governance mechanisms are components of the nexus of contracts (Watts & Zimmerman, 1986). This is because auditors assure as to the integrity of the accounting numbers and information produced by the company's accounting technology (Simunic, 1980).

Box 5
Climate-related considerations are relatively new to auditors. Embedding these into the audit process requires knowledge acquisition and a mind-set shift.

As far as the audit fees are concerned, the results of previous studies on the determinants of audit fees (Hay et al., 2006; Simunic, 1980) find that the audit fee is budgeted by estimating the hours required to conduct an audit. Also, other studies reveal more factors that are directly related to audit fees determination, such as the auditor's effort, the working risks, and complexity (Causholli et al., 2011; Hay et al., 2006).

Next, this chapter examines whether the level of disclosed carbon information might affect audit fees by improving the information environment. It is claimed that increased corporate disclosure levels can reduce information asymmetry and the cost of capital (Bamber et al., 2018). If the quantity of carbon disclosure improves the information environment, this should reduce the audit risk, and hence, the audit premium will decrease.

Taking these factors into consideration, our first hypothesis is:

H1: The quantity of carbon disclosures is likely to decrease the level of audit fees.

The state-owned enterprises (SOEs) are significant to China's economy and have economic, political, and social responsibilities (Atkinson & Stiglitz, 1980). Like other businesses, SOEs must also acquire profits to keep the enterprise running. Meanwhile, SOEs must also satisfy employment demands, provide public services and facilities, maintain social stability and order, and achieve balanced societal development, economy, and environment. Due to these particular characteristics, SOEs are obliged to undertake more social responsibilities than non-state-owned enterprises (Non-SOEs), which increases the social responsibility information disclosure, including carbon information disclosure. The SOEs also have agency problems. Specifically, state owners do not oversee daily operations. Thus, they do not know everything about the company's operations, and managers may likely take actions to maximise their benefits at the expense of both state and minority shareholders. The increase in disclosed information can reduce the information asymmetry between them. Also, suppose the SOEs disclose more carbon information.

In that case, auditors will have more information to assess the company. They will need less time to collect evidence to verify the figures and other information in the annual report. Therefore, audit premiums for SOEs should be lower than non-SOEs.

Box 6
SOEs are obliged to undertake more social responsibilities than non-SOEs, which increases the social responsibility information disclosure (i.e., carbon information disclosure). If they disclose more carbon information, auditors will have more information to assess the company. They will need less time to collect evidence to verify the figures and other information in the annual report.

Therefore, we propose the second hypothesis:
H2: The relationship between the amount of carbon disclosure and the audit fee in H1 is more pronounced for SOEs than non-SOEs.

4 Methodology

4.1 Corporate Carbon Emission Disclosure

Content analysis involves codifying qualitative and quantitative information into pre-defined categories to derive patterns in the presentation and reporting of information (Guthrie & Abeysekera, 2006). This research will adopt the content analysis to evaluate what type of carbon information is disclosed in the sample firm's CSR report.

The measurement of carbon emission disclosure follows Ding et al. (2023). Where their paper uses firm annual reports to measure the level of carbon disclosure, we extract carbon emission information from annual reports. The keywords include 'climate opportunity', 'carbon emission', 'GHG emission', 'greenhouse gas', 'carbon', 'CO2', 'greenhouse', 'climate change', 'climate risk', and 'global warming. These terms appear most often in the collocation of 'climate' or 'carbon'. Recent studies support the importance of annual reports for climate information disclosure. For example, Guay et al. (2016) find that voluntary disclosure in annual reports helps managers communicate effectively with investors.

Moreover, Hahn et al. (2015) conducted a systematic literature review on carbon disclosure research. They found that CDP was the most popular data source among the 42 quantitative carbon disclosure empirical studies reviewed. Still, the annual report was the least popular data source for quantitative studies.

4.2 Sample and Data

This chapter obtains the accounting and financial data for Chinese-listed firms from 2017 to 2021 from the China Stock Market Accounting Research (CSMAR) database to test the predicted hypotheses. In addition, we hand-collect the carbon discourse level data from the annual financial report. Following the previous literature (Chen et al., 2010; Gul et al., 2013; Li and Guo., 2022), we exclude firms in the financial sector because they are specially regulated, and their financial ratios are not comparable with other industry sectors. The final sample includes 16,703 firm-year observations from 4058 firms from 2017–2021.

4.3 Research Model

The regression model is specified as follows:

$$\text{Audit}_{i,t+1} = ?+?_1\,\text{Carbon}_{i,t} + ?\,\text{Controls}_{i,t} + \text{Industry FEs} + \text{Year FEs} + ?_{i,t} \quad (1)$$

where i indexes firms, and t indexes time, the dependent variable is *Audit fees (Audit)*, the natural log of audit fees. The primary independent variable, carbon trading disclosure (*Carbon*), is the level of carbon information disclosure. It is a dummy variable; if the listed firm's disclosure, the carbon information equals 1; otherwise, it is zero.

$\text{Control}_{i,t}$ is a vector of control variables which have been found to affect audit fees. Control variables include firm size, measured as the logarithm of total assets (Francis et al., 2013). According to Bamber et al. (2018), we also control for the ratio of long-term debt to total assets (*Leverage*), return on assets (*ROA*), current ratio, quick ratio, inventories to assets (*Inv_asset*), sales growth (*Growth*), and receivables to total assets (*Rece_assets*). The number of subsidiaries is to capture audit complexity (*Subsidiary*).

4.3.1 Summary Statistics

Table 2 shows the summary statistics of the variables for the overall sample. The mean value of *Audit* is 14.022. The average for *Audit* is 13.911. The mean value of *Carbon* is 0.77, and the average of *Carbon* is 1.

Table 2 Summary statistics. This table presents summary statistics for a sample of Chinese-listed firms from 2017 to 2022. It reports the number of observations, mean, standard deviation, 25th percentile, median, and 75th percentile statistics of corporate governance variables. All variables are defined in Appendix

	N	Mean	St. Dev	p25	Median	p75
Audit	12,281	14.022	0.656	13.58	13.911	14.375
Carbon	12,281	0.77	0.421	1	1	1
Leverage	12,281	0.439	0.198	0.286	0.432	0.58
Firm_size	12,281	22.471	1.317	21.531	22.285	23.21
ROA	12,281	0.026	0.086	0.011	0.034	0.064
Inv_asset	12,281	0.039	0.06	0.009	0.024	0.046
Subsidiary	12,216	27.408	34.771	8	16	32
Growth	12,281	0.137	0.339	−0.031	0.099	0.25
Rece_assets	12,281	0.127	0.103	0.045	0.107	0.184
Current ratio	12,281	2.174	1.825	1.143	1.598	2.476
Quick ratio	12,281	1.723	1.641	0.792	1.207	1.951
Cash ratio	12,281	0.631	0.832	0.176	0.349	0.704
Debt asset	12,281	0.439	0.198	0.286	0.432	0.58

4.3.2 Correlation

Table 3 presents the correlation coefficients between the total audit fees and carbon disclosure. The coefficient of *Audit* is negative and significant at the 1% level, which is consistent with the hypothesis. When firms disclose carbon information in their annual reports, the total audit fees will be reduced.

5 Empirical Findings

5.1 The Relationship Between Total Audit Fees (Audit) and Carbon Trading Disclosure

Table 4 (column 1) presents the results for the total sample of the listed firms. We find that the coefficient of *Carbon* is −0.082 and statistically significant at the 1% level. This result is consistent with the hypothesis 1. The findings indicate that if the listed firm disclosure information is related to the carbon emission in the annual report, these firms' financial transparency is better than that of non-disclosure firms. Such firm's auditors may spend less time acquiring knowledge of carbon emissions. Auditors should understand how climate-related issues could impact the entity's annual report and how this needs to be incorporated into the audit work being performed. The results also support Bamber et al.'s (2018) view that a better corporate disclosure level can reduce information asymmetry and audit risk, decreasing audit fees.

Table 3 Correlation matrix. This table reports the correlation matrix among the audit fees, carbon disclosure, and control variables. ***, **, and * indicate the significance of correlation coefficient at the 1%, 5%, and 10% levels, respectively. All variables are defined in Appendix

	Audit	Carbon	Leverage	Firm_size	ROA	Inv_asset	Subsidiary	Growth	Rece_assets	Current ratio	Quick ratio	Cash ratio	Debt asset
Audit	1												
Carbon	−0.047***	1											
Leverage	0.390***	−0.056***	1										
Firm_size	0.749***	0.054***	0.474***	1									
ROA	−0.052***	0.187***	−0.334***	0.082***	1								
Inv_asset	0.002	0.098***	0.105***	0.036***	−0.001	1							
Subsidiary	0.544***	−0.123***	0.328***	0.549***	−0.036***	0.041***	1						
Growth	0.005	0.089***	−0.003	0.055***	0.308***	0.031***	0.007	1					
Rece_ assets	−0.132***	−0.039***	0.067***	−0.232***	−0.094***	−0.065***	−0.086***	0.028***	1				
Current ratio	−0.317***	0.008	−0.686***	−0.351***	0.203***	−0.008	0.206***	−0.029***	−0.036***	1			
Quick ratio	−0.307***	−0.026***	−0.677***	−0.347***	0.194***	−0.116***	−0.208***	−0.032***	−0.003	0.972***	1		
Cash ratio	−0.223***	−0.035***	−0.580***	−0.252***	0.196***	−0.091***	−0.159***	−0.021**	−0.167***	0.796***	0.818***	1	
Debt asset	0.390***	−0.056***	1.000***	0.474***	−0.334***	0.105***	0.328***	−0.003	0.067***	−0.686***	−0.677***	−0.580***	1

Table 4 The relationship between total audit fees and carbon information disclosure. This table reports the results of the OLS regressions for the relationship between the total audit fees and carbon disclosure in 2017–2022. The dependent variable, *Audit*, is the total audit fees. The independent variable is carbon disclosure, which is the level of carbon information disclosure. It is a dummy variable; if the listed firm's disclosure, the carbon information equals 1; otherwise, it is zero. SOEs represent firms controlled by the state, while non-SOEs represent firms controlled by private owners. All models include year and industry fixed effects, whose coefficients are suppressed based on calendar years and CSRC 2012 industry classification, respectively. All variables are defined in Appendix. T-statistics are reported in parentheses. ***, **, and * indicate significance at the 1%, 5%, and 10% levels, respectively

	(1)	(2)	(3)
	Audit	Audit	Audit
Carbon	−0.083***	−0.124**	−0.066
	(−4.122)	(−5.101)	(−1.939)
Leverage	−0.082	−0.048	0.060
	(−0.570)	(−0.701)	(0.543)
Client_size	0.348***	0.385***	0.315***
	(85.153)	(77.888)	(89.855)
ROA	−0.751***	−0.816***	−0.697***
	(−14.523)	(−11.123)	(−7.508)
Inv_asset	0.036	0.219**	−0.218*
	(0.498)	(4.390)	(−2.586)
Growth	−0.006	−0.017	−0.001
	(−0.526)	(−0.834)	(−0.090)
Rece_assets	0.192***	0.308**	0.087**
	(4.490)	(3.423)	(3.494)
Current ratio	−0.009	0.011	−0.026**
	(−0.732)	(1.282)	(−5.587)
Quick ratio	0.027***	0.016	0.028***
	(3.200)	(1.877)	(5.936)
Cash ratio	−0.055	−0.226*	−0.055
	(−0.406)	(−2.608)	(−0.516)
Subsidiary	0.003***	0.004***	0.003***
	(25.256)	(26.161)	(42.517)
Constant	6.261***	5.551***	6.907***
	(66.936)	(46.966)	(255.356)
Year	Yes	Yes	Yes
Ind	Yes	Yes	Yes
N	12,148	5167	6981
R^2	0.620	0.641	0.571

5.2 *The Role of State Ownership in the Relationship Between Total Audit Fees and Carbon*

Columns (2) and (3) of Table 4 examine the role of state ownership in the relationship between the total audit fees and carbon disclosure. Column (2) presents results for the SOEs and column (3) shows results for non-SOEs.

For SOEs, in column (2), the coefficient of *Audit* is −0.124 and statistically significant at the 5% level. The result indicates a negative relationship between carbon emission information and total audit fees. The total audit fees will be decreased for firms that disclose carbon emissions. Column (4) examines the relationship between the total audit fees and carbon disclosure in the non-SOEs. However, the coefficient of *Carbon* is −0.066, but statistically insignificant.

Unlike non-SOEs, SOEs prefer to disclose more carbon information in the annual report. The results are consistent with the hypothesis 2. For SOEs, in addition to pursuing economic interests, state-owned enterprises bear more social responsibilities, such as satisfying the demands of employment, providing public services and facilities, maintaining social stability and order, and achieving balanced developments among society, economy, and environment (Jiang and Kim, 2020). The disclosure of carbon information will also be affected by government intervention. Thus, the main objective is that SOEs are obliged to undertake more social responsibilities than non-SOEs, which increases the social responsibility information disclosure, including carbon information disclosure. Furthermore, non-SOEs show a stronger profit orientation, which is unfavourable for social responsibility information disclosure (Liu & Zhang, 2017). Thus, the relationship between carbon emission information and total audit fees in SOEs is stronger than in non-SOEs.

5.3 *Industry Effect*

We further investigate the relationship between carbon discourse and total audit fees in different industries among the Chinese-listed firms. Samples are classified according to the *Industry Classification Standard of CSRC (2012)*, divided into 18 industry samples from A to S.[1] Then, we run the same model (1) for different industries and examine the differences among Chinese-listed firms.

[1] 'A' represents agriculture, forestry, animal husbandry, and fishery. 'B' represents mining. 'C' represents manufacturing ('C1': food, clothing, textile; 'C2': Furniture, printing, paper making, petroleum, chemistry; 'C3': Metal, nonmetal, machinery; 'C4': Instruments, equipment). 'D' represents the electricity, heat, gas, and water production and supply industry. 'E' represents the construction industry. 'F' represents wholesale and retail; 'G' means transportation, warehousing, and postal services. 'H' represents the accommodation and catering industry. 'I' represents Information transfer, software and information technology services. 'J' represents finance. 'K' represents real estate. 'L' represents rental and business services. 'M' represents scientific research and technology services. 'N' represents water conservancy, environment and public facilities management. 'O' describes residential services, repairs, and other services. 'P' represents education. 'Q' represents health and social work. 'R' represents culture, sports, and entertainment industry. 'S' represents comprehensive.

Table 5 reports the number and the percentage of sample firms in different industries. The CSRC 2012 divides all firms into 18 sectors; the sample only involves 16 industries,[2] except the accommodation and catering industry and residential services, repairs, and other services industries, which do not disclose the carbon information.

Table 6 presents the results in the scientific research and technology services industry. The coefficient of *Carbon* is −0.217, which is statistically significant at the 10% level. Table 7 presents results in the metal, nonmetal, and machinery industries. The coefficient of *Carbon* is −0.101, which is statistically significant at the 1% level. The results show a meaningful relationship between carbon emissions and total audit fees in heavily polluting listed enterprises and technology companies.

Based on social identity theory and signal theory (Hu et al., 2020; Zhang et al., 2020), the enterprises' CSR activities, like carbon emission disclosure, can effectively transmit positive signals to the outside world and gain more stakeholders' attention, enhance customer loyalty, reduce negative government constraints, and help enterprises meet stakeholders' needs well (Akbari et al., 2021). In addition, CSR activities can effectively improve the efficiency of enterprises in obtaining more social capital and development opportunities (Zhu & Lai, 2019), thus reducing

Table 5 Disclosure percentage of sample firms in different industries. This table presents the number and the percentage of sample firms in different industries among the listed Chinese firms from 2017 to 2021. Samples are classified according to the *Industry Classification Standard of CSRC (2012)*, divided into 18 industries

Industry	Number of firms	Percentage
Agriculture, forestry, animal husbandry, and fishery	42	0.011
Mining	78	0.021
Manufactory	2366	0.647
Electricity, heat, gas, and water production and supply industry	113	0.031
Construction industry	105	0.029
Wholesale and retail	172	0.047
Transportation, warehousing, and postal services	103	0.028
Information transfer, software and information technology services	294	0.080
Real estate	124	0.034
Rental and business services	55	0.015
Scientific research and technology services	54	0.015
Water conservancy, environment, and public facilities management	58	0.016
Education	1	0.000
Health and social work	12	0.003
Culture, sports, and entertainment industry	59	0.016
Comprehensive	21	0.006

[2] We exclude the financial industry because the regulation differs from other sectors.

Table 6 The relationship between total audit fees and carbon information disclosure in scientific research and technology services industry. This table reports the results of the OLS regressions for the relationship between the total audit fees and carbon disclosure in 2017–2022. The dependent variable, *Audit*, is the total audit fees. The independent variable is carbon disclosure, which is the level of carbon information disclosure. It is a dummy variable; if the listed firm's disclosure, the carbon information equals 1; otherwise, it is zero. All models include year and industry fixed effects, whose coefficients are suppressed based on calendar years and CSRC 2012 industry classification, respectively. All variables are defined in Appendix. T-statistics are reported in parentheses. ***, **, and * indicate significance at the 1%, 5%, and 10% levels, respectively

	Audit
Carbon	−0.217*
	(−1.776)
Leverage	−0.271
	(−0.796)
Client_size	0.298***
	(5.169)
ROA	−1.147**
	(−2.140)
Inv_asset	−0.172
	(−0.149)
Growth	0.205*
	−1.938
Rece_assets	−0.105
	(−0.317)
Current ratio	0.291
	−1.447
Quick ratio	−0.246
	(−1.226)
Cash ratio	−0.096
	(−1.040)
Subsidiary	0.008***
	(4.476)
Constant	7.239***
	(6.072)
Year FEs	Yes
Industry FEs	Yes
N	146
R^2	0.482

operational risk and operating costs and promoting improving their corporate financial performance (Yang et al., 2020). Also, implementing CSR activities enhances the company's external reputation, releases excellent signals to the market, and attracts more investors and cooperation opportunities (Cui et al., 2018).

In China, 40% of Chinese rivers are polluted, and heavily polluting companies are responsible for the pollution (Miao et al., 2015). Heavily polluting industries, represented by the metal, nonmetal, and machinery industries, are essential to China's economic development (Ang et al., 2022).

Table 7 The relationship between total audit fees and carbon information disclosure in metal, nonmetal, machinery industry. This table reports the results of the OLS regressions for the relationship between the total audit fees and carbon disclosure in 2017–2022. The dependent variable, *Audit*, is the total audit fees. The independent variable is carbon disclosure, which is the level of carbon information disclosure. It is a dummy variable; if the listed firm's disclosure, the carbon information equals 1; otherwise, it is zero. The regression model only includes year-fixed effects, whose coefficients are suppressed.. All variables are defined in Appendix. T-statistics are reported in parentheses. ***, **, and * indicate significance at the 1%, 5%, and 10% levels, respectively

	Audit
Carbon	−0.101***
	(0.033)
Leverage	0.107
	(0.263)
Client_size	0.327***
	(0.007)
ROA	−0.714***
	(0.084)
Inv_asset	0.256
	(0.185)
Growth	−0.029
	(0.020)
Rece_assets	0.041
	(0.069)
Current ratio	0.016
	(0.023)
Quick ratio	−0.055**
	(0.026)
Cash ratio	0.029**
	(0.014)
Subsidiary	0.004***
	(0.000)
Year FEs	Yes
Constant	6.690***
	(0.145)
Observations	4679
R^2	0.591

For heavy pollution Chinese-listed companies, it is necessary to disclose the carbon emissions in the annual report. The auditor will spend less time finding information and balancing the firm risk. Thus, the relationship between carbon emissions and audit fees is significant in the heavy pollution industry.

In addition to the heavy pollution industry, there is a significant negative relationship between carbon emissions and audit fees in the scientific research and technology services industry. The characteristics of this industry determine such a relationship in China. Within companies in this sector, supply chains are geographically dispersed, with production processes often spanning multiple countries and continents. Such sectors must consider serving many needs in diverse consumer, business, and governmental sectors (stakeholders). The stakeholder theory focuses on the social disclosure aspect of environmental, social, and governance (ESG) disclosure, which comprises primarily CSR engagement with two critical stakeholders—employees and the community. Thus, for scientific research and technology services firms that prefer to disclose carbon information, it is easier for the auditors to find related information and balance the firms' risk.

6 Conclusion

This paper examines whether the level of disclosed carbon information might affect audit fees by improving the information environment. Bamber et al. (2018) suggest that increasing corporate disclosure levels can reduce information asymmetry and the cost of capital. The findings of this chapter show a significant negative relationship between carbon disclosure and audit fees in Chinese-listed firms. The results suggest that firms disclosing carbon emissions will have better financial transparency, and it will reduce information asymmetry. Thus, auditors can access more information related to carbon emissions in the annual report. It can help auditors make a final decision. Second, this paper also examines the role of state ownership.

Regarding the two sub-samples (SOEs and non-SOEs), the relationship between carbon disclosure and audit fees is stronger for the former group than the latter. In addition, the effect of industry is found. Samples are divided into 18 sectors. A negative relationship between carbon disclosure and audit fees only occurred in the metal, nonmetal, machinery, and scientific research and technology services industries. Specifically, heavy pollution and high technology firms prefer to disclose their carbon emissions to consider and meet stakeholders' needs, which can attract investment and gain a good reputation.

Overall, while this chapter contributes to literature related to carbon information disclosure and audit fees, it has some limitations in this study. First, this paper uses a dummy variable to measure the carbon information; the results from this chapter may not reflect how the company manages carbon emissions. Second, this chapter only considers the audit fees; it is not sure whether such ESG reports affect the auditor selection. Given the rapid development of the Chinese audit market, researchers should consider other audit variables.

Those limitations allow future researchers to conduct further research in this area. Future researchers can use the disclosure index to measure the disclosure level of carbon information, and from this, they can analyse how Chinese companies manage carbon. Also, future researchers can conduct carbon disclosure studies in other emerging market contexts.

List of Accounting Standards IFRS S1 General Requirements for Disclosure of Sustainability-related Financial Information.

IFRS S2 Climate-related Disclosures.

Declaration of Generative AI and AI-Assisted Technologies in the Writing Process for This Chapter The editor only used ChatGPT (Premium GPT4.0) and Grammarly to proof-read and check for typos and inconsistencies. There is no further declaration from the authors.

Appendix: Definition of Variable

Variables	Definition
Audit	The natural log of audit fees
Carbon	If the listed firm's disclosure the carbon information is equals to 1, otherwise is zero
Firm_size	The natural log of the total assets
Leverage	(Long-Term Debt + Short-Term Debt & Current Portion of Long-Term Debt)/(Long-Term Debt + Short-Term Debt and Current Portion of Long-Term Debt + Common Equity)
ROA	Net profit/Total assets
Current ratio	Current assets/Current liabilities
Quick ratio	(Current assets – inventories)/Current liabilities
Cash ratio	Cash and cash equivalent/Current liabilities
Inv_asset	Inventory/Assets
Subsidiary	Number of subsidiaries of the listed firms
Growth	Sales growth
Debt/Asset	Total debt/Total assets

References

Aboody, D., & Lev, B. (2000). Information asymmetry, R&D, and insider gains. *Journal of Finance, 55*(6), 2747–2766.

Akbari, M., Nazarian, A., Foroudi, P., Seyyed Amiri, N., & Ezatabadipoor, E. (2021). How corporate social responsibility contributes to strengthening brand loyalty, hotel positioning and intention to revisit? *Current Issues in Tourism, 24*(13), 1897–1917.

Ang, R., Shao, Z., Liu, C., Yang, C., & Zheng, Q. (2022). The relationship between CSR and financial performance and the moderating effect of ownership structure: Evidence from Chinese heavily polluting listed enterprises. *Sustainable Production and Consumption, 30*, 117–129.

Ares, E., & Hirst, D. (2016). The Paris Climate Change Conference. Available at: https://commonslibrary.parliament.uk/research-briefings/cbp-7393/. Accessed 14 August.

Atkinson, A. B., & Stiglitz, J. E. (1980). *Lectures in public economics*. McGraw-Hill.

Bamber, M., McMeeking, K., & Petrovic, N. (2018). Mandatory financial reporting processes and outcome. *International Journal of Accounting, 53*, 227–245.

Beattie, V. (2014). Accounting narratives and the narrative turn in accounting research: Issues, theory, methodology, methods and a research framework. *British Accounting Review, 46*(2), 111–134.

Beattie, V., & Thomson, S. J. (2007). Lifting the lid on the use of content analysis to investigate intellectual capital disclosures. *Accounting Forum, 31*(2), 129–163.
Beyer, A., Cohen, D. A., Lys, T. Z., & Walther, B. R. (2010). The financial reporting environment: Review of the recent literature. *Journal of Accounting and Economics, 50*(2–3), 296–343.
Bodansky, D. (2016). The Paris climate change agreement: A new hope? *American Journal of International Law, 110*(2), 288–319.
Bukh, P. N., Nielsen, C., Gormsen, P., & Mouritsen, J. (2005). Disclosure of information on intellectual capital in Danish IPO prospectuses. *Accounting, Auditing & Accountability Journal, 18*(6), 713–732.
Causholli, M., De Martinis, M., Hay, D., & Knechel, W. (2011) Audit markets, fees, and production: Towards an integrated view of empirical audit research. *Journal of Accounting Literature, 29*, 167–215.
Chen, S., Sun, S.Y., & Wu, D. (2010). Client importance, institutional improvements, and audit quality in China: An office and individual auditor level analysis. The Accounting Review, 85, 127-158.
China Banking Regulatory Commission (CBRC). (2013). Green credit statistics system. CRBC General Office.
Cormier, D., & Magnan, M. (1999). Corporate environmental disclosure strategies: Determinants, costs and benefits. *Journal of Accounting, Auditing & Finance, 14*(4), 429–451.
Cui, J., Jo, H., & Na, H. (2018). Does corporate social responsibility affect information asymmetry? *Journal of Business Ethics, 148*, 549–572.
Depoers, F. (2000). A cost benefit study of voluntary disclosure: Some empirical evidence from French listed companies. European Accounting Review, 9, 245-263.
Depoers, F., Jeanjean, T., & Jérôme, T. (2016). Voluntary disclosure of greenhouse gas emissions: Contrasting the carbon disclosure project and corporate reports. *Journal of Business Ethics, 134*(3), 445–461.
Ding, D., Liu, B., & Chang, M. (2023). Carbon Emissions and TCFD Aligned Climate-Related Information Disclosures. Journal of Business Ethics, 182, 967-1001.
Dhaliwal, D., Li, O. Z., Tsang, A., & Yang, Y. G. (2014). Corporate social responsibility disclosure and the cost of equity capital: The roles of stakeholder orientation and financial transparency. *Journal of Accounting and Public Policy, 33*(4), 328–355.
Eisenhardt, K. M. (1989). Agency theory: An assessment and review. *Academy of Management Review, 14*(1), 57–74.
Francis, J. R., Michas, P. N., & Yu, M. D. (2013). Office size of Big 4 auditors and client restatements. *Contemporary Accounting Research, 30*(4), 1626–1661.
Garanina, T., & Kim, O. (2023). The relationship between CSR disclosure and accounting conservatism: The role of state ownership. *Journal of International Accounting, Auditing and Taxation, 50*, 100522.
García-Meca, E., & Sanchez-Ballesta, J. P. (2010). The association of board independence and ownership concentration with voluntary disclosure: A meta-analysis. *European Accounting Review, 19*(3), 603–627.
Guay, W., Samuels, D., & Taylor, D. (2016). Guiding through the fog: Financial statement complexity and voluntary disclosure. Journal of Accounting and Economics, 62 (2-3), 234-269.
Gul, F.A., Wu, D., & Zhang, Z. (2013). Do individual auditors affect audit quality? Evidence from archival data. The Accounting Review, 88, 1993-2023.
Guthrie, J., & Abeysekera, I. (2006). Content analysis of social, environmental reporting: What is new? *Faculty of Commerce - Papers, 10*. https://doi.org/10.1108/14013380610703120
Hahn, R., Reimsbach, D., & Schiemann, F. (2015). Organizations, climate change, and transparency: Reviewing the literature on carbon disclosure. Organisation and Environment, 28(1), 80-102.
Hay, D. C., Knechel, W. R., & Wong, N. (2006). Audit fees: A meta-analysis of the effect of supply and demand attributes. *Contemporary Accounting Research, 23*, 141–191.

Healy, P. M., & Palepu, K. G. (2001). Information asymmetry, corporate disclosure, and the capital markets: A review of the empirical disclosure literature. *Journal of Accounting and Economics, 31*(1–3), 405–440.

Hu, B., Liu, J., Zhang, X. (2020). The impact of employees' perceived CSR on customer orientation: An integrated perspective of generalized exchange and social identity theory. International Journal of Contemporary Hospitality Management, 32(7), 2345–2364.

Jensen, M. C., & Meckling, W. H. (1976). Theory of the firm: Managerial behavior, agency costs and ownership structure. *Journal of Financial Economics, 3*(4), 305–360.

Jiang, F., & Kim, K. (2020). Corporate governance in China: A survey. Review of Finance, 24, 733-772.

Jizi, M. I., Salama, A., Dixon, R., & Stratling, R. (2014). Corporate governance and corporate social responsibility disclosure: Evidence from the US banking sector. *Journal of Business Ethics, 125*, 601–615.

Keasey, K., & Wright, M. (1993). Issues in corporate accountability and governance: An editorial. *Accounting and Business Research, 23*(sup1), 291–303.

Kim, J.-B., Liu, X., & Zheng, L. (2012). The impact of mandatory IFRS adoption on audit fees: Theory and evidence. *Accounting Review*. Forthcoming, Available at SSRN.

Kim, Y., Park, M. S., & Wier, B. (2011). Is earnings quality associated with corporate social responsibility? *The Accounting Review, 87*. https://doi.org/10.2308/accr-10209

KPMG. (2022). Survey of Sustainability Reporting 2022—China Insights. Available at: https://kpmg.com/cn/en/home/insights/2023/01/survey-of-sustainability-reporting-2022-china-insights.html. Accessed 24 August.

Leuz, C., & Wysocki, P. D. (2016). The economics of disclosure and financial reporting regulation: Evidence and suggestions for future research. *Journal of Accounting Research, 54*(2), 525–622.

Li, J., Pike, R., & Haniffa, R. (2008). Intellectual capital disclosure and corporate governance structure in UK firms. *Accounting and Business Research, 38*(2), 137–159.

Li, Q., & Guo, M. (2022). Do the resignations of politically connected independent directors affect corporate social responsibility? Evidence from China. Journal of Corporate Finance, 73, art.102174.

Liobikienė, G., & Butkus, M. (2017). The European Union possibilities to achieve targets of Europe 2020 and Paris agreement climate policy. *Renewable Energy, 106*, 298–309. https://doi.org/10.1016/j.renene.2017.01.036

Liu, X., & Zhang, C. (2017). Corporate governance, social responsibility information disclosure, and enterprise value in China. *Journal of Cleaner Production, 142*, 1075–1084.

Miao, X., Tang, Y., Wong, C. W., & Zang, H. (2015). The latent causal chain of industrial water pollution in China. *Environmental Pollution, 196*, 473–477.

Nekhili, M., Nagati, H., Chtioui, T., & Rebolledo, C. (2017). Corporate social responsibility disclosure and market value: Family versus nonfamily firms. *Journal of Business Research, 77*, 41–52.

Roos, G., & Roos, J. (1997). Measuring your company's intellectual performance. *Long Range Planning, 30*(3), 413–426.

Simunic, D. (1980). The pricing of audit services: Theory and evidence. *Journal of Accounting Research, 18*(1), 161–190.

Sun, Y., Xu, C., Li, H., & Cao, Y. (2022). What drives the innovation in corporate social responsibility (CSR) disclosures? An integrated reporting perspective from China. *Journal of Innovation & Knowledge, 7*, 100267.

Watts, R., & Zimmerman, J. (1986). *Positive accounting theory*. Prentice Hall.

Yang, Y., Yao, C., & Li, Y. (2020). The impact of the amount of environmental information disclosure on financial performance: The moderating effect of corporate internationalization. *Corporate Social Responsibility and Environmental Management, 27*(6), 2893–2907.

Zhang, Q., Cao, M., Zhang, F., Liu, J., & Li, X. (2020). Effects of corporate social responsibility on customer satisfaction and organizational attractiveness: A signaling perspective. *Business Ethics: A European Review, 29*(1), 20–34.

Zhu, Q., & Lai, K. H. (2019). Enhancing supply chain operations with extended corporate social responsibility practices by multinational enterprises: Social capital perspective from Chinese suppliers. *International Journal of Production Economics, 213*, 1–1.

Chengruizhi Ma is Lecturer in Accounting at Department of Accounting and Finance of the Open University. Prior to this, he held teaching assistant positions at the University of Bradford and University of Hull. His research interests include International Financial Reporting Standards 9 [IFRS 9], voluntary disclosure, auditor function, corporate governance, business law, sustainable accounting, and corporate social responsibility (CSR). He has experience of working in audit, tax, employment law and insolvency law areas.

Dr Yifei Bi currently holds a position at the School of Economics and Finance, Queen Mary University of London. Yifei has a Ph.D. in Accounting and Finance. Her research interests mainly cover empirical topics in corporate social responsibility (CSR), sustainable accounting, corporate finance (i.e., mergers and acquisitions), corporate governance, and financial reporting quality.

Business Ecosystem and Sustainable Innovative Practices

Meryem Altaf and Nosheen Jawaid Khan

Abstract This chapter provides evidence of how the business ecosystem affects companies adopting innovative approaches for sustainable outcomes. We contend that companies alone cannot achieve sustainable outcomes and require collaborative approaches to innovate processes. We identify various internal and external factors in the business ecosystem which could either facilitate or hinder the company's sustainable innovation approaches. Using multiple case study designs, documentary analysis, and semi-structured interviews, we explore various crucial external factors, e.g., the country's regulatory framework, culture, available resources, and collaboration of companies with stakeholders, in developing sustainable, innovative approaches. These sustainable innovations (e.g., digitisation, training on health, education, drip irrigation, and water sense technologies) help firms improve their existing products and processes and contribute positively to the environment and society.

1 Introduction

DURING THE LAST THREE DECADES, the term "*sustainability*" has gained attraction from academia, industries, governments, media, and other practitioners. Research demonstrates that business organisations are among the most important drivers of environmental degradation and social distress due to their massive resource utilisation and production operations (Ullah et al., 2022). These issues highlight the need for business organisations to explore new technologies and develop business models and innovative ways to minimise their environmental and

M. Altaf (✉)
Leicester Castle Business School, De Montfort University, Leicester, UK
e-mail: meryem.altaf@dmu.ac.uk

N. J. Khan
Newcastle University Business School, Newcastle University, Newcastle upon Tyne, UK
e-mail: nosheen.khan@ncl.ac.uk

V. Q. Trinh (ed.), *Climate Governance and Corporate Eco-innovation*, Sustainable Finance, https://doi.org/10.1007/978-3-031-56423-9_10

social impacts in the long run (Cillo et al., 2019). Many companies have recognised the pressing need to reduce greenhouse gas emissions, conserve natural resources, invest in energy-efficient measures, create jobs, and take other actions to develop greener and more inclusive economies. However, transitioning into resilient, greener, and just economies requires companies to align their economic, social, and environmental outcomes through innovative approaches. Cillo et al. (2019) state that innovation should focus on gaining a competitive advantage and devise approaches to minimise environmental degradation and social distress. Various internal and external factors impact companies' strategies for sustainable innovation (Chen et al., 2014; Cillo et al., 2019; Seuring & Gold, 2013). In this chapter, we focus on the role of the business ecosystem as an external factor to the company, which could either facilitate or hinder the company's innovative approaches to sustainability.

Moore (1998) defines the business ecosystem as an "extended system of mutually supportive organizations, communities of customers, suppliers, lead producers, and other stakeholders, financing, trade associations, standard bodies, labour unions, governmental and quasi-governmental institutions, and other interested parties" (p. 168). These heterogeneous stakeholders intentionally or unintentionally interact with each other and co-evolve (Yoon et al., 2022). This is a comprehensive definition of the business ecosystem, highlighting the intentions of various stakeholders and their interrelationships. These mutually developed relationships help companies to evolve and redesign their business models (Amit & Zott, 2015).

Box 1
The business ecosystem is an "extended system of mutually supportive organisations, communities of customers, suppliers, lead producers, and other stakeholders, financing, trade associations, standard bodies, labour unions, governmental and quasi-governmental institutions, and other interested parties". These heterogeneous stakeholders intentionally or unintentionally interact with each other and co-evolve.

The business ecosystem in Pakistan is evolving because of changing trends in the external environment. According to the World Bank report (2022), within the complex business ecosystem of Pakistan, multiple stakeholders compete and collaborate on available resources, co-evolve, and jointly adapt to external disruption. The unstable political situation of Pakistan, along with the long-fought battle related to terrorism, also impacts the day-in and day-out of businesses, as they are directly related to economic growth and national security in particular. Both the policies set by government agencies and leaders can affect the legal framework within which businesses operate, as well as the market conditions that influence consumer buying behaviours (Kosar et al., 2022). Thus, multiple factors and actors in Pakistan's business ecosystem make it a complex survival, growth, and evolution system. Within such a system, joint actions are required, as no single company can sustain itself in isolation (Herrero-Luna et al., 2022; Parida et al., 2019). Mutual efforts from stakeholders within the business environment are non-trivial, either it is for running a conventional business or engaging in a circular economy to reuse, recycle, and regenerate resources (Gregory et al., 2020). Therefore, organisations are now going beyond their boundaries and collaborating with the actors within an ecosystem to synergize diverse resources (Frishammar & Parida, 2019; Yi et al., 2022). Companies are exploring innovative ways to minimise their environmental impact while maximising revenue and growth simultaneously.

Previous studies highlight the role of stakeholder ties in organisations' sustainable innovations (Yi et al., 2022). However, there is still a lack of studies investigating the diverse factors and actors in the business ecosystem that could affect companies' sustainable, innovative strategies (Yi et al., 2022). Moreover, it is also necessary to understand Pakistan's sustainability landscape as it is still underdeveloped. We aim to explore various factors in the business ecosystem that impact companies' sustainable, innovative strategies in Pakistan.

Box 2

Mutual efforts from stakeholders within the business environment are non-trivial, either for running the conventional business or engaging in a circular economy to reuse, recycle, and regenerate resources. Therefore, organisations are now going beyond their boundaries and collaborating with the actors within an ecosystem to synergise diverse resources.

With the rise in global environmental issues and social distress, it has become critical for companies to develop sustainable, innovative strategies. To fulfil the desired aim of the study, we ask two key questions: (RQ1) Who are key stakeholders, and how do they engage with companies? And (RQ2) How do external factors in the business ecosystem facilitate or hinder the company's sustainable innovation approaches? We have employed a multiple case study research design to answer our research questions. The cases are selected from the FMCG sector of a developing economy, Pakistan. Documentary analysis and semi-structured interviews are used for the collection of data. The findings highlight two important aspects: (a) external factors in a business ecosystem, such as regulatory framework, culture, and available resources, and (b) sustainable innovative approaches by businesses. Sustainable innovations such as packaging waste reduction, greenhouse gas emission strategies, drip irrigation, water sense technologies, etc. help companies improve their existing products and processes and contribute positively to the environment and society.

The remainder of the chapter is divided into four sections: Sect. 2 sheds light on how we understand sustainable innovation in the context of our study and its relation within the business ecosystem framework. Section 3 explains the reasoning behind the case study approach, multiple data collection methods, and thematic analysis techniques for understanding and explaining the phenomenon. Section 4 accentuates two main themes: *The role of the business ecosystem* and *Sustainable, innovative practices* that are interrelated and interdependent in explaining companies' sustainability efforts. Lastly, Sect. 5 concludes the chapter by highlighting the research's theoretical, methodological, and empirical contributions and the study's limitations.

2 Literature Review

2.1 *Business Ecosystem*

Changing consumer tastes and preferences, rapid technological advancements, resource scarcity, and an uncertain environment indicate that businesses cannot survive in isolation. Businesses are the components of a more extensive system where they are connected with multiple actors and factors "who depend on each other for their mutual effectiveness and survival" (Iansiti & Levien, 2004, p. 8). Such a system is called a business ecosystem, a term coined by Moore. He defines the business ecosystem as a network of groups, including customers, suppliers, and organisations formed intentionally and incidentally (Moore, 1998). Moore's comprehensive definition of the business ecosystem highlights various stakeholders and the intentions of their interrelationships. Stakeholder relationships are rooted in collaborations within the ecosystem, and they are guided by superordinate institutions, such as religious, cultural, or political institutions, as also expressed by Greer et al. (2016). Studies argue that stakeholders require an ecosystem where all resources are transformed, augmented, and utilised for various purposes (Pera et al., 2016).[1]

Along with collaborations, stakeholders also compete with each other in a business ecosystem. Riquelme-Medina et al. (2022) highlight that coopetition, where cooperation and competition coexist, indirectly leads to superior organisational performance. Complex networks and stakeholder relationships within an ecosystem help an organisation gain resources (Yi et al., 2022). These resources, either operant or operand, support organisations in growing and innovating their products and processes. Moore (1998) also narrates that various actors and factors in an ecosystem "work cooperatively and competitively to support new products, satisfy customer needs, and incorporate the next round of innovation" (Moore, 1998, p. 76). Frow et al. (2014) state that negotiation between and among actors can provide a platform for stakeholders to offer and seek resources with collaborators. Hence, it is observed that stakeholder ties within an ecosystem help organisations gain resources through cooperation or competition and utilise them to survive in the long run.

[1] Constantin and Lusch (1994) divide resources into two categories, which are operand and operant resources. Where operand resources are physical, for example, natural resources, and materials. Meanwhile, operant resources are processional or non-physical, for example, knowledge and skills.

However, organisations' profit focus has changed since the emergence of the concept of sustainability. Today, they are finding approaches to making profits without harming the environment and society (Elkington, 1997). Organisations require networks and stakeholders' relationships to seek avenues for developing a sustainable future (Yi et al., 2022). We are identifying the role of the business ecosystem in influencing companies to innovate their products, processes, or business models to ensure sustainability. Both business ecosystems and sustainable innovation are complementary terms as business ecosystem provides a framework to collaborate and help businesses to innovate and develop sustainable practices. With the rise in awareness and need for sustainable practices, companies are seeking ways to innovate their products and processes to reduce the negative impact of their operations on the environment and society (Shakeel et al., 2020). We argue that a single organisation cannot protect the environment and work for social well-being. Organisations interact with actors and factors within the business ecosystem that influence companies to gain resources and knowledge and develop new ways to achieve sustainable, innovative outcomes. Here, the critical question is how can we define sustainable innovation, and how can sustainable innovation be achieved? The following section will help us understand sustainable innovations and how they relate to the business ecosystem framework.

Box 3

Both business ecosystems and sustainable innovation are complementary terms as business ecosystem provides a framework to collaborate and help businesses to innovate and develop sustainable practices. With the rise in awareness and need for sustainable practices, companies are seeking ways to innovate their products and processes to reduce the negative impact of their operations on the environment and society.

2.2 *Understanding Sustainable Innovation*

There has been growing debate over the past 15 years regarding "sustainability"—intertwining economic, environmental, and social goals (Adams et al., 2015). There is immense pressure on businesses to implement sustainable initiatives and measure, monitor, and report sustainability performance for accountability. However, within the existing literature, precisely what sustainability means or how it can be achieved remains uncertain. A variety of conceptualisations exist, and there is no single definition for sustainability (Blättel-Mink, 1998; Blowfield et al., 2007; Bos-Brouwers, 2010; Elkington, 1994; Fussler & James, 1996; George et al., 2016; Gladwin et al., 1995). It mainly refers to the ability to meet the needs of the present generation without compromising the ability of future generations to meet their own needs. It encompasses environmental, social, and economic dimensions, seeking to balance ecological preservation, social equity, and economic prosperity. Where sustainability is the end, we believe sustainable innovation is the means to achieve the end. This is why our chapter is interested in sustainable-orientated innovation activities and how they become effective in helping companies achieve sustainable goals.

Box 4
The existing literature remains uncertain about what sustainability means or how it can be achieved. Various conceptualisations exist, and there is no single definition for sustainability. However, it could be said that sustainability mainly refers to the ability to meet the needs of the present generation without compromising the ability of future generations to meet their own needs. It encompasses environmental, social, and economic dimensions, seeking to balance ecological preservation, social equity, and economic prosperity.

2.2.1 Definition of Sustainable Innovation

Innovation plays a crucial role by fostering a greater level of sustainability in company activities (e.g., Crossan & Apaydin, 2010; Dangelico & Pujari, 2010; Hansen et al., 2009; Hansen & Große-Dunker, 2013; Snider et al., 2003). A confusing array of labels applied to innovation that contributes to sustainability: sustainability-oriented innovations (SIs) (Klewitz & Hansen, 2014); corporate social responsibility; green-, eco-, or ecological innovation; social, environmental management; and/or responsible innovation (Carroll & Shabana, 2010). The most researched concepts, "green innovation" or "eco-innovation", highlight that the environmental orientation of an innovation is often considered to be the most important by the company because of both its innovative potential and economic impact (e.g., Carrillo-Hermosilla et al., 2010; Horbach, 2008; Horbach et al., 2012; Kesidou & Demirel, 2012; Schiederig et al., 2012). However, this perspective on sustainable innovation neglects the social dimensions of both innovation and sustainability.

We argue that innovation and sustainability guarantee a competitive advantage for companies, provide environmental benefits, and produce social well-being (Cillo et al., 2019; Garcia & Calantone, 2002). Literature suggests that Sustainability (Elkington, 1997), Sustainable Development (WCED, 1987), and innovation are all contested and controversial concepts. Consequently, no clear or unified definition of "sustainable innovation" has been published (Rauter et al., 2017). However, two well-cited definitions highlight the holistic impact of innovation on all three dimensions of sustainability, which is similar to how we approach this concept. For example, Boons et al. (2013) define sustainability innovation as "innovation that improves sustainability performance" (p. 2), where performance includes all three dimensions of sustainability: environmental, economic, and social. Similarly, Clark and Charter (2007, p. 99) define sustainability innovation as "a process where sustainability considerations (environmental, social, and financial) are integrated into company systems from idea generation through to research and development (R&D) and commercialisation. This applies to products, services, and technologies, as well as to new business and organizational models".

This latter definition includes managerial innovations and innovations generally associated with sustainability, namely, those related to products, processes, services, and business models (Schiederig et al., 2012). For this chapter, we have adopted the following broad definition: "*Sustainable innovation considers all sustainability dimensions, including environmental, social, and economic during the whole innovation process that applies to products, services, technologies, processes, strategies and business models to avoid or reduce negative impacts on the environment while considering social aspects and simultaneously aim to sustain the profitability of the business*". In simplest terms, sustainable innovation involves developing and implementing novel ideas, products, services, or processes that contribute to sustainability goals of all three dimensions of sustainability (Tello & Yoon, 2008, p. 165). It goes beyond incremental improvements and aims to create transformative changes in how society interacts with the environment, addresses social issues, and manages economic resources. We use the terms "sustainability-oriented innovation" and "sustainable innovation" interchangeably throughout the chapter, which most researchers have supported to conceptualise the above-stated concept (e.g., Hansen et al., 2009; Klewitz & Hansen, 2014).

Box 5
Sustainable innovation considers *"all sustainability dimensions, including environmental, social, and economic during the whole innovation process that applies to products, services, technologies, processes, strategies and business models to avoid or reduce negative impacts on the environment while considering social aspects and simultaneously aim to sustain the profitability of the business"*. In simplest terms, sustainable innovation involves developing and implementing novel ideas, products, services, or processes that contribute to sustainability goals of all three dimensions of sustainability.

2.2.2 Effectiveness of Sustainable Innovation

Until now, we understand sustainable innovation and why it is essential in achieving companies' sustainable goals. Now, the question arises of "how" sustainable innovation can effectively implement and fulfil its purpose. In line with the general innovation model, several authors have recognised that the effectiveness of sustainable innovation can be ascribed to both internal and external factors. The former relates to managing new products and services' development, commercialisation, and dissemination phases (Kemp et al., 1998; Lee et al., 2022). Instead, other studies have underlined the pivotal role of external factors and actors, especially highlighting the relational aspects of sustainability innovation (Foxon & Pearson, 2008;

Seuring & Gold, 2013). Bansal and DesJardine (2014, p. 71) state that "firms are systems nested within larger macro-systems". It means that business models create the infrastructure of business ecosystems, which we define as networks of interconnected actors (e.g., government, suppliers, customers, regulatory bodies, and NGOs) that depend on one another for the exchange of resources, expertise, as well as their mutual effectiveness and survival (see Ansari et al., 2016; Iansiti & Levien, 2004; Laasch, 2019; Moore, 1998). We similarly argue in this chapter that an organisation is an entity that has interrelation with other entities in the business ecosystem and fosters sustainable innovation. Organisations must embrace a collaborative approach among diverse stakeholders, such as businesses, governments, academia, and civil society. This perspective in the extant literature of sustainable innovation is studied as external relational, systems thinking, system building, stakeholders' governance, and ecosystem innovation (see Adams et al., 2016; Hermundsdottir & Aspelund, 2021; Lupova-Henry & Dotti, 2019; Snihur & Bocken, 2022).

Regarding the external relational perspective, some studies have emphasised that a company's innovation ability is strongly influenced by its relational capital and the intangible value present in the relations (Thompson & Heron, 2006). It implies that market stakeholders no longer perceive profit-making as necessary for a company to be legitimised (Forstater et al., 2010). Products or services certified as ethical, socially responsible, and made from a sustainable chain might become more attractive for stakeholders demonstrating a growing interest in sustainable performance. Thus, companies must consider stakeholders' expectations and decisions while developing their products and services. An increasing number of scholars have studied the involvement of stakeholders and their role in the strategic management of organisations by stakeholder theory, which explains that the interactions with the market and nonmarket players affect a company's performance (Freeman, 1984).

Similarly, Werther and Chandler (2010) have indicated that stakeholder engagement influences a firm's economic and social value in the medium and long-term goals. A key element especially emerging from these considerations is the external stakeholders' expectations as a prerequisite to understanding environmental and social actions for innovations (Alkemade & Suurs, 2012; Seuring & Gold, 2013). For example, by including internal stakeholder expectations, companies can improve workplace health and safety, employee motivation, and sustainability-oriented organisational practices (Hutchins & Sutherland, 2008).

Box 6

A company's ability to innovate is strongly influenced by its relational capital and the intangible value present in the relations. It implies that market stakeholders no longer perceive profit-making as necessary for legitimising a company. Products or services certified as ethical, socially responsible, and made from a sustainable chain might become more attractive for stakeholders demonstrating a growing interest in sustainable performance. Thus, companies must consider stakeholders' expectations and decisions while developing their products and services.

Another prominent perspective highlights collaborative efforts explained by the sustainability system thinking framework (Williams et al., 2017). According to this aspect, sustainable innovation is challenging to achieve within a single organisation and thus requires collaboration with other relevant organisations to create valuable products and services for customers continually (Anttonen et al., 2013; Cappa et al., 2016; Desouza et al., 2008). In line with this concept, the systems-building perspective brings a radical shift in the philosophy of responsible business, thinking beyond the firm and reframing the purpose of business in society: "doing good by doing new things with others". A key feature is that sustainability cannot logically be thought of as an attribute of a single firm but can only correctly be applied globally (Lamming et al., 1999); this puts linkages at the heart of sustainable-oriented innovation activity.

Moreover, sustainable innovation is not a linear or mechanical process but an ecosystem formed by continuous interactions between the economy, society, and other aspects (Hsieh et al., 2017; Vollenbroek, 2002). The context is characterised by a shift towards networks of relations in which sustainability value is created collaboratively rather than individually (Mulgan & Leadbeater, 2013). Hence, we could probably refer to our previous argument that collaboration between a company and external organisations in a business ecosystem facilitates sustainable innovation, where sustainable innovation takes a strategic role in achieving sustainable outcomes (Foxon & Pearson, 2008).

Box 7

The systems-building perspective brings a radical shift in the philosophy of responsible business, thinking beyond the firm and reframing the purpose of business in society: "doing good by doing new things with others". A key feature is that sustainability cannot logically be thought of as an attribute of a single firm but can only correctly be applied globally; this puts linkages at the heart of sustainable-oriented innovation activity.

One critical aspect of the relational perspective is including stakeholders and integrating their expectations (Seuring & Gold, 2013). It owes to the involvement and engagement of several stakeholders in sustainable innovation processes (Alkemade & Suurs, 2012). The involvement of internal and, in particular, external stakeholders could improve the orientation towards sustainable innovation and enable the creation of innovative and sustainable ideas. With this in mind, a key question is how firms should collaborate and engage with stakeholders (internally and externally) in the innovation process and seek to influence sustainability goals and what factors hinder or facilitate the process. To address this challenge of sustainable innovation, this chapter will primarily focus on the business ecosystem and related factors, such as the role of institutions, collaborators, resources, and stakeholders' engagement with companies to achieve sustainable outcomes.

Overall, understanding sustainability and sustainable innovation requires a shift in mindset, embracing a relational approach that considers the interconnectedness of social, environmental, and economic factors and actors. It entails recognising the complex interactions between human activities and the natural world and an ongoing commitment to learning, adaptation, and continuous improvement as we navigate the challenges and opportunities of a rapidly changing world.

3 Methodology: Data Collection and Analysis Technique

This chapter focuses on fast-moving consumer goods (FMCG), which are used to fulfil the everyday demands of consumers and account for the most frequent consumer expenditure. FMCGs typically include goods with a shorter useful life and a wide range of diverse products that consumers usually find in supermarkets (Kenton, 2023). The FMCG industry is segmented based on product types, for example, food and beverages, personal care, healthcare care, and home care (Statista, 2023). This industry continuously adapts due to changes in consumer tastes, sustainable and healthy habits, and inflation (Statista, 2023). Dinesh et al. (2023) reported that the FMCG industry is expected to grow at a rate of 5.1% from 2022 to 2031. Asia-Pacific region is dominating in escalating the growth of the global FMCG industry. Pakistan is located in the Asia-Pacific region with a vast population and an increasing demand for consumer products. The reason for selecting this sector in Pakistan is the rising consumption of FMCG products and their significant contribution to environmental waste production. However, the current political situation in Pakistan is unstable, which led to a rise in the inflation rate and changes in the overall ecosystem, particularly the cost of production, consumer buying patterns, and international collaborations. There are several associated challenges for businesses to be sustainable in such a turbulent environment. Therefore, we are intrigued to understand the business ecosystem within Pakistan and how it influences companies to inculcate sustainable, innovative approaches.

We have used multiple case study research designs to understand the role of the business ecosystem and collaborative approaches used by companies to orient sustainable innovation efforts. Five top companies from Pakistan's FMCG industry have been selected through purposive sampling (Bryman & Bell, 2015). Documentary analysis and semi-structured interviews are used to collect data from each established company. In the first order, documentary analysis was used to partly address RQ1: Who are the key stakeholders (internally and externally), and how do they engage with companies? Further interview protocol was designed to address RQ2: What are the critical factors in the business ecosystem, and how do they hinder or facilitate the process? Face-to-face and telephone interviews were conducted with 14 internal stakeholders (company representatives) from the selected companies, and each interview time ranged from 30 to 45 min. Respondents were asked about their understanding of sustainability practices, factors in the ecosystem, and engagement with stakeholders and how this collectively facilitates or hinders their sustainable innovation activities and sustainable outcomes.

Thematic analysis is used to analyse the data from documents and interviews. An essential activity involved in thematic analysis is coding, which then requires qualitative data to be organised into conceptual/theoretical categories (Miles & Huberman, 1994). This study is theory-driven because we have preconceptions about the social reality or phenomenon. We claim that categories are empirically grounded in the field studied and theoretically grounded in concepts related to business ecosystems and sustainable innovation (see Kempster & Perry, 2014). We identified diverse codes from the empirical data, and themes are drawn to the business ecosystem and sustainable, innovative practices categories. This approach to data analysis demonstrates the utility of abductive inference in this qualitative research. Abduction is a process of "an inference or thought operation, implying that a particular phenomenon or event is interpreted from a set of general ideas or concepts or theories" (Danermark, 2002, p. 205). It is also known for theoretical redescription, exploring different theoretical perspectives and explanations that differ from deductive or inductive inference (Danermark, 2002). The following section demonstrates the step-by-step process of coding and driving themes.

4 Analysis

Our analysis of selected companies' documents and interview transcripts revealed the aspects of the business ecosystem that influence adopting sustainable innovative practices. We have followed the open coding process by Strauss and Corbin (1998), which is more inductive. The process involves identifying and managing diverse codes, called pre-code manually (Layder, 1998), then putting those codes into provisional codes that are identified as empirically grounded categories from the data (Fletcher, 2017). We identified 25 pre-codes that are grouped into five empirical categories. Lastly, we label theoretical themes using concepts derived from the literature review. In steps 2 and 3 of the analysis process, these theoretical categories are re-interpreted to explain how the business ecosystem and stakeholders' interactions impact sustainable, innovative practices and outcomes. The process is iterative, allowing us to look at the themes with a holistic and unbiased approach throughout the data. The themes are labelled using framework categories that seemed relevant to the redescription of the data, a process called abduction. Table 1 shows pre-codes and theoretical and empirical categories identified through analysis.

Our analysis highlights that the business ecosystem involves external factors common to all stakeholders to enable or obstruct the company's sustainable, innovative practices and outcomes. Sustainable, innovative practices involve innovation, collaborative efforts, activities, and sustainable outcomes.

Table 1 Coding of data

Theoretical categories	Empirical categories	Pre-codes
Sustainable innovative approaches and outcomes	Innovative practices	Companies' internal practices for sustainable innovation
		Companies' external practices for sustainable innovation
	Sustainability	Sustainability defined
		Stakeholders engagement in innovative practices
		Sustainable outcomes
		Socio-economic impact
		Targeted beneficiaries
Business ecosystem	Diverse factors in the business ecosystem	Local and international regulations
		Differences from other countries
		Non-compliance and penalties
		Religious impact
		Miscellaneous factors in the ecosystem such as currency devaluation
		Changing business ecosystem in terms of technology and competition
		Resource scarcity
		Perception of stakeholders
		Cultural influence
		Limitations from the ecosystem
		Lack of awareness
		Certifications
		Global pressure
	Resources	Resources required for innovation
		Resource acquisition
	Stakeholders	Internal stakeholders such as employees, founders
		External stakeholders, such as customers, associations, NGOs, government regulatory offices
		Nature of the relationship between stakeholders

4.1 Role of Business Ecosystem

The analysis highlights various factors in the ecosystem, mainly regulations, resources, culture, religion, and stakeholders. Stakeholders are considered actors in the ecosystem. Both actors and factors in an ecosystem can either facilitate or hinder companies' sustainable, innovative practices explained below:

4.1.1 Stakeholders

Stakeholders are individuals or organisations associated with companies for sustainable innovation, identified through documents and interviews. We broadly categorise them into internal stakeholders and external stakeholders. Internal stakeholders are mainly company employees and founders. One of the selected companies' employees mentions that: "[...] "Stakeholders inside include departments like production, QFS, and AGRO (Sustainable Agriculture), and they are responsible for various activities". Another respondent points out internal stakeholders and narrates that: "[...] internal stakeholders include management, operations, Supplier management, Finance and accounting, key accounts and marketing". Company representatives also elaborate that internal stakeholders work collaboratively for sustainable, innovative practices. One of them describes it as: "[...]Team sustainability is leading sustainable innovative practices with the cross-functional group". The company reports and interviews also highlight that linkages with external stakeholders are non-trivial in identifying and executing sustainable approaches. External stakeholders include business partners, government bodies, research collaborations, suppliers, and customers. Company representatives mention external stakeholders as "[...] suppliers, business partners, recyclers, NGOs, schools, communities, Alliances, etc." and "[...]local community, local legislative bodies [EPA, PFA, etc.]".

Businesses interact with stakeholders to gain resources and mutual benefits. Companies can improve their business practices by actively examining their relationships with stakeholders and resources. Cultivating existing relationships and resources enables them to foster financial stability and embrace sustainable innovation.

4.1.2 Nature of Relationship

Various stakeholders have formal and informal ties with companies, depending upon the nature of the relationship. Companies also establish a good relationship with each stakeholder, enabling them to benefit from each other mutually. One of the company representatives describes that: "[...] for example if I talk to you about a supplier, a vendor, we should treat him as a business partner, and it should not be like that we expect him to provide us anything on a very basic low cost and in that low cost that supplier is not providing us the quality that we expect and he is not getting sufficient profit out of it that then it is not going to be a mutually beneficial relationship".

Companies have varying relationships with stakeholders that differ in duration, degree of concern, and expectations. Business partners and suppliers have a formal relationship with these companies, where both parties are responsible for sharing resources and disseminating information. The benefits of these partnerships depend on the nature and type of relationship. For instance, the benefits would differ if a large corporation partners with a start-up. Start-ups lack financial resources, while large corporations may not have the innovation or time to explore a new market. Start-ups have the time and innovation to focus on resolving one issue. At the same time, large corporations can offer financial resources and support due to their reputation and access to large numbers of customers. Similar formal ties are developed between companies and regulatory bodies. However, companies' relationships with regulatory bodies have two sides.

On the one hand, regulatory bodies provide guidelines and standards for companies, and on the other hand, they also do joint projects with companies. Fieldwork reveals that multinationals are found to be careful about their working standards and comply with the rules and regulations of the country in which they are operating. For example, from the environmental point of view, the biggest concern is the disposal of wastewater by the FMCGs and it is noticed by the Environmental Protection Agency (EPA) that companies studied have good wastewater treatment plants at their facilities. They do chlorination of their wastewater before disposal.

Companies are engaged with stakeholders for various activities, such as: "[...] Major activities are creating awareness among stakeholders and make them prepared for the season. Stay involved throughout the season and become a guiding star for the farmers". Another representative highlights "[...] Training, awareness, sessions for generating new ideas with the community, customers, suppliers, sister companies and employees from all cadre". Along with these actors, various factors in the business ecosystem can impact sustainable, innovative practices. Some of them are regulations, culture, religion, and resources.

4.1.3 Regulations

Regulations are national and international laws and standards to be followed by companies in a territory. The regulatory environment substantially drives companies' behaviour towards sustainability (Lozano, 2015). Various government authorities work in Pakistan with different industries on sustainability initiatives driven by welfare and reputational motives. Institutional regulatory arrangements externally legitimise companies' sustainable, innovative practices, reshape the competitive landscape, and pose specific pressures on companies to engage in sustainability initiatives (Ortiz-de-Mandojana et al., 2016). Documentary analysis and interviews highlight that the following regulatory bodies are witnessed to have direct linkage with the company's sustainability efforts: EPA, Food Authority (PFA), Intellectual Property Organization (IPO), and Ministry of Water Resources.

Companies must comply with these regulations to maintain their competitive position and secure themselves from any legal sanctions, as explained by Ortiz-de-Mandojana et al. (2016). These authorities provide general guidelines and standards to the industries and are involved with them on specific projects. For example, companies in Pakistan are legally bound to submit an environmental assessment report to EPA and take NOC before starting any new project. Also, EPA is involved with different companies on tree plantation and water replenishment projects. Similarly, any company cannot commence its business unless it has taken intellectual property rights from IPO, which ensures that there are no counterfeit products in the market through its enforcement agencies. One of the Empirical illustrations related to compliance with the regulatory environment narrates that: "[...] as it is our company policy that although we are a global company, we have to follow the rule of the land. So, we try our best to comply with all the policies of the government". Another company representative also narrates, "[...] we follow all the local regulations like if there is food safety requirement from PFA so that we will follow that".

All the multinational companies stress their compliance with local laws and admit to preferring local laws if they differ from international ones. Along with these local regulations, companies also report to comply with international laws; for example, PepsiCo is following American anti-corruption law. Companies are also following the regulations of the Securities and Exchange Commission of Pakistan, regulations by the Ministry of Commerce related to imports, tariffs, and customs-related duties, and the Industrial Ministry. These regulatory bodies monitor the activities of companies, and in case of non-compliance, they are allowed to take any legal action or impose penalties on them. However, company representatives also mentioned clashes in regulations regarding separate water standards, effluent discharge, and transboundary movement of hazardous waste. That is why companies need help to comply with conflicting regulations due to the lack of homogenous national regulations. One of the company's representatives talks about difficulties arising due to clashes in regulations and narrates that: "[...] at times it becomes very difficult for the organizations like Nestlé, as it has such vast presence over the country. We are in Sindh, Baluchistan, Punjab, Khyber Pakhtunkhwa, and Gilgit-Baltistan, but we have to follow the rules and policies and things like that. So, it's high time that we need some sort of harmonization among policies and services in Pakistan". The issue's complexity makes it challenging for companies to operate and comply with all the regulations and introduce and implement sustainable, innovative practices.

4.2 Culture and Religion

Another critical factor identified from our analysis is culture, which means shared ideas and beliefs that set standards for "perceiving, believing, evaluating, and acting" (Christie et al., 2003, p. 265). Culture guides a society's understanding and shared ideas about the meaning of life. As a part of society, organisations are primarily influenced by cognitive institutional pressures (Ortiz-de-Mandojana et al., 2016), which are reflected in an organisation's activities. Here, culture refers to the culture of a society, which significantly impacts the ethical reasoning of people, thus shaping the ethical conceptualisation of the society, as expressed by Christie et al. (2003). Pakistan's culture shows diversity in its ethnic groups regarding language, clothing, food, arts, and religion. One of the company representatives expresses an opinion on cultural impact on people's perception and narrates that "It can totally change your way of operating, gradual change in culture and steadfast the growth of the organisation". Sustainability is not widely recognised in Pakistani culture, and many small and medium-sized companies do not understand the term. While larger companies and multinationals often view sustainability as part of their social responsibility, it is not always integrated into their business models. Customers, business partners, and suppliers expect companies to use the country's resources for sustainability ethically, but there is a lack of knowledge about whether this is being done.

Along with culture, religion has a substantial impact on companies' practices. For example, Islam is the dominant religion in Pakistan, provides points of reference for evaluating any conduct, and has a substantial impact on the ethical conceptualisation of companies. For example, every local and international food and beverage company in Pakistan is religiously and legally bound to use halal ingredients in their products.[2] From July 2019, the government of Pakistan has made mandatory halal labelling requirements for all the food and beverage companies in Pakistan.[3] By implementing this rule, Pakistan has become the first Islamic state to make halal labelling requirements mandatory for a wide range of products produced inside the country or imported from any other country. On the one hand, halal certification labelling directly impacts the financial cost of food and beverage products, and on the other hand, it socially affects the company's image. Although this labelling is mandatory as per the legal notification from the government, some of the company representatives are unaware of these legal bindings. As one of the company representatives explains: "[...] So far I don't know if there is anything like that. Some of our products already have it and some of our products don't have it in written form. But we don't have any product that is not halal. If somebody is doing anything which is not halal then it would be difficult for that person to operate".

The excerpt also highlights a lack of awareness about current legal requirements by the companies. Thus, we can infer from the fieldwork that a country's cultural and religious elements impact the overall regulatory landscape of a country and shape the minds and perceptions of people in a community. Cultural elements tacitly or explicitly influence most stakeholders in a business ecosystem. Fieldwork reveals that culture, religion, regulatory landscape, and stakeholder perception are interconnected and influenced by each other.

4.2.1 Resources in the Ecosystem

Demand for resources is one of the driving forces for companies to interact and communicate with various stakeholders. Documents and interviews highlight that plenty of resources, such as physical and intellectual resources, are exchanged among companies and stakeholders. One of the company representatives mentions, "It depends upon the activity we are doing, but common resources utilised are

[2] Halal means permissible and lawful. Halal foods are foods allowed to be consumed under Islamic dietary guidelines. The foods that are not permitted are called haram, meaning "forbidden" in Arabic. (https://www.thespruceeats.com/what-is-halal-food-2355726, accessed on 05/08/ 2019).

[3] See full report at: https://bit.ly/3rqnNuI (Assessed on18/07/2019).

human resources and technology". Another representative describes that "[…]We already have well-versed human resources dedicated to sustainable innovative activities". Companies manage their resources internally or acquire them from external stakeholders. As one of the company representatives highlights, "[…] "Company has its internal resources to manage this. Yes. We do exchange resources with sister concerns companies, who are also our suppliers in some cases […] by being part of alliances with a common purpose. Internal and external benchmarking".

Along with the resources mentioned above, natural resources in an ecosystem are common and available to all stakeholders, for example, water, land, and air. All these resources also have a limit and are subject to diminish with their usage. It requires stakeholders to develop policies and guidelines for efficiently utilising these resources. For example, Pakistan is facing water-related problems, and water scarcity is one of the central issues, which requires its major users to recognise the need to ensure its sustainability. According to the International Monetary Fund (IMF) report, Pakistan is ranked third in countries with acute water shortages worldwide. United Nations Development Programme (UNDP) and the Pakistan Council of Research in Water Resources (PCRWR) also report that severe water crises will create an absolute water scarcity in the South Asian region by 2025 (Baloch, 2018). Sources also identify that the per capita water availability has dropped from "5,000 cubic metres per annum in 1951 to about 1,000 cubic metres in 2014", further reducing (Dawn, 2018). This alarming situation highlights that the water crises are not new, but the stakeholders, especially the government, have recently started taking action.

Currently, regulatory bodies and NGOs are motivating businesses to work closely with them to battle the issue of water scarcity. National Water Policy 2018,[4] chief justice drives for water consumption,[5] AWS certification, and water replenishment projects by companies are stepping stones towards securing water resources and using these resources efficiently. After 2018, regulatory bodies started playing their role in securing water resources; for example, aquifer charges by the government were implemented to prevent the overuse of groundwater resources. One of the company representatives narrates that: "[…] our sustainability goal in water is that we have to be 100% neutral which means whatever water that we are extracting from the ground we are able to replenish back the same amount of water into the ground". The urgency of the water crisis is a wake-up call for industries and dramatically influences Pakistan's sustainability landscape. However, changing regulations, culture, and scarcity of resources add complexities to the business ecosystem for sectors.

---

[4] National water policy was introduced in 2018 as a genesis of the Pakistan Water Charter, which outlines an integrated water management strategy for the sustainable use of water resources. Available at: https://bit.ly/3c2Mqaj, assessed on 05/03/2021.

[5] In 2018, the chief justice of Pakistan highlighted the issue of the exploitation of water resources by bottled water companies in Pakistan. It charged those companies to pay a suitable fee for using water resources. Available at: https://www.dawn.com/news/1433034, accessed on 05/03/2021.

Companies studied also highlight other business ecosystem factors that can impact sustainable, innovative approaches. As one of the representatives mentions, "[...] Customer focus, Government policies, Leadership commitment, Community/ stakeholder pressure, International certifications, Adapting to new ways of working to continue working as market leader in Pakistan". Another respondent mentioned that there are factors that obstruct the sustainability landscape of a country, such as "[...] Lack of awareness among community and internal customers/ employees to adapt to new approaches of sustainable working" and "lack of motivation from the government side". It depicts that the business ecosystem is a complex system of external actors and factors, such as stakeholders, regulations, culture, religion, resources, and the relationships among them. The following section highlights how companies consider these relationships to develop sustainable, innovative approaches.

4.3 Sustainable Innovative Practices

Our data from interviews and documents determine that the companies studied are part of the complex business ecosystem impacting their involvement in sustainable, innovative practices, collaborative efforts, diverse activities, and sustainable outcomes. These are explained below:

4.3.1 Activities and Collaborative Efforts

Companies can identify areas for sustainable innovation through relationships with stakeholders and factors within the business ecosystem, whether independently or collaboratively. Companies' relationships with stakeholders mainly depend on each other for mutually beneficial outcomes. The benefits sought and achieved vary according to the scope of work of each stakeholder. As one of the company representatives describes their relationship with stakeholders and narrates: "[...] most of the benefits are intangible, and it's again that we would like to better serve our stakeholders so that they can grow, and we can grow". Interviews and documents emphasise the importance of engaging stakeholders to identify and address unsustainable issues. For example, PepsiCo's official reports claim continuous stakeholder engagement, feedback, and global goals to reduce unhealthy ingredients. Interviews with company representatives also shed light on companies' various activities to sustainably use resources. As one of the representatives mentions, "We are demotivating the use of papers through E-Documents, we are demotivating the use of individual plastic bottles, instead we recommend larger bottles where everyone can access the water". Another excerpt pinpoints various "activities including research and development and engagement of teams from all organizational functions starting from supply chain to operations".

Companies utilise various platforms to engage with external stakeholders, including formal and informal channels. Additionally, these platforms are utilised to exchange resources to address unsustainable issues. One of the company representatives highlights that the "Company has its internal resources to manage various sustainability-related activities. Yes. We do exchange resources with sister concerns companies, who are also our suppliers in some cases [...] being part of alliances with a common purpose. Internal and external benchmarking". The companies' commitment to sustainability is evident in their collaborative efforts, which encourage innovative approaches.

4.4 Sustainable Innovative Approaches and Outcomes

We have identified that companies are finding ways to innovate their practices while contributing to sustainability. A representative from the company explained their move towards innovating their practices while maintaining focus towards sustainability and explained that "[...] we are working extensively on water and energy conservation in our processes and investing in renewable resources, reducing the grammage of plastic packaging, suspending the use of diesel or petrol driven material handling equipment with electric equipment". Analysis shows that FMCG companies are trying to reduce environmental waste, conserve energy, improve supply chain sustainability, and benefit communities.

The empirical excerpt highlights various practices that demonstrate companies studied focus towards transforming their ways to conserve energy: "[...] Inclusion of Solar power into the central power grid of the company, operation of Biomass boiler to produce low-cost steam, replacement of old air conditioning units with the new environment-friendly refrigerants, circularity and recycling of packaging portfolio, carbon emission reduction and net zero road maps, Biodiversity targets including Social Sustainability". Another company representative also mentions their approach towards innovating processes such as: "[...] recyclable PET (for plastic bottles used in beverages), sustainable farming (100% biodegradable items used in potato farming for Lays), Net Zero in terms of carbon footprint.—Net Zero in terms of water losses—2 Mega Watt solar electricity production plant".

The analysis shows sustainable, innovative approaches by selected companies that benefit women, communities, farmers, and the environment. For instance, companies offer micro-financing, nutrition and digital skill training, and scholarships for women. The results show significant improvements over the years. One FMCG has helped 8000 women become entrepreneurs, trained 400 women with digital skills, and committed to achieving a 50/50 gender balance in the company. Table 2 displays various sustainable, innovative approaches, their beneficiaries, and outcomes identified from documents and interviews.

Several programs are implemented to address unsustainable issues. For example, one company planted over a million trees and transformed 200 acres of land into a forest with 270,000 trees to offset about 6 KT of CO_2 annually. Another company

Table 2 Innovative approaches and their outcomes

Sustainable Innovation Practices	Beneficiaries	Outcomes
Micro-financing, job opportunities, training, scholarships	Women	Microloans of an average PKR 10,000–20,000 were disbursed, enrolled sales agents, more than 8000 women became entrepreneurs, more than 400 women were uplifted with digital skills, EDI commitment to have increased gender balance in the company
Training programs for teachers, students, and drivers Welfare funds for students and police Sharing and developing best practices, digital engagement	Communities	Trained 1750 teachers and 320,000 children, Trained 31,000 drivers, promoting good consumer and marketing practices, health and safety, including fighting COVID-19. Invested in skills training programs such as Technical Training College (TTC). Initiatives on Digitisation, mobile-enabled customer-centric application to book orders online, 24/7
Training for farmers, establishing farming centres, funding for farmers	Farmers	Agricultural internship program, the Shandaar-Kissan program, Hamdam programs sustainably sourced raw materials used for farmers, training areas include pre- and post-harvest horticulture, plant propagation and varietal assessment, installation of soil moisture sensors on agriculture value chain, drip irrigation
Renewable energy, waste management programs Tree plantation Sustainable packaging, Commitments to a sustainable environment	Environment	More than one million tree project, reduction in total water consumption, replenishment water, plastic waste collected and recycled, renewable energy sources, use of purified wastewater for cleaning roads and watering green areas, shifted from polystyrene cups for our yogurts to PET cups, water savings as a result of drip irrigation and smart soil moisture sensors installation

reduced total water usage at their site by around 85%. These sustainable innovations, such as drip irrigation, water sense technologies, waste reduction in packaging, greenhouse gas emission strategies, etc., not only help companies enhance their existing products and processes but also positively impact the environment and society.

5 Discussion and Conclusion

This section elaborates on the learning from the analysis using the multiple case study approach. Overall, the research focuses on understanding the role of the business ecosystem and its influence on companies' sustainable innovation practices and outcomes. The research also aimed to explain the engagement of multiple stakeholders and factors in the ecosystem that can enable or hinder the company's efforts towards sustainability. To summarise the findings and contributions of this study, this section is divided into two subsections: (a) sheds light on the approaches to understanding each research question by explaining the methodological, empirical, and practical contributions of this study, and (b) suggests directions for some future research opportunities. This chapter contributes to the academic literature on sustainability and sustainable innovation practices. The research has made significant contributions at three levels: methodological, empirical, and practical. Methodologically, this research has used multiple case studies to analyse the data from five selected companies in Pakistan. Theoretically, this study has extended our understanding of sustainable innovation practices by integrating the business ecosystem concept. The study analyses five FMCG companies' context and sustainable practices as an empirical contribution while focusing on sustainability outcomes. Lastly, the study contributes to practice from the organisational and stakeholders' perspectives. The following subsections explain these contributions in detail:

5.1 Methodological Contribution

Our study employed a multiple case study methodology to focus on factors and actors in the business ecosystem that impact companies' pursuit of sustainability. We have attempted to demonstrate a detailed process of data collection, a theory-driven analytical approach, and abduction as a data inference strategy. The step-by-step process contributes to the empirical application of the research and methods used in the data collection and analysis. The first step was the desk research that helped us to identify the cases (sample companies) based on their active involvement in sustainability efforts. Documents and interviews were used as methods of collecting data. We gathered secondary data-existing sustainability reports (from 2016 to 2021) produced by companies being studied (documents, websites) in the first instance. This helped us identify and group stakeholders into categories: internal stakeholders (company representatives), external stakeholders (customers, associations, NGOs, Government regulatory offices), and recognise sustainable practices and outcomes. The documentary analysis helped us in formulating and conducting interviews. We developed interview questions based on our pre-existing knowledge from documentary analysis and literature review. For example, we aimed to start the conversation with respondents knowing their collaborative activities and sustainable practices; however, the focus was to evaluate the reasoning and explanation of their involvement and factors that impact their activities. An essential consideration in our research design was closely monitoring ethical and methodological aspects while preparing interview questions, contacting respondents, and recording and analysing interviews. Extended study analysis is utilised to maintain the rigour and depth of the study, enabling us to identify patterns in our findings.

5.2 Empirical Contribution

The study has also made an empirical contribution by examining the role of the business ecosystem and its impact on companies' efforts towards developing sustainable approaches. The analysis unfolds relational aspects of different factors and actors in the ecosystem and their influence on sustainable, innovative approaches by companies. This study argues that companies cannot achieve sustainability goals alone and require a collaborative innovation approach. Our research concluded that companies need an understanding of various factors in the business ecosystem, including identifying critical stakeholders for sustainable outcomes. Moore (1998) suggested that stakeholder collaboration is crucial for organisational success. This study also reaffirms the significance of stakeholder collaboration in acquiring resources that enable companies to innovate sustainable practices.

Furthermore, factors in the ecosystem, such as religion, regulations, resources, and culture, impact the stakeholders' perception and engagement process in sustainable innovation. This study shows how sustainable outcomes benefit disadvantaged groups in Pakistan, including women, farmers, communities, and the environment. However, analysis of global sustainability reports demonstrates that the focal sustainability areas and beneficiaries vary among economies. The beneficiaries in the context of Pakistan are targeted based on companies' global sustainability agendas, local environment and regulations, and mutually beneficial outcomes. Overall, companies are engaged in innovating their practices, such as digitisation of customers shopping online, drip irrigation, smart soil moisture sensor installation for farmers, and digital skills training programs for women (see Table 2 for more details), are among a few initiatives introduced in Pakistan for the very first time. Several external enablers, which are structural and resource-based, help companies overcome social and environmental distress and increase their capacity to act and create impact. Findings show that companies develop resources in collaboration with stakeholders, including knowledge, monetary, relational, and technological resources, which benefit individuals such as women, communities, support environment, and farmers. To summarise, the interaction between factors and actors in the ecosystem plays a crucial role in helping companies innovate and impact sustainability outcomes.

5.3 Practical Contribution

The research findings contribute to practice from an organisational and stakeholder perspective. Significant categories of stakeholders that make collective efforts and provide resources to companies when needed have been identified. Companies and stakeholders can gain valuable insights from these findings on collectively achieving sustainable goals. The study also informs the nature of the relationship and resource exchange between companies and stakeholders and innovative processes targeting various beneficiaries. Additionally, the study provides insights on how to enhance the effectiveness of sustainable efforts in the field. Evidence suggests companies can access physical or intangible resources for sustainable innovation through stakeholder relationships. Some relations are formalised through a Memorandum of Association (MOU) or agreements, while others are informal.

5.4 Limitations of the Study and Direction for Future Research

During the course of our study, we faced issues, especially in the data collection phases. For example, due to time constraints, we only conducted interviews with internal stakeholders who were conveniently available to participate in our research. Initially, we planned to conduct face-to-face interviews. Still, due to a lack of response within the given timeframe, we resorted to other means of interaction, such as telephonic and web-based interviews. It's worth noting that relying solely on interviews can be limiting, as Bryman and Bell (2015) point out. Therefore, we gathered data from documents and websites and conducted semi-structured interviews to understand the issue under study better. Moreover, none of the companies selected for the study publish local sustainability reports, so we relied on regional and global sustainability reports to collect data. The research opens avenues for future research, such as:

- A comprehensive study will be conducted in a developing or developed economy, focusing more on sustainable, innovative practices and outcomes.
- A comparative analysis will also help understand the differences in the sustainability landscapes of different economies and their target areas and beneficiaries.
- Various factors in the business ecosystem, such as culture, religion, and market forces, must be studied more to understand their impact on companies' sustainable, innovative practices and outcomes.

Declaration of Generative AI and AI-Assisted Technologies in the Writing Process for This Chapter The editor only used ChatGPT (Premium GPT4.0) and Grammarly to proof-read and check for typos and inconsistencies. There is no further declaration from the authors.

Declaration by Dr. Meryem Altaf This chapter is inspired by and derived from some theoretical and empirical parts of my doctoral (Ph.D.) thesis, titled "Corporate sustainability: The role of co-creation of value by multiple stakeholders in the food and beverage sector of Pakistan". However, it is important to note that this book chapter contains new insights, additional data collection, and updated perspectives contributing to the on-going field discourse. The electronic version of the thesis is published in the Newcastle University e-Thesis Repository. This work is licensed under the following licence: Creative Commons Attribution-Noncommercial-No Derivative Works 3.0.

References

Adams, R., Jeanrenaud, S., Bessant, J., Denyer, D., & Overy, P. (2016). Sustainability-oriented innovation: A systematic review. *International Journal of Management Reviews, 18*(2), 180–205.

Alkemade, F., & Suurs, R. A. (2012). Patterns of expectations for emerging sustainable technologies. *Technological Forecasting and Social Change, 79*(3), 448–456.

Amit, R., & Zott, C. (2015). Crafting business architecture: The antecedents of business model design. *Strategic Entrepreneurship Journal, 9*(4), 331–350.

Ansari, S., Garud, R., & Kumaraswamy, A. (2016). The disruptor's dilemma: TiVo and the US television ecosystem. *Strategic Management Journal, 37*(9), 1829–1853.

Anttonen, M., Halme, M., Houtbeckers, E., & Nurkka, J. (2013). The other side of sustainable innovation: Is there a demand for innovative services? *Journal of Cleaner Production, 45*, 89–103.

Baloch, S. M. (2018). Water crisis: Why is Pakistan running dry? Available at: https://www.dw.com/en/water,crisis-why-is-pakistan-running-dry/a-44110280. Accessed 5 Aug 2019.

Bansal, P., & DesJardine, M. R. (2014). Business sustainability: It is about time. *Strategic Organization, 12*(1), 70–78.

Blättel-Mink, B. (1998). Nachhaltige Entwicklung: Leitbild und Indikatoren. In U. Becher, H. Frenzel, & U. Schirmer (Eds.), *Handbuch Nachhaltige Entwicklung: Wie ist nachhaltiges Wirtschaften machbar?* (pp. 23–38). Oekom Verlag.

Blowfield, M., Frynas, J. G., & Yamahaki, C. (2007). Setting new agendas: Critical perspectives on corporate social responsibility in the developing world. *International Affairs, 83*(3), 499–513.

Boons, F., Montalvo, C., Quist, J., & Wagner, M. (2013). Sustainable innovation, business models and economic performance: An overview. *Journal of Cleaner Production, 45*, 1–8.

Bos-Brouwers, H. E. J. (2010). Corporate sustainability and innovation in SMEs: Evidence of themes and activities in practice. *Business Strategy and the Environment, 19*(7), 417–435.

Bryman, A. and Bell, E., 2015. Business research methods. *Oxford university press*.

Cappa, F., Del Sette, F., Hayes, D., & Rosso, F. (2016). How to deliver open sustainable innovation: An integrated approach for a sustainable marketable product. *Sustainability, 8*(12), 1341.

Carrillo-Hermosilla, J., Del Río, P., & Könnölä, T. (2010). Diversity of eco-innovations: Reflections from selected case studies. *Journal of Cleaner Production, 18*(10–11), 1073–1083.

Carroll, A. B., & Shabana, K. M. (2010). The business case for corporate social responsibility: A review of concepts, research and practice. *International Journal of Management Reviews, 12*(1), 85–105.

Chen, Y. S., Chang, C. H., & Lin, Y. H. (2014). The determinants of green radical and incremental innovation performance: Green shared vision, green absorptive capacity, and green organizational ambidexterity. *Sustainability, 6*(11), 7787–7806.

Christie, P. M. J., Kwon, I. W. G., Stoeberl, P. A., & Baumhart, R. (2003). A cross-cultural comparison of ethical attitudes of business managers: India Korea and the United States. *Journal of Business Ethics, 46*, 263–287.

Cillo, V., Petruzzelli, A. M., Ardito, L., & Del Giudice, M. (2019). Understanding sustainable innovation: A systematic literature review. *Corporate Social Responsibility and Environmental Management, 26*(5), 1012–1025.

Clark, T., & Charter, M. (2007). Sustainable innovation: Key conclusions from sustainable innovation conferences 2003–2006 organised by the centre for sustainable design.

Constantin, J. A., & Lusch, R. F. (1994). *Understanding resource management*. The Planning Forum.

Crossan, M. M., & Apaydin, M. (2010). A multi-dimensional framework of organizational innovation: A systematic review of the literature. *Journal of Management Studies, 47*(6), 1154–1191.

Danermark, B. (2002). Interdisciplinary research and critical realism the example of disability research. *Alethia, 5*(1), 56–64.

Dangelico, R. M., & Pujari, D. (2010). Mainstreaming green product innovation: Why and how companies integrate environmental sustainability. *Journal of Business Ethics, 95*, 471–486.

Dawn. (2018) Audit report finds profit margins in bottled water sale unjustified. Available at: https://www.dawn.com/news/1442464. Accessed 19 Oct 2019.
Desouza, K. C., Awazu, Y., Jha, S., Dombrowski, C., Papagari, S., Baloh, P., & Kim, J. Y. (2008). Customer-driven innovation. *Research-Technology Management, 51*(3), 35–44.
Dinesh, T., Indranil, C., & Vidit, G. (2023). *FMCG market*. Allied Market Research. Available at: https://www.alliedmarketresearch.com/fmcg-market
Elkington, J. (1994). Towards the sustainable corporation: Win-win-win business strategies for sustainable development. *California Management Review, 36*(2), 90–100.
Elkington, J. (1997). *Cannibals with forks: The triple bottom line of 21st century business*. Capstone Publishing Ltd.
Fletcher, A. J. (2017). Applying critical realism in qualitative research: Methodology meets method. *International Journal of Social Research Methodology, 20*(2), 181–194.
Forstater, M., Zadek, S., Guang, Y., Yu, K., Hong, C. X., & George, M. (2010). Corporate responsibility in African development: Insights from an emerging dialogue. *Corporate Social Responsibility Initiative Working Paper, 60*, 1–55.
Foxon, T., & Pearson, P. (2008). Overcoming barriers to innovation and diffusion of cleaner technologies: Some features of a sustainable innovation policy regime. *Journal of Cleaner Production, 16*(1), 148–161.
Freeman, R. (1984). *Strategic management: A stakeholder's approach*. Pitman.
Frishammar, J., & Parida, V. (2019). Circular business model transformation: A roadmap for incumbent firms. *California Management Review, 61*(2), 5–29.
Frow, P., McColl-Kennedy, J. R., Hilton, T., Davidson, A., Payne, A., & Brozovic, D. (2014). Value propositions: A service ecosystems perspective. *Marketing Theory, 14*(3), 327–351.
Fussler, C., & James, P. (1996). *Driving eco-innovation: A breakthrough discipline for innovation and sustainability*. Pitman Publishing.
Garcia, R., & Calantone, R. (2002). A critical look at technological innovation typology and innovativeness terminology: A literature review. *Journal of Product Innovation Management, 19*(2), 110–132.
George, G., Howard-Grenville, J., Joshi, A., & Tihanyi, L. (2016). Understanding and tackling societal grand challenges through management research. *Academy of Management Journal, 59*(6), 1880–1895.
Gladwin, T. N., Kennelly, J. J., & Krause, T. S. (1995). Shifting paradigms for sustainable development: Implications for management theory and research. *Academy of Management Review, 20*(4), 874–907.
Greer, C. R., Lusch, R. F., & Vargo, S. L. (2016). A service perspective. *Organizational Dynamics, 1*(45), 28–38.
Gregory, A. J., Atkins, J. P., Midgley, G., & Hodgson, A. M. (2020). Stakeholder identification and engagement in problem structuring interventions. *European Journal of Operational Research, 283*(1), 321–340.
Hansen, E. G., & Große-Dunker, F. (2013). Sustainability innovation archetype: A tool for managing innovation in a complex adaptive system. *Journal of Cleaner Production, 45*, 20–30.
Hansen, E. G., Grosse-Dunker, F., & Reichwald, R. (2009). Sustainability innovation cube—A framework to evaluate sustainability-oriented innovations. *International Journal of Innovation Management, 13*(04), 683–713.
Hermundsdottir, F., & Aspelund, A. (2021). Sustainability innovations and firm competitiveness: A review. *Journal of Cleaner Production, 280*, 124715.
Herrero-Luna, S., Latorre-Martinez, M., & Ferrer-Serrano, M. (2022). Circular economy and innovation: A systematic literature review. *Central European Business Review*, ART-2022-128647.
Horbach, J. (2008). Determinants of environmental innovation—New evidence from German panel data sources. *Research Policy, 37*(1), 163–173.
Horbach, J., Rammer, C., & Rennings, K. (2012). Determinants of eco-innovations by type of environmental impact—The role of regulatory push/pull, technology push and market pull. *Ecological Economics, 78*, 112–122.

Hsieh, Y. C., Lin, K. Y., Lu, C., & Rong, K. (2017). Governing a sustainable business ecosystem in Taiwan's circular economy: The story of spring pool glass. *Sustainability, 9*(6), 1068.

Hutchins, M. J., & Sutherland, J. W. (2008). An exploration of measures of social sustainability and their application to supply chain decisions. *Journal of Cleaner Production, 16*(15), 1688–1698.

Iansiti, M., & Levien, R. (2004). Strategy as ecology. *Harvard Business Review, 82*(3), 68–78.

Kemp, R., Schot, J., & Hoogma, R. (1998). Regime shifts to sustainability through processes of niche formation: The approach of strategic niche management. *Technology Analysis & Strategic Management, 10*(2), 175–198.

Kempster, S., & Perry, K. (2014). Critical realism and grounded theory. In P. Edwards, J. O'Mahoney, & S. Vincent (Eds.), *Studying organisations using critical realism: A practical guide* (pp. 86–108).

Kenton, W. (2023). Fast-moving consumer goods (FMCG) industry: Definition, types, and profitability, investopedia. Available on: https://www.investopedia.com/terms/f/fastmoving-consumer-goods-fmcg.asp. Accessed 17 May 2023.

Kesidou, E., & Demirel, P. (2012). On the drivers of eco-innovations: Empirical evidence from the UK. *Research Policy, 41*(5), 862–870.

Klewitz, J., & Hansen, E. G. (2014). Sustainability-oriented innovation of SMEs: A systematic review. *Journal of Cleaner Production, 65*, 57–75.

Kosar, F., Khan, S. M., & Brohi, A. F. (2022). Financial crisis in the Muslim world. *Pakistan Journal of International Affairs, 5*(2), 481.

Laasch, O. (2019). An actor-network perspective on business models: How 'being responsible' led to incremental but pervasive change. *Long Range Planning, 52*(3), 406–426.

Lamming, R., Faruk, A., & Cousins, P. (1999). Environmental soundness: A pragmatic alternative to expectations of sustainable development in business strategy. *Business Strategy and the Environment, 8*(3), 177–188.

Layder, D. (1998). Sociological practice: Linking theory and social research. *Sociological Practice*, 1–208.

Lee, T. R., Lin, K. H., Chen, C. H., Otero-Neira, C., & Svensson, G. (2022). A framework of firms' business sustainability endeavours with internal and external stakeholders through time across oriental and occidental business contexts. *Asia Pacific Journal of Marketing and Logistics, 34*(5), 963–986.

Lupova-Henry, E., & Dotti, N. F. (2019). Governance of sustainable innovation: Moving beyond the hierarchy-market-network trichotomy? A systematic literature review using the 'who-how-what' framework. *Journal of Cleaner Production, 210*, 738–748.

Lozano, R., 2015. A holistic perspective on corporate sustainability drivers. *Corporate social responsibility and environmental management, 22*(1), pp.32–44.

Miles, M. B., & Huberman, A. M. (1994). *Qualitative data analysis: An expanded sourcebook*. Sage.

Moore, J. F. (1998). The rise of a new corporate form. *Washington Quarterly, 21*(1), 167–181.

Mulgan, G., & Leadbeater, C. (2013). *Systems innovation*. Nesta.

Ortiz-de-Mandojana, N., Aguilera-Caracuel, J., & Morales-Raya, M. (2016). Corporate governance and environmental sustainability: The moderating role of the national institutional context. *Corporate Social Responsibility and Environmental Management, 23*(3), 150–164.

Parida, V., Burström, T., Visnjic, I., & Wincent, J. (2019). Orchestrating industrial ecosystem in circular economy: A two-stage transformation model for large manufacturing companies. *Journal of Business Research, 101*, 715–725.

Pera, R., Occhiocupo, N., & Clarke, J. (2016). Motives and resources for value co-creation in a multi-stakeholder ecosystem: A managerial perspective. *Journal of Business Research, 69*(10), 4033–4041.

Rauter, R., Perl-Vorbach, E., & Baumgartner, R. J. (2017). Is open innovation supporting sustainable innovation? Findings based on a systematic, explorative analysis of existing literature. *International Journal of Innovation and Sustainable Development, 11*(2–3), 249–270.

Riquelme-Medina, M., Stevenson, M., Barrales-Molina, V., & Llorens-Montes, F. J. (2022). Coopetition in business ecosystems: The key role of absorptive capacity and supply chain agility. *Journal of Business Research, 146*, 464–476.

Schiederig, T., Tietze, F., & Herstatt, C. (2012). Green innovation in technology and innovation management–An exploratory literature review. *R&D Management, 42*(2), 180–192.

Seuring, S., & Gold, S. (2013). Sustainability management beyond corporate boundaries: From stakeholders to performance. *Journal of Cleaner Production, 56*, 1–6.

Shakeel, J., Mardani, A., Chofreh, A. G., Goni, F. A., & Klemeš, J. J. (2020). Anatomy of sustainable business model innovation. *Journal of Cleaner Production, 261*, 121201.

Snider, J., Hill, R. P., & Martin, D. (2003). Corporate social responsibility in the 21st century: A view from the world's most successful firms. *Journal of Business Ethics, 48*(2), 175–187.

Snihur, Y., & Bocken, N. (2022). A call for action: The impact of business model innovation on business ecosystems, society and planet. *Long Range Planning, 55*(6), 102182.

Statista. (2023). Consumer Goods & FMCG. Available at: https://www.statista.com/markets/415/consumer-goods-fmcg/. Accessed 17 May 2023.

Strauss, A., & Corbin, J. (1998). *Basics of qualitative research techniques*. Sage Publications, Inc.

Tello, S. F., & Yoon, E. (2008). Examining drivers of sustainable innovation. *International Journal of Business Strategy, 8*(3), 164–169.

Thompson, M., & Heron, P. (2006). Relational quality and innovative performance in R&D based science and technology firms. *Human Resource Management Journal, 16*(1), 28–47.

Ullah, S., Khan, F. U., & Ahmad, N. (2022). Promoting sustainability through green innovation adoption: A case of manufacturing industry. *Environmental Science and Pollution Research*, 1–21.

Vollenbroek, F. A. (2002). Sustainable development and the challenge of innovation. *Journal of Cleaner Production, 10*(3), 215–223.

WCED, S. W. S. (1987). World commission on environment and development. *Our Common Future, 17*(1), 1–91.

Werther, W. B., Jr., & Chandler, D. (2010). *Strategic corporate social responsibility: Stakeholders in a global environment*. Sage Publications, Inc.

Williams, A., Kennedy, S., Philipp, F., & Whiteman, G. (2017). Systems thinking: A review of sustainability management research. *Journal of Cleaner Production, 148*, 866–881.

World Bank. (2022). Long-standing structural challenges pose risks to Pakistan's sustained growth: World Bank bi-annual Pakistan development update report. Available at: https://www.worldbank.org/en/news/press-release/2022/04/19/long-standing-structural-challenges-pose-risks-to-pakistan-s-sustained-growth-world-bank-bi-annual-pakistan-development-. Accessed 31 Aug 2023.

Yi, Y., Chen, Y., & Li, D. (2022). Stakeholder ties, organizational learning, and business model innovation: A business ecosystem perspective. *Technovation, 114*, 102445.

Yoon, C., Moon, S., & Lee, H. (2022). Symbiotic relationships in business ecosystem: A systematic literature review. *Sustainability, 14*(4), 2252.

Dr. Meryem Altaf is a Lecturer in Business & Management at De Montfort University, UK with more than 5 years of experience mainly in academia. Her areas of expertise are sustainability and multiple stakeholder studies; she is also interested in Equality, Diversity, and Inclusion (EDI) and innovation. She has a PhD in category A1 from Newcastle University, UK, and was awarded Newcastle University Business School studentship for her PhD. She has experience in teaching in the areas of management, marketing, and research at both undergrad and postgrad levels in Pakistan and the UK, and has also been involved in research and administrative roles. Dr. Meryem is a multidisciplinary early career researcher with experience in both qualitative and quantitative data collection and analysis techniques. She is currently engaged in multiple research projects focusing on corporate sustainability, sustainable innovation, and EDI.

Dr. Nosheen Jawaid Khan is a Lecturer in Human Resource Management at Newcastle University. Her areas of expertise are Equality, Diversity, and Inclusion; She is also interested in having a multidisciplinary approach to research in the future. She is an early career researcher (ECR) currently engaged in several research projects (funded and non-funded) focusing on diversity and inclusion, third-sector organisations and women's career outcomes, women mentoring, and sustainable innovation. She has experience of more than 6 years in academia, the banking industry, and research. She is also a Fellow of Higher Education Academy, UK. Dr. Khan is a PhD in Management from Newcastle University, UK. She was awarded a Research Excellence Award (REA) and Postgraduate Studentship Award for her PhD program at Newcastle University Business School, UK. She also holds a double Master's from renowned institutes in Pakistan and a Bachelor in Computer Science (with Honours) from Pakistan.

The Challenges in Constructing Effective Climate Governance in Southeast Asia: Evidence from Vietnam

Phuong Dung Nguyen and Truc Hanh Vu

Abstract This chapter provides readers with an overview of regional climate governance in Southeast Asia and climate governance in Vietnam. It then identifies and examines existing shortcomings in climate governance in this country, focusing on its current legal framework and practice of corporate responsibility for climate change adaptation. Based on the analyses and evaluations in the preceding parts, the chapter discusses and proposes practical solutions for policymakers and stakeholders to improve the legal framework and monitoring and enforcement mechanisms, which, in turn, enhance and strengthen effective climate governance.

1 Introduction

IN A COMMENCEMENT ADDRESS at the Munich Security Conference in February 2022, UN Secretary-General António Guterres reminded us that the international community is now encountering a global threat which is worsening and becoming increasingly complex (United Nations, 2022). Climate change has risen to the 'number one threat to mankind' (Parry, 2007), and its impact is 'accelerating at an alarming rate' (Ban, 2011). Undoubtedly, climate change poses a significant threat to the survival of the human race. Climate change has engendered the scarcity of natural resources crucial to the existence of all creatures on Earth, such as energy, water, arable land, and others, causing failures in implementing policies or even disputes (Parry, 2007). The pressing circumstances surrounding climate change

P. D. Nguyen (✉)
Department of Economics and Finance, The Business School, RMIT University Vietnam, Hanoi, Vietnam
e-mail: dung.nguyen118@rmit.edu.vn; p.d.nguyen1812@gmail.com

T. H. Vu
The School of Law, University of Economics Ho Chi Minh City (UEH), Ho Chi Minh City, Vietnam
e-mail: hanhvt@ueh.edu.vn; truchanhvu@gmail.com

V. Q. Trinh (ed.), *Climate Governance and Corporate Eco-innovation*, Sustainable Finance, https://doi.org/10.1007/978-3-031-56423-9_11

highlight the imperative of establishing effective climate change governance. There is an increased emphasis on regional-level climate change governance in the contemporary landscape. The essential need for collaborative efforts among states to address transboundary environmental concerns and achieve sustainability objectives underscores the active participation of diverse stakeholders. The ambit of climate governance is defined by its encompassment of various mechanisms and institutions dedicated to policy formulation, such as (i) state commitments through treaty agreements, (ii) mechanisms for dispute resolution, (iii) entities tasked with shaping rules to facilitate treaty execution; (iv) policies and regulations instituted by individual states; and (v) the involvement of other entities and institutions from both the public and private sectors (Carlarne, 2008).

In the context of global climate change, encompassing nations on a broad scale and specifically emphasising developing regions like Southeast Asia, a compelling urgency has emerged to adapt to the consequences of climate shifts to mitigate their adverse impacts. Establishing robust climate governance is a potentially pivotal solution for Southeast Asian nations amid their development trajectory, empowering them to tackle and reduce the effects of climate change effectively. This chapter seeks to delve comprehensively into the climate change scenario in Southeast Asia while also exploring the establishment and operational dynamics of climate change governance within the region.

Box 1
The ambit of climate governance is defined by its encompassment of various mechanisms and institutions dedicated to policy formulation, particularly:

1. state commitments through treaty agreements;
2. mechanisms for dispute resolution;
3. entities tasked with shaping rules to facilitate treaty execution;
4. policies and regulations instituted by individual states;
5. the involvement of other entities and institutions from both the public and private sectors.

Vietnam's political framework about climate change and environmental conservation stands as a noteworthy exemplar, particularly when contrasted with the contexts of other emerging economies. Over a significant period, the nation has meticulously constructed a comprehensive legal foundation and established instrumental institutions, all with a keen focus on addressing environmental challenges and propelling sustainable development. Our study provides a comprehensive overview of the central legislative enactments and governmental entities that assume pivotal roles in shaping Vietnam's governance paradigm for climate change. From the inception of national strategies to the orchestration of climate-centric endeavours across diverse hierarchical tiers, we shed light on Vietnam's unwavering commitment to effectively grappling with the pressing challenges posed by climate change with a focus on regulating the engagement of business entities in the private sector and the implications for development and enhancement.

2 Overview of Climate Change Situation in Southeast Asian and Vietnam

2.1 *Climate Change Situation in Southeast Asia*

Southeast Asia is one of the regions most severely impacted by climate change. Myanmar, the Philippines, Bangladesh, Vietnam, and Thailand have been documented as nations enduring severe weather events attributable to climate change throughout 1999–2018 and 2000–2019 (Eckstein et al., 2019; Eckstein et al., 2021). Within the last two decades, the reports rank Myanmar as one of the countries suffering the most brutal impact of climate change, ascribed to extreme weather events such as Cyclone Nargis in 2008. Because of its geographical location, the Philippines is frequently influenced by catastrophic events, mainly tropical cyclones such as Bopha 2012, Haiyan 2013, and Mangkhut 2018 (Eckstein et al., 2019; Eckstein et al., 2021).

The devastating impacts of climate change, exemplified by the heightened frequency of intense rainfall resulting in floods and landslides, have had adverse consequences for Southeast Asia. The decrease in precipitation, coupled with the emergence of El Niño events triggered by the cyclic elevation of sea surface temperatures in the central and eastern equatorial Pacific Ocean, has precipitated severe droughts and average temperatures (Eckstein et al., 2021). These calamities exert significant detrimental effects on the economy, particularly within agriculture and food security. Under the impact of the El Niño event in 2015–2016, a substantial reduction of 15 million tonnes in rice production, a fundamental staple in Southeast Asia, was attributed to elevated temperatures and severe droughts. Contributing factors, such as salinity intrusion, prolonged droughts, and water scarcity, were responsible for diminishing rice productivity in Vietnam's Mekong Delta region, leading to a financial loss of $674 million (equivalent to 0.35% of the country's GDP). Furthermore, the Philippines encountered declines in rice and corn yields, experiencing a notable 11-percent contraction in production. Presently, Southeast Asian nations are contending with an ongoing El Niño event spanning the years 2023–2024, giving rise to concerns about a substantial deficit in rice production and posing a palpable threat to food security (Ludher & Teng, 2023).

Recent reports have underscored the region's vulnerability to climate-related challenges. At a 1.5 °C global warming scenario, the projections indicate that heavy precipitation and associated flooding will intensify and become more frequent, with Southeast Asia particularly susceptible to extreme weather events. Southeast Asian countries are already experiencing a noticeable rise in summer temperatures, leading to a surge in energy demand for cooling, compounded by the region's rapid population growth. Southeast Asia is witnessing a shift towards energy-intensive methods such as desalination and underground water pumping for water supply due to decreased precipitation, further straining the energy demand. The impact of climate change is also placing food production systems in jeopardy. The average temperature rise and erratic shifts in weather patterns would have a domino effect. Studies suggest that Southeast Asia would consistently sustain extreme heat, giving rise to incidents like wildfires, droughts, and water scarcity.

Moreover, owing to the heightened intensity of the global hydrological cycle resulting from global warming, heavy rainfall would become more frequent, leading to dramatic flooding, erosion, and landslides. As a result of these severe weather events instigated by climate change, agricultural production would be impeded, presenting an elevated concern for food security in the region. Alongside the risks posed by severe weather events, gradual processes exacerbated by climate change, such as rising sea levels, desertification, land degradation, and biodiversity loss, are also of notable concern to the region (ADB, 2017; Eckstein et al., 2021; IPCC, 2021, 2022).

Climate change may substantially degrade and stagnate the economic growth of the region. Projections indicate that Southeast Asia's overall GDP could experience a decline of 11% by 2100 if current trends continue without significant intervention (Raitzer et al., 2015). The region would sustain detrimental repercussions within the agricultural sector, which serves as the fundamental economic driver of the area. Research predicts Southeast Asia will witness a GPD loss of 0.1% due to a sea rise level of 25 cm by 2050 (ADB, 2017). The anticipated decrease in rice yield within the Mekong River Delta could range from 6 to 12%, accompanied by a corresponding decline of 3–26% in the yield of other crops by the year 2050. Countries such as Indonesia, the Philippines, Thailand, and Vietnam face the potential consequence of climate change, leading to a substantial reduction of up to 50% in rice production (ADB, 2017; Seah & Martinus, 2021).

2.2 Climate Change Situation in Vietnam

The climate change scenario in Vietnam can be characterised as profoundly disconcerting. Recent investigations into climate change reveal compelling evidence pointing to significant alterations in Vietnam's climatic conditions. More specifically, spanning the last century, there has been a distinct warming trend in the average monthly temperature by approximately 0.4 °C nationwide. This increase is evident when comparing the temperature of 27.1 °C documented during the 1901–1930 period with the elevated mean temperature of 27.5 °C registered between 1991 and 2015 (CRU, 2018; Nguyen & Nguyen, 2022). The maximum monthly precipitation displayed a noticeable upward trend, escalating from 270 mm between 1901 and 1930 to 281 mm from 1991 to 2015. However, the precipitation levels showcased intricate fluctuations marked by a decrease in the northern geographic zones and a simultaneous increase in the southern territorial areas (CRU, 2018; Nguyen & Nguyen, 2022).

Furthermore, from 1993 to 2018, a noticeable yearly increase of 4.05 ± 0.6 mm in the sea level within the East Sea was observed. In parallel, the mean sea level showcased an ascending trend, exhibiting an average rise of about 3.5 ± 0.7 mm annually. In Central Vietnam, especially along the South Central coast, a substantial rise in sea levels was observed, manifesting as elevations of 4 mm/year and 5.6 mm/year, respectively (Nguyen & Nguyen, 2022; Tran et al., 2016; Woillez et al., 2021). Over the past decade, Vietnam has also encountered catastrophes, including Typhoon Nock Ten in 2011 and Typhoon Haiyan in 2013. These occurrences led to the displacement of several thousand people, significantly influencing migration patterns within the Vietnamese population and imposing substantial pressures on major metropolitan areas (Nguyen & Nguyen, 2022). The General Statistics Office (GSO) documented a financial shortfall amounting to VND 14.2 trillion, attributed to various natural disasters such as storms, sea level elevation, tropical depressions, floods, droughts, landslides, salt incursion, and other relevant events (GSO, 2022).

The climate change scenario in Vietnam appears bleak, with a consistent increase in average temperatures of up to 3.4 °C from 2080 to 2100. The most severely impacted region is projected to be southern Vietnam (WB & ADB, 2021). In parallel, prognostications point towards significant alterations in precipitation patterns, encompassing a projected increase in precipitation levels coupled with a heightened frequency of intense precipitation events. The Red River Delta and the Mekong River Delta, critical regions for agricultural cultivation and livestock farming, face significant vulnerability due to rising sea levels induced by climate change. This susceptibility notably involves the risk of inundation and salinity intrusion. In a 100 cm rise in sea levels, approximately 16.8% of the Red River Delta and 38.9% of the Mekong River Delta would be exposed to flooding, endangering staple crops and the local populace. Projections suggest that a sea level increase of 100 cm, which could lead to severe salinisation and flooding, might result in the loss of nearly half of the agricultural land, displacement of around seven million residents, and the demolition of over 14.2 million homes (Nguyen & Nguyen, 2022; Tran et al., 2016). With an expansive coastline spanning over 3200 km and encompassing a substantial number of low-lying urban centres and river delta regions, Vietnam's coastal cities face the recurrent challenges of being prone to natural disasters, including storms, floods, droughts, and salinity intrusion. The direct exposure to heightened flood risks places approximately $1 billion worth of GDP and about 1.5 million workers in a precarious situation. Evidencing an upward trajectory, the costs associated with climate-induced disasters are mounting rapidly, inflicting an increasingly profound impact on human lives, tangible assets, livelihoods, and intricate ecological systems (World Bank, 2022).

In the absence of comprehensive adaptation and mitigation strategies, climate change is forecasted to yield an economic impact ranging from approximately 12–14.5% of Vietnam's GDP on an annual basis by 2050. Moreover, a disquieting prospect emerges wherein up to one million individuals could find themselves trapped in conditions of extreme poverty by the year 2030 (World Bank, 2022).

3 Climate Governance in Southeast Asia

3.1 Climate Governance under the Auspices of ASEAN

At the regional level, effective coordination by regional institutions is imperative for the advancement and fortification of climate change governance within the area, offering a collaborative forum for member states to access and explore information, exemplary practices, and valuable lessons aimed at enhancement. In Southeast Asia, apart from Timor-Leste, which is currently undergoing the membership evaluation process, the remaining nations have demonstrated proactive engagement in various collaborative endeavours in different areas, such as environmental protection and adaptation to climate change, through their participation in the Association of Southeast Asian Nations (ASEAN) (ASEAN, n.d.).

Diverging from the European Union, despite the absence of a central parliament, ASEAN has endeavoured to establish a framework for environmental cooperation to enhance the efficiency of implementation, coordination, and resource mobilisation. The ASEAN Summit assumes the highest authority within this hierarchical organisational structure, taking responsibility for policy formulation. It is supported by the ASEAN Coordinating Council, which is crucial in executing its agreements and decisions. The organisational framework comprises three distinct Community Councils: the ASEAN Political-Security Community Council, the ASEAN Economic Community Council, and the ASEAN Socio-Cultural Community Council. The ASEAN Socio-Cultural Community inter alia incorporates a focus on environmental sustainability, and within this context, it encompasses the ASEAN Working Group on Climate Change (AWGCC) (Koh & Bhullar, 2011).

Box 2
The ASEAN Socio-Cultural Community inter alia incorporates a focus on environmental sustainability, and within this context, it encompasses the ASEAN Working Group on Climate Change (AWGCC).

Within the framework of ASEAN, dating back to 1978, establishing strategic Plans of Action marked the initiation of regional collaboration under the aegis of the ASEAN Sub-regional Environment Programme. The ASEAN Ministerial Meeting on Environment (AMME) and the ASEAN Senior Officials Meeting on Environment (ASOEN) are the entities instituted to oversee and synchronise regional cooperation concerning environmental matters. Although the AMME was initially mandated to deal with transboundary haze pollution in Indonesia, its function was subsequently broadened to address environmental management issues. This expansion followed the endorsement of the Singapore Declaration on Climate Change, Energy and the Environment at the 12th ASEAN Summit (Boer, 2016; Seah & Martinus, 2021).

Box 3
The ASEAN Ministerial Meeting on Environment (AMME) and the ASEAN Senior Officials' Meeting on Environment (ASOEN) are the entities instituted to oversee and synchronise regional cooperation concerning environmental matters.

The ASEAN member states (AMS) established the AWGCC to research climate issues, devise policies, and coordinate. The AWGCC's responsibility centres on providing updates on advancing the group's action plan. This comprehensive plan entails initiatives aimed at enhancing the connection between scientific insights and policy formulation, conducting a scoping study for the creation of a monitoring, verification, and reporting (MRV) mechanism tailored for greenhouse gas (GHG) emissions at the facility/company level, and fostering capacity development to establish an Enhanced Transparency System (ETS), conducting a study to assess financing requirements, and improving capacity of ASEAN climate change negotiation teams (Seah & Martinus, 2021).

The ASEAN Socio-Cultural Community (ASCC) Blueprint, a strategic framework that prominently focuses on 'environmental sustainability', directs ASEAN's collaborative efforts concerning climate change. The ASCC Blueprint 2016–2025 encapsulates four fundamental dimensions: biodiversity and natural resources, developing environmentally sustainable cities, fostering climate sustainability, and promoting sustainable consumption and production practices. These four fundamental pillars serve as the bedrock for the primary objectives outlined by the AWGCC. These objectives are primarily focused on amplifying regional cooperation in climate change endeavours, achieved through the meticulous implementation of the Action Plan, nurturing harmonious collaborations across a spectrum of ASEAN sectoral entities, and adeptly conveying the pivotal concerns and priorities of the ASEAN community on the global platform. While the AWGCC has successfully implemented several collaborative projects with Dialogue Partners in recent times, its specific jurisdiction to address matters extending beyond the domain of AMME working groups remains ambiguously delineated (Koh & Bhullar, 2011; Seah & Martinus, 2021).

Box 4
The ASCC Blueprint 2016–2025 encapsulates four fundamental dimensions:

- Biodiversity and natural resources
- Developing environmentally sustainable cities
- Fostering climate sustainability
- Promoting sustainable consumption and production practices

These four fundamental pillars serve as the bedrock for the primary objectives outlined by the AWGCC.

Established in 2010 as a regional consultative platform, the ASEAN Climate Change Initiative (ACCI) aims to synchronise regional concerns and foster collaboration at both regional and international levels to tackle climate challenges. The ACCI draws its foundation from ASEAN's responsibilities enshrined in the ASEAN Charter, enabling ASEAN to assert its rightful role in advocating and negotiating for its collective interests within UNFCCC deliberations. However, there remains a lack of clarity regarding the operational efficacy of the ACCI in the years since its establishment and the precise consensus positions that ASEAN has adopted in the international arena (Seah & Martinus, 2021).

Box 5
The ASEAN Climate Change Initiative (ACCI) aims to synchronise regional concerns and foster collaboration at both regional and international levels to tackle climate challenges.

With the region's growing recognition of its vulnerability to climate change and the corresponding risks, conversations and initiatives related to climate change have progressively expanded beyond the confines of the AMME and the ASCC Blueprint in different fields. Relevant to the topic matter of this chapter, by sector, ASEAN's statutory framework interconnects energy security and climate change. In parallel with the development and promotion of transitioning to renewable energy sources, the AMS place a particular emphasis on the reduction of carbon emissions by curbing the utilisation of fossil fuels, including coal, natural gas, and oil, for electricity generation. This initiative aims to address a pivotal contributor to the generation of GHG emissions in the region. Adopting the Singapore Declaration on Climate Change, Energy, and the Environment in 2007 paved the way for acknowledging the interconnections among climate challenges, energy provision, and other environmental issues within the context of sustainable development and regional energy security. ASEAN has articulated a more precise objective in its latest guiding document. In particular, the ASEAN Plan of Action for Energy Cooperation (APAEC) 2016—2025 envisages a target of achieving a renewable energy share of 23% of the total primary energy supply by 2025. Additionally, it is firmly committed to reducing energy intensity by 20% by 2020 and 32% by 2025, based on the 2005 levels (ACE, 2020; Seah & Martinus, 2021).

Box 6
Adopting the Singapore Declaration on Climate Change, Energy, and the Environment in 2007 paved the way for acknowledging the interconnections among climate challenges, energy provision, and other environmental issues within the context of sustainable development and regional energy security.

In finance, the adoption of sustainable investments is witnessing a significant rise. Particularly, the engagement of ASEAN's business communities in dialogues aimed at supporting the private sector to refine and complement its environmental, social, and governance (ESG) mechanisms. These mechanisms now progressively incorporate climate change resilience into business and investment determinations. Furthermore, initiatives such as the ASEAN Green Bond standards advanced by the ASEAN Capital Markets Forum (ACMF) in alignment with the ASEAN Finance Ministers are designed to facilitate sustainable regional development and satisfy investor demand for environmentally responsible investments (Seah & Martinus, 2021).

Box 7
Initiatives such as the ASEAN Green Bond standards advanced by the ASEAN Capital Markets Forum (ACMF) in alignment with the ASEAN Finance Ministers are designed to facilitate sustainable regional development and satisfy investor demand for environmentally responsible investments.

Since its foundation in 1967, environmental protection has not been a priority within ASEAN, whose initial mandate revolved around fostering cooperation to preserve peace, security, and stability. Nevertheless, despite not being initially prioritised, in recent decades, all the AMS have come to recognise the significance of building resilience to climate change following their participation in the United Nations Conference on the Human Environment in Stockholm in 1972 (Koh & Robison, 2002). This acknowledgement has culminated in sustained, enduring political commitments to comprehensive environmental management throughout the region, underscoring their collective resolve to effectively navigate the challenges of climate change adaptation (Boer, 2016). All member states of ASEAN are participants of the United Nations Framework Convention on Climate Change (UNFCCC) (UNFCCC, n.d.) and have ratified the Paris Agreement (UNTC) and the Kyoto Protocol (UNTC). In alignment with these global undertakings, each of the AMS has formulated and submitted their respective Nationally Determined Contributions (NDCs), outlining their commitment to devising strategies that facilitate sustained low-emission development and undertaking actions to pursue and attain climate aspirations. Except for Brunei and the Philippines, which have solely submitted their initial NDCs, other member countries have furnished updated or enhanced NDCs (United Nations Climate Change, n.d.). Singapore notably emerged as a frontrunner, pledging to a comprehensive long-term plan for low-emission development. Although all the members have fulfilled their obligations under the UNFCCC, ASEAN must acknowledge the commonalities and challenges the member states have encountered in performing their NDC objectives (Seah & Martinus, 2021).

Furthermore, as part of the ASCC Blueprint framework, mechanisms have been established to facilitate the incorporation of these commitments into the implementation at the national level. Nevertheless, a significant observation in federal environmental legislation is the lack of precise alignment with the assumed international obligations. Moreover, Southeast Asian nations have exhibited a hesitancy to embrace regional legally binding instruments about environmental matters, which stands in contrast to their active engagement in Multilateral Environmental Agreements (MEAs) (Boer, 2016).

Box 8
All member states of ASEAN are participants of the United Nations Framework Convention on Climate Change (UNFCCC) and have ratified the Paris Agreement (UNTC) and the Kyoto Protocol (UNTC). In alignment with these global undertakings, each of the AMS has formulated and submitted their respective Nationally Determined Contributions (NDCs), outlining their commitment to devising strategies that facilitate sustained low-emission development and undertaking actions to pursue and attain climate aspirations.

3.2 Shortcomings and Implications for Enhancing Climate Governance within the ASEAN's Regional Framework

Although it appears that the governments in Southeast Asia are dedicated to taking effective measures against climate change and are actively engaged within the international climate framework of the UNFCCC, primarily conveyed through ASEAN's expressions of concern regarding the escalated climate risks confronting the region, a more detailed examination of the regional instruments and declarations conducted under the auspices of ASEAN reveals the presence of several notable issues. Despite their active participation in the international climate governance framework initiated by the UNFCCC, there persists an ambiguity surrounding the substantive actions and commitments undertaken by the AMS in climate change mitigation. The absence of well-defined targets exemplifies this ambiguity, specified financial allocations, or concrete action plans. By the prevailing stance among most developing nations, the AMS assert that the onus of climate action and the provision of financial support for facilitating mitigation and adaptation endeavours in the Global South primarily rest upon industrialised countries. In their capacity as developing nations, the AMS restrict their commitments to voluntary Nationally Appropriate Mitigation Actions (NAMAs) while recurrently alluding to the emissions trading mechanism—Reducing Emissions from Deforestation and Forest Degradation (REDD+) (Pye, 2021).

Box 9
Despite their active participation in the international climate governance framework initiated by the UNFCCC, there needs to be more clarity surrounding the substantive actions and commitments undertaken by the AMS in climate change mitigation. The absence of well-defined targets exemplifies this ambiguity, specified financial allocations, or concrete action plans.

Addressing the complexities of instituting robust climate change governance within ASEAN is a formidable task due to the foundational structure that underpins the association. The roots of ASEAN can be traced back to the establishment of the ASEAN Economic Community (AEC). This construct was erected upon the foundational framework of the ASEAN Free Trade Area (AFTA). The core focal points of ASEAN encompass the enhancement of security, socio-cultural integration, and fostering economic collaboration, all strategically aligned to facilitate the seamless trade flow among member nations within ASEAN. The genesis of ASEAN was primarily driven by economic motivations, diverging from more pronounced political or socio-cultural underpinnings (Rachiminawati, 2010). The principles of national sovereignty and non-interference are enshrined in the ASEAN Charter (ASEAN, 1967). These principles establish the basis for the characteristic approach known as the 'ASEAN way'. Despite promoting values such as justice and adherence to the rule of law upon adopting the ASEAN Vision 2020, the practical reality within various AMS often deviates from these stated commitments. While there is an acknowledgement of the importance of the rule of law, its effective application is frequently diluted due to the prevailing influence of the 'ASEAN way'. Additionally, the AMS prefer independent implementation of programmes rather than an extensive reliance on a centralised regional bureaucracy. This approach emphasises that the AMS avoid meddling in each other's domestic matters and instead prioritise collaboration over strict legal obligations (Boer, 2016).

Box 10

Despite promoting values such as justice and adherence to the rule of law upon adopting the ASEAN Vision 2020, the practical reality within various AMS often deviates from these stated commitments. While there is an acknowledgement of the importance of the rule of law, its effective application is frequently diluted due to the prevailing influence of the 'ASEAN way'.

The prevailing trend observed among instruments within the ASEAN framework distinctly leans towards a state-centric orientation, potentially prompting the requisite reconsideration of sovereign principles in managing cross-border environmental concerns. The 'ASEAN way' concept frequently revolves around the principle of sovereignty, wherein the AMS consistently reject direct involvement in each other's internal affairs. This disposition is prominently evident in various agreements adopted within the ASEAN framework. This approach is noticeably reflected in various agreements adopted within ASEAN. It is argued that many Asian nations are willing participants in multilateral environmental agreement negotiations, demonstrating their readiness to assume the attendant responsibilities. The argument posits that universally acknowledged norms, even if they seemingly clash with culturally ingrained short-term economic objectives, generally find acceptance among the political and bureaucratic leadership in the Asia-Pacific region. However, the practical application of these obligations exhibits variance across diverse legal systems. Although the 'ASEAN way' is influenced by cultural and political sensitivities in Southeast Asia, it prompts inquiry into whether this approach remains tenable in rationalising the gradual progress towards achieving satisfactory, durable environmental and social outcomes that do not align with global developments (Boer, 2016; Koh & Bhullar, 2011).

Furthermore, there is an increasing call for nations to align their policies and actions with the 17 Sustainable Development Goals (SDGs). This notable influence of the SDGs is mirrored by indicators suggesting a shift in the approaches to legal standards within Southeast Asia. These signs include the introduction of the ASEAN Charter in 2007, the acknowledgement of the necessity for stronger regional actions related to climate change and biodiversity conservation, a greater emphasis on environmental security, the establishment of the ASEAN Commission on Human Rights in 2010, and the agreement on the ASEAN Human Rights Declaration in 2012, which acknowledges environmental rights. Additionally, establishing specialised environmental courts across several ASEAN jurisdictions signals an escalating determination to enforce environmental legislation nationwide throughout the region (Boer, 2016; Koh & Bhullar, 2011).

Box 11

Although the 'ASEAN way' is influenced by cultural and political sensitivities in Southeast Asia, it prompts inquiry into whether this approach remains tenable in rationalising the gradual progress towards achieving satisfactory, durable environmental and social outcomes that do not align with global developments.

This prospect implies a possible relaxation of the principle of sovereignty. The recalibration of the traditional 'ASEAN way' emerges as an essential step in response. Furthermore, the emergent phenomenon of new regionalism, propelled by the forces of globalisation and underscored by the incorporation of non-traditional security issues, such as climate change or human rights crises, rather than conventional state security, indicates a discernible transition towards a paradigm of multifunctional cooperation. This cooperative shift transcends geographical limitations and engages various stakeholders, encompassing entities like ASEAN's Dialogue Partners. The pragmatic implementation of this collaborative framework takes on heightened significance during times of crisis, particularly due to the inherent nature of issues like climate change, which inherently surpass the individual capacities of the AMS to address effectively on their own (Koh & Bhullar, 2011).

ASEAN embarked on integrating environmental considerations as a pivotal aspect within its intricate network of regional dialogues, driven by the overarching aspiration to cultivate collaborative endeavours spanning economic, social, technical, and scientific advancement. Since ASEAN's inception, the evolution of environmental law has witnessed the majority of regional nations signing and ratifying significant multilateral environmental agreements (MEAs). However, this process has brought forth diverse approaches to implementing the obligations mandated by these MEAs, influenced by both shared socio-cultural ties and divergent legal systems shaped by historical, economic, and political factors. Similar to many developing regions, legal systems in Southeast Asia exhibit legal pluralism, a consequence of the coexistence of traditional pre-colonial laws, colonial regulations, and post-colonial developments. This intricacy creates complex legal landscapes within and across jurisdictions. A preference for non-binding 'soft law' over legally binding 'hard law' is evident within the ASEAN framework. This preference is mirrored in unenforceable declarations and charters concerning environmental management, climate change, and sustainable development. This approach is commonly called the 'ASEAN way' and is founded on non-interference and national sovereignty principles. The inclination towards 'soft law' is also reflected in the absence of robust legal and institutional frameworks for regional environmental management and cross-border dispute resolution within ASEAN. The formulation of planning and cooperative programmes within ASEAN is solidly rooted in consultative processes and consensus-building (Boer, 2016; Koh & Robison, 2002).

Box 12
Since ASEAN's inception, the evolution of environmental law has witnessed the majority of regional nations signing and ratifying significant multilateral environmental agreements (MEAs). However, this process has brought forth diverse approaches to implementing the obligations mandated by these MEAs, influenced by both shared socio-cultural ties and divergent legal systems shaped by historical, economic, and political factors. Similar to many developing regions, legal systems in Southeast Asia exhibit legal pluralism, a consequence of the coexistence of traditional pre-colonial laws, colonial regulations, and post-colonial developments. This intricacy creates complex legal landscapes within and across jurisdictions.

It is argued that formulating a soft law document is considerably more feasible than engaging in formal treaty negotiations that encompass binding legal obligations, and soft law texts serve as foundational elements for the eventual emergence of robust hard law instruments over time (Boer, 2016). Nonetheless, the preference for a 'soft' approach has acted as a barrier to implementing effective strategies to tackle regional issues (Koh & Bhullar, 2011; Koh & Robison, 2002). Furthermore, how decisions are reached, hinged on consensus (ASEAN, 1967), has significantly contributed to shaping ASEAN's reputation as an entity that does not proactively address environmental issues. Upon reflection of its history, ASEAN has frequently faced criticism for its lack of proactive engagement when directly confronting environmental challenges. This notable inertia can be traced partly to the group's hesitance in committing to legally binding instruments designed to uphold environmental protection. This shared stance has contributed to the perception of ASEAN's apparent inactivity in effectively addressing urgent environmental matters. For example, the region has experienced recurrent haze, reaching levels deemed equivalent to an 'environmental disaster'.

Contrary to other AMS, Indonesia chose not to ratify the Agreement on Transboundary Haze Pollution in 2002 despite being the primary location of these fires. This decision invited criticism from neighbouring nations adversely affected by the annual haze, further compounding the delay in finding a solution to the transboundary haze issue. The process of Indonesia's eventual ratification of the Agreement took nearly 12 years, serving as a reminder that compelled all AMS to collaboratively forge ahead in establishing a framework underpinned by legally binding obligations (Bell, 2014; Habib, 2019; Hermawan & Astuti, 2021).

Box 13
The preference for a 'soft' approach has acted as a barrier to the implementation of effective strategies to tackle regional issues.

In addition, the Intended Nationally Determined Commitments (INDCs) submitted by certain AMS to the UNFCCC within the architecture of the Paris Agreement, indicating their commitments to reducing GHG emissions exhibit a resemblance. Specifically, Vietnam (8%), Thailand (20%), Cambodia (27%), Indonesia (29%), Malaysia (35%), Singapore (36%). With financial support from developed countries, Indonesia plans to increase its reduction target to 41%, Malaysia aims for 45%, and Thailand and Vietnam each aspire to achieve a 25% reduction. On the other hand, the Philippines has committed to reducing emissions by 70% only by receiving financial support from developed countries. Singapore and Cambodia, however, have yet to make any further commitments beyond their initial pledges. The reduction objectives of these AMS are questioned in which context as it appears that they have committed to reducing emissions, but when viewed generally, there is a potential for an overall increase in emissions.

In most cases, countries refer to a baseline scenario for 2030, which is the expected emissions if nothing changes (business-as-usual or BAU). For example, when Indonesia promises a 29% reduction, it means they plan to reduce the expected increase in emissions by 2030, which would have been 2.9 billion tonnes of carbon dioxide equivalent per year (CO2e/a) in the BAU scenario. So, this 29% reduction implies that Indonesia aims to increase its annual GHG emissions by 200 million tons of CO2 equivalent per year (MtCO2e/a) compared to the 2005 baseline of 1.8 billion tonnes. Similarly, Viet Nam's 8% reduction is about the expected 787 MtCO2e/a in 2030. An 8% reduction would mean 724 MtCO2e/a, which is 293% higher compared to the 2010 baseline of 247 MtCO2e/a. Malaysia and Singapore are exceptional cases in that they have only pledged to reduce their 'emissions intensity of GDP' by 45% and 35% by 2030, respectively. In practical terms, over the next 15 years, there could be an increase of 759 MtCO2e/year compared to the amount documented in 2005. Likewise, Singapore is expected to emit an additional

25 $MtCO_2e$ in GHG emissions compared to 2005, signifying an increase of over 60% (Pye, 2021).

In general, although ASEAN serves as a foundational platform for regional collaboration, the primary impetus for orchestrating suitable measures and establishing requisite support systems lies within the purview of national, regional, and local governance. In their nascent stages, a preponderance of developing nations accorded precedence to economic expansion and poverty alleviation, relegating climate change considerations to a secondary stance. However, a perceptible shift is underway, aligning policy trajectories towards a more holistic paradigm. Recognising the diversity of climate risks and adaptation priorities across regions, countries, and sectors is crucial. A uniform adaptation strategy cannot effectively address the unique circumstances of all situations; hence, approaches should be customised based on local resources and constraints. This significance is especially pronounced in Southeast Asia, where the effectiveness of regional entities like ASEAN, coupled with regional, national, and local adaptation initiatives, hinges on access to international funding and technology transfer.

Such resources are indispensable for conducting vital research and development activities in critical domains such as climate and economic modelling, technological advancements, and support for vulnerability assessments and impact analyses. These efforts aim to generate high-quality insights that bolster understanding of climate change, its implications, adaptation requirements, and the precise design and execution of adaptation measures. However, more than the mere formulation of adaptation, political policies are required to bring about desired outcomes. Numerous instances indicate policies conceived at different governance levels are not achieving their goals. Thus, vigilant monitoring of their implementation becomes paramount. With ASEAN's restructured governance framework and the establishment of new working groups, the potential emerges for a more resilient governance structure that can effectively address these challenges (Koh & Bhullar, 2011; Koh & Robison, 2002).

Box 14

Although ASEAN serves as a foundational platform for regional collaboration, the primary impetus for orchestrating suitable measures and establishing requisite support systems lies within the purview of national, regional, and local governance. In their nascent stages, a preponderance of developing nations accorded precedence to economic expansion and poverty alleviation, relegating climate change considerations to a secondary stance. However, a perceptible shift is underway, aligning policy trajectories towards a more holistic paradigm.

4 Vietnamese Governance and Statutory Policies in Response to Climate Change

4.1 Key Policies and Legislation

The increasing impacts of climate change in Vietnam are compelling the Communist Party within the country to drive the government's investments towards climate change adaptation. Over the recent years, the Vietnamese government has diversified its strategies for managing the consequences of climate change. These strategies encompass a deliberate emphasis on long-term and meticulously planned climate change adaptation measures. These measures are pursued alongside other policy initiatives, including disaster risk reduction, developmental aid, and sustainable development.

Commencing in the 1990s, Vietnam embarked on a proactive trajectory of engagement in global climate change negotiations, substantiated by its affiliation with the UNFCCC in 1994 (UNFCCC, n.d.) and its subsequent ratification of the Kyoto Protocol in 2002 and the Paris Agreement in 2016 (UN, n.d.). Vietnam has enacted institutional frameworks to execute its obligations under these treaties effectively. Additionally, with international backing, the country submitted its 'initial communication' to the UNFCCC in 2003. Participation in the global climate process during the 1990s and the early 2000s was primarily limited to experts specialising in climatology, hydrology, energy, industry, waste management, forestry, and agriculture. This limitation was attributed to the imperative of monitoring GHG emissions in these sectors. The scope of climate-related policies and actions remained restricted at the national level.

Nonetheless, governmental agencies did monitor meteorological conditions, sea-level fluctuations, and river flow patterns. Furthermore, there were instances of international cooperation concerning research into vulnerabilities associated with climate change (Neefjes, 2021, p. 208). The integration of climate change considerations into Vietnamese policies did not transpire until 2008. This juncture marked a pivotal advancement within Vietnam's national policy framework, characterised by the deliberate and formal inclusion of climate change concerns through the inauguration of the National Target Programme to Address Climate Change (NTP-RCC) (Strauch et al., 2018). The validation and authorisation of this commitment were explicitly accentuated through Decision 158/2008/QD-TTg (Gverdtsiteli, 2023).

Beyond the endorsement of the NTP-RCC, this decision distinctly underscored the imperative indispensability of allocating resources towards climate change response, thereby positioning it as a quintessential cornerstone for ensuring the enduring viability of developmental trajectories (Gverdtsiteli, 2023). Successive strategic frameworks, exemplified by the National Climate Change Strategy (NCCS), the National Green Growth Strategy (NGGS), and the National Green Growth Action Plan (NGGAP), have consistently reinforced the priority accorded to mitigation efforts. Within these approaches, defined targets for curbing emissions have been set, concomitantly advocating for the propulsion of environmentally sound economic growth. Notably, the NGGAP imparted substantial autonomy to provinces in formulating their own Provincial Green Growth Action Plans, seamlessly integrating these localised strategies into broader developmental frameworks (Prime Minister of Vietnam, 2022). Consequently, this approach facilitated the efficient mobilisation of financial resources from the national budget to underpin strategic climate action at the regional level.

Box 15
Vietnam embarked on a proactive trajectory of engagement in global climate change negotiations, substantiated by its affiliation with the UNFCCC in 1994 and its subsequent ratification of the Kyoto Protocol in 2002 and the Paris Agreement in 2016 (UN, n.d.). Vietnam has enacted institutional frameworks to execute its obligations under these treaties effectively.

In 2013, a significant achievement was reached in Vietnam when environmental protection and climate change prevention were officially incorporated into the country's Constitution (Tin, 2019). Embedded within specific sections, including Articles 43 (which address the realisation of the right to a healthy environment for all citizens) and Articles 50 and 63 (which underscore commitments to development harmonised with environmental protection and the creation and execution of policies centred on ecological preservation), Vietnam's Constitution 2013 established a comprehensive framework, outlining the principles and duties of the Government related to safeguarding the environment, conserving natural resources, and proactively tackling climate change (National Assembly of Vietnam, 2013). As the highest legal document, the Constitution firmly established the nation's dedication to addressing these vital concerns.

Box 16
Vietnam's Constitution 2013 established a comprehensive framework outlining the principles and duties of the Government related to safeguarding the environment, conserving natural resources, and proactively tackling climate change. As the highest legal document, the Constitution firmly established the nation's dedication to addressing these vital concerns.

In alignment with the environmental rights enshrined in Constitutional Law, the National Assembly recently enacted the Environment Protection Law (EPL) 2014, subsequently succeeded by the EPL 2020. These are primary laws overseeing activities that pose environmental harm, explicitly focusing on business and investment operations. In the past, the EPL 2014 merely outlined general criteria These included projects that required approval for investment intentions, a decision that rested within the authority of the National Assembly, the Government, and the

Prime Minister. The law also encompassed projects that utilised land within wildlife sanctuaries, national parks, historical-cultural monuments, world heritage sites and ranked scenic areas of beauty. Furthermore, it contained projects that could give rise to adverse environmental effects.

Box 17
In alignment with the environmental rights enshrined in Constitutional Law, the National Assembly recently enacted the Environment Protection Law (EPL) 2014, subsequently succeeded by the EPL 2020. These are primary laws overseeing activities that pose environmental harm, explicitly focusing on business and investment operations.

Indicating further improvements, the EPL 2020 has introduced more precise and delimited environmental criteria. This has led to a narrower scope, specifying the projects requiring environmental licences and approvals. In the classification paradigm of investment projects, a multifaceted array of criteria comes into contemplation, in particular (National Assembly of Vietnam, 2020):

1. the project's scale, capacity, the distinctive nature of its production, commercial, or service-oriented facets;
2. the amplitude of land utilisation, ranging from terrestrial domains to areas contiguous with water bodies and extending even to maritime zones, concurrent with an evaluation of the magnitude of natural resource exploitation; and
3. 'sensitive environmental factors', including but not limited to densely populated residential zones, water sources essential for domestic water supply, areas designated for natural preservation, forests, physical and cultural legacies along with other elements of the natural heritage, land allocated for the cultivation of wet rice involving two or more crops, significant wetlands, as well as prerequisites regarding the process of relocation and resettlement.

These criteria serve as the foundation for classifying and arranging investment projects into distinct clusters, contingent upon the extent of their deleterious influence on the environment, notably delineated as Group I (Significant), Group II (Moderate), Group III (Minor), and Group IV (Negligible). Moreover, these criteria intricately determine the essential licences and approvals requisite for these projects, encompassing vital procedures such as the environmental impact preliminary assessment (EIPA), the comprehensive environmental impact assessment (EIA), and the acquisition of environmental permits (National Assembly of Vietnam, 2020).

Following the enactment of the EPL, the Government promulgated Decree 06/2022/ND-CP and Decree 08/2022/ND-CP, furnishing comprehensive directives for the effective execution of the EPL 2020 and Decision 01/2022/QD-TTg, focusing on the reduction of GHG emissions and the preservation of the ozone layer.

Decree 06/2022/ND-CP has introduced a particular legal framework for the carbon market in Vietnam. In the initial phase from 2023 to 2027, its principal objectives revolve around the meticulous formulation of regulations governing carbon credit management, quota exchange activities, and the comprehensive carbon credit framework. Furthermore, it encompasses the development of precise operational guidelines for carbon credit trading platforms. Within this phase, there are also plans to initiate a pilot programme designed for the exchange and clearance of carbon credits, scheduled to commence in 2025. Subsequently, starting from 2028 and onwards, the formal operation of the carbon credit trading platform is envisioned. Vietnam aims to establish meaningful connections between its domestic carbon market and analogous markets operating in Asia and the global sphere. As a pivotal component of this framework, companies and industrial facilities that cannot curtail their carbon emissions will be mandated to procure carbon credits to offset their environmental impact. Non-compliance with this obligation may result in these entities incurring administrative fines (Government of Vietnam, 2022).

Decision 01/2022/QD-TTg enumerates a comprehensive list of 21 sectors and 1912 establishments obligated to conduct GHG inventory assessments. This list, as specified within this decision, will undergo a biennial reassessment process. The entities encompassed by this directive are compelled to devise and execute plans to curtail GHG emissions by the prescribed quotas established by the Ministry of Natural Resources and Environment (MONRE). Furthermore, these entities are granted the authority to participate in the exchange, sale, and acquisition of GHG emission quotas and carbon credits through designated carbon credit exchanges, all in the context of the forthcoming 2026–2030 period (Prime Minister of Vietnam, 2022).

In addition to the EPL 2020, a constellation of other noteworthy legislation contributes to Vietnam's legal framework to tackle environmental challenges (Nachmany et al., 2015). Among these statutes, the Forest Protection and Development Law 2004 stands out, seeking to safeguard and prudently manage forest resources. The Law on Economic and Efficient Use of Energy 2010 is dedicated to advancing energy conservation and efficiency. The Law on Water Resources 2012 assumes a crucial role in managing the nation's water resources, ensuring their sustainable utilisation and preservation. Furthermore, the Law on Natural Disaster Prevention and Control 2013 aims to enhance disaster preparedness and response measures to mitigate the impact of natural catastrophes.

An essential development in Vietnam's statutory framework was the 2015 Penal Code (amended in 2017) (Penal Code), which addressed environmental crimes in Chapter 19 from Article 235 to Article 246. This amendment introduced significant changes, particularly in the realm of environmental offences. Article 238 of the Penal Code represents a significant milestone as it presents, for the first time, criminal liability for business legal entities (referred to as *pháp nhân thương mại* in Vietnamese) concerning environmental crimes (Ha & Tran, 2022a). Although the scope of this criminal liability remains limited, it facilitates the legal pursuit of business entities engaged in activities culminating in environmental pollution. This has contributed significantly to the nation's efforts in combating and preventing activities that harm the environment, meeting international requirements, and promoting sustainable development.

4.2 Institutional Governance

Establishing the National Council of Sustainable Development in 2005 marked a significant step towards implementing sustainable development in Vietnam (Vo, 2019). Led by the Prime Minister, the National Steering Committee on Climate Change (NCCC) includes key ministers from various government bodies responsible for climate change-related activities (ADB, 2013). The National Climate Change Committee (NCCC) is vested with a set of core objectives, which encompass assuming a leadership role, orchestrating and overseeing the formulation and execution of national strategies and programmes about climate change, green growth, energy efficiency, REDD+, as well as other climate change-related issues. Furthermore, the NCCC is actively engaged in negotiations about international treaties on climate change. The NCCC's standing office, situated within the MONRE, holds responsibility for formulating the NCCC's agenda and monitoring the execution of climate change mitigation and adaptation measures. Operational from the MONRE, the NCCC's standing office assumes responsibility for formulating the committee's agenda and monitoring the execution of climate change mitigation and adaptation measures. Focal points from pertinent ministries were designated to take responsibility for climate change affairs, such as REDD+ (within the Ministry of Agriculture and Rural Development—MARD) and green growth (housed within the Ministry of Planning and Investment—MPI). Moreover, Climate Change Coordination Offices were set up by several provincial and municipal authorities to address climate-related challenges in localities (Neefjes, 2021).

Box 18

The NCCC's standing office, situated within the MONRE, holds responsibility for formulating the NCCC's agenda and monitoring the execution of climate change mitigation and adaptation measures. Operational from the MONRE, the NCCC's standing office assumes responsibility for formulating the committee's agenda and monitoring the execution of climate change mitigation and adaptation measures.

The MONRE plays a central role in managing climate change response and is responsible for implementing international agreements, such as the UNFCCC and the Kyoto Protocol (ADB, 2013). The MONRE's Department of Meteorology, Hydrology, and Climate Change coordinates climate-related activities. At the same time, the Department of Legal Affairs advises on the legal aspects of climate change, including legislation development and implementation (ADB, 2013).

The MARD supervises climate change matters related to rural development and serves as the national coordinating body for Disaster Risk Management (Strauch et al., 2018). With a nationwide network of 63 provincial offices and a significant field staff, the MARD has the capacity for targeted local-level implementation of adaptation and mitigation measures (ADB, 2013). It assists the Climate Change Steering Committee in supervising, guiding, and facilitating climate-change-responsive projects in various areas under its responsibility, including irrigation, water management, forest and marine biodiversity management, and flood control, all of which are vulnerable to climate change (ADB, 2013).

Box 19
The MARD supervises climate change matters related to rural development and serves as the national coordinating body for Disaster Risk Management.

The MPI coordinates Vietnam's overall development strategies, national planning, and investments, including mobilising and managing climate finance and Official Development Assistance (ODA) (Strauch et al., 2018). It is responsible for formulating and overseeing the implementation of the NGGAP. It acts as the National Designated Authority for the Green Climate Fund while leading efforts to achieve the Sustainable Development Goals in Vietnam (Strauch et al., 2018). Meanwhile, other line ministries, such as the Ministry of Industry and Trade (MIT) and the Ministry of Construction (MOC), have specific responsibilities related to climate change, including managing carbon-intensive industries and planning urban infrastructure development (Strauch et al., 2018). Additionally, the Ministry of Transport, Ministry of Foreign Affairs, Ministry of Science and Technology (MOST), and Ministry of Education and Training (MOET) play significant roles in climate change activities aligned with their respective functions.

Box 20
Other line ministries, such as the Ministry of Industry and Trade (MIT) and the Ministry of Construction (MOC), have specific responsibilities related to climate change, including managing carbon-intensive industries and planning urban infrastructure development (Strauch et al., 2018). Additionally, the Ministry of Transport, Ministry of Foreign Affairs, Ministry of Science and Technology (MOST), and Ministry of Education and Training (MOET) play significant roles in climate change activities aligned with their respective functions.

Overall, Vietnam has made commendable strides in developing a solid legal framework for climate change and environmental protection, evidenced by its membership in international agreements and establishment of crucial legislation. The involvement of multiple ministries demonstrates a comprehensive approach to addressing these critical issues. The ministries steered the helm of national climate change governance, with local authorities and their climate change coordination offices playing a pivotal role in this landscape. Moreover, climate governance underscores active involvement with non-state actors. The MARD has forged a collaborative REDD+ partnership under the UN's guidance. This initiative has garnered active participation from national and provincial departments, international agencies, and non-governmental organisations (NGOs). Receiving assistance from the EU, the MOIT assumes a leadership role in the Vietnam Energy Partnership Group (VEPG). VEPG's primary focus revolves around shaping energy efficiency and renewable energy policies. International NGOs and UN agencies have collaborated with the MARD, notably within working groups dedicated to disaster management. This enduring collaboration has substantially strengthened coordination in this domain. These partnership endeavours are mainly centred on coordinating aid efforts, exchanging critical information, and conducting substantive policy and technical dialogues, thereby exerting varying degrees of influence on the landscape of climate change governance. Furthermore, a memorandum of understanding was jointly formalised between international and Vietnamese NGOs and the MONRE. This memorandum establishes a structured framework for sustained dialogue and information sharing, with a specific emphasis on community-driven responses to climate change and the invaluable insights they offer for national and international climate policy (Neefjes, 2021).

Box 21

Overall, Vietnam has made commendable strides in developing a solid legal framework for climate change and environmental protection, evidenced by its membership in international agreements and establishment of crucial legislation. The involvement of multiple ministries demonstrates a comprehensive approach to addressing these critical issues. The ministries steered the helm of national climate change governance, with local authorities and their climate change coordination offices playing a pivotal role in this landscape. Moreover, climate governance underscores active involvement with non-state actors.

However, the effectiveness of these measures hinges on successful implementation. Challenges persist in translating policies into tangible actions on the ground. Many experts and observers have pointed out the gap between policy intent and actual execution (Schirmbeck, 2017). Therefore, this highlights the need to enhance the application and implementation for greater effectiveness in achieving the desired impact in mitigating climate change and protecting the environment. Examining specific instances of environmental breaches will provide a practical illustration of potential improvements, emphasising the need for further actions to ensure more effective governance in addressing the challenges of climate change. Moreover, recognising the constraints faced by corporations and local communities in climate change governance provides an opportunity to address specific limitations in policy formulation and implementation, which is discussed in the subsequent section of this chapter.

Box 22
Many experts and observers have identified the gap between policy intent and actual execution. Therefore, this highlights the need to enhance the application and implementation for greater effectiveness in achieving the desired impact in mitigating climate change and protecting the environment.

5 Deficiencies and Implications for Strengthening Climate Governance in Vietnam

5.1 Enhancing Governmental Coordination for Climate Change Initiatives

In emerging economies such as Vietnam, effective climate change adaptation demands a holistic strategy encompassing the entire nation and economy, transcending specific sectors. In Vietnam, the allocation of duties concerning climate change is divided among different ministries. The MONRE is primarily responsible for orchestrating the coordination of climate change efforts, whereas the MPI is entrusted with the facilitation of initiatives for promoting green growth. Concurrently, the MARD assumes a leadership role in steering disaster risk reduction and management endeavours. As for climate-related matters like urban infrastructure, energy, and transportation, these are overseen by the respective ministries dedicated to those sectors. The coordination of climate-related funding is under the purview of the MPI, while the MOST plays a role in the realm of climate forecasting. Assigning climate change responsibilities across various ministries necessitates robust inter-ministerial collaboration to ensure a unified and efficient approach to addressing climate challenges. Nonetheless, multiple studies have characterised the Vietnamese government structure as notably fragmented, suggesting a potential requirement for enhanced horizontal coordination (Strauch et al., 2018).

Box 23
In emerging economies such as Vietnam, effective climate change adaptation demands a holistic strategy encompassing the entire nation and economy, transcending specific sectors. In Vietnam, the allocation of duties concerning climate change is divided among different ministries. The MONRE is primarily responsible for orchestrating the coordination of climate change efforts, whereas the MPI is entrusted with the facilitation of initiatives for promoting green growth.

Vietnam's hierarchical multilevel structure establishes a range of conditions that both facilitate and constrain the implementation of adaptation measures at the local level. These challenges include vague institutional frameworks concerning structure, roles, and accountability mechanisms, coupled with a lack of clarity in coordination within and across levels. Additionally, human, financial, and legal resource scarcity pose challenges, alongside a limited comprehension of climate change and its consequences among individual policy actors. While these issues are prominently evident at the district and community levels, the hierarchical nature of the governance system means that many of these limitations extend across various tiers of the government structure. The established collaboration between national and local levels for executing climate change adaptation efforts currently faces challenges. There also exists a necessity for mechanisms for cross-sectoral and cross-scale coordination among agencies, to prevent potential overlapping or omitted responsibilities (Le et al., 2018).

Box 24

Vietnam's hierarchical multilevel structure establishes a range of conditions that both facilitate and constrain the implementation of adaptation measures at the local level. These challenges include vague institutional frameworks concerning structure, roles, and accountability mechanisms, coupled with a lack of clarity in coordination within and across levels. Additionally, human, financial, and legal resource scarcity pose challenges, alongside a limited comprehension of climate change and its consequences among individual policy actors. While these issues are prominently evident at the district and community levels, the hierarchical nature of the governance system means that many of these limitations extend across various tiers of the government structure.

This scenario often leads to policy inaction in hierarchical governance systems, where only some actors feel accountable for initiating measures (Le et al., 2018). The environmental policymaking process in Vietnam is characterised by a strong hierarchical structure, where policies are predominantly formulated at the central government level, often needing more involvement or engagement from lower-level governments or civil society organisations (Schirmbeck, 2017). This development and approval of most strategies in a top-down approach have led to several institutional constraints in Vietnam's environmental and climate governance. The lack of involvement of subnational levels in the decision-making process results in strategies and policies that may not fully address their specific needs and capacities, which hinder effective implementation, as lower levels often lack the necessary resources and motivation to carry out strategies that do not consider their local context (Schirmbeck, 2017).

Box 25
The environmental policymaking process in Vietnam is characterised by a strong hierarchical structure, where policies are predominantly formulated at the central government level, often without sufficient involvement or engagement from lower-level governments or civil society organisations.

This situation is evident in climate change and adaptative measures when the top-down steering of adaptation implementation poses significant institutional constraints. Policies and guidelines designed at the national level may not align with the priorities and vulnerabilities of lower levels. This could be because the centralised approach to developing new adaptation policies has yet to involve lower levels of government (Phuong et al., 2018). Consequently, mismatches occur between central government directives and local needs, making it difficult for lower levels to tailor the adaptation measures to their specific climate change impacts, which will eventually cause tensions between top-down policies and existing practices at the local level (Phuong et al., 2018).

Furthermore, the need for more dedicated institutions can enhance resilience to maladaptation. Existing research highlights the opportunity to harness certain bureaucratic traits in hierarchical systems to empower managers and personnel to collaboratively devise initiatives that extend beyond the confines of individual agencies. Despite the ongoing process of opening up Vietnam's policy landscape, substantial transformations in the institutional framework are imperative to pave the way for fundamental shifts. A notable policy approach significantly influencing localities in Vietnam is the mainstreaming strategy embedded within the Socio-Economic Development Plans (SEDPs). However, refining the effective implementation of mainstreaming and determining how to effectively structure and execute climate change adaptation measures at the local level in alignment with SEDPs remains an ongoing endeavour (Le et al., 2018). The absence of effective intergovernmental communication and collaboration allowed the local authorities to disregard the concerns raised at the national level. This is evident in the Formosa case. Despite receiving a warning from the MPI regarding Formosa's 'insufficient environmental impact assessment' and its potential adverse effects, the local Ha Tinh People's Committee proceeded with the project without heeding the concerns raised (Nguyen, 2016). This inadequacy in coordination resulted in a significant oversight in assessing the potential environmental risks of the Formosa project more properly.

The incident also brought attention to a more extensive challenge of divergent priorities and incentives between local and national governments. The pressure for economic development and investment at the local level overshadowed the need for rigorous environmental assessments and adherence to federal environmental regulations. As an illustration, during the Vedan incident, the then Minister of the MONRE,

Mr. Pham Khoi Nguyen, faced immense pressure (Minh Tien, 2008). On the one hand, Vedan provided jobs to numerous individuals and supported the economies of underprivileged neighbouring regions through substantial raw material consumption. On the other hand, the Minister faced complaints from certain local leaders demanding lower environmental standards to attract foreign investment. These conflicting interests added to the situation's complexity, creating a situation where local governments might prioritise short-term economic gains over long-term environmental sustainability. The case also exposed the challenges of enforcement and monitoring mechanisms at the local level. Even when national authorities raised concerns, there was a need for the establishment of more effective means to ensure compliance and accountability at the local level. This inadequacy resulted in the continuation of the project despite the warnings.

The prospect of enhancing coordination and positive competition among the ministries tasked with climate change adaptation can facilitate more streamlined and efficient policy development and execution. In the absence of a unified approach and clear direction from the executive branch, efforts to combat climate change can become disjointed and less impactful. This situation can result in duplicated projects, conflicting strategies, and gaps in the response to climate-related challenges. As a result, the nation's ability to comprehensively address the impacts of climate change across various sectors and communities could be undermined. This, in turn, hampers the advancement of resilience and sustainability objectives, accentuating the necessity for substantive reforms within the ambit of governance. Civil society wields the potential for substantial influence over governmental decisions and the advancement of sustainable development. This is increasingly evident as civil society asserts itself and actively addresses various environmental challenges. One notable aspect is the public demonstrations in response to issues like coal-fired power plants, environmental pollution, and air quality concerns. Analysing the responses of local communities to corporate' violations, as observed in cases like Thi Vai-Vedan or Formosa, reveals that environmental controversies have the potential to negatively impact climate change efforts and the overall perception of climate change governance. As environmental concerns mount, they exert significant pressure on the government to enhance its governance practices. This scenario underscores a compelling opportunity for Vietnamese policymakers and enforcement authorities to harness civil society's active participation in environmental issues and respond to their apprehensions regarding environmental regulations (Strauch et al., 2018).

Box 26

The prospect of enhancing coordination and positive competition among the ministries tasked with climate change adaptation can facilitate more streamlined and efficient policy development and execution.

5.2 *Enhancing Monitoring and Procedures: A Necessity in Focus*

The need for robust enforcement of statutory policies and regulations, coupled with a heightened emphasis on industrialisation, industry growth, and attracting foreign investments to bolster national and local economies, presents an opportunity for Vietnam to address the environmental consequences caused by human activities more effectively.

The Vedan environmental case in Vietnam is a significant incident that involved pollution and environmental violations. Vedan Vietnam Enterprise Corp., a Taiwanese-owned company, operated a monosodium glutamate (MSG) and starch processing plant in the southern province of Dong Nai. In 2008, it was discovered that Vedan, a company with Taiwanese investment, was discharging untreated sewage into the Thi Vai River. This improper disposal had dire consequences, causing severe pollution across approximately 77% of the Thi Vai River. The aftermath resulted in extensive harm to farmers' crops, cultivable lands, and aquatic farms and also gave rise to the occurrence of digestive and respiratory ailments, along with the development of malignant tumours among the local population (Nguyen & Nguyen, 2021; TN News, 2010a).

Another particularly significant case is the Formosa incident, recognised as one of Vietnam's most prominent environmental disasters. The Formosa environmental incident, also identified as the Formosa steel plant pollution case, unfolded in 2016 and centred on the activities of the Formosa Ha Tinh Steel Corporation. This entity operates as a subsidiary of the Formosa Plastics Group (FPG), a Taiwanese conglomerate. This incident originated in Ha Tinh province, positioned along the central coast of Vietnam, where the Formosa steel plant was situated. Subsequent revelations revealed that the company had been directly discharging toxic industrial waste, encompassing heavy metals and other hazardous substances, directly into the ocean via underwater conduits. This mismanagement resulted in severe contamination of the coastal marine environment, leading to extensive fish fatalities and causing profound disruptions to the local marine ecosystem (Agence France-Presse, 2016; Associated Press, 2016). To be more specific, in an official report submitted to the National Assembly, it is estimated that the disaster resulted in the death of 140 tons of fish and directly affected 41,000 fishermen and over 176,000 people (VnExpress, 2016a). Over 100 individuals are believed to have become ill from consuming contaminated fish so far (Ngo, 2017). Experts predict that the ecosystem may take over a century, possibly more, to recover fully (Ngo, 2017).

Box 27

The need for robust enforcement of statutory policies and regulations, coupled with a heightened emphasis on industrialisation, industry growth, and attracting foreign investments to bolster national and local economies, presents an opportunity for Vietnam to address the environmental consequences caused by human activities more effectively.

In 2016, the actions of seafood processing businesses in Tan Hai commune, Tan Thanh district, Ba Ria—Vung Tau province, led to a devastating environmental catastrophe (Viet Nam News, 2016a). Their waste discharge transformed a once vibrant flood-release area and brackish water lagoon into a lifeless expanse, resulting in the tragic mass die-off of fish. Surprisingly, records show these businesses had a history of severe environmental violations, with some even facing temporary suspension. After the accident, 35 affected households in fish farming in floating cages sought justice through a legal battle to claim compensation for their substantial losses (Viet Nam News, 2016b). Despite the passage of time and a court decision favouring the affected households, the situation remains dire, as the Cha Va River continues to witness repeated mass fish deaths (Truong, 2021).

Without accessible legal recourse for local communities and individuals adversely impacted by pollution, they resorted to extrajudicial mechanisms to vindicate their rights and seek compensation. These informal strategies operated beyond the confines of formal legal channels and included measures such as orchestrating large-scale boycotts against the offending company's products, as evidenced in the Vedan case in Thi Vai (TN News, 2010b). The Vedan case incited public anger, as citizens called for guilt and restitution for the incurred damages. The Thi Vai-Vedan case provoked widespread public indignation, eliciting demands from citizens for accountability and restitution for the incurred damages (Bui, 2015). In response, the Vietnamese government instituted legal proceedings against Vedan, culminating in monetary penalties and an obligation for the company to compensate affected individuals and communities (Government News, 2008).

Additionally, organised protests were staged against the responsible entities, exemplified by the Formosa case. At the same time, media channels were leveraged to broadly disseminate particulars of these cases, aiming to heighten public awareness and exert pressure on the offenders for therapeutic action. In the Formosa case, the culpable party committed to disbursing $500 million in compensation to all affected individuals as a measure to ameliorate the adverse impact on their livelihoods (Hoang, 2016; Nguyen & Nguyen, 2021; VnExpress, 2016b). Nevertheless, fulfilling compensation for the aggrieved citizens and communities enduring the repercussions of pollution-related harm remains uncertain (ASEAN Today, 2019).

Box 28

Without accessible legal recourse for local communities and individuals adversely impacted by pollution, they resorted to extrajudicial mechanisms to vindicate their rights and seek compensation. These informal strategies operated beyond the confines of formal legal channels and included measures such as orchestrating large-scale boycotts against the offending company's products.

The Thi Vai-Vedan case revealed a deficiency in the customary legal mechanisms, encompassing aspects such as guidance, human resources, and the capacity to facilitate class action lawsuits within Vietnam's legal framework. In response to the Thi Vai-Vedan case, the Vietnamese Government undertook measures to enhance and establish formal legal avenues, such as class action suits, to furnish augmented legal protection to individuals whose rights have been encroached upon and to serve as a deterrent against unlawful activities by private entities (Larkin & Tran, 2010). Nonetheless, despite these endeavours, when the subsequent Formosa case transpired in the following years, it became evident that limited groundwork had been laid in the wake of the Thi Vai-Vedan incident, and the progress in legal protection remained modest. This fact is exemplified by the subsequent initiation of class action lawsuits by thousands of victims affected by the Formosa case, pursued against FPG and falling under the jurisdiction of Taiwan (ASEAN Today, 2019).

The absence of provisions for class action lawsuits in Vietnam's legal system presents a consequential hurdle. This challenge becomes particularly pronounced within the context of the Formosa incident and its repercussions on endeavours about environmental protection. Unlike several other legal jurisdictions, the legislative landscape of Vietnam does not explicitly embrace the concept of class actions (Apolat Legal, 2023). Instead, the prevailing legal framework accommodates collective remedies through legal actions initiated by representative entities acting on behalf of employees or consumers to uphold their rights and interests. When faced with cases involving multiple plaintiffs with similar claims, the court can decide whether to consolidate these individual cases into a single proceeding. The guiding principle behind such consolidation is maintaining adherence to the law and ensuring fair treatment for all parties involved, as stated in Article 41 of the Civil Procedure Code 2015. An illustrative example of this practice occurred in 2017 when the People's Court of Ba Ria—Vung Tau Province considered 33 cases involving fish farming households. These households sought compensation from 11 seafood processing companies due to significant losses from fish mortality. To streamline the proceedings and avoid duplicative efforts, the court decided to handle these cases as one proceeding (People's Court of Ba Ria-Vung Tau Province, 2022).

Nevertheless, it is essential to note that the decision to consolidate or merge multiple cases is not solely determined by objective criteria or the needs of the plaintiffs. Instead, it lies within the trial court's discretion, relying on their subjective judgement and consideration of the specific circumstances of each case. The absence of a well-established system for class action lawsuits could present a significant hurdle in situations such as the Thi Vai-Vedan and Formosa incidents. In these cases, it is crucial to address class action matters and ensure that major corporations are held responsible for the environmental harm they cause. The absence of a class action framework could also present practical difficulties. Even when multiple individuals empower a single attorney to represent them, each case must be initiated separately, and the court handles them individually. Consequently, this leads to prolonged timelines and increased costs associated with pursuing separate legal actions, which can dishearten individuals seeking restitution for damages.

Box 29
The absence of provisions for class action lawsuits in Vietnam's legal system presents a consequential hurdle. This challenge becomes particularly pronounced within the context of the Formosa incident and its repercussions on endeavours about environmental protection. Unlike several other legal jurisdictions, the legislative landscape of Vietnam does not explicitly embrace the concept of class action. Instead, the prevailing legal framework accommodates collective remedies through legal actions initiated by representative entities acting on behalf of employees or consumers to uphold their rights and interests.

Additionally, the Thi Vai-Vedan case highlighted the need for criminal law to cover environmental crimes committed by companies. However, similar to the Formosa case, there were no legal mechanisms to prosecute companies causing environmental pollution. This limitation was due to the Penal Code 1999, which was applicable then, not including provisions for the criminal prosecution of commercial legal entities for committing offences. Formosa was only fined administratively and required to pay compensation. While administrative sanctions were available, they were considered less deterrent than criminal sanctions. Only with the introduction of the Penal Code 2015 (later amended in 2017) was a criminal liability established for commercial legal entities in environmental offences. Despite this, in 2020, there were 25,256 cases of environmental law violations detected involving 3093 offending organisations, some of which were very serious (Nguyen, 2020). However, no legal entities have been held criminally accountable for these violations. This suggests significant obstacles exist to prosecuting legal entities for environmental violations. Most cases are prosecutions of individuals—the primary reasons related to difficulties in proving damages and identifying culpable parties.

The Formosa incident also revealed a significant issue regarding the overlapping jurisdictions of executive and judicial authorities in Vietnam's legal system. After the incident, affected individuals filed 506 lawsuits against the Formosa company, which were sent to the local People's Court in Ky Anh Town. However, the court returned all 506 petitions, citing that the matter had already been addressed through an effective decision made by a competent state agency, as per Article 192.1(c) of the Civil Procedure Code 2015 (Thanh Nien, 2016). This decision was the Prime Minister's Decision 1880/QD-TTg, issued on 29 September 2016, concerning the compensation rates for the affected parties in Ha Tinh, Quang Binh, Quang Tri, and Thua Thien-Hue provinces due to the marine environmental incident (Prime Minister of Vietnam, 2016).

Deciding without involving the court's deliberation in line with proper procedures has left uncertainties in handling environmental incidents. The decision-making process could benefit from greater inclusivity and enhanced transparency, ensuring a more comprehensive reflection of the perspectives of impacted individuals and communities. Specifically, providing more clarity on the government's role and methodology for determining fault, damage extent, and compensation in the 'Compensation List for Environmental Incidents in Four Central Provinces', issued together with Decision 1880, would prevent overlapping with the court's role and resolution. Furthermore, a more transparent approach could clarify the extent of public consultation, thereby addressing certain current practical drawbacks.

Box 30

Deciding without involving the court's deliberation in line with proper procedures has left uncertainties in handling environmental incidents. It could be seen that the voices of affected individuals were not heard, and the decision-making process lacked transparency.

The first drawback is that the compensation amount needs to be considered sufficient to cover the damages suffered fully. Seafood traders assert that their average income, in the absence of any disaster, far exceeds the compensation amount of VND2,910,000/person/month, while fishing vessel owners and fishermen argue that their income exceeds the compensation amount of VND3,690,000/month (Green Trees, 2017). Furthermore, when the compensation dossier is processed at the commune or district level, cases are occasionally removed from the list without reason, leading to protests in specific communities where people found their names mistakenly omitted without any notice or explanation (Green Trees, 2017).

Moreover, the existing legal framework necessitates the presentation of concrete and substantiated evidence of actual damages as a prerequisite for accepting compensation claims. This requirement significantly burdens affected individuals, particularly those with limited resources, who may struggle to assemble the requisite evidence to substantiate their claims. Local citizens seeking redress and support for the seafood industry, which has suffered adverse effects from a marine environmental incident, often find it arduous to satisfy the stipulated conditions and furnish comprehensive evidence to address their grievances (Ha & Tran, 2022b). In the Formosa case, one contributing factor leading to the dismissal of petitions was the plaintiffs' incapacity to furnish extensive documentation and evidence that could substantiate the actual damages, as stipulated by Article 189(5) of the Civil Procedure Code. Understandably, this situation has generated frustration among the fishermen, particularly those affected by the Formosa incident. As articulated by Nguyen So Menh, a local fisherman from Tan An village, who questioned, 'We are jobless, four people are dead because of fish poisoning, and a whale was found dead on Cua Lo beach, only 50 km from here. What other proof do they need?' (Cantera, 2017).

Box 31
The existing legal framework necessitates the presentation of concrete and substantiated evidence of actual damages as a prerequisite for accepting compensation claims. This requirement significantly burdens affected individuals, particularly those with limited resources, who may need help to assemble the requisite evidence to substantiate their claims.

Due to their belief that their compensation is insufficient or nonexistent, affected individuals are reluctant to comply with Decision 1880 and instead opt for legal recourse through the courts. However, pursuing justice in Vietnamese courts may no longer be feasible for them, leading some to consider filing lawsuits in foreign courts. For example, in the Formosa case, 7875 Vietnamese citizens filed a lawsuit against FPG and its partner investors in the Taipei District Court, where Formosa is headquartered after their petition was rejected in the Vietnamese court (The News Lens, 2019). This, in turn, results in much higher expenses, such as legal representation and translation services. Since many individuals seeking legal action cannot navigate this process alone, they rely on external assistance to protect their rights. Moreover, this raises the question of what happens if the party responsible for the environmental disaster is not a foreign corporation like Formosa but a Vietnamese company.

In a similar situation where the government promptly issues a compensation decision, the avenue for accessing justice through the Vietnamese courts for the affected individuals is almost entirely closed. With that being said, even when bringing the cases to the courts is an option, Vietnam's legal system exhibits a complex and challenging litigation process. People often do not resort to litigation unless it is the last resort, which aligns with the Vietnamese saying: *Vô phúc đáo tụng đình* (to be involved in court is a misfortune). When environmental disasters occur, it indicates that the preceding legal measures were not adhered to, and the executive authorities failed to exercise adequate supervision. At this point, pursuing legal action, while far from ideal, appears to be the sole viable solution. However, this solution frequently leads to disappointment. As a result, the lack of active engagement from the judicial system becomes a clear impediment to the enforcement of laws.

The Formosa environmental case, the Thi Vai-Vedan pollution incident, and the extensive fish die-off in the Cha Va River provide valuable insights into Vietnam's expansive spectrum of environmental and climate governance challenges. These occurrences epitomise how reckless corporate conduct can precipitate substantial ecological degradation, leading to considerable adversity for local communities. These instances accentuate the compelling necessity for an all-encompassing and harmonised approach to climate and environmental governance characterised by robust regulatory structures, rigorous enforcement mechanisms, and seamless coordination among various governmental bodies.

6 Conclusion

This chapter commences its investigation with a comprehensive analysis of the intricate climate change dynamics prevalent in Southeast Asia, a region profoundly affected by the manifold repercussions of climate change. Within this expansive geographical domain, numerous nations, including prominent examples such as Myanmar, the Philippines, Bangladesh, Vietnam, and Thailand, have indisputably experienced the advent of severe weather events directly linked to the overarching climate change phenomenon in recent history. It is imperative to underscore that this chapter places a discernible emphasis on Vietnam, where the climate change scenario assumes an especially disquieting character, substantiated by a substantial body of empirical evidence affirming significant deviations in its climatic conditions. This phenomenon has posed considerable challenges to Vietnam's economic development trajectory.

In the broader Southeast Asian context, climate governance initiatives led by ASEAN aim to address environmental protection and climate adaptation. While ASEAN has made progress in establishing frameworks for environmental cooperation, the state-centric approach of these efforts presents challenges in effectively managing transboundary environmental issues. Southeast Asia's ability to tackle climate challenges relies on access to international support for research, technology, and adaptation efforts. However, policies formulated must be comprehensive and closely monitored during implementation.

This chapter focuses on Vietnam's climate governance and discusses critical policies and legislation. Vietnam has shown a substantial commitment to addressing climate change, as evidenced by many legal documents and the assignment of responsibilities to relevant ministries. Nonetheless, there is room for improvement in Vietnam's climate change governance. The allocation of responsibilities among various ministries, although fragmented, opens avenues for improved coordination. Given the crucial roles these ministries play in climate change initiatives, fostering and promoting enhanced collaboration between them can lead to more coherent policies and more effective enforcement.

Additionally, a critical imperative lies in enhancing monitoring and enforcement mechanisms. Vietnam's consistent emphasis on industrialisation and foreign investments has often taken precedence over environmental considerations, resulting in adverse ecological consequences. The exemplification of these challenges can be discerned in the Thi Vai-Vedan and Formosa cases. These environmental crises serve as a clarion call to the government, highlighting the imperative to strengthen climate change governance and mitigate pollutive activities by private corporations. This underscores that the environment should not be sacrificed in pursuing economic development at any price.

In summary, this chapter underscores both the regional and domestic facets of climate governance within Southeast Asia and Vietnam, offering insights into potential areas for enhancement. While Vietnam has demonstrated notable progress in acknowledging the significance of climate change mitigation and adaptation, it is necessary to continuously commit to addressing and improving any identified shortcomings. To fortify climate change governance in Vietnam, it is imperative to enhance inter-ministerial coordination, refine monitoring and enforcement mechanisms, and rectify legal inadequacies in handling environmental transgressions committed by corporations. These challenges bear implications for Vietnam's environmental sustainability and hold broader ramifications for the entire region and global endeavours in climate mitigation.

Former UN Secretary-General Ban Ki-moon, in his address at the 'Momentum for Change' Initiative, emphasised that 'Climate change does not respect borders, it does not respect who you are—rich and poor, small and big. Therefore, this is what we call global challenges which require global solidarity' (Ban, 2011). Establishing effective governance to address climate change is a multifaceted undertaking that necessitates the active participation of governments and various non-governmental actors. Among these actors, corporate entities, often the primary contributors to environmental degradation through pollution, wield significant influence. Climate change governance necessitates the development and enhancement through international cooperation that surpasses national boundaries and jurisdictional confines.

Declaration of Generative AI and AI-assisted Technologies in the Writing Process for this Chapter from Authors The authors of this chapter have used ChatGPT and Grammarly to proofread certain parts of the chapter. However, they declared that they did not use AI to create or write original and new manuscript content. The manuscript also underwent a proofreading process by a native speaker.

References

ACE. (2020). ASEAN Plan of Action for Energy Cooperation (APAEC) 2016–2025—Phase II: 2021–2025. Retrieved September 15, 2023, from https://aseanenergy.sharepoint.com/PublicationLibrary/Forms/AllItems.aspx?id=%2FPublicationLibrary%2F2020%2FPublication%2FBooklet%20APAEC%20Phase%20II%20%28Final%29%2Epdf&parent=%2FPublicationLibrary%2F2020%2FPublication&p=true&ga=1

ADB. (2013). Viet Nam: Environment and climate change assessment. Retrieved September 15, 2023, from https://www.adb.org/sites/default/files/institutional-document/33916/files/viet-nam-environment-climate-change.pdf

ADB. (2017). *A region at risk: The human dimensions of climate change in Asia and the Pacific*. Asian Development Bank (ADB). Retrieved September 15, 2023, from https://www.adb.org/sites/default/files/publication/325251/region-risk-climate-change.pdf

Agence France-Presse. (2016). *Vietnam investigates mass fish deaths*. The Guardian. Retrieved September 15, 2023, from https://www.theguardian.com/environment/2016/apr/21/vietnam-investigates-mass-fish-deaths-pollution

Apolat Legal. (2023). In review: Court procedure in Vietnam. Retrieved September 15, 2023, from https://www.lexology.com/library/detail.aspx?g=85374810-db2b-4131-bde5-a211ddf15676

ASEAN. (1967). Charter of the Association of Southeast Asian Nations. Retrieved September 15, 2023, from https://asean.org/wp-content/uploads/images/archive/publications/ASEAN-Charter.pdf

ASEAN. (n.d.). ASEN Member States. Association of Southeast Asian Nations - A community of opportunities for all. Retrieved February 28, 2023, from https://asean.org/member-states/

ASEANToday.(2019). *Vietnamesefishingcommunitiesseekjusticeinlawsuitagainst Taiwanesecorporation*.ASEANToday.RetrievedSeptember15,2023,fromhttps://www.aseantoday.com/2019/06/vietnamese-fishing-communities-seek-justice-in-lawsuit-against-taiwanese-corporation/

Associated Press. (2016). *Vietnam blames toxic waste water from steel plant for mass fish deaths*. The Guardian. Retrieved September 15, 2023, from https://www.theguardian.com/environment/2016/jul/01/vietnam-blames-toxic-waste-water-fom-steel-plant-for-mass-fish-deaths

Ban, K. (2011). *Remarks at "momentum for change" initiative*. United Nations - Secretary-General. Retrieved September 15, 2023, from https://www.un.org/sg/en/content/sg/speeches/2011-12-06/remarks-momentum-change-initiative

Bell, L. (2014). *After 12 years, Indonesia finally ratifies transboundary haze agreement*. Mongabay - News and Inspiration from Nature's Frontline. Retrieved September 15, 2023, from https://news.mongabay.com/2014/09/after-12-years-indonesia-finally-ratifies-transboundary-haze-agreement/

Boer, B. (2016). Environmental law in Southeast Asia. In P. Hirsch (Ed.), *Routledge handbook of the environment in Southeast Asia* (pp. 115–132). Taylor & Francis Group.

Bui, H. T. (2015). Civil society and governance in Vietnam's one party system.

Cantera, A. L. M. (2017). *"We are jobless because of fish poisoning": Vietnamese fishermen battle for justice*. The Guardian. Retrieved September 15, 2023, from https://www.theguardian.com/global-development/2017/aug/14/vietnamese-fishermen-jobless-fish-poisoning-battle-justice

Carlarne C.P. (2008). Good Climate Governance: Only a Fragmented System of International Law Away?, *30*(4), 450–480. https://doi.org/10.1111/j.1467-9930.2008.00289.x

CRU. (2018). *Average monthly temperature for Vietnam from 1901-2015*. Climatic Research Unit (CRU), University of East Anglia (UEA). Retrieved September 15, 2023, from https://data.vietnam.opendevelopmentmekong.net/en/dataset/nhi-t-d-va-lu-ng-mua-trung-binh-hang-thang-t-i-vi-t-nam-t-1901-2015

Eckstein, D., Kunzel, V., & Schafer, L. (2021). *Global climate risk index 2021 - Who suffers Most from extreme weather events? Weather-related loss events in 2019 and 2000 to 2019*. Germanwatch e.V. Retrieved September 15, 2023, from https://www.germanwatch.org/sites/default/files/Global%20Climate%20Risk%20Index%202021_2.pdf

Eckstein, D., Kunzel, V., Schafer, L., & Winges, M. (2019). *Global climate risk index 2020 - Who suffers most from extreme weather events? Weather-related loss events in 2018 and 1999 to 2018*. Germanwatch e.V. Retrieved September 15, 2023, from https://www.germanwatch.org/sites/default/files/20-2-01e%20Global%20Climate%20Risk%20Index%202020_14.pdf

General Statistics Office of Vietnam (GSO). (2022). *Statistical Yearbook of Vietnam 2022, General Statistics Office of Vietnam (GSO)*. General Statistics Office of Vietnam.

Government News. (2008). VN to strictly punish Vedan's law-breaking ac. Retrieved September 15, 2023, from https://en.baochinhphu.vn/vn-to-strictly-punish-vedans-law-breaking-act-1112274.htm

Government of Vietnam. (2022). Decree No. 06/2022/ND-CP on Mitigation of Green House Gas (GHG) Emissions and Protection of Ozone Layer. Retrieved September 15, 2023, from https://climate-laws.org/documents/decree-no-062022nd-cp-on-mitigation-of-green-house-gas-ghg-emissions-and-protection-of-ozone-layer-5a50?id=decree-no-06-2022-nd-cp-on-mitigation-of-green-house-gas-ghg-emissions-and-protection-of-ozone-layer_d8ff

Green Trees. (2017). Formosa disaster, one year look back. Retrieved September 15, 2023, from https://en.greentreesvn.org/2017/07/formosa-disaster-one-year-look-back_18.html

Gverdtsiteli, G. (2023). Authoritarian environmentalism in Vietnam: The construction of climate change as a security threat. *Environmental Science & Policy, 140*, 163–170.

Ha, L. T., & Tran, C. T. (2022a). Penal liability of legal persons for polluting acts under Vietnam's penal code. Retrieved September 15, 2023, from https://vietnamlawmagazine.vn/penal-liability-of-legal-persons-for-polluting-acts-under-vietnams-penal-code-48695.html

Ha, L. T., & Tran, C. T. (2022b). Trách nhiệm hình sự của pháp nhân đối với hành vi gây ô nhiễm môi trường theo luật hình sự Việt Nam [in English: Criminal liability of legal entities for environmental offences according to the Criminal Code of Vietnam]. *Legislative Studies, 05*, 453. Retrieved September 15, 2022, from http://www.lapphap.vn/Pages/tintuc/tinchitiet.aspx?tintucid=211046#

Habib, F. H. (2019). *What to expect from ASEAN's new agreement on marine debris*. The Diplomat. Retrieved September 15, 2023, from https://thediplomat.com/2019/07/what-to-expect-from-aseans-new-agreement-on-marine-debris/

Hermawan, S., & Astuti, W. (2021). Analysing several ASEAN countries' policy for combating marine plastic litter. *Environmental Law Review, 23*(1), 9–22.

Hoang, V. N. (2016). Enhancing mechanism for protection of constitutional rights in Vietnam today. *Asia-Pacific Journal on Human Rights and the Law, 17*(1), 28–41.

IPCC. (2021). *Climate Change 2021: The physical science basis*. Contribution of Working Group I to the Sixth Assessment Report of the Intergovernmental Panel on Climate Change. Intergovernmental Panel on Climate Change (IPCC). Retrieved October 4, 2022, from https://www.ipcc.ch/report/ar6/wg1/downloads/report/IPCC_AR6_WGI_FullReport.pdf

IPCC. (2022). *Climate change 2022: Impacts, adaptation and vulnerability*. Intergovernmental Panel on Climate Change (IPCC). Retrieved October 4, 2022, from https://www.ipcc.ch/report/ar6/wg2/

Koh, K. L., & Bhullar, L. (2011). Governance on adaptation to climate change in the Asean region. *Carbon & Climate Law Review, 5*(1), 82–90.

Koh, K. L., & Robison, N. A. (2002). Strengthening sustainable development in regional intergovernmental governance: Lessons from the "ASEAN way". *Singapore Journal of International & Comparative Law, 6*, 640–682.

Larkin, A. T., & Tran, T. S. (2010). *Lessons learned from Vedan: A call for class action suits in Vietnam*. Vietnam Law & Legal Forum. Retrieved September 15, 2023, from https://vietnamlawmagazine.vn/lessons-learned-from-vedan-a-call-for-class-action-suits-in-vietnam-3633.html, archived in the Issue No. 192/Aug

Le, T. H. P., Robbert, B. G., & Wals, A. E. J. (2018). Barriers and enablers to climate change adaptation in hierarchical governance systems: the case of Vietnam. *Journal of Environmental Policy and Planning, 20*(4), 518–532. https://doi.org/10.1080/1523908X.2018.1447366

Ludher, E., & Teng, P. (2023). Rice production and food security in Southeast Asia under threat from El Niño. *ISEAS Perspective, 2023*(53), 14.

Minh Tien. (2008). Xử lý hình sự các vi phạm của Công ty Vedan là cần thiết [in English: Criminal handling of Vedan's violations is necessary]. Public Security News. Retrieved September 15, 2023, from https://cand.com.vn/Su-kien-Binh-luan-antg/Xu-ly-hinh-su-cac-vi-pham-cua-Cong-ty-Vedan-la-can-thiet-i293545/

Nachmany, M., Fankhauser, S., Davidová, J., Kingsmill, N., Landesman, T., Roppongi, H., Schleifer, P., Setzer, J., Sharman, A., Singleton, C. S., Sundaresan, J. & Townshend, T.. (2015). Climate change legislation in Vietnam. An excerpt from the 2015 Global Climate Legislation Study. A review of climate change legislation in 99 countries. Retrieved September 15, 2023, from https://www.lse.ac.uk/GranthamInstitute/wp-content/uploads/2015/05/VIETNAM.pdf

National Assembly of Vietnam. (2013). The 2013 Constitution of the Socialist Republic of Vietnam. Retrieved September 15, 2023, from https://vietnamlawmagazine.vn/the-2013-constitution-of-the-socialist-republic-of-vietnam-4847.html.

National Assembly of Vietnam. (2020). Law No. 72/2020/QH14 dated 17 November 2020 on Environmental Protection. Retrieved October 31, 2022, from http://extwprlegs1.fao.org/docs/pdf/vie168513.pdf

Neefjes, K. (2021). Climate change governance in Viet Nam: Party leadership, decentralization, and transitions. In J. Marquardt et al. (Eds.), *Governing climate change in Southeast Asia: Critical perspectives* (pp. 205–223). Taylor & Francis Group.

Ngo, J. (2017). Choosing fish over steel: Ample protests and the large-scale death of fish in Central Vietnam.

Nguyen, K. (2016). Formosa's US$500 million settlement set to usher in new era for environmental enforcement. Vietnam Briefing. Retrieved September 15, 2023, from https://www.vietnam-briefing.com/news/formosa-500-million-settlement-mean-investors.html/

Nguyen, V. H.. (2020). Nhiều pháp nhân vi phạm về môi trường nhưng chưa truy cứu trách nhiệm hình sự? [in English: Many legal entities have committed environmental violations but have not been prosecuted for criminal liability?]. Communist Party of Vietnam Online Newspaper. Retrieved September 15, 2023, from https://dangcongsan.vn/thoi-su/nhieu-phap-nhan-vi-pham-ve-moi-truong-nhung-chua-truy-cuu-trach-nhiem-hinh-su-567313.html

Nguyen, T. H. Y., & Nguyen, P. D. (2021). Climate change and the challenges for developing countries in the implementation of the human right to a healthy environment: Case of Vietnam. *Asia-Pacific Journal on Human Rights and the Law, 22*(2), 222–254.

Nguyen, T. H. Y., & Nguyen, P. D. (2022). The efforts to respond to climate change and implementation of the sustainable development goals (SDGs) from the hardest-affected countries: Vietnam case analysis. *Brazilian Journal of International Law, 19*(1), 164–191.

Parry, E. J. (2007). The greatest threat to global security: Climate change is not merely an environmental problem. The UN Chronicle, vol. XLIV, no. 2. Retrieved August 31, 2023, from https://www.un.org/en/chronicle/article/greatest-threat-global-security-climate-change-not-merely-environmental-problem.

People's Court of Ba Ria-Vung Tau Province. (2022). Judgment No. 84/2017/DS-PT dated 01 August 2017 on compensation for damage caused by environmental pollution.

Phuong, L. T. H., Biesbroek, G. R., & Wals, A. E. J. (2018). Barriers and enablers to climate change adaptation in hierarchical governance systems: The case of Vietnam. *Journal of Environmental Policy & Planning, 20*(4), 518–532.

Prime Minister of Vietnam. (2016). Decision No. 1880 on the compensation to the provinces of Ha Tinh, Quang Binh, Quang Tri, and Thue Thien-Hue, following the marine environmental incident. Retrieved September 15, 2023, from https://datafiles.chinhphu.vn/cpp/files/vbpq/2016/09/1880.signed.pdf

Prime Minister of Vietnam. (2022). Decision No. 01/2022/QD-TTg on the list of greenhouse gas emitting facilities that must conduct greenhouse gas inspections.

Pye, O. (2021). Fossil capitalism the ASEAN way. In J. Marquardt et al. (Eds.), *Governing climate change in Southeast Asia: Critical perspectives* (pp. 227–248). Taylor & Francis Group.

Rachiminawati. (2010). Lesson learned for ASEAN from the integration of human rights in the European Union (the EU). *Indonesian Journal of International Law, 6*(3), 490–515.

Raitzer, D. A., Bosello, F., Tavoni, M., Orecchia, C., Marangoni, G., & Samson, J. N. G. (2015). *Southeast Asia and the economics of global climate stabilization*. Asian Development Bank (ADB). Retrieved September 15, 2023, from https://www.adb.org/sites/default/files/publication/178615/sea-economics-global-climate-stabilization.pdf

Schirmbeck, S. (2017). Vietnam's environmental policies at a crossroads salinated rice fields, hunted-out national parks, and eroding beaches—and what we can do about it.

Seah, S., & Martinus, M. (2021). *Gaps and opportunities in ASEAN's climate governance*. ISEAS Publishing. Retrieved September 15, 2023, from https://www.iseas.edu.sg/wp-content/uploads/2021/03/TRS5_21.pdf

Strauch, L., Robiou du Pont, Y., & Balanowski, J.. (2018). Multi-level climate governance in Vietnam: Bridging national planning and local climate action. Berlin. Retrieved September 15, 2023, from https://adelphi.de/system/files/mediathek/bilder/Multi-level%20climate%20governance%20in%20Vietnam%20-%20adelphi.pdf

Thanh Nien. (2016). Tòa án trả lại 506 đơn khởi kiện Formosa của người dân [in English: Court returns 506 people's petitions against Formosa]. Retrieved September 15, 2023, from https://thanhnien.vn/toa-an-tra-lai-506-don-khoi-kien-formosa-cua-nguoi-dan-185599236.htm

The News Lens. (2019). *Taipei Court dismisses lawsuit filed by 8,000 Vietnam marine disaster victims*. The News Lens. Retrieved September 15, 2023, from https://international.thenewslens.com/article/126835

The World Bank (WB), & The Asian Development Bank (ADB) (2021). Climate Risk Country Profile: Viet Nam, The World Bank (WB) and the Asian Development Bank (ADB).

Tin, V. T. (2019). Assessing Vietnam's environmental laws and direction for improvement. *Vietnamese Journal of Legal Sciences, 1*(1), 64–76.

TN News. (2010a). *Vedan responsible for 77 pct of Thi Vai River pollution*. Thanh Nien News. Retrieved September 15, 2023, from http://www.thanhniennews.com/society/vedan-responsible-for-77-pct-of-thi-vai-river-pollution-17302.html

TN News. (2010b). *Boycott fear forces river polluter payout*. Thanh Nien News. Retrieved September 15, 2023, from http://www.thanhniennews.com/society/boycott-fear-forces-river-polluter-payout-15358.html

Tran, T., Nguyen, V. T., Huynh, T. L. H., Mai, V. K., Nguyen, X. H., & Doan, H. P. (2016). *Climate change and sea level rise scenarios for Vietnam*. Ministry of Natural Resources and Environment (MONRE). Retrieved October 4, 2022, from https://data.opendevelopmentmekong.net/dataset/k-ch-b-n-bi-n-d-i-khi-h-u-va-m-c-nu-c-bi-n-dang-c-a-vi-t-nam-2009-2016/resource/a354c3e0-3cfe-4d07-ad03-d24713792d37/view/dcc6d854-4a84-4636-856e-8a5b0cfe8103

Truong, H. (2021). *Detention basin adopts alien color, releases foul smell*. VnExpress. Retrieved September 15, 2023, from https://e.vnexpress.net/news/news/detention-basin-adopts-alien-color-releases-foul-smell-4257051.html

UN. (n.d.). *Status of ratification of the Kyoto protocol and Paris agreement: Vietnam*. United Nations Climate Change. Retrieved September 22, 2023, from https://unfccc.int/node/61236

UNFCCC. (n.d.). Parties to the United Nations Framework Convention on Climate Change. Retrieved September 15, 2023, from https://unfccc.int/process/parties-non-party-stakeholders/parties-convention-and-observer-states

United Nations. (2022). Threat to global security more complex, probably higher than during cold war, secretary-general warns Munich security conference. In *Meetings coverage and press releases, Munich, Germany*. Retrieved August 31, 2023, from https://press.un.org/en/2022/sgsm21146.doc.htm

United Nations Climate Change. (n.d.). *Nationally determined contributions registry*. United Nations Climate Change. Retrieved September 15, 2023, from https://unfccc.int/NDCREG

Viet Nam News. (2016a). Farmers disagree with Chà Và fish death report. Retrieved September 15, 2023, from https://vietnamnews.vn/society/344804/farmers-disagree-with-cha-va-fish-death-report.html

Viet Nam News. (2016b). Industrial pollution tests people's patience. Retrieved September 15, 2023, from https://vietnamnews.vn/society/344804/farmers-disagree-with-cha-va-fish-death-report.html

VnExpress. (2016a). *Formosa's toxic disaster: are fish safe to eat now in central Vietnam?* VnExpress. Retrieved September 15, 2023, from https://e.vnexpress.net/news/news/formosa-s-toxic-disaster-are-fish-safe-to-eat-now-in-central-vietnam-3456368.html

VnExpress. (2016b). *Formosa offers $500 mln to compensate Vietnam for catastrophic environmental damage*. VnExpress International. Retrieved September 15, 2023, from https://e.vnexpress.net/news/news/formosa-offers-500-mln-to-compensate-vietnam-for-catastrophic-environmental-damage-3428656.html

Vo, T. S. (2019). Integrating sustainable development into national policy: The practice of Vietnam. Retrieved September 15, 2023, from https://repository.vnu.edu.vn/bitstream/VNU_123/136837/1/KY_20211109235756.pdf

Woillez, M.-N., Espagne, E., Ngo, D. T., Nguyen, M. H., Pannier, E., Drogoul, A., Huynh, T. P. L., Le, T. T., Nguyen, T. T. H., Nguyen, T. T., Nguyen, T. A., Thomas, F., Truong, Q. C., Vo, Q. T., & Vu, C. T. (2021). *Climate change in Vietnam, impacts and adapta-*

tion. AFD Group. Retrieved October 4, 2022, from https://www.afd.fr/en/ressources/gemmes-vietnam-climate-change-impacts-and-adaptation
World Bank. (2022). *Vietnam country climate and development report*. World Bank Group. Retrieved September 15, 2023, from https://reliefweb.int/report/viet-nam/vietnam-country-climate-and-development-report

Nguyen Phuong Dung earned her LL.B. degree from Hanoi Law University (Class of 2009–2013) in Hanoi, Vietnam, and subsequently pursued an LL.M. in International Business Law at Newcastle Law School (Class of 2013–2014) at Newcastle University in Newcastle upon Tyne, England, United Kingdom. Currently, she holds the position of Associate Lecturer (Law) at the Department of Economics and Finance, the Business School—RMIT University Vietnam. Previously, she worked as a legal practitioner specialising in international business law. Her scholarly pursuits are anchored in the realm of public international law and comparative law, specifically international human rights, international environmental law, international law of the seas, climate change, migrant workers' rights, and related areas. She has co-authored numerous publications featured in prestigious national and international journals and publishers. Additionally, she is a qualified solicitor licensed to practice law in Vietnam. For additional information, please visit: https://orcid.org /0000-0002-1882-2956

Vu Truc Hanh attained her LL.B. degree from Ho Chi Minh University of Law in Vietnam, followed by an LL.M. in Globalisation and Law with a specialisation in Corporate and Commercial Law from Maastricht University, the Netherlands. She is currently pursuing her second LL.M. at Ghent University. Prior to this, she served as a Law Lecturer at the University of Economics, Ho Chi Minh City, Vietnam (UEH), and held the position of Associate Lecturer (Law) at the Department of Economics and Finance, the Business School of RMIT University Vietnam. Additionally, she gained practical experience in a law firm, focusing on company law. Her research interests lie in public international law and comparative law, with a specific emphasis on international human rights, international environmental law, and climate change. For additional information, please visit: https://orcid.org/0000-0002-1812-5077

Eco-Innovative Actions and Small Business Performance

Olubiyi Timilehin Olasoji, Ravinder Rena, Valerie Onyia Babatope, Omoyele Olufemi Samuel, Jubril Bolaji, and Akinlabi Hameed Babatunde

Abstract This chapter presents evidence regarding the association between eco-innovative actions and the sustainability performance of small businesses in Nigeria, which is Africa's largest economy. It also examines the extent to which small businesses implement eco-innovative actions. Based on a survey of 480 owners-managers, we identify a significant relationship between eco-innovative actions and the sustainability performance of Nigerian small businesses. These eco-innovative actions are found to enhance the resources needed for sustainability performance. Therefore, it is recommended that businesses incorporate eco-innovative actions and sustainability practices into their strategic vision. This alignment with SDG13 is critical and may offer advantages for the environment.

O. T. Olasoji (✉)
Department of Business Administration & Marketing, School of Management Sciences, Babcock University, Ilishan-Remo, Ogun State, Nigeria

Babcock University, Business Administration and Marketing Dept, Ilishan-Remo, Nigeria

R. Rena
DUT Business School, Durban University of Technology, Durban, South Africa

V. O. Babatope
Degroote School of Business, McMaster University, Hamilton, ON, Canada

O. O. Samuel
Department of Entrepreneurial Studies, Faculty of Management Sciences, Osun State University, Osogbo, Osun State, Nigeria

J. Bolaji
Department of Marketing and Sales, University of Portsmouth, Portsmouth, UK

A. H. Babatunde
School of Creative and Cultural Business, Robert Gordon University, Aberdeen, Scotland, UK

V. Q. Trinh (ed.), *Climate Governance and Corporate Eco-innovation*, Sustainable Finance, https://doi.org/10.1007/978-3-031-56423-9_12

1 Introduction

THE COVID-19 PANDEMIC has had a devastating impact on the global economy, affecting businesses across all sectors. Small and medium-sized enterprises (SMEs) have been particularly vulnerable to the pandemic's negative effects. Concerns about environmental degradation are now pervasive among businesses worldwide, especially SMEs. In recent years, global awareness and discussions about environmental issues have escalated in the literature. Nevertheless, environmental damage resulting from human and business activities continues to persist.

The COVID-19 pandemic has exacerbated economic challenges globally, making it imperative for businesses to seek competitive advantages to enhance their performance in an increasingly environmentally conscious landscape. Environmental protection is an integral component of sustainable development, as multiple studies have emphasized (Halpern et al., 2019). Issues such as air and water pollution, noise pollution, waste management, and carbon footprints generated by economic production and business activities are gaining significance, especially in regions like sub-Saharan Africa, with Nigeria being no exception (Zhang et al., 2022).

Small businesses, while often viewed as significant contributors to pollution and threats to environmental sustainability, also hold potential as drivers of eco-innovation and economic development (Adomako & Tran, 2022; Meng et al., 2022). Eco-innovation and environmental collaboration are expected to play pivotal roles in addressing environmental challenges and enhancing business performance. Considering that small businesses constitute the majority of enterprises in most countries, both developed and developing, their role in addressing environmental concerns cannot be overlooked (Olubiyi, 2022). By embracing eco-innovation, small business stakeholders and management can explore innovative approaches to producing eco-friendly products and contributing to environmental sustainability.

The performance of business activities, specifically the production and consumption of products and services, plays a crucial role in economic development, environmental preservation, and climate action. Businesses have historically depleted the world's finite natural resources at a rate that not only degrades and pollutes the environment but also presents a growing concern. To address these environmental challenges, the majority of countries within the Organization for Economic Cooperation and Development (OECD) have recognized eco-innovation as a key tool for mitigating negative impacts on the environment. They are actively promoting innovations that focus on renewable resource utilization, environmental protection, pollution control, and waste management, among other factors. The Sustainable Development Goals (SDGs), also referred to as Global Goals or the 2030 Agenda (UNDP, 2017), include Goal 13, which calls for urgent action to combat climate change and its impacts.

Research conducted by Almeida and Wasim (2023) indicates that eco-innovation can help businesses achieve sustainable competitive advantages and align with UN Sustainable Development Goal 13. It enhances brand reputation and fosters increased customer loyalty. In essence, eco-innovation is closely linked to environmental innovation within the business sphere. From a sustainability perspective, ecological innovation, often referred to as eco-innovation, represents an appropriate strategy for businesses seeking to contribute to sustainable development while enhancing their overall performance. To operate in a sustainable and environmentally friendly manner, businesses must embrace organizational, process, and product eco-innovation strategies.

Eco-innovative actions hold significant value for businesses as they enable differentiation from competitors and enhance both operational efficiency and environmental impact. Eco-innovation capabilities encompass process innovation, product innovation, and organizational innovation (Arranz et al., 2019; Šūmakaris et al., 2023; Wang & Yang, 2022). This need for eco-innovative action extends beyond large firms, as small businesses also stand to benefit. Despite the various challenges faced by small enterprises, opportunities exist for them to enhance their performance through eco-innovation. Numerous organizations advocate for eco-innovative actions, including environmental management innovation programs aimed at effectively reducing waste and optimizing resource utilization (Adomako & Tran, 2022; Cheng et al., 2014; Janahi et al., 2021; Zulkiffli et al., 2022).

Box 1
Eco-innovation can help businesses achieve sustainable competitive advantages and align with UN Sustainable Development Goal 13. It enhances brand reputation and fosters increased customer loyalty. In essence, eco-innovation is closely linked to environmental innovation within the business sphere. From a sustainability perspective, ecological innovation, often referred to as eco-innovation, represents an appropriate strategy for businesses seeking to contribute to sustainable development while enhancing their overall performance. To operate in a sustainable and environmentally friendly manner, businesses must embrace organizational, process, and product eco-innovation strategies.

While there has been growing interest in the concept of eco-innovation, it remains relatively unexplored in developing nations like Nigeria. In developed countries, having an effective eco-innovation program and integrating it into a company's management practices is crucial due to increasing pressure from both government regulations and market demands for sustainable service, production, and manufacturing practices. However, many developing nations have yet to adopt such programs. Previous studies examining the relationship between eco-innovation and business performance (Kumar & Ayedee, 2021; Keshminder & Chandran, 2017; Larbi-Siaw et al., 2022) have predominantly focused on developed nations and the performance of individual eco-innovation initiatives. Furthermore, the literature has reported conflicting findings regarding this relationship (Cai & Li, 2018; Cheng et al., 2014; Janahi et al., 2021; Šūmakaris et al., 2023; Wang & Yang, 2022).

Numerous studies have established a positive correlation between eco-innovation and business performance (Kumar & Ayedee, 2021; Munodawafa & Johl, 2019; Zulkiffli et al., 2022). However, there is a lack of research on eco-innovation in small and medium-sized firms (SMEs) in Nigeria. The role of eco-innovation in the sustainability and performance of businesses post-COVID-19 pandemic remains underexplored (Guo et al., 2020; Sanchez-Henriquez & Pavez, 2021). Despite the relevance and interest in eco-innovation, the area of eco-innovative actions has not been thoroughly explored in the scientific literature in Nigeria. There is limited evidence of a connection between eco-innovation and a company's environmental performance in the country. This chapter addresses this research gap and investigates the association between eco-innovative actions and the sustainability performance of small businesses in Lagos State, Nigeria. The study also examines the extent to which small businesses implement eco-innovative actions in Africa's largest economy.

Box 2
In developed countries, having an effective eco-innovation program and integrating it into a company's management practices is crucial due to increasing pressure from both government regulations and market demands for sustainable service, production, and manufacturing practices. However, many developing nations have yet to adopt such programs.

2 Literature Review

2.1 Sustainable Development Goals (SDGs)

Sustainable development is not new and has been defined numerous times (Olubiyi et al., 2023). Sustainable development is described as 'development that meets present demands without jeopardizing future generations' ability to meet their own needs'. The United Nations (UN) approved 17 goals for sustainable development in 2015 (Table 1). 2030 is set to deliver the goals agenda for People, the Planet, and the Profit of businesses. According to Adams, Sustainable Development Goals are a tool for maximizing and creating organizational value and improving business operations' impact on sustainable development. The SDGs are a potent action guide for ensuring a more sustainable planet. The SDGs address many concerns by encouraging healthy living and well-being for all. Therefore, incorporating these SDG activities into businesses is essential for regulators, investors, governments, and millions of consumers since it helps achieve equitable and safe enterprises, future social development, and sustainable economic growth.

United Nations' adoption of the 17 sustainable development goals (SDGs) has provided new opportunities for socially responsible businesses and large entities.

Table 1 The 17 Sustainable Development Goals (SDGs). Source: United Nations website

SDG	Objectives
Goal 1	No poverty
Goal 2	Zero hunger
Goal 3	Good health and Well-being
Goal 4	Quality education
Goal 5	Gender equality
Goal 6	Clean water and sanitation
Goal 7	Affordable and clean energy
Goal 8	Decent work and economic growth
Goal 9	Industry, innovation, and infrastructure
Goal 10	Reduced inequalities
Goal 11	Sustainable cities and communities
Goal 12	Responsible consumption and production
Goal 13	Climate action
Goal 14	Life below water
Goal 15	Life on land
Goal 16	Peace, justice, and strong institutions
Goal 17	Partnership for the goals

Goal 10 is significant and the focus of this study because sustainable development cannot be achieved if any part of the world's population is excluded. Therefore, the reference of the Goal 10 objective in the workplace is ethically justifiable for business effectiveness and various socioeconomic and political outcomes. Therefore, achieving the SDGs, particularly goal 10, requires global collaboration from all stakeholders, including governments, businesses, academic institutions, and the general public (Olubiyi et al., 2023).

Box 3

Sustainable Development Goals are a tool for maximizing and creating organizational value and improving business operations' impact on sustainable development. The SDGs are a potent action guide for ensuring a more sustainable planet. The SDGs address many concerns by encouraging healthy living and well-being for all. Therefore, incorporating these SDG activities into businesses is essential for regulators, investors, governments, and millions of consumers since it helps achieve equitable and safe enterprises, future social development, and sustainable economic growth.

2.2 Eco-Innovative Actions

According to its definition, eco-innovation is the production, assimilation, or exploitation of a product, production process, service, or management or business methods that are novel to the organization (developing or adopting them) and which results, throughout its life cycle, in a reduction of environmental risk, pollution, and other negative impacts of resources used (Adomako & Tran, 2022; Almeida & Wasim, 2023). Eco-innovation refers to developing new processes, products, and services that positively impact the environment. Research has shown that eco-innovation can help firms achieve sustainable competitive advantages, enhance brand reputation, and increase customer loyalty (Hermundsdottir & Aspelund, 2021).

To elucidate its meaning, the OECD highlighted the two characteristics distinguishing eco-innovation from innovation. The first advantage is that it is an innovation that reflects the concept's explicit emphasis on reducing environmental impact, whether or not this effect was intended. According to the second tenet, it also encompasses innovation in social and institutional structures, products, processes, and organizational methods. Eco-innovation can be a viable strategy from a sustainability perspective and help businesses develop sustainably while enhancing their performance. The environmental impact of eco-product innovations arises from their use (e.g., fuel consumption and $CO2$ emissions of automobiles) and disposal (e.g., heavy metals in batteries) instead of their production. Then, to function sustainably and eco-friendly, businesses must implement organizational, process, and product eco-innovation approaches.

Box 4

OECD highlighted the two characteristics distinguishing eco-innovation from innovation. The first advantage is that it is an innovation that reflects the concept's explicit emphasis on reducing environmental impact, whether or not this effect was intended. According to the second tenet, it also encompasses innovation in social and institutional structures, products, processes, and organizational methods. Eco-innovation can be a viable strategy from a sustainability perspective and help businesses develop sustainably while enhancing their performance. The environmental impact of eco-product innovations arises from their use (e.g., fuel consumption and $CO2$ emissions of automobiles) and disposal (e.g., heavy metals in batteries) instead of their production.

2.3 Eco-Organizational Structure

Eco-organization structure implementation refers to the competencies and commitment of organizational members to implement new forms of eco-innovation management. Eco-organizations cannot directly reduce environmental impact but can help implement eco-processes (e.g., in manufacturing) and eco-product innovations. Businesses implementing novel strategies to manage resource usage and pollution effectively are more dedicated to addressing climate change. Further, climate governance is positively correlated with corporate commitment to combating climate change, indicating that businesses with a governance framework that incorporates climate change into corporate strategies can better address climate change-related issues and increase corporate commitment to combating them (Erdoğan et al., 2020; Lin & Zhu, 2019).

Box 5
Eco-organization structure implementation refers to the competencies and commitment of organizational members to implement new forms of eco-innovation management. Climate governance is positively correlated with corporate commitment to combating climate change, indicating that businesses with a governance framework that incorporates climate change into corporate strategies can better address climate change-related issues and increase corporate commitment to combating them.

2.4 *Eco-Product Action*

United Nations Environment Programme (UNEP) has been assisting SMEs from various countries in creating and implementing a business model that integrates sustainability into all business activities based on life cycle thinking and in collaboration with partners across the value chain through its eco-innovation approach. To improve a company's performance and competitiveness, eco-innovation comprises a coordinated set of changes or creative solutions to products (goods/services), processes, market strategy, and organizational structure. SMEs can benefit from this strategy in several ways, including increased productivity, profitability across the value chain, and staying ahead of rules and standards (Gerged et al., 2021). It can also help SMEs access new and expanding markets. When examining a product's life cycle, one must consider all its stages, from raw material extraction through processing, production, distribution, use, repair, and maintenance to disposal or reuse. Utilizing this strategy enables businesses to assess areas where notable advancements can be made about the primary market difficulties and foresee and mitigate upcoming ones. Adopting this perspective in collaboration with suppliers, clients, and other partners along the value chain is best.

Box 6
To improve a company's performance and competitiveness, eco-innovation comprises a coordinated set of changes or creative solutions to products (goods/services), processes, market strategy, and organizational structure. SMEs can benefit from this strategy in several ways, including increased productivity, profitability across the value chain, and staying ahead of rules and standards.

2.5 *Eco-Business Process Action*

Eco-innovation is often considered a foundation for fostering and nurturing SMEs, given the growth these companies have experienced. It has become essential for them to commit to achieving environmental performance, as they originally aimed for economic effectiveness. This shift towards environmental responsibility has become crucial for these institutions.

Organizational, process, and product eco-innovation, which can significantly impact corporate performance, requires dynamic capabilities from a resource-based view (RBV) as proposed by Hair et al. (2018). In addition to reducing environmental risks, environmental innovation and performance improvements lead to cost savings, increased sales of unique products, improved profit margins, enhanced brand value, and a better company reputation within the community.

Environmental regulations have evolved to consider economic, social, and environmental factors (Shah & Ahmad, 2019). Large corporations, due to their substantial investments in research and development, find it easier to adapt to changing environmental legislation. On the other hand, micro and small businesses incorporate innovation into their processes and products through recycling and reusing materials. This environmentally friendly industrial innovation not only benefits the environment but also saves production costs.

Developing an eco-innovation process necessitates the integration of components that consider human health, minimize environmental impacts, and comply with legislative laws. Environmental advancements focus on the product's life cycle, reducing environmental impact through material and energy efficiency improvements, thereby increasing production efficiency (Hair et al., 2018). It is crucial for decision-makers to understand that the only viable path for business growth and expansion is through the adoption of environmental innovation. Given the increasing importance of environmental innovation in raising consumer awareness, both domestic and international customers demand that their suppliers provide products free of dangerous and harmful ingredients. Similarly, businesses are exploring ways to manufacture products with reduced energy and material input (Vaitoonkiat & Charoensukmongkol, 2019).

Box 7

Developing an eco-innovation process necessitates the integration of components that consider human health, minimize environmental impacts, and comply with legislative laws. Environmental advancements focus on the product's life cycle, reducing environmental impact through material and energy efficiency improvements, thereby increasing production efficiency.

2.6 Eco-Technological Capability Action

Along with the innovativeness of the product and the procedures used by SMEs, technology has been seen to impact a company's sustainable business performance significantly. Despite the cost, businesses invest in new technology for its perceived more significant benefits and values. One of the reasons enterprises implement eco-technology capability within the organization is to ensure employee safety. In addition, technological capability is one of the best ways for businesses to meet customer needs, and this can be achieved by developing eco-friendly products that can garner more consumer interest in the modern market. Eco-technology innovation reduces environmental pollutants in the pursuit of sustainability (Sukri et al., 2023; Zhang et al., 2021).

Box 8
One of the reasons enterprises implement eco-technology capability within the organization is to ensure employee safety. In addition, technological capability is one of the best ways for businesses to meet customer needs, and this can be achieved by developing eco-friendly products that can garner more consumer interest in the modern market. Eco-technology innovation reduces environmental pollutants in the pursuit of sustainability.

2.7 Climate Change Action (SDG 13) and Eco-Innovation

An undeniable hazard to our entire civilization is climate change. Without immediate action, the impacts are already apparent and will be disastrous. We can bring the essential reforms to protect the environment via education, innovation, and adherence to our climate obligations. The worldwide community, managers, consumers, media, suppliers, and experts have all expressed worry about climate change as a serious environmental issue in recent years (Krieger & Zipperer, 2022). Additionally, there is a growing call for businesses to demonstrate their accountability and obligation to stakeholders by improving corporate practices connected to climate change commitments from shareholders and governments (Afrifa et al., 2020; Hollindale et al., 2019). Eco-innovation can include the technological advancement that allows businesses to introduce new procedures, techniques, and goods to prevent or lessen environmental harm and promote trash recycling and energy conservation. It is referred to as innovation, which includes creating novel concepts, methods, practices, goods, or methods that lessen environmental burdens while enhancing economic performance (Krieger & Zipperer, 2022).

Box 9
Eco-innovation can include the technological advancement that allows businesses to introduce new procedures, techniques, and goods to prevent or lessen environmental harm and promote trash recycling and energy conservation. It is referred to as innovation, which includes creating novel concepts, methods, practices, goods, or methods that lessen environmental burdens while enhancing economic performance.

3 Empirical Review

The OECD identify four distinct categories of eco-innovation in the Oslo Manual: product innovation, process innovation, organizational innovation, and marketing innovation. The literature suggests that when examining internal innovation, it is advisable to focus on eco-process, eco-products, and eco-organizational innovation activities (Horbach, 2008; Triguero et al., 2013).

Eco-innovation plays a catalytic role in the development of both process and product eco-innovation, and these two types of eco-innovation significantly impact a company's environmental performance. Several researchers have found a positive correlation between eco-innovation and business performance. For instance, Chan et al. (2016) provide evidence showing a positive correlation between Product Design Efficiency (PDE) and a firm's financial performance. Hojnik and Ruzzier (2016) find that Process Carbon Efficiency (PCE) positively impacts the financial performance of businesses, and Weng et al. (2015) demonstrate a positive impact of both process and product eco-innovation on business performance.

However, studies on the implications of eco-innovation, especially concerning climate change, are limited at both macro and micro levels, and they often produce contradictory findings compared to studies on the determinants of eco-innovation (Afrifa et al., 2020; Erdoğan et al., 2020; Ge et al., 2018; Lin & Zhu, 2019; Mongo et al., 2021). Lin and Zhu (2019) argue that innovation can enhance energy efficiency, reducing energy consumption and carbon emissions during production. Mongo et al. (2021) discover that such effects are more noticeable in the long term, but in the short term, the effect may be reversed based on their 23-year research in the most developed European nations. Additionally, Du et al. (2019), using panel data from 71 economies between 1996 and 2012, observe that the mitigating benefits of eco-innovation are primarily present in high-income economies.

Erdoğan et al. (2020) note that the sectoral effects of emission reduction vary, with the energy and transportation sectors showing no discernible impact, the industrial sector showing a negative effect, and the construction sector showing a favourable outcome. Most of the available research on the effects of eco-innovation on reducing carbon emissions is currently conducted at the macro level, with micro-level studies still being relatively rare.

At the micro level, eco-innovative actions are pivotal in helping businesses gain a sustainable competitive advantage (Ge et al., 2018). These actions also enhance environmental management performance, enabling companies to meet stringent ecological protection criteria. Despite the significant implications of eco-innovation for corporate social and environmental responsibility, the relationship between eco-innovation and corporate engagement in climate change initiatives still needs to be explored.

In contrast to traditional innovation, eco-innovative actions tend to be more costly, less predictable, require a longer payback period, and often exhibit a higher failure-to-success ratio (Zaman et al., 2021). Additionally, while startups often dedicate themselves to green missions and focus on eco-innovation, transitioning into green markets and aligning green technological potential with internal competencies can be complex for established organizations (Wicki & Hansen, 2019). Therefore, eco-innovation necessitates increased involvement of top-level management, heightened managerial environmental awareness, the development of internal organizational capacities (Salim et al., 2019), and access to a diverse range of knowledge resources (Conti et al., 2018; Martínez-Ros & Kunapatarawong, 2019).

Box 10
In contrast to traditional innovation, eco-innovative actions tend to be more costly, less predictable, require a longer payback period, and often exhibit a higher failure-to-success ratio.

General innovation theory emphasizes the importance of a corporation's physical and intellectual capital stock, including its technological capacities for creating new products and processes. Technological capabilities, such as accumulated human capital and knowledge, are known to stimulate innovation. Similarly, we propose that eco-innovative actions result from resource orchestration and reflect a firm's capacity and expertise in addressing environmental challenges, such as climate change.

From a legitimacy perspective, recent studies on climate change indicate that companies are taking action to manage the legitimacy gap arising from growing public concern about climate change (Talbot & Boiral, 2018) and to avoid potential financial penalties. Some companies must comply with regulatory policies and stakeholder pressure regarding climate change before making substantial commitments to reduce carbon emissions (Haque & Ntim, 2018).

4 Theoretical Review and Hypotheses Development on Eco-Innovative Actions and Sustainability Performance

Theory of Equity
John Stacey Adams, a workplace and behavioural psychologist, propounded equity theory in 1963 when he established his job incentive theory, according to Davlembayeva and Alamanos. The theory was developed against the lack of theoretical explanation of the psychological basis of inequity perception. Further, Adams contends that people use social comparison by relating their efforts and rewards to those of relevant individuals. Individuals' motivation is influenced by their perceptions of how equitable their rewards are compared to others. The inability to explain the perception of fairness was the top concern for employers and governments, as it revealed the behaviour and attitudes of employees towards organizations. Three social science and psychological theories, namely Social Exchange Theory, Social

Comparison Theory, and the Theory of Cognitive Dissonance, served as the foundation for Equity Theory. People consider equity when they believe their effort-to-reward ratio is identical to those they associate with. When people perceive that their effort-to-reward ratio differs from those they compare themselves to (typically in a negative way), they experience inequality.

Equity theory was employed as the foundation for this study because it advocates the idea of developing a viable workforce based on equity and justice. According to theory, workers are less exploited; there is a greater incentive and better interrelationships among workers. This guarantees that the workforce remains viable and ready to improve performance in the future. According to equity theory, employees need to be treated equally and fairly compensated for their contributions to the bank's performance. The Equity Theory has been criticized for oversimplifying the normative foundation of individuals' social exchange behaviour. Employees develop beliefs about what constitutes a fair and equitable return for their contributions to their jobs. Employees are said to equate what they receive from their employers in exchange for their contributions with what their counterparts obtain. According to the equity hypothesis, employees would be forced to do something about workplace inequity if they believe their care is not equal in comparison to what they believe others are making, resulting in negative outcomes such as job dissatisfaction, lack of interest, and difficulty communicating citizenship behaviours. See Fig. 1 for Authors' Conceptual Model.

$\mathbf{H_{o1:}}$ There is no significant relationship between eco-innovative actions and the business sustainability performance of SMEs in Lagos State, Nigeria post-pandemic.

5 Model Specification

The model sheds light on the relationship between eco-innovative actions and business performance which is the research framework. Given, the mathematical derivative function which gives the value of the slope at any value (x-------$x_{n)}$ since intuition explains that as $\Delta x \rightarrow 0$, then $\Delta y \rightarrow 0$. This can be deduced mathematically since a firm's business performance is a function of eco-innovative actions; $Y = f$ (x_1-----------x_n).

The model specification is given as follows: Eco-innovative actions as it relate to eco-products (EP), eco-business process (EBP), eco-organizational structure (EOS), and eco-technological capability (ETC). This can be expressed in a functional relationship as EA $= f$ (EP, EBP, EOS, ETC). The functional relationship was tested using the Pearson product-moment correlation. The functional relationship is therefore stated:

$$\mathrm{EO} = f\left(\mathrm{EP,EBP,EOS,ETC}\right) \tag{1}$$

where:

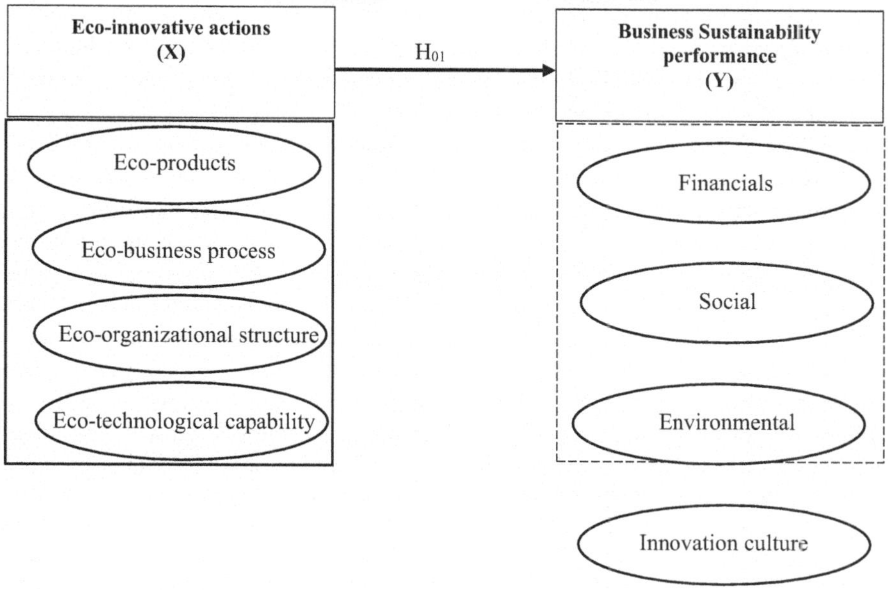

Fig. 1 Authors' conceptual model (2023)

EO = Eco-actions
EP = Eco-products
EBP = Eco-business process
EOS = Eco-organization structure
ETC = Eco-technological capability

Ho$_1$: It is expected that innovative actions (eco-products, eco-business process, eco-organizational structure, and eco-technological capability) will have a positive and significant effect on sustainability performance of SMEs in Lagos State, Nigeria.

6 Methodology

The research context is the structured small businesses, and the study adopted the survey research design. The justification for adopting the survey is its usefulness in assessing the thoughts, opinions, and feelings of different groups of individuals and allowing them to give more valid and honest feedback on the study area. Researchers such as Adeyemi and Olubiyi, Olubiyi et al. (2023), Olubiyi, Egwakhe, and Akinlabi (2019), Olubiyi, Egwakhe, and Egwuonwu (2019), Olubiyi, Lawal, and Adeoye (2022a), Olubiyi (2019), Olubiyi, Lawal, and Adeoye (2022b), Olubiyi (2022a, 2022b), Olubiyi, Jubril et al. (2022), Ukabi et al. (2023), and Uwem et al. (2021) with cross-sectional have adopted and employed a survey research design, which this study is relying on and found it useful. The population comprised 22,466 owners/managers registered with the Small and Medium Enterprises Development Agency of Nigeria (SMEDAN) as of 2021 in Lagos State, the economic hub of Nigeria with the highest number of SMEs.

The Research Advisors Table was adopted to determine the sample size. Using the Research Advisors Table of sample size, given as 378 with a confidence level of 95% and a margin error of 5% from the target population of 22,466. Furthermore, non-responses, improperly filled surveys, and unreturned copies of the questionnaire are common problems in research; therefore, adequate provision is given to this envisaged limitation. As a result, a 30% additional provision was made to cover such differences if they arise, based on the expert's advice (Israel, 2010). As a result, 113 will be added to 378. When this was added to the sample size, it ended up as 491 respondents. The study was contextualized to the small businesses—SMEs in Nigeria due to their contribution to employment and economic growth, and more because of data availability. Nigeria is also the continent of Africa's largest economy, and many of the African countries are emerging economies.

7 Data Analysis, Results, and Discussion of Findings

The main aim was to analyse and clarify the link between workplace inequalities and business effectiveness in selected listed companies in Nigeria. Copies of the questionnaire were distributed to the respondents 491 in total by the researcher and with the help of three research assistants. Then, 480 completed copies of the questionnaire were returned and were found suitable for the study. This corresponds to a response rate of approximately 97.76%. The rest either had unreturned or missing responses; the details of the responses are shown in Table 2.

Restatement of Research Objective and Research Question

Objective: To investigate the combined effect of innovative actions (eco-products, eco-business process, eco-organizational structure, and eco-technological capability) on the sustainability performance of Selected SMEs in Lagos State, Nigeria.

Research Question: How does the combined effect of innovative actions (eco-products, eco-business process, eco-organizational structure, and eco-technological capability) affect the sustainability performance of Selected SMEs in Lagos State, Nigeria?

The objective assessed the combined effect of innovative actions (eco-products, eco-business process, eco-organizational structure, and eco-technological capability) on the sustainability performance of Selected SMEs in Lagos State, Nigeria. On a six-point Likert Scale, the respondents were asked to rate their perception of various items comprising eco-technological capability and SME growth. Frequencies, percentages, mean, and standard deviation were used to summarize the study findings. The findings of the results were previously presented. The findings revealed that (eco-products, eco-business process, eco-organizational structure, and eco-technological capability) and sustainability performance of Selected SMEs in Lagos State, Nigeria. This provides the answer to the research question and enables the researcher to achieve the objective of the study as well.

Restatement of Hypothesis

H_{01}: The combined effect of innovative actions (eco-products, eco-business process, eco-organizational structure, and eco-technological capability) does not significantly affect the sustainability performance of selected SMEs in Lagos State, Nigeria.

Discussion and Findings

Table 3 presents the regression result of the combined effect of innovative actions on the sustainability performance of selected SMEs in Lagos State, Nigeria. Results presented in Table 2 show that the combination of eco-innovative activities (eco-products, eco-business process, eco-organizational structure, and eco-technological capability) significantly sustainability performance development of selected SMEs in Lagos State, Nigeria (Adj. R = 0.678; F = 568.330, $p < 0.05$). The F-statistic, a measure of joint determination, has an estimated value of 568.330 and $p < 0.05$. This implies that eco-innovative action components are jointly crucial in explaining the changes in the sustainability performance of SMEs in Lagos State. This, therefore, means that the regression model has a confidence level of over 95%, hence the high reliability of the results.

Further, the value of Adjusted R-squared was 0.678, implying that strategic innovation components collectively explained 67.8 per cent of the variations in the sustainability performance of SMEs in Lagos State, Nigeria. Based on this result, the null hypothesis (H_{01}), which states that eco-innovative action components do not have significant combined effects on the sustainability performance of SMEs in Lagos State, Nigeria, is hereby rejected. The established regression equation:

$$Y = 28.608 + 1.391EP + 0.807EBP + 0.380EOS + 1.762ETC \tag{2}$$

where:

Y = Sustainability performance
EP = Eco-products
EBP = Eco-business process
EOS = Eco-organization structure
ETC = Eco-technological capability

From the above regression model, the effect of eco-innovative actions (eco-products, eco-business process, eco-organizational structure, and eco-technological

Table 2 Response Rate. Source: Researchers' computation (2023)

Response rate	Frequency	Percentage
Fully filled and returned	480	97.76%
Incomplete or unreturned	11	2.24%
Total	491	100%

Table 3 Multiple Regression result of innovative actions (eco-products, eco-business process, eco-organizational structure, and eco-technological capability) and sustainability performance of SMEs in Lagos State, Nigeria. Source: Researchers Software computation (2023)

Model	Unstandardized Coefficients B	Std. Error	Standardized coefficients Beta	T	Sig.
(Constant)	28.608	3.303		8.660	0.000
Eco-products	1.391	0.053	0.476	26.451	0.000
Eco-business process	0.807	0.064	0.236	12.578	
Eco-organizational structure	0.380	0.060	0.121	6.306	0.000
Eco-technological capability	1.762	0.099	0.330	17.868	0.000
$R^2 = 0.680$; Adj. $R^2 = 0.678$; $F(5,1340) = 568.330$[a]					

[a]Dependent Variable: sustainability performance Researchers computation (2023)

capability) is constant; sustainability performance would be achieved at a unit of 28.608. The regression result shows that eco-innovative actions have a positive relationship with the sustainability performance of SMEs in Lagos State, Nigeria. The coefficient of this variable is 1.391, with a t-value of 26.451. According to the results, the coefficient of this variable is statistically significant at a 5 per cent significance level. The result shows that a unit increase in eco-innovative action would result in a 1.391 increase in the sustainability performance of SMEs in Lagos State, Nigeria. The regression results also show that organizational structure has a positive relationship with sustainability performance. The coefficient of this variable is 0.807 with a t-value of 12.578 ($p < 0.05$). This implies that the coefficient of organizational structure is statistically significant, confirming that organizational structure is an essential determinant of sustainability performance. The result shows that a unit increase in the organizational structure would result in a 0.807 increase in the sustainability performance of SMEs in Lagos State, Nigeria.

Furthermore, the estimation results show a positive relationship between innovation culture and sustainability performance. According to the estimation results, the coefficient of this variable is 0.380. The parameter has a t-statistic of 6.306 and a corresponding p-value of 0.000. This implies that the coefficient of innovative actions is positive and statistically significant at a 5 per cent significance level. The result shows that a unit increase in innovative actions would lead to a 0.380 increase in the sustainability performance of SMEs in Lagos State, Nigeria. The finding revealed that innovative actions (eco-products, eco-business process, eco-organizational structure, and eco-technological capability) combined affected the sustainability performance of SMEs in the state of Lagos.

Also, the finding revealed that eco-technological capability is the most significant determinant of the sustainability performance of SMEs in Lagos State, Nigeria. The result is consistent with Zulkiffli et al. (2022). Also, the study of Adeoti and Adeoti examined eco-technological capability, innovation capacity, and agro-industry development in Nigeria. The study revealed that the global competitiveness of any company depends on its science, technology, and innovation capabilities. However, organizational innovation and collaborations had a weak relationship with organizational performance. Maktoba et al. found that technological innovation capabilities positively influenced the performance of firms in Liaoning and Henan provinces. The study also argues that enhanced innovative ability is associated with competitor orientation, knowledge enhancement, and management capability. This argument supports the position that customers are often only conscious of their needs once they are triggered through marketing efforts. The findings reveal that internal and external factors influence the design of an eco-innovation strategy. However, the relevance of external factors is more significant for SMEs in Nigeria. The findings suggest that small and medium-sized enterprises (SMEs) should prioritize eco-innovation and environmental collaboration to improve their financial, environmental, and social performance, especially during the COVID-19 pandemic. Investing in eco-innovation can reduce costs and increase market competitiveness for small and medium-sized enterprises.

In addition, SMEs can improve their environmental and social performance by collaborating with their suppliers to manage the environment strategically. During the COVID-19 pandemic, the results inform policymakers and stakeholders in developing nations about the significance of eco-innovation and environmental collaboration for small and medium-sized enterprises (SMEs). Policymakers can encourage small and medium-sized enterprises (SMEs) to implement eco-innovation and collaborate with suppliers to enhance their environmental and social performance. The study's limitations suggest that future research should investigate other variables, such as firm size and industry sector, that may influence the relationship between eco-innovation, environmental collaboration, and SME performance. In addition, the findings are limited to a particular nation (Nigeria) and small businesses in Lagos State, Nigeria. Therefore, additional research is required to analyse the topic across countries using various businesses.

8 Policy Implication and Recommendations

The findings from the research have shown critical implications in the area of a direct impact of eco-innovative actions on business sustainability performance in Lagos State, Nigeria. Consequently, it contributes to a broad spectrum of existing research and clarifies prior findings. The study has practical and theoretical implications for businesses in developing economies, particularly in Africa. The study shows that despite the relevance attached to the sustainable development goals and goal thirteen (13), which is reducing climate degradation and pollution, in almost all the SMEs, the awareness among the respondents is low. The organizations' sustainable development goals (SDGs) coverage is very low. The results confirm that SDG awareness levels are low within the SME sector in Lagos State, Nigeria, because many African businesses are yet to realize the relevance and government regulations are only persuasive. Drawing on supporting evidence by the equity theory and prior performance (Arranz et al., 2019; Šūmakaris et al., 2023; Wang & Yang, 2022 Kumar & Ayedee, 2021; Zulkiffli et al., 2022). This study recommends that companies consider and revise their missions, strategies, and management methods to include urgent action to combat climate change and its impacts and emphasize sustainability.

Furthermore, applying best practices in organizational structure is necessary to reduce climate degradation and pollution. This research will aid investors and government agencies in comprehending the relationship between eco-innovative actions (eco-products, eco-business process, eco-organizational structure, and eco-technological capability) and business sustainability performance in various industries, especially in determining the efficacy of goal thirteen (13) sustainable decisions. This study recommends that proper environmental regulations from the government could compel or incentivize the SME sector to make eco-decisions that result in greater resource productivity and efficiency. Therefore, policymakers should establish regulations or provide incentives to encourage businesses to design and implement eco-innovation programmes more effectively.

This study contributes to the existing body of knowledge regarding incorporating SDGs into corporate plans for enhanced sustainability performance within business organizations, particularly SMEs. Implementing eco-innovation in eco-organizations includes co-training programs, eco-product design programs, eco-learning techniques, and creating management teams to deal with eco-issues and eco-management systems. Since eco-innovation is an essential component of businesses' responses to changing environmental conditions, it entails developing and implementing novel concepts for products, processes, behaviours, and regulations. Therefore, companies are encouraged to adopt eco-innovative actions as part of the business strategy, along with collaboration between multiple organizations and civil society, and promote eco-innovations for performance improvement.

9 Conclusion

The capability of adopting eco-innovative actions may support small businesses in overcoming the challenges of environmental or economic changes. This study contributes to the literature devoted to eco-innovative actions by providing insights into what to focus on when implementing eco-innovative actions and capabilities. The impact of eco-innovative actions within the small business space, particularly in SMEs in Lagos State Nigeria, was demonstrated in this study. This investigation increases knowledge and comprehension of implementing eco-innovative actions of businesses in Lagos State, Nigeria. This study's findings assist government agencies, policymakers, and top-tier manufacturing SMEs construct an exceptional innovation platform on which SMEs can rely for assistance and support in preserving their business performance in the future and beyond. The study established a significant relationship between eco-innovative actions and business sustainable performance (Arranz et al., 2019; Šūmakaris et al., 2023; Wang & Yang, 2022 Kumar & Ayedee, 2021; Munodawafa & Johl, 2019; Zulkiffli et al., 2022). SMEs must also collaborate with policymakers, suppliers, and related government agencies to develop eco-innovation capabilities to ensure that the innovation will be adopted more efficiently. These initiatives could give Nigerian SMEs more opportunities to sustain environmental and sustainability difficulties.

Managers should be able to handle this situation in a way that benefits both the individual and the organization. Organizations in sub-Saharan Africa should adopt strategic managerial actions, corporate policies, and human resource practices that can decrease inequalities, improve the shift to sustainable activities, and raise awareness of sustainable development goal ten to prevent inequality-related issues and business ineffectiveness.

The study encountered some methodological restrictions, which posed some limitations to the findings. These limitations thus suggest the need for further studies. The first limitation is that, despite the proposed model providing insight into eco-innovative actions sub-variables and the linkage to affect business sustainability performance in Lagos State, Nigeria. The study model should be replicated in other countries to determine whether it is location sensitive. Therefore, researchers should undertake cross-country comparative studies to compare and contrast the societal context. The second limitation relates to the sample selection and data considered. There may be additional factors influencing workplace inequalities and business effectiveness in other sectors or industries that this study did not account for in previous research. In addition, similar studies may be conducted qualitatively in other nations to provide valuable insights into the factors that may significantly impact workplace inequality and business effectiveness. Future research can expand upon the conclusions of this study.

Declaration of Generative AI and AI-Assisted Technologies in the Writing Process for This Chapter The editor only used ChatGPT (Premium GPT4.0) and Grammarly to proof-read and check for typos and inconsistencies. There is no further declaration from the authors.

References

Adomako, S., & Tran, M. D. (2022). Environmental collaboration, responsible innovation, and firm performance: The moderating role of stakeholder pressure. *Business Strategy and the Environment, 31*(4), 1695–1704.

Afrifa, G. A., Tingbani, I., Yamoah, F., & Appiah, G. (2020). Innovation input, governance and climate change: Evidence from emerging countries. *Technological Forecasting and Social Change, 161*, 120256.

Almeida, F., & Wasim, J. (2023). Eco-innovation and sustainable business performance: Perspectives of SMEs in Portugal and the UK. *Society and Business Review, 18*, 28–50.

Arranz, N., Arroyabe, M. F., Molina-Garcia, A., & Arroyabe, J. C. F. D. (2019). Incentives and inhibiting factors of eco-innovation in the Spanish firms. *Journal of Cleaner Production, 220*, 167–176.

Cai, W., & Li, G. (2018). The drivers of eco-innovation and its impact on performance: Evidence from China. *Journal of Cleaner Production, 176*, 110–118.

Chan, H. K., Yee, R. W. Y., Dai, J., & Lim, M. K. (2016). The moderating effect of environmental dynamism on green product innovation and performance. *International Journal of Production Economics, 181*, 384–391.

Cheng, C. C. J., Yang, C.-L., & Sheu, C. (2014). The link between eco-innovation and business performance: A Taiwanese industry context. *Journal of Cleaner Production, 64*, 81–90.

Conti, C., Mancusi, M. L., Sanna-Randaccio, F., Sestini, R., & Verdolini, E. (2018). Transition towards a green economy in Europe: Innovation and knowledge integration in the renewable energy sector. *Research Policy, 47*(10), 1996–2009.

Du, K., Li, P., & Yan, Z. (2019). Do green technology innovations contribute to carbon dioxide emission reduction? Empirical evidence from patent data. *Technological Forecasting and Social Change, 146*, 297–303.

Erdoğan, S., Yıldırım, S., Yıldırım, D. Ç., & Gedikli, A. (2020). The effects of innovation on sectoral carbon emissions: Evidence from G20 countries. *Journal of Environmental Management, 267*, 1–10.

Ge, B., Yang, Y., Jiang, D., Gao, Y., Du, X., & Zhou, T. (2018). An empirical study on green innovation strategy and sustainable competitive advantages: Path and boundary. *Sustainability, 10*(10), 3631.

Gerged, A. M., Albitar, K., & Al-Haddad, L. (2021). Corporate environmental disclosure and earnings management—The moderating role of corporate governance structures. *International Journal of Finance & Economics, 10*, 1002.

Guo, J., Chen, M., Sun, X., Wang, Z., & Xue, J. (2020). Leveraging indstrial-technological innovation to achieve sustainable development: A systems thinking perspective. *PLoS One, 15*(12), e0242981.

Hair, J. F., Babin, B. J., Anderson, R. E., & Black, W. C. (2018). *Multivariate data analysis* (8th ed.). Cengage India.

Halpern, B., Frazier, M., Afflerbach, J., Lowndes, J. S., Micheli, F., O'Hara, C., Scarborough, C., & Selkoe, K. A. (2019). Recent pace of change in human impact on the world's ocean. *Scientific Reports, 9*(11609), 1–8.

Haque, F., & Ntim, C. G. (2018). Environmental policy, sustainable development, governance mechanisms and environmental performance. *Business Strategy and the Environment, 27*(3), 415–435.

Hermundsdottir, F., & Aspelund, A. (2021). Sustainability innovations and firm competitiveness: A review. *Journal of Cleaner Production, 280*, 124715.

Hojnik, J., & Ruzzier, M. (2016). The driving forces of process eco-innovation and its impact on performance: Insights from Slovenia. *Journal of Cleaner Production, 133*, 812–825.

Hollindale, J., Kent, P., Routledge, J., & Chapple, L. (2019). Women on boards and greenhouse gas emission disclosures. *Accounting and Finance, 59*(1), 277–308.

Horbach, J. (2008). Determinants of environmental innovation-new evidence from German panel data sources. *Research Policy, 37*, 163–173.

Janahi, N. A., Durugbo, C. M., & Al-Jayyousi, O. R. (2021). Eco-innovation strategy in manufacturing: A systematic review. *Cleaner Engineering and Technology, 5*, 100343.

Keshminder, J. S., & Chandran, V. G. R. (2017). Eco-innovation in the chemical manufacturing firms—Insights for policy response. *Institutions and Economies, 9*, 21–42.

Krieger, B., & Zipperer, V. (2022). Does green public procurement trigger environmental innovations? *Research Policy, 51*(6), 104516.

Kumar, A., & Ayedee, N. (2021). An interconnection between COVID-19 and climate change problem. *Journal of Statistics and Management Systems, 24*, 281–300.

Larbi-Siaw, O., Xuhua, H., Owusu, E., Owusu-Agyeman, A., Fulgence, B. E., & Frimpong, S. A. (2022). Eco-innovation, sustainable business performance and market turbulence moderation in emerging economies. *Technology in Society, 68*, 101899.

Lin, B., & Zhu, J. (2019). The role of renewable energy technological innovation on climate change: Empirical evidence from China. *Science of the Total Environment, 659*, 1505–1512.

Martínez-Ros, B., & Kunapatarawong, R. (2019). Green innovation and knowledge: The role of size. *Business Strategy and the Environment, 28*(6), 1045–1059.

Meng, S., Yan, H., & Yu, J. (2022). Global value chain participation and green innovation: Evidence from Chinese listed firms. *International Journal of Environmental Research and Public Health, 19*, 8403.

Mongo, M., Belaïd, F., & Ramdani, B. (2021). The effects of environmental innovations on CO2 emissions: Empirical evidence from Europe. *Environmental Science & Policy, 118*, 1–9.

Munodawafa, R. T., & Johl, S. K. (2019). A systematic review of eco-innovation and performance from the resource-based and stakeholder perspectives. *Sustainability, 11*, 6067.

Olubiyi, T. O. (2019). Knowledge management practices and family business profitability: Evidence from Lagos State, Nigeria. *Global Journal of Management and Business Research, 19*(A11), 21–31.

Olubiyi, T. (2022). Pandemic environment and small businesses. *This Day Newspaper*, 31 January 2022, p. 33.

Olubiyi, T. O. (2022a). Measuring technological capability and business performance post-COVID era: Evidence from small and medium-sized enterprises (SMEs) in Nigeria. *Management & Marketing Journal, xx*(2), 234–248.

Olubiyi, T. O. (2022b). An investigation of sustainable innovative strategy and customer satisfaction in small and medium-sized enterprises (SMEs) in Nigeria. *Covenant Journal of Business and Social Sciences, 13*(2), 1–24.

Olubiyi, T. O., Adeoye, O. O., Jubril, B., Adeyemi, O. S., & Eyanuku, J. P. (2023). Measuring inequality in sub-Saharan Africa post-pandemic: Correlation results for workplace inequalities and implication for sustainable development goal ten. *International Journal of Professional Business Review, 8*(4), e01405.

Olubiyi, T. O., Egwakhe, J., & Akinlabi, B. H. (2019). Knowledge management and family business continuity: The moderating effect of length of time in existence. *Global Journal of Management and Business Research, 19*(5), 29–35.

Olubiyi, T. O., Egwakhe, A. J., & Egwuonwu, T. K. (2019). Managerial roles and competitive advantage: SMEs perspective from Lagos State, Nigeria. *International Journal of Small Business and Entrepreneurship Research, 7*(3), 1–14.

Olubiyi, T. O., Jubril, B., Sojinu, O. S., & Ngari, R. (2022). Strengthening gender equality in small business and achieving sustainable development goals (SDGs), comparative analysis of Kenya and Nigeria. *Sawala Jurnal Administrasi Negara, 10*(2), 168–186.

Olubiyi, O., Lawal, A. T., & Adeoye, O. O. (2022a). Succession planning and family business continuity: Perspectives from Lagos State, Nigeria. *Organization and Human Capital Development, 1*(1), 40–52.

Olubiyi, O. T., Lawal, A. T., & Adeoye, O. O. (2022b). Succession planning and family business continuity: Perspectives from Lagos State, Nigeria. *Organization and Human Capital Development, 1*(1), 40–52.

Salim, N., Ab Rahman, M. N., & Abd Wahab, D. (2019). A systematic literature review of internal capabilities for enhancing eco-innovation performance of manufacturing firms. *Journal of Cleaner Production, 209*, 1445–1460.

Sanchez-Henriquez, F., & Pavez, I. (2021). The effect of open innovation on eco-innovation performance: The role of market knowledge sources. *Sustainability, 13*(7), 3890.

Shah, S. Z. A., & Ahmad, M. (2019). Entrepreneurial orientation and performance of small and medium-sized enterprises. *Competitiveness Review: An International Business Journal, 29*(5), 551–572.

Sukri, N., Zulkiffli, S., Mat, N. H. N., Omar, K., Mawardi, M. K., & Zaidi, N. F. Z. (2023). An analysis of eco-innovation capabilities among small and medium enterprises in Malaysia. *Administrative Sciences, 13*(4), 113.
Šūmakaris, P., Kovaitė, K., & Korsakienė, R. (2023). An integrated approach to evaluating eco-innovation strategies from the perspective of strategic green transformation: A case of the Lithuanian furniture industry. *Sustainability, 15*(11), 8971.
Talbot, D., & Boiral, O. (2018). GHG reporting and impression management: An assessment of sustainability reports from the energy sector. *Journal of Business Ethics, 147*(2), 367–383.
Triguero, A., Moreno-Mondéjar, L., & Davia, M. (2013). Drivers of different types of eco-innovation in European SMEs. *Ecological Economics, 92*, 25–33.
Ukabi, O. B., Uba, U. J., Ewum, C. O., & Olubiyi, T. O. (2023). Measuring entrepreneurial skills and sustainability in small business enterprises post-pandemic: Empirical study from Cross River State, Nigeria. *International Journal of Business, Management and Economics, 4*(2), 132–149.
United Nations Development Programme. (2017). What are the sustainable development goals? www.undp.org
Uwem, E. I., Oyedele, O. O., & Olubiyi, O. T. (2021). Workplace green behavior for sustainable competitive advantage. *Human Resource Management Practices for Promoting Sustainability IGI Global*, 248–263.
Vaitoonkiat, E., & Charoensukmongkol, P. (2019). Interaction effect of entrepreneurial orientation and stakeholder orientation on the business performance of firms in the steel fabrication industry in Thailand. *Journal of Entrepreneurship in Emerging Economies, 12*(4), 453–473.
Wang, Y., & Yang, Y. (2022). Analyzing the green innovation practices based on sustainability performance indicators: A Chinese manufacturing industry case. *Environmental Science and Pollution Research, 28*, 1181–1203.
Weng, H. H., Chen, J. S., & Chen, P. C. (2015). Effects of green innovation on environmental and corporate performance: A stakeholder perspective. *Sustainability, 7*, 4997–5026.
Wicki, S., & Hansen, E. G. (2019). Green technology innovation: Anatomy of exploration processes from a learning perspective. *Business Strategy and the Environment, 28*(6), 970–988.
Zaman, R., Atawnah, N., Haseeb, M., Nadeem, M., & Irfan, S. (2021). Does corporate eco-innovation affect stock price crash risk? *British Accounting Review, 53*(5), 101031.
Zhang, X., Meng, Q., & Le, Y. (2022). How do new ventures implementing green innovation strategy achieve performance growth? *Sustainability, 14*, 2299.
Zhang, Y., Yanying, M., Liudan, J., Chenyang, S., & Heshan, Z. (2021). Eco-efficiency, eco-technology innovation and eco-Well-being performance to improve global sustainable development. *Environmental Impact Assessment Review, 89*, 1–11.
Zulkiffli, S. N. A., Zaidi, N. F. Z., Padlee, S. F., & Sukri, N. K. A. (2022). Eco-innovation capabilities and sustainable business performance during the COVID-19 pandemic. *Sustainability, 14*, 7525.

Olubiyi Timilehin Olasoji is a well-known author, senior government official, researcher, and business expert. Dr. Timi Olubiyi, as he is affectionately known, is a seasoned professional and a scholar of high repute. A Chartered Member of the Chartered Institute for Securities & Investment (CISI) England and Member Institute of Directors(M.IoD) UK with M.Phil. and Ph.D. Degrees in Business Administration. He has relevant expertise in the Nigerian financial industry and academia, including public service. His background includes stockbroking, fund management, consulting, and education. An affiliate of Babcock University Nigeria's Department of Business Administration and Marketing, an adjunct lecturer at the National Open University of Nigeria Department of Business Administration, and also an adjunct lecturer at the Department of Business Administration, Caleb University, Imota, Lagos, Nigeria. Dr. Timi Olubiyi has several papers, monographs, and opinions published in high-impact academic journals and several renowned newspapers worldwide on small business, entrepreneurship, sustainability, innovation, knowledge management, enterprise continuity, succession, strategy, policy, and leadership. An academic, a peer reviewer, and a member of the editorial board of many high-impact academic journals, including Scopus, EBSCO, and DOAJ-indexed.

Ravinder Rena is a profound academician and distinguished scholar in economics with over 31 years of teaching and research experience. Prof Rena is a Professor of Economics at the DUT Business School, Faculty of Management Sciences, Durban University of Technology, South Africa. He also serves as an Adjunct Professor of Economics at Monarch Business School, Monarch University, Switzerland. He published widely in development economics, especially on African issues. He published over 150 peer-reviewed articles in reputable journals and 50 chapters in edited books across the globe. He is the founding Editor-in-Chief of the International Journal of Education, Economics and Development. He supervised over 60 PhDs, M.Phils, and Masters' theses and dissertations across the globe. He served on many academic and professional committees as a chairman and panel member. He has also been an external examiner/moderator for Masters and PhD at different universities in Africa, Europe, Asia, America, and Australia.

Valerie Onyia Babatope is an experienced scholar who currently works in McMaster University, a prestigious university in Canada. She is also an HR consultant with a demonstrated history of working in the higher education industry and offering solutions to HR needs in organizations. Skilled in Youth Leadership, Human Resource Management, Business Intelligence, and Business Management, she is a strong higher education professional with a Doctor of Philosophy in Business Administration and focused on research interests such as Mentoring, Sustainable business, and Organizational Behaviour. She teaches future HR professionals and designs HR course content, writes curriculum, and facilitates online learning in business and HR courses.

Omoyele Olufemi Samuel is a Senior Lecturer at the Department of Entrepreneurial Studies, Osun State University, Osogbo, Oyo State, Nigeria. President/Chairman Governing Council at the Chartered Institute of Human Resource Management. A former Director, Centre for Entrepreneurial Skills and Development, Redeemer's University, Ede, Osun State, Nigeria. The Chairman, Conference Committee, Faculty of Management Sciences, Osun State University, Osogbo Osun State Nigeria and Chairman, Faculty Journal verification committee, Osun State University, Osun State, Nigeria. Member, Central Journal verification committee, Osun State University, Osogbo, Osun State, Nigeria.

Bolaji Jubril studied Sales Management at the Department of Marketing and Sales, University of Portsmouth. With almost two decades of professional service in marketing communications in Nigeria. Bolaji is currently doing research in Sustainable development, Social Stratification, Sharing Economy, Entrepreneurship and innovation, Communication and Media and Qualitative Social Research.

Akinlabi Hameed Babatunde is an accomplished lecturer at Edinburgh Napier University, Edinburgh. He holds a degree in Economics, Business Administration, Business Analytics, Transport Planning, and Operations Research. With 11 years of teaching experience, Babatunde has published over 100 articles in local and international journals, earning him over 1600 Google Scholar citations. He possesses strong analytical skills in statistical software and is a member of the reviewer's committee for an international journal. His academic achievements, teaching experience, and dedication to research make him a highly respected professional in business administration and operations research fields.

Unboxing Eco-Innovation and ESG for Circular Economy

Md. Abu Toha, Parvez Alam Khan, Fatima Irfan, Mohd Salim, and Mantasha Khan

Abstract This chapter provides empirical evidence on the association between eco-innovation and ESG in Malaysia. First, this study proposes an econometric model based on the emerging Malaysian economy with the resource-based view theory. It then develops a multiple regression for the panel data for 6 years from 2016 to 2021 to test the econometric model and proposed hypothesis. The analysis reveals a positive and significant relationship between eco-innovation and ESG. This finding indicates that eco-innovation enhances ESG practices in the firm and contributes to circular economy practices in the industrial sector.

1 Introduction

Globally, corporations are increasingly encouraged to broaden their operational scope by proactively addressing ecological, social, and governance (ESG) challenges within the context of eco-innovation and the circular economy (De Jesus et al., 2018; De Jesus & Mendonça, 2018; Smol et al., 2017). The endorsement of the 2030 Agenda marked a pivotal step towards integrating ESG considerations with circular economy principles into organisational objectives and contemporary

M. A. Toha
National University, Gazipur, Bangladesh

P. A. Khan (✉)
Management and Humanities Department, University Technology PETRONAS, Seri Iskandar, Perak, Malaysia
e-mail: parvez.khan@utp.edu.my

F. Irfan
Department of Commerce and Business Management, Integral University, Lucknow, India

M. Salim
Department of Commerce, Aligarh Muslim University, Aligarh, India

M. Khan
Faculty of Commerce, KMCL University, Lucknow, India

V. Q. Trinh (ed.), *Climate Governance and Corporate Eco-innovation*, Sustainable Finance, https://doi.org/10.1007/978-3-031-56423-9_13

business models (Demirel et al., 2019; Maldonado-Guzmán et al., 2020; Vence & Pereira, 2019). This transition is further substantiated by recent research from Bloomberg Intelligence (2021), which predicts that global ESG assets could reach $41 trillion by 2022 and $50 trillion by 2025, constituting roughly one-third of the total global assets (BI, 2021). This trend continues the trajectory observed when ESG assets surpassed the $35 trillion mark in 2020. Additionally, the practice of resource reuse is seen as economically advantageous. According to statistics from Bloomberg Intelligence (2021) related to the circular economy, recycling solid waste can result in $101 more in salary per ton than disposing of it in a landfill (BI, 2021).

Two distinct forces drive this study. Firstly, the globe is grappling with a pressing environmental crisis characterised by the rapid acceleration of global warming and climate change (Yusuf et al., 2023), which poses significant obstacles to societal development. It is estimated that climate change endangers the lives of approximately 2.7 billion individuals worldwide. Secondly, many corporations continue to employ outdated business models in the context of the Internet of Things, machine intelligence, and the information age. This obsolete approach produced 36.83 million tons of carbon dioxide and 7.70 million metric tons of solid waste in 2018, accompanied by a 2.3% increase in energy consumption (Qureshi et al., 2022). Consequently, to enhance the current pace of social development, replacing these conventional business models with sustainable practices is imperative.

Much literature has contributed to eco-innovation, ESG, or the circular economy. However, only a few studies have simultaneously addressed all three factors, as Table 1 (see below) illustrates. Furthermore, most have focused on developed economies at the macroeconomic level, with very few investigations into micro-level factors in emerging economies such as Malaysia. Therefore, our chapter fills the gap by investigating how eco-innovation influences the circular economy in Malaysia and further exploring the mediating role of ESG in such a relationship, with the underlying theoretical framework rooted in the resource-based view theory. We believe that introducing ESG as a mediating variable represents a novel approach, being the first to explore its role in mediating the relationship between eco-innovation and the circular economy.

Our study carries some important practical implications. Firstly, senior-level managers should promote a strong business identity to customers by demonstrating their commitment to environmental concerns by offering eco-friendly products. This proactive stance can enhance their companies' environmental reputation. Furthermore, a robust ecological image is anticipated to impact the company's financial performance positively. Consequently, by building such reputations, firms can strengthen their relationships with internal and external stakeholders. This research recommends that businesses adopt eco-innovation strategies to promote ESG and Circular Economy principles within their operational processes.

Additionally, eco-innovation can contribute to the economic dimension of the circular economy by improving cost-effectiveness by introducing eco-friendly products and utilising recycled waste materials. Implementing organisational eco-innovation and green human resource management practices within an organisation

Table 1 Brief literature

Authors	Year	Study brief overview
Blinova et al. (2022)	2022	The philosophical underpinnings of corporate sustainability, features and categorisation of definitions, and the interaction between corporate sustainability, sustainability at the micro level, and CE are all covered in this article. From the perspective of sustainability, the impact of the mining sector on the environmental, economic, and social development of both a nation with a resource-based economy and specific mining areas is demonstrated via the analysis of the case of Russia.
N. Cudečka-Puriņa et al. (2022)	2022	The current study focused on Industry 4.0 as one of the circular economy's business models. It assessed the advantages of symbiosis and the promotion of collaboration across industries, and as a result, it significantly affected resource efficiency ratios. The study employs both quantitative and qualitative research techniques, including a triangulation method application, evaluation, and a literature review.
Hadro et al. (2022)	2022	This study examines the most often revealed subjects regarding the environmental, social, and governance (ESG) dimensions to determine if non-financial disclosure inside the construction industry satisfies stakeholders' information demands.
Alkaraan et al. (2022)	2022	Quantitative analysis is also used to investigate how CTTI 4.0 data affects financial performance. According to the report, strategic investment decision-making (SIDM) procedures for CTTI4.0 have become more advanced over time and differ according to industry sectors. Additionally, it discovers that CTTI4.0 disclosure enhances financial performance. The study also reveals that environmental, social, and governance (ESG) policies modify the association between CTTI4.0 disclosure and financial performance.
Whenish and Ramakrishna (2022)	2022	In order to attain a zero-carbon economy in the foreseeable future, governments and industries are encouraged to embrace circular economy principles based on the three sustainability pillars of environmental, social, and governance (ESG). The primary contributors to carbon emissions are the extraction, processing, and subsequent waste management of resources. The implementation of circular economy ideas by major technology companies and their deliberate shift towards a commitment to zero-carbon emissions through the 3R (reduce, reuse, and recycle) principles were explored from this perspective.
Krause et al. (2022)	2022	An industry CE framework should be developed to provide direction to decision-makers in assessing promising initiatives.
Morea et al. (2022)	2022	Even though ESG ratings do not represent superior performance per se, writers discover whether ESG profiles have such a beneficial influence on stock performance. The analysis also reveals that there is currently no proof that CE initiatives may affect stock returns.
Sepetis (2021)	2021	At the global financial and commercial level, there is a need for a collaborative effort between the public and private sectors to transition towards sustainable financing and circular business models. ESG and circular risks are discussed within this idea's context, and financial changes are suggested.

(continued)

Table 1 (continued)

Authors	Year	Study brief overview
Sparacino et al. (2021)	2021	Companies may measure their influence on the 17 SDGs and the three ESG aspects using a qualitative examination of the interdependence amongst nine categories, grouping many environmental, social, and governance variables.
Toha et al. (2020)	2020	This study aims to investigate five dimensions of eco-innovation with societal development focusing on the fishbone eco-innovation.
García-Granero et al. (2018)	2021	This study suggested the eco-innovation indicators measure four types of eco-innovation at the micro level.

can enhance the social dimension of the circular economy. Moreover, proactive technical eco-innovation for green pollution management can assist companies in enhancing their environmental performance in the context of the circular economy (Khan et al., 2023). The overall performance across these three dimensions of the circular economy aims to enhance the environmental standing of the company. Consequently, this research is designed to assist businesses in developing sustainable business strategies and taking initial steps towards embracing eco-innovation and ESG principles.

The study's structure is as follows: It begins with a brief introduction, followed by a comprehensive literature review covering eco-innovation, ESG, and the circular economy. The third section presents the conceptual and theoretical framework, followed by a discussion of the methodology. The fourth section includes data analysis and model discussion, along with the presentation of findings. Finally, the study concludes with a relevant summary of significant contributions and recommendations.

2 Related Work

2.1 Eco-Innovation and Its Dimensions

There are five specific dimensions of eco-innovation (Toha et al., 2020), which are summarised as below:

Product eco-innovation refers to creating or developing products to reduce environmental risks and improve sustainability (Toha et al., 2022). This term encompasses using resources to manufacture goods with a reduced environmental impact while enhancing product quality and sustainability. Such products and services often prioritise eco-design to minimise the overall environmental footprint of production, earning them the label of 'eco-products' and attracting consumers' attention (Akhtar et al., 2020; Khan and Johl, 2019). Product eco-innovation involves the creation of products or services that are either novel or significantly more efficient for their intended purposes (Johl & Toha, 2021; Toha et al., 2020; Toha & Johl, 2021a).

Process eco-innovation involves the application of new or significantly improved manufacturing or distribution methods aimed at accelerating the reduction of environmental impacts through substantial changes. Research has identified several characteristics that enhance and optimise a company's clean production processes, including using fewer materials, reducing risks, and cost savings (Khan et al., 2020; Khan et al., 2021). Two commonly used terms in process eco-innovation are 'cleaner production' in manufacturing and 'end-of-pipe technology' in the production line. It has been suggested that process eco-innovation encompasses 'end-of-pipe technology and cleaner manufacturing technologies' (Johl & Toha, 2021). Additionally, recent developments in process eco-innovation now encompass implicit environmental improvements focusing on sustainability and explicit ecological performance.

Technological eco-innovation: Rapid technological advancements drive the fourth industrial revolution, leading to significant global transformation. Examples of technological eco-innovation within companies include investments in environmentally friendly machinery and the adoption of innovative green production techniques (De Jesus et al., 2021; Demirel et al., 2019; Maldonado-Guzmán et al., 2020). Usman et al., (2023) and Khan et al., (2023) emphasise the importance of technological eco-innovations in managing credentials and data and providing information for comprehensive material-saving programs. The literature suggests that businesses require substantial internal competencies and physical resources to undertake technological eco-innovation, given its complexity (Johl & Toha, 2021; Toha et al., 2022; Toha & Johl, 2021b).

Organisational eco-innovation involves changes in management structure, workplace arrangements, or external interactions to allocate responsibilities and decision-making regarding the division of labour within and across client activities. Organisational eco-innovation entails establishing various ecological rules and guidelines to reduce environmental impact and enhance sustainability (Johl & Toha, 2021; Toha et al., 2020).

Marketing eco-innovation involves using novel marketing strategies linked to material product positioning, promotion, pricing, or design changes. These changes aim to mitigate the negative ecological impact on society while aligning with sustainability goals. Researchers aim to identify these critical marketing strategies that motivate consumers to make eco-friendly purchases and support sustainability efforts. Marketing eco-innovation can manifest in various forms, including product positioning, pricing strategies, eco-labelling, and product design or packaging.

Box 1

There are five specific dimensions of eco-innovation: Product eco-innovation; Process eco-innovation; Technological eco-innovation; Organisational eco-innovation; and Marketing eco-innovation.

2.2 Circular Economy

The circular economy (CE) represents a strategic approach promoting sustainable and cyclical resource utilisation (see Demirel et al., 2019; Vence & Pereira, 2019). CE has gained recent prominence as a strategy to reduce environmental burdens while fostering economic growth. It is a comprehensive concept centred on minimising material consumption and waste generation to derive economic benefits from resource utilisation. Numerous countries worldwide are now embracing CE, employing methods such as material flow analysis, energy performance evaluation, and input–output analysis to monitor its implementation on a large scale (De Jesus et al., 2018; Demirel et al., 2019; Vence & Pereira, 2019).

The foundations of the CE can be traced back to the work of Stahel and Reday, who emphasised aspects of industrial economics. They introduced the concept of a 'loop economy' to illustrate strategies for reducing industrial waste, promoting local employment, improving resource efficiency, and achieving dematerialisation. According to Stahel, the most effective and sustainable business strategy involves selling services rather than just products. This approach allows businesses to generate profits without externalising the costs and risks associated with waste disposal to the public. The modern conception of the 'Circular Economy' incorporates principles and ideas from diverse disciplines, aiming to achieve closed-loop processes in business and economics (Demirel et al., 2019; Vence & Pereira, 2019). Notably, the cradle-to-cradle theory has had a significant theoretical influence (Maldonado-Guzmán et al., 2020; Stankevičienė et al., 2020; Vence & Pereira, 2019).

Box 2
The circular economy represents a strategic approach promoting sustainable and cyclical resource utilisation. It has gained recent prominence as a strategy to reduce environmental burdens while fostering economic growth. It is a comprehensive concept centred on minimising material consumption and waste generation to derive economic benefits from resource utilisation.

2.3 The Mediating Role of ESG

Corporate ESG disclosures related to the SDGs and the Paris Agreement provide information on a company's environmental, social conscience, and governance operations (Khan et al., 2023; Elgharbawy et al., 2024; Elgharbawy et al., 2023) ESG initiatives and transparent reporting can offer an additional strategy for addressing societal problems and enhancing business value (Khan et al, 2021). Developing a well-modelled framework that various stakeholders can understand is the first step in creating ESG initiatives for a sustainable future. To achieve this, it is essential to establish an adaptable ESG model for each country, considering its unique economic and social conditions.

There are several contributing factors and anticipated outcomes of corporate ESG adoption. Firstly, management may decide to implement ESG at a strategic level. A company's sustainability efforts can increase firm value, promote sustainability, differentiate it from competitors, reduce costs, enhance employee engagement, and foster consumer loyalty.

Secondly, implementing ESG can help manage risk and opportunity, benefiting management, staff, stakeholders in the supply chain, and clients. According to Nam et al., corruption poses a survival threat to newly established businesses and can negatively impact profitability and stock values (Salim et al., 2023). Effective risk management can be a preventive measure that supports companies in becoming more sustainable (Khan et al., 2022; Khan, Johl, Singh, et al., 2021). When management can address or prevent issues from occurring in the first place, costs are reduced. Corporate reputation should also be part of risk management. Negative news reports about criminal activity have a more significant impact on business revenues than operational offences (De Jesus et al., 2021; Kiefer et al., 2021; Patil et al., 2021; Senadheera et al., 2021).

Thirdly, embracing ESG is a company's responsibility as a member of society, regardless of whether it is mandated by law or regulation. Adopting ESG disclosures alone does not make a corporation ethical, but it does make it more ethically conscious when making relevant decisions (Cudečka-Puriņa et al., 2022; Dicuonzo et al., 2022; Montalbetti, 2022). ESG rating companies and other financial institutions can be seen as change agents when evaluating company practices.

A crucial point is that corporate adoption of ESG can benefit the company's stakeholders. Institutional investors are increasingly interested in mainstream ESG investing for two reasons (Jalil et al., 2023). Firstly, ESG investing actively promotes ethical investment practices. Secondly, ESG investments are believed to enhance managed portfolio performance, increase returns, and reduce portfolio risk. After considering the research gaps discussed in the introduction and literature review sections, the following two hypotheses could be developed (Morea et al., 2022; Sepetis, 2022; Triguero et al., 2022).

H1: Eco-innovation has a significant and positive relationship with a Circular economy in emerging economies.

H2: ESG mediates the relationship between eco-innovation and Circular economy in emerging economies.

3 Theoretical Framework and Model Development

The conceptual and theoretical framework of eco-innovation represents an enhanced model that incorporates ESG and CE. Building on identified research gaps and guided by the resource-based view theory, the current study proposes a novel model to explore the influence of eco-innovation on CE, with ESG serving as a mediating factor.

In our proposed model, eco-innovation is the independent variable and encompasses five dimensions: product eco-innovation, process eco-innovation, technology eco-innovation, organisational eco-innovation, and marketing eco-innovation. Concurrently, ESG functions as the mediating variable, comprising three dimensions: environmental, social, and governance. Specifically, products, processes, and technology are linked to the ecological dimension, while organisational and marketing dimensions are associated with the governance and social dimensions.

The ultimate dependent variable in this proposed model is the CE, and this relationship aligns with the resource-based view theory. The proposed model posits that eco-innovation, with its five dimensions focusing on environmental aspects, is intricately linked to the broader context of CE. Moreover, ESG is recognised as an integral component of emerging economic sustainable development in the foreseeable future.

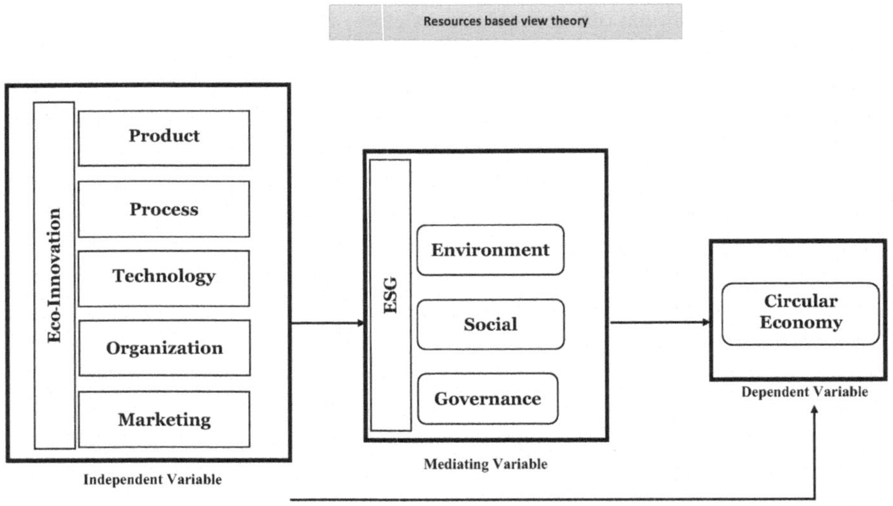

4 Methodology

Our study adopts a quantitative approach, explicitly focusing on emerging economies. Malaysia is among the prominent emerging economies in the global economic landscape. Therefore, the research was conducted on publicly listed Malaysian companies, specifically the top 50, selected based on their market capitalisation on the Bursa Malaysia stock exchange.

This study employs panel data spanning the years from 2016 to 2021, forming a sample of 300 firm-year observations. The use of panel data is preferred as it provides a more transparent and robust foundation for empirical investigations related to Eco-innovation, ESG, and CE. To measure these variables, the study draws upon existing indices: eco-innovation (Toha & Johl, 2021a), ESG (Gutiérrez-Ponce et al., 2022), and CE (Moraga et al., 2019).

However, it is important to note that all items within these indices were carefully adapted and modified to suit the context of emerging economies, with input from academic and industry experts. Subsequently, panel data were collected from the annual and sustainability reports of the respective companies.

Two econometric models were developed per this study's research problem and objective. The first model was based on the relationship between eco-innovation and CE. The second model was based on the mediating role of ESG between eco-innovation and CE.

The two models are as follows.

$$CE_{it} = \beta_0 + \beta_1 \, eco-innovation_{it} + \varepsilon \tag{1}$$

$$CE_{it} = \beta_0 + \beta_1 \, eco-innovation_{it} + \beta 2 ESG_{it} + \varepsilon \tag{2}$$

The selection of the most appropriate regression model should, as suggested by Borenstein et al., be primarily based on how well the model aligns with the distribution of effect sizes and accounts for relevant sources of error. The process of choosing the best regression model involves two phases. Firstly, to decide between the Pooled OLS (Ordinary Least Squares) regression model and the GLS (Generalised Least Squares) model, this study conducts the Breusch-Pagan Lagrangian multiplier tests. Secondly, the Hausman Test is employed to determine whether a fixed or random effect model should be used. Based on the outcomes of these model selection tests, the GLS random effect model was chosen for testing the hypothesis.

5 Findings and Discussion

Table 2 reports the random effect GLS regression model co-efficient findings. It shows a positive beta = 0.496 with a p-value = 0.000 (> 0.05) with Z statistics 9.060 for model 1. In addition to checking the goodness-of-fit of model 1, this study applied Wald Chi2 (2) and Prob > Chi2 test. The figures of Wald Chi2 (1) = 82.00, with Prob > Chi2 = 0.000, are revealed in Table 2. The meaning of the result (Prob > Chi2 = 0.000) approves the goodness-of-fit for model 1 of the study, and it means that the overall model is significant in the forecast of increasing the CE. It is inferred that eco-innovation has a significant positive effect on CE. This result also supports hypothesis H1.

The second model was based on mediation analysis. The model's mediation could be investigated in four steps. Several authors advise following these four steps. The following are general guidelines for these steps: Step 1: In path (a), the independent variable (X) should have a significant effect on the mediating variable

Table 2 Eco-innovation and Circular Economy

	CE
Eco_innovation	0.496*** (0.000)
Firm_age	0.622*** (0.000)
Firm_size	0.591*** (0.000)
Constant	0.245*** (0.000)
No of observations	300
R-square	0.0891
Wald Chi 2	82***

This table reports the regression results on the association between Eco-innovation and Circular Economy. P-values are reported in parentheses. ***, **, and * denote the significance level of 1%, 5%, and 10%, respectively

Table 3 The mediating effect of ESG

Independent variable	Mediating variable	Dependent variable	Step 1	Step 2	Step 3	Step 4	Type of mediation
Eco-innovation	ESG	Circular economy	Coef.	Coef.	Coef.	Coef.	Full mediation
			0.496*** (0.000)	0.513*** (0.000)	0.733*** (0.000)	0.154*** (0.001)	
						0.662*** (0.000)	

This table reports the regression results on the mediating effect of ESG on the association between Eco-innovation and Circular Economy. *P*-values are reported in parentheses. ***, **, and * denote the significance level of 1%, 5%, and 10%, respectively

(M); Step 2: In path (b), the mediating variable (M) should have a significant impact on the dependent variable (Y); Step 3: In path (c) independent variables (X) have a significant impact on dependent variables (Y). Step 4: In path (c'), the effect of independent variables (X) must change on the dependent variables (Y) after controlling the effect of mediating variable (M). Table 3 illustrates the result of the mediation of ESG between eco-innovation and CE. It was inferred from Table 3 that there is a full mediation of ESG in the relationship. Therefore, this result supports the H2 hypothesis in this study.

6 Conclusion

Our research indicates a positive association between eco-innovation and the circular economy. Additionally, it was observed that ESG plays a mediating role in the relationship between eco-innovation and the circular economy. The study suggests that companies adopting a proactive approach to eco-innovation, along with its specific dimensions, can significantly enhance and accelerate the development of the micro-level circular economy in emerging economies. Furthermore, it was noted that ESG itself positively impacts the circular economy, as eco-innovation contributes positively to ESG. The three pillars of ESG also play a role in promoting circular economy concepts in emerging economies.

Like any study, this research has its limitations. Future investigations into the mentioned relationships could employ mixed methods to yield more comprehensive results. Researchers may also consider studying ESG as a dependent variable, focusing on individual factors in a comparative analysis between developed and developing economies. Additionally, conducting a meta-analysis and systematic literature review on eco-innovation, ESG, and the circular economy could shed light on future research directions in these domains.

Declaration of Generative AI and AI-Assisted Technologies in the Writing Process for This Chapter The editor only used ChatGPT (Premium GPT4.0) and Grammarly to proof-read and check for typos and inconsistencies. There is no further declaration from the authors.

References

Akhtar, S., Khan, T., & Khan, P. A. J. J. o. C. R. (2020). Examine the key drivers affecting bottom line: A panel estimation study of Indian commercial bank. *Journal of Critical Reviews, 7*(9), 2020.

Alkaraan, F., Albitar, K., Hussainey, K., & Venkatesh, V. G. (2022). Corporate transformation toward industry 4.0 and financial performance: The influence of environmental, social, and governance (ESG). *Technological Forecasting and Social Change, 175*, 121423.

Blinova, E., Ponomarenko, T., & Knysh, V. (2022). Analyzing the concept of corporate sustainability in the context of sustainable business development in the mining sector with elements of circular economy. *Sustainability (Switzerland), 14*(13), 8163.

Cudečka-Puriņa, N., Atstāja, D., Koval, V., Purviņš, M., Nesenenko, P., & Tkach, O. (2022). Achievement of sustainable development goals through the implementation of circular economy and developing regional cooperation. *Energies, 15*(11), 4072.

De Jesus, A., Antunes, P., Santos, R., & Mendonça, S. J. J. (2018). Eco-innovation in the transition to a circular economy: An analytical literature review. *Journal of Cleaner Production, 172*, 2999–3018.

De Jesus, A., Lammi, M., Domenech, T., Vanhuyse, F., & Mendonça, S. J. S. (2021). Eco-innovation diversity in a circular economy: Towards circular innovation studies. *Sustainability, 13*(19), 10974.

De Jesus, A., & Mendonça, S. J. E. (2018). Lost in transition? Drivers and barriers in the eco-innovation road to the circular economy. *Ecological Economics, 145*, 75–89.

Demirel, P., Danisman, G. O. J. B. S., & Environment, T. (2019). Eco-innovation and firm growth in the circular economy: Evidence from European small-and medium-sized enterprises. *Business Strategy and the Environment, 28*(8), 1608–1618.

Dicuonzo, G., Donofrio, F., Ranaldo, S., & Dell'Atti, V. J. M. A. R. (2022). The effect of innovation on environmental, social and governance (ESG) practices (ahead-of-print).

Elgharbawy, A. A., Syed Putra, S. S., Khan, H. W., Azmi, N. A. N., Sani, M. S. A., Ab Llah, N., et al. (2023). Menthol and fatty acid-based hydrophobic deep eutectic solvents as media for enzyme activation. *PRO, 11*(2), 547.

Elgharbawy, A. A., Khan, H. W., Noor, N. M., Putra, S. S. S., Ismail, E. N. E., Hizaddin, H. F., et al. (2024). Antibacterial performance enhancement using hydrophobic deep eutectic solvents: COSMO-RS prediction, experimental validation, and synergistic action with antibiotics. *Journal of Molecular Liquids, 396*, 124008.

García-Granero, E. M., Piedra-Muñoz, L., & Galdeano-Gómez, E. (2018). Eco-innovation measurement: A review of firm performance indicators. *Journal of Cleaner Production, 191*, 304–317.

Gutiérrez-Ponce, H., Chamizo-González, J., & Arimany-Serrat, N. J. S. (2022). Disclosure of environmental, social, and corporate governance information by Spanish companies: A compliance analysis. *Sustainability, 14*(6), 3254.

Hadro, D., Fijałkowska, J., Daszyńska-Żygadło, K., Zumente, I., & Mjakuškina, S. (2022). What do stakeholders in the construction industry look for in non-financial disclosure and what do they get? *Meditari Accountancy Research, 30*(3), 762–785. https://doi.org/10.1108/MEDAR-11-2020-1093

Johl, S. K., & Toha, M. A. J. S. (2021). The nexus between proactive eco-innovation and firm financial performance: A circular economy perspective. *Sustainability, 13*(11), 6253.

Khan, P. A., Johl, S. K., Akhtar, S. J. J., & Management, F. (2022). Vinculum of sustainable development goal practices and firms' financial performance: A moderation role of green innovation. *Journal of Risk and Financial Management, 15*(3), 96.

Khan, P. A., Johl, S. K., Kumar, A., & Luthra, S. (2023). Hope-hype of green innovation, corporate governance index, and impact on firm financial performance: a comparative study of Southeast Asian countries. *Environmental Science and Pollution Research, 30*(19), 55237–55254.

Khan, P. A., Johl, S. K., Johl, S. K. J. B. S., & Environment, T. (2021). Does adoption of ISO 56002-2019 and green innovation reporting enhance the firm sustainable development goal performance? An emerging paradigm. *Business Strategy and the Environment, 30*(7), 2922–2936.

Khan, P. A., Johl, S. K., & Akhtar, S. (2021). Firm sustainable development goals and firm financial performance through the lens of green innovation practices and reporting: a proactive approach. *Journal of Risk and Financial Management, 14*(12), 605.

Khan, H. W., Elgharbawy, A. A., Shah, M. U. H., Negash, B. M., Khan, M. K., Khan, K., et al. (2023). Exploring ionic liquids for formaldehyde separation via computational COSMO-RS screening. *Chemical Engineering Research and Design, 196*, 588–598.

Khan, P. A., Johl, S. K. J. C. B., & Management. (2019). Nexus of comprehensive green innovation, environmental management system-14001-2015 and firm performance. *Cogent Business & Management, 6*(1), 1691833.

Khan, P. A., Johl, S. K., Singh, P., Johl, S. K., Shamim, A., Nurhayadi, Y., Wijiharjono, N., Al-Azizah, U. S. (2021). *Injecting green innovation reporting into sustainability reporting.* Paper presented at the SHS web of conferences.

Khan, P. A., Johl, S. K. J. B., & Updates, E. R. (2020). Firm performance from the lens of comprehensive green innovation and environmental management system ISO 14001. *Processes, 8*(9), 1152.

Kiefer, C. P., del Río, P., Carrillo-Hermosilla, J. J. B. S., & Environment, T. (2021). On the contribution of eco-innovation features to a circular economy: A microlevel quantitative approach. *Business Strategy and the Environment, 30*(4), 1531–1547.

Krause, S., Drusche, O., & Kretschmann, J. (2022). Circular business model innovation in mining: Towards a sector-specific framework. In *SME annual conference and expo 2022*.

Maldonado-Guzmán, G., Garza-Reyes, J. A., & Pinzón-Castro, Y. J. B. A. I. J. (2020). Eco-innovation and the circular economy in the automotive industry. *Benchmarking: An International Journal, 28*(2), 621–635.

Jalil, N. A., Khan, P. A., & Shad, M. K. (2023). Digitalization, Sustainability and Development in Business. Business Intelligence-The Innovative Solutions for Business Sustainability, Equality, and Green Initiatives of Long-Term Organisational Performance. *KnE Social Sciences*, 286–298.

Montalbetti, C. (2022). Consortium company, circular economy and ESG: The Comieco case study. In *Climate change adaptation, governance and new issues of value* (pp. 95–106). Springer.

Moraga, G., Huysveld, S., Mathieux, F., Blengini, G. A., Alaerts, L., Van Acker, K., & Dewulf, J. (2019). Circular economy indicators: What do they measure? *Resources, Conservation and Recycling, 146*, 452–461.

Morea, D., Mango, F., Cardi, M., Paccione, C., & Bittucci, L. (2022). Circular economy impact analysis on stock performances: An empirical comparison with the Euro Stoxx 50® ESG Index. *Sustainability (Switzerland), 14*(2), 843. https://doi.org/10.3390/su14020843

Qureshi, F., Yusuf, M., Pasha, A. A., Khan, H. W., Imteyaz, B., & Irshad, K. (2022). Sustainable and energy efficient hydrogen production via glycerol reforming techniques: A review. *International Journal of Hydrogen Energy, 47*(98), 41397–41420.

Patil, R. A., Ghisellini, P., & Ramakrishna, S. (2021). Towards sustainable business strategies for a circular economy: Environmental, social and governance (ESG) performance and evaluation. In *An introduction to circular economy* (pp. 527–554). Springer.

Salim, M., Khan, P. A., Jalil, N. A., Johl, S. K., Jafar, S. H., Irfan, F., & Khan, M. (2023). Fusion of Blockchain and Sustainable Development Goals: A Bibliometric Analysis for Future Trends. *KnE Social Sciences*, 633–654.

Senadheera, S. S., Withana, P. A., Dissanayake, P. D., Sarkar, B., Chopra, S. S., Rhee, J. H., & Ok, Y. S. J. S. E. (2021). Scoring environment pillar in environmental, social, and governance (ESG) assessment. *Sustainable Environment, 7*(1), 1960097.

Sepetis, A. (2021). Sustainable finance and circular economy. In *Circular economy and sustainability: Volume 1: Management and policy* (pp. 207–226). Elsevier.

Sepetis, A. (2022). Sustainable finance and circular economy. In *Circular economy and sustainability* (pp. 207–226). Elsevier.

Smol, M., Kulczycka, J., Avdiushchenko, A. J. C. T., & Policy, E. (2017). Circular economy indicators in relation to eco-innovation in European regions. *Clean Technologies and Environmental Policy, 19*(3), 669–678.

Sparacino, E., Bologni, E., Rossi, A., Agostinelli, C., Madeo, D., & Mocenni, C. (2021). An integrated model for supporting aware decisions of companies in a circular and sustainable economy transition. *Procedia Environmental Science, Engineering and Management, 8*(3), 705–714.

Stankevičienė, J., Nikanorova, M. J. V. T., & Practice. (2020). Eco-innovation as a pillar for sustainable development of circular economy. *Verslas: teorija ir praktika, 21*(2), 531–544.

Toha, M. A., Akter, R., & Uddin, M. S. J. P. S. P. (2022). Paradigm of sustainable process safety management for industrial revolution 4.0: A circular economy and sustainability perspective. *Process Safety Progress, 41*, S17–S26.

Toha, M. A., & Johl, S. K. (2021a). *Does proactive eco eco-innovation matter in the energy sector?* Paper presented at the European conference on management, leadership & governance.

Toha, M. A., & Johl, S. K. J. D. (2021b). Panel dataset to assess proactive eco-innovation in the paradigm of firm financial progression. *Data, 6*(12), 131.

Toha, M., Johl, S. K., & Khan, P. A. J. P. (2020). Firm's sustainability and societal development from the lens of fishbone eco-innovation: A moderating role of ISO 14001-2015 environmental management system. *Processes, 8*(9), 1152.

Triguero, Á., Cuerva, M. C., Sáez-Martínez, F. J. J. B. S., & Environment, T. (2022). Closing the loop through eco-innovation by European firms: Circular economy for sustainable development. *Business Strategy and the Environment, 31*(5), 2337–2350.

Usman, B. M., Johl, S. K., & Khan, P. A. (2023). Reshaping Tomorrow through Green Governance and Circular Economy: An Emerging Paradigm. *KnE Social Sciences*, 239–256.

Vence, X., & Pereira, Á. J. C. (2019). Eco-innovation and circular business models as drivers for a circular economy. *Contaduría y administración, 64*(SPE1), 0.

Whenish, R., & Ramakrishna, S. (2022). BigTech befriending circular economy. In *Vol. 1591 CCIS. 5th international conference on emerging technologies in computer engineering: Cognitive computing and intelligent IoT, ICETCE 2022* (pp. 111–126). Springer Science and Business Media Deutschland GmbH.

Yusuf, M., Khan, H. W., Beg, M., Ekeoma, B. C., Nishat, A., & Al-Othman, A. L. (2023). Effect of climate change on air quality: a Nigerian perspective. In *Climate Change Impacts on Nigeria: Environment and Sustainable Development* (pp. 19–38). Springer International Publishing.

Mr Md. Abu Toha is working as an assistant professor at the Accounting and Information Systems (AIS) department under the Business Studies group at the National University, Bangladesh. Mr. Abu has completed his M.Phil. in Management from the University of Technology Petronas, Malaysia, with a Graduate on Time (GOT) research award. He was also awarded a full scholarship for his M.Phil. degree from the Ministry of Higher Education, Malaysia, under FRGS Grand. Previously, he completed a BBA and MBA from the AIS department at Jagannath University, Bangladesh, with a distinctive position. Mr. Abu Toha is a naive researcher in strategic management and green innovation. He has participated in and attended a few international conferences and seminars in the last few years. Further, his name was listed in the AD scientific index for the last 3 years.

Dr. Parvez Alam Khan is a Lecturer at the Management Department & Humanities, University Technology PETRONAS, with 4 years of industry and 5 years of research experience. He has completed his PhD in Management from Universiti Teknologi PETRONAS, Malaysia. His research has been featured in leading journals, including Business Strategy and the Environment, Cogent Business and Management, Environmental Science and Pollution Research and Journal of Risk and Financial Management. His research interests include sustainable innovation, green innovation, social innovation, SDG, and corporate governance. He teaches accounting, sustainability, sustainable finance, corporate governance, and strategic management courses.

Fatima Irfan is student at the Department of Commerce and Business Management Integral University Lucknow, India

Dr. Mohd Salim , working as an Assistant Professor at GCMT College, Aligarh, India, actively lectures, administers assessments, and contributes to curriculum development. Furthermore, Dr. Mohd Salim possesses over 3 years of practical experience in the corporate sector and a 2-year tenure in teaching within the Indian academic landscape. His educational journey includes an MBA in Finance, completed at Aligarh Muslim University, and a Bachelor of Commerce (Hons.) degree from the same institution. Dr. Salim's research focused on 'Evaluation and Impact Assessment of ASPIRE Scheme', showcasing his dedication to original research and mentoring students. He has contributed significantly to scholarly literature by disseminating high-quality book chapters, research papers, and conference papers in journals indexed by reputable databases such as Scopus and Web of Science. Moreover, his active engagement in academic discourse is evident through his participation in diverse forums, including seminars, conferences, workshops, and colloquia.

Mantasha Khan is student at the Faculty of Commerce, KMCL University, Lucknow, India.

SPRINGER NATURE

GPSR Compliance

The European Union's (EU) General Product Safety Regulation (GPSR) is a set of rules that requires consumer products to be safe and our obligations to ensure this.

If you have any concerns about our products, you can contact us on ProductSafety@springernature.com

In case Publisher is established outside the EU, the EU authorized representative is:

Springer Nature Customer Service Center GmbH
Europaplatz 3
69115 Heidelberg, Germany

The manufacturer's authorised representative in the EU is Springer Nature Customer Service Centre GmbH, Europaplatz 3, 69115 Heidelberg, Germany. If you have any concerns regarding our products, please contact ProductSafety@springernature.com

Printed and bound by CPI Group (UK) Ltd, Croydon, CR0 4YY
01/10/2026
02225862-0011